The World's Classics

313
FIVE RESTORATION
TRAGEDIES

Oxford University Press, Amen House, London E.C. 4.

GLASGOW NEW YORK TORONTO MELBOURNE WELLINGTON
BOMBAY CALCUTTA MADRAS CAPE TOWN

Geoffrey Cumberlege, Publisher to the University

Five
RESTORATION
TRAGEDIES

Edited with an INTRODUCTION

by

BONAMY DOBRÉE

The World's Classics

Geoffrey Cumberlege
OXFORD UNIVERSITY PRESS
London New York Toronto

This volume of Five Restoration Tragedies *was first published in* The World's Classics *in* 1928 *and reprinted in* 1935, 1941, *and* 1951.

CONTENTS

INTRODUCTION

THE title given to this choice of plays from the period which may roughly be named 'the Restoration' calls for remark, or even apology. Many readers, no doubt, will open this book expecting to find a group of plays written in the rhyming 'heroic couplet', as being the most representative of the age which bred 'heroic tragedy'. But our English ear, so alert to catch a repetition, has never taken very happily to a dramatic poem in rhyme, and a tragedy written in this manner has always seemed to the 'common reader' coldly artificial. This is not the place in which to plead the virtues of that form of verse; here it will only be said that unrhymed plays have been chosen so as not to assault popular prejudice: but it is hoped that, should this volume meet with a welcome, another one of tragedies written in the rhymed form will be added to the World's Classics.

Yet though the title gives promise of the book being more racy of its time than the contents show it to be, it may be defended on the ground that there is no real difference between rhymed and unrhymed Restoration tragedy, in that they both belong to the same 'heroic' school. Its elements differ something from those of other tragedies in that the emotions appealed to are not the general terror and pity of the kind—Aristotle or no Aristotle—we are used to have stirred in us by great tragedy of any age or country, but these emotions led along definite channels. It is

admiration rather than terror that is appealed to on
the one hand, while on the other, the pity is almost
entirely centred about the distresses of love. Whereas
the same analysis can be applied with almost startling
rigour to Sophocles, Shakespeare, and Racine, we are
aware of being faced, in these plays, with a different
theory of tragedy, a theory which, because it implied
bounds to the elements in life with which tragedy
might deal, has unavoidably made these tragedies of
secondary importance in the literature of the world.
By secondary, however, is meant something very good,
something indeed better than any country has since
brought forth, with the doubtful exception of Ibsen.

The theory of admiration came from France,
through Corneille; but it must be remembered that
theory always comes after, if not practice, at any
rate after the impulse towards practice. Admiration
corresponded to an emotional need due to the events
of the time. It must never be forgotten that the period
was one of disillusion—it is that which makes it more
real to us than it ever has been before—a period in
which Utopian hopes had not borne fruit, or where
hopes, even if realized, had lost some of their bloom.
Again, one of two conditions must be present if a
hero is to be recognized: either direct contact with
a big magnetic personality, or the distance in time
which lends enchantment. Now the Great Rebellion
had had its heroes, but it was being followed by a
period of licence in some quarters, and fierce puritan-
ism in others, by the horrors of the Popish Plot, by
the tyranny of James, and by the comparative flatness

of the Revolution. Thus the names of Brutus, Cicero, or Cato, so freely bestowed upon men in that age, until all men ' grew Consuls in their wine ', were, in view of human flesh and rasping fact, seen to be hollow mockeries. Few idealisms can stand the test of actuality. But the nation had acquired a taste for heroes, it needed noble sentiments, and it seemed natural that the theatre should gratify a craving life itself did not seem able to assuage. Therefore the greatness of a tragedy came to depend too much upon the ' fortunes ', the great place, of the chief characters, instead of being merely incidental, and it is worth notice that an eighteenth-century editor was to praise Otway for obtaining his response from the emotions of his characters rather than from their high rank.[1] Yet the theory still had this advantage over all that have come in its train: it did make a cleavage between art and life. Once George Lillo had made a tragedy out of everyday happenings, there began the descent of the drama into a naturalism from which it yet shows small signs of recovery. The complaint sometimes to be heard that modern drama is too ' literary ' is a reaction against this, but it is nevertheless a profound error. The disease from which modern drama is suffering is not literature, but literalness ; it is not literary enough—a complaint which cannot be urged against Restoration tragedy.

The love motive may have gained support from a misunderstanding of Racine, but that too was of fatal growth in Restoration society; it was a result of

[1] But see Rowe's prologue.

chaotic values, and it is best reflected in the comedy of the period. And love, perhaps because it is of necessity a private emotion, a man's attitude towards it biased by all sorts of accidents, is weak as a main element in tragedy. Aristophanes showed a right instinct when he resented its introduction by Euripides. Tragic terror and pity, however, are elemental emotions; complicate them, and the balance is lost. Pope, a very acute critic on some points, was exactly right when he said in the prologue to *Cato*:

> In pitying love we but our weakness show,

and that the really tragic was to portray

> A brave man struggling in the storms of Fate,

though whether Addison succeeded in doing this must be left to the reader to decide.

These dramas, then, have been chosen with a view to displaying the most typical streams of the time, their growth and fluctuations, with the final partial rebellion against them. The choice is, perhaps, rather the obvious one, but it falls in pat. It may be objected that there is no Lee, but the terrific and continued, one may say high-falutin', tension of his plays, is not quite to our modern taste, though he must certainly figure in the ' heroic ' volume if it should ever be put together. Were it not that *The Mourning Bride* appears in the second volume of Congreve's works in this series, it would have replaced *Oroonoko*, which is included here in spite of its comic scenes, as being very representative of its period, showing the method resorted to to check the growing romanticism, even sentimentality, of the age. It may, I venture to think, with all modesty be claimed, that the plays here printed give a very fair, and by no means uninteresting, chilly, or unamusing view of the tragedy of the Restoration.

All for Love is beyond doubt a proud and lovely masterpiece; it is the fine flower of Dryden's genius. It was at one time, indeed for a very long time, fashionable to decry it in comparison with *Antony and Cleopatra*, but Dryden was not trying to do at all the same kind of thing as Shakespeare. Free opinion will be forced to admit that though Shakespeare's play contains finer poetry than Dryden could ever write—as he would have been the first to admit— Dryden's has a more tragic effect. Shakespeare's play, indeed, suffers from the disadvantage of all ' histories ' in being overcrowded with themes and events. Closely founded upon North's translation of Plutarch, it is a piece of magnificent poetic journalism, and it is extraordinary how little any formative capacity is brought to bear on it, either in design or character. The only person at all ' created ' by Shakespeare is Enobarbus, the episode of his remorse being perhaps the most moving scene in the play. Dryden, on the other hand, carefully selected and moulded his material. Instead of copying North's characters, he re-created them. Antony becomes more grandiose, more heroic; Ventidius, who is nothing in Shakespeare, becomes the pattern of a noble, loyal Roman; Cleopatra, from being the flashy vulgarian described by Plutarch, and taken over whole by Shakespeare, becomes the type of tragedy queen. And these variations show very clearly the difference in the conception of tragedy. Whereas the terror in Shakespeare is felt to be part of the fatal warp of life, in the fact that the tremendous energy of Antony and Cleopatra ends in death, that of Dryden is transmuted into admiration for the hero or heroes. In the same way the pity in Shakespeare is a general thing—except in the already mentioned remorse scene of Enobarbus— but in Dryden the pity is almost entirely contained in Cleopatra's emotions about Antony. Right though Dryden may have been to limit his ' fable ', he was wrong in limiting the scope of his emotional material, though in this matter he errs far less than his contemporaries. At all events the internal movement of his drama, the way the emotions of his characters, and our own emotions, are ordered and modulated; the dignity of the poetry which though full of sentiment is never sentimental, make of the play a sublime piece of organ music, a gem of literature which may be read again and again, and which does not lose upon the stage.

With Otway's *Venice Preserv'd* we seem to enter a new realm of sensibility, of that extreme abandonment to the emotions of love, or indeed to the emotions in general, we find in eighteenth-century French literature, in the letters of Mademoiselle de Lespinasse, and the *Confessions* of Rousseau. The pains and tortures of love are indeed the main subjects of Otway's plays, for he himself was obsessed in life by a hopeless passion for Mrs. Barry, who acted in his plays, but who pre-

ferred the homage of Rochester and Etherege to his
own. It is a mistake to think that Otway shadows
a return to the Elizabethans, for his discontent with
the forms of his time is due not to his hankering after
a past age, but to his belonging to a future one;
though he may with some profit be compared with
Ford. The play which represents him here is taken
from a story of the Abbé Saint Réal, which has no
historical basis. It is a splendid, gloomy tragedy of
betrayed friendship with its consequent remorse; and
of ruined love, the latter too much overbalancing the
former. There is enough of pity, indeed, in the
friendship motive to make Belvidera and the love-
pity she arouses almost superfluous, but in this Otway
was a child of his time. The heroism of this play is
on the Restoration model, but Otway, with recent
memories of the Popish Plot, is a trifle satirical about
his heroes in their ' Romane-cast similitude '. The
Nicky-Nacky scenes, of course, are a deliberate satire
upon Antony Ashley Cooper, Lord Shaftesbury,
included perhaps at the King's request, and Otway,
who appears to have been a stout Tory, was by no
means averse from scathing the great fallen Whig
chieftain. The scenes may appear a little too harsh
for modern taste, but something of the nature was
needed if the play was to be given some strong
element to redeem it from sentimentality; and though
virility seems hardly the word to describe these scenes
of revolting decadence, they make possible the conception of a virile element lying between the two
extremes. The audiences probably felt this, for the

public was not yet ready for the frankly sentimental
either in tragedy or comedy.

Southerne also seems to have felt this, for he, again,
redeemed the somewhat too soft love-pity element in
Oroonoko by alternating with it scenes of the typical
Restoration comedy, though on the second-rate level.
To us they seem in glaring contradiction to the roman-
tic story of the African prince, which Southerne
borrowed from Mrs. Aphra Behn, who may be said
to have invented the ' noble savage ' ; but the
struggle to maintain a balance is significant, as showing that by that time the admiration-cum-love-pity
mixture, wonderfully exemplified in the Oroonoko
portions of the play, was felt to be inadequate. Thus
we are not surprised when in Rowe we come to a
modification. Heroism is by no means so heavily
stressed, and not so much is made of love, though it
is still the most important theme. *The Fair Penitent*,
derived from Massinger's *The Fatal Dowry*, really
contains the broader elements of great tragedy more
than *Venice Preserv'd* does, but being written by a far
lesser poet, is by no means such a great play; another
illustration of the fact that the drama is essentially
a literary form. Indeed, it must be confessed that
the adjective which best suits Rowe's tragedies is
' agreeable ', and that in the effort to achieve something more, he sometimes rose merely to the ridiculous, as when Callista says,

Is it the Voice of Thunder, or my Father ?

But again we must remember that the ' gay Lothario '
was an important figure of speech for two cen-

turies, and perhaps the forebear of Richardson's Lovelace.

With Addison we may say that we come to the end of heroic drama, for heroism had become a formula, not a need of the age. Cato is certainly enough of a hero, but he is a moral, not a passionate one; and in this play the theme of love is only introduced, one feels, because managers in every age insist that plays should have a love *motif*. But the contemporary excitement about the play was purely of a political nature. What would Addison, the notable Whig, say at a time of Tory triumph? Which party would be able to draw profit from the utterances of Mr. Spectator? Addison managed the matter very cleverly. Both sides should applaud the unexceptionable speeches about liberty, indeed neither side would be able to afford not to do so; and in the event Bolingbroke did take the wind out of the Whig sails by giving Booth, who acted the part of Cato, a fifty-pound purse for so well defending the cause of personal liberty. Yet Addison was in terror, although he had dined with Bolingbroke, got Pope, a notorious Tory, to write the prologue, and Dr. Garth, an equally notorious Whig, to scribble an epilogue. The actors were to be given his profits, so no expense was spared; Juba had a splendid gold waistcoat, Cato a brand-new fifty-pound wig, and Steele undertook to pack the house. Thus all went well, and both parties acclaimed the play as a masterpiece; they durst not do otherwise. It appears a little lifeless to us, just as do those of Voltaire, who praised it; it seems too much a thing made according to Horatian rules. But to contemporary audiences it was packed with allusions, and must have seemed full of vital matters. Indeed, it is just because it was so significant to its own day, that it has ceased to be so to ours.

And if in the structure and emotional make-up of these plays we run through a complete cycle, in versification also we traverse a period. Dryden's verse is admirable, an extremely well-wrought stage instrument, capable of sonority, of grandeur even, and also of lightness. It is at once concise and rich. It never rises to the rhetorical heights of Shakespeare's, but it is modulated and adaptable. It can achieve:

> How I lov'd
> Witness ye Days and Nights, and all ye Hours
> That danc'd away with Down upon your Feet,
> As all your business were to count my Passion,

as well as:

> O Horror, Horror !
> Egypt has been; our latest hour is come.
> The Queen of Nations from her ancient Seat,
> Is Sunk for ever in the dark Abyss:
> Time has unrolled her Glories to the last,
> And now closed up the Volume,

and no one on reading this play can doubt that Dryden was a great poet. But his verse lacks the marvellous flexibility of Shakespeare's, those undertones which, indeed, only Shakespeare has; and the reason for this is largely historical. For Shakespeare's flexibility had in his successors become chaos; with them blank verse had become irregularly cadenced prose, and Dryden, with his school, by imposing the disci-

pline of the rhymed 'heroic couplet' on it, had once
more made it a fitting, an honourable, vehicle for
the drama. Dryden, however, was a technician far
more efficient than any one of that age of technicians;
he was superior as only a great poet can be superior,
and when the new medium came into smaller hands,
it once more began to collapse. There is no need to
quote passages here for comparison, an almost
cursory reference to the plays in this volume will
illustrate the argument; but look at Otway's verse.
Otway himself, in his earlier tragedies, had submitted
to the discipline of the rhymed couplet, but as soon
as he allowed himself the freedom of blank verse he
began to become diffuse, so diffuse that he often
let the idea be lost in verbiage which carried him
into falsity. He was still a good poet; the emotion
and the thought behind his writings would always
maintain him at that level; but we feel that with him
the medium is in decline. There is no longer that strict
correspondence of word and image with emotion that
there is in Dryden, and in all the greater Elizabethans.

Southerne carried the process a step farther; his
verse lacks bone, as well as thought. That is what
invariably happens in periods when poets think that
poetry can be made out of the emotions alone.
Otway never fell into this error; he was always
striving for that marriage of thought and feeling
which produces good poetry; but Southerne took it all
too easily. His verse is rich and fluid, but it is like
an embroidered garment covering a flimsy frame.
Rowe's verse is not much more than passable.   With

him we see verse becoming more precise, certainly, but more polite, under the influence of Augustan theory; it exactly suits his polite tragedy, in which we never stagger over the abyss, as we do with Otway, nor enter the imaginative realm of Dryden. And when we come to Addison, something very peculiar happens. Read such passages as these, chosen almost at random:

> Coarse are his meals, the fortune of the chase,
> Amid the running streams he slakes his thirst,
> Toils all the day, and at th' approach of night
> On the first friendly bank he throws him down.

> *　　　　*　　　　*

> Believe me, Prince, you make old *Syphax* weep
> To hear you talk—but 'tis with tears of joy.
> If e'er your father's crown adorn your brows,
> *Numidia* will be blest by *Cato's* lectures.

The ear is continually deceived. With astonishment we discover that Addison has been writing rhymed couplets *without the rhymes*! This becomes all the more apparent when at the end of each act he allows the rhymes ingress for a few lines, and we greet them with relief. The heroic couplet had taken its revenge. But we see what had come about. Just as Addison had returned to the old form of heroic play, leaving out one element in it, so, in a like effort to redeem the vehicle of the drama, he had returned to the old form of verse, omitting one of the important factors. It is an object-lesson in what blank verse is not. Thus in medium, as well as in form and matter, Addison may be said to have closed a cycle of dramatic writing, which had its rise under peculiar conditions, and flickered out in *Cato* when those conditions had for some years ceased to exist.

ALL for LOVE:

OR, THE

World Well Loſt.

A

TRAGEDY,

As it is Acted at the

THEATRE - ROYAL;

AND

Written in Imitation of *Shakepſeare's* Stile.

Written by Mr. *Dryden*.

---

*Facile eſt verbum aliquod ardens (ut ita dicam) notare : Idque re-
ſtinctis animorum incendiis irridere.* Cicero.

In the SAVOY:

Printed for H. *Herringman*, and Sold by R. *Bently*, *J. Tonſon*,
F. *Saunders*, and T. *Bennet*. 1692.

To the Right Honourable,

THOMAS Earl of *Danby*, Viscount *Latimer*, and Baron *OSBORNE* of *Kiveton* in *York-shire*, Lord High Treasurer of *England*, One of His Majesties most Honourable Privy Council, and Knight of the Most Noble Order of the Garter, *&c.*

My L O R D,

The Gratitude of Poets is so troublesome a Virtue to Great Men, that you are often in danger of your own Benefits: For you are threaten'd with some Epistle, and not suffer'd to do Good in quiet, or to compound for their Silence whom you have Oblig'd. Yet, I Confess, I neither am, nor ought to be surpriz'd at this Indulgence; For your Lordship has the same Right to Favour Poetry which the Great and Noble have ever had.

Carmen amat, quisquis carmine digna gerit.

There is somewhat of a tye in Nature betwixt those who are Born for Worthy Actions, and those who can transmit them to Posterity: And though ours be much the inferiour

Danby] (1631–1712), afterwards Duke of Leeds. He succeeded to the baronetcy of his father, Sir Edward Osborne, in 1647, and being unsuccessful in his courtship of his cousin, Dorothy Osborne, who married Sir William Temple, he married the daughter of the Earl of Lindsey. At one time almost omnipotent, and much hated, he fell over the French intrigues and the Popish Plot. He was one of the seven lords who invited William—whose marriage with Mary he had arranged—to come over. He was once more Lord Treasurer (a post which corresponds with our Prime Minister), 1690–5. His last public appearance of any importance was at the Sacheverell trial in 1710.

part, it comes at least within the Verge of Alliance; nor are we unprofitable Members of the Commonwealth, when we animate others to those Virtues, which we Copy and Describe from you.

'Tis indeed their Interest, who endeavour the Subversion of Governments, to discourage Poets and Historians; for the best which can happen to them is to be forgotten: But such, who, under KINGS, are the Fathers of their Country, and by a Just and Prudent ordering of Affairs preserve it, have the same Reason to Cherish the Chroniclers of their Actions, as they have to lay up in safety the Deeds and Evidences of their Estates: For such Records are their undoubted Titles to the Love and Reverence of After-Ages. Your Lordships Administration has already taken up a considerable part of the English Annals; and many of its most happy Years are owing to it. His MAJESTY, the most knowing Judge of Men, and the best Master, has acknowledg'd the Ease and Benefit he Receives in the Incomes of His Treasury, which you found not only Disorder'd, but Exhausted. All Things were in the Confusion of a Chaos, without Form or Method, if not reduc'd beyond it, even to Annihilation: So that you had not only to separate the Jarring Elements, but (if that boldness of Expression might be allow'd me) to Create them. Your Enemies had so Embroil'd the Management of your Office, that they look'd on your Advancement as the Instrument of your Ruine. And as if the clogging of the Revenue, and the Confusion of Accounts, which you found in your Entrance, were not sufficient, they added their own weight of Malice to the Public Calamity, by forestalling the Credit which shou'd Cure it: Your Friends on the other side were only capable of Pitying, but not of Aiding you: No farther Help or Counsel was remaining to you, but what was founded on your Self; And that indeed was your Security: For your Diligence, your Constancy, and your Prudence, wrought more surely within, when they were not disturb'd by any outward Motion. The highest Virtue is best to be trusted with its Self, for Assistance only can be given by a Genius Superiour to that which it Assists. And 'tis the Noblest kind of Debt,

when we are only oblig'd to God and Nature. This then,
My Lord, *is your just Commendation, That you have
wrought out your Self a way to Glory, by those very Means
that were design'd for your Destruction: You have not
only restor'd, but advanc'd the Revenues of your Master
without Grievance to the Subject: And as if that were little
yet, the Debts of the* Exchequer, *which lay heaviest both on
the* Crown, *and on* private Persons, *have by your Conduct
been Establish'd in a certainty of Satisfaction. An Action
so much the more Great and Honourable, because the Case
was without the ordinary Relief of Laws; above the Hopes
of the Afflicted, and beyond the Narrowness of the Treasury
to Redress, had it been manag'd by a less able Hand. 'Tis
certainly the Happiest, and most Unenvy'd part of all your
Fortune, to do Good to many, while you do Injury to none:
To receive at once the Prayers of the Subject, and the Praises
of the Prince: And by the care of your Conduct, to give Him
Means of Exerting the chiefest, (if any be the chiefest) of
His Royal Virtues: His distributive Justice to the Deserving,
and His Bounty and Compassion to the Wanting. The
Disposition of Princes towards their People, cannot better be
discover'd than in the choice of their Ministers; who, like
the Animal Spirits betwixt the Soul and Body, participate
somewhat of both Natures, and make the Communication
which is betwixt them. A King, who is Just and Moderate
in his Nature, who Rules according to the Laws, whom God
made Happy by Forming the Temper of His Soul to the
Constitution of His Government, and who makes us Happy,
by assuming over us no other Sovereignty than that wherein
our Welfare and Liberty consists; A Prince, I say, of so
excellent a Character, and so suitable to the Wishes of all
Good Men, could not better have convey'd Himself into His
Peoples Apprehensions, than in your Lordships Person; who
so lively express the same Virtues, that you seem not so much
a Copy, as an Emanation of Him. Moderation is doubtless
an Establishment of Greatness; but there is a steadiness of
Temper which is likewise requisite in a Minister of State:
So equal a mixture of both Virtues, that he may stand like*

an Isthmus *betwixt the two Encroaching Seas of Arbitrary Power, and Lawless Anarchy.* The Undertaking would be difficult to any but an *Extraordinary* Genius, to stand at the *Line*, and to divide the *Limits*; to pay what is due to the *Great Representative of the Nation*, and neither to inhance, nor to yield up the undoubted *Prerogatives of the Crown.* These, My Lord, are the proper *Virtues of a Noble Englishman*, as indeed they are properly *English Virtues*: No People in the World being capable of using them, but we who have the Happiness to be Born under so equal, and so well-pois'd a Government. A Government which has all the Advantages of *Liberty* beyond a *Commonwealth*, and all the Marks of *Kingly Sovereignty* without the danger of a *Tyranny.* Both my Nature, as I am an Englishman, and my Reason, as I am a Man, have bred in me a Loathing to that specious Name of a *Republick*; That mock-appearance of a *Liberty*, where all who have not part in the Government, are *Slaves*; And *Slaves* they are of a viler Note than such as are *Subjects* to an absolute Dominion. For no *Christian Monarchy* is so Absolute, but 'tis Circumscrib'd with Laws: But when the Executive Power is in the Law-Makers, there is no farther check upon them; and the People must suffer without a Remedy, because they are Oppress'd by their Representatives. If I must serve, the number of my *Masters*, who were Born my *Equals*, would but add to the Ignomiy of my Bondage. The Nature of our Government above all others, is exactly Suited both to the Situation of our Country, and the Temper of the Natives: An Island being more proper for *Commerce* and for *Defence*, than for extending its *Dominions* on the Continent: For what the Valour of its Inhabitants might gain, by Reason of its Remoteness, and the Casualties of the Seas, it cou'd not so easily preserve: And therefore, neither the *Arbitrary Power* of one in a *Monarchy*, nor of many in a *Commonwealth*, could make us greater than we are. 'Tis true, that vaster and more frequent Taxes might be gather'd, when the Consent of the People was not Ask'd or Needed; but this were only by Conquering abroad to be Poor at home: And the Examples of our Neighbours teach us, that they are

*not always the Happiest Subjects whose Kings extend their
Dominions farthest. Since therefore we cannot win by an
Offensive War, at least a Land-War, the Model of our
Government seems Naturally contriv'd for the Defensive
part: And the Consent of a People is easily obtain'd to
contribute to that Power which must protect it.* Felices
nimium bona si sua nôrint, Angligenæ![1] *And yet there
are not wanting Malecontents amongst us, who Surfeiting
themselves on too much Happiness, wou'd perswade the
People that they might be Happier by a Change. 'Twas
indeed the Policy of their old Forefather, when himself was
fallen from the Station of Glory, to seduce Mankind into
the same Rebellion with him, by telling him he might yet
be freer than he was: That is, more free than his Nature
wou'd allow, or (if I may so say) than God cou'd make him.
We have already all the Liberty which Free-Born Subjects
can enjoy; and all beyond it is but License. But if it be
Liberty of Conscience which they pretend, the Moderation of
our Church is such, that its Practice extends not to the
severity of Persecution, and its Discipline is withal so easie,
that it allows more freedom to Dissenters than any of the
Sects wou'd allow to it. In the mean time, what Right can
be pretended by these Men to attempt Innovations in Church
or State? Who made them the Trustees, or (to Speak a little
nearer their own Language) the Keepers of the Liberty of
England? If their Call be extraordinary, let them Convince us by working Miracles; for ordinary Vocation they
can have none to disturb the Government under which they
were Born, and which protects them. He who has often
chang'd his Party, and always has made his Interest the
Rule of it, gives little Evidence of his Sincerity for the
Publick Good: 'Tis manifest he changes but for himself, and
takes the People for Tools to work his Fortune. Yet the
Experience of all Ages might let him know, that they who
trouble the Waters first, have seldom the benefit of the
Fishing: As they who began the late Rebellion, enjoy'd not*

[1] The original quotation is ' O fortunatos nimium, sua
si bona norint '.

the *Fruit* of their *Undertaking*, but were crush'd themselves by the *Usurpation* of their own *Instrument*. Neither is it enough for them to *Answer*, that they only intend a *Reformation* of the *Government*, but not the *Subversion* of it: On such pretences all *Insurrections* have been founded; 'Tis striking at the *Root* of *Power*, which is *Obedience*. Every *Remonstrance* of private Men, has the seed of *Treason* in it; and *Discourses* which are couch'd in ambiguous *Terms*, are therefore the more dangerous, because they do all the Mischief of open *Sedition*, yet are safe from the *Punishment* of the *Laws*. These, My Lord, are Considerations which I should not pass so lightly over, had I room to manage them as they deserve: for no Man can be so inconsiderable in a Nation, as not to have a share in the welfare of it; and if he be a true Englishman, he must at the same time be fir'd with Indignation, and revenge himself as he can on the Disturbers of his Country. And to whom could I more fitly apply my self, than to your Lordship, who have not only an inborn, but an Hereditary Loyalty? The memorable constancy and sufferings of your Father, almost to the ruine of his Estate for the Royal Cause, were an earnest of that, which such a Parent and such an Institution wou'd produce in the Person of a Son. But so unhappy an occasion of manifesting your own Zeal in suffering for his present Majesty, the Providence of God, and the Prudence of your Administration, will, I hope, prevent. That as your Fathers Fortune waited on the unhappiness of his Sovereign, so your own may participate of the better Fate which attends his Son. The Relation which you have by Alliance to the Noble Family of your Lady, serves to confirm to you both this happy Augury. For what can deserve a greater place in the English Chronicle, than the Loyalty and Courage, the Actions and Death of the General of an Army Fighting for his Prince and Country? The Honour and Gallantry of the Earl of Lindsey, is so illustrious a Subject, that 'tis fit to adorn an Heroick Poem; for He was the Proto-Martyr of the Cause, and the Type of his unfortunate Royal Master.

Yet, after all, My Lord, if I may speak my thoughts, you

*are happy rather to us than to your self: for the Multiplicity,
the Cares, and the Vexations of your Imployment, have
betray'd you from your self, and given you up into the
Possession of the Publick. You are Robb'd of your Privacy
and Friends, and scarce any hour of your Life you can call
your own. Those who envy your Fortune, if they wanted not
good Nature, might more justly pity it; and when they see
you watch'd by a Croud of Suitors, whose importunity 'tis
impossible to avoid, would conclude with Reason, that you
have lost much more in true Content, than you have gain'd
by Dignity; and that a private Gentleman is better attended
by a single Servant, than your Lordship with so clamorous a
Train. Pardon me, My Lord, if I speak like a Philosopher
on this Subject; the Fortune which makes a Man uneasie,
cannot make him Happy: and a Wise Man must think
himself uneasie, when few of his Actions are in his Choice.*

*This last Consideration has brought me to another, and
a very seasonable one for your Relief; which is, That while
I pity your want of leisure, I have impertinently Detain'd
you so long a time. I have put off my own Business, which
was my Dedication, till 'tis so late, that I am now asham'd
to begin it: And therefore I will say nothing of the Poem,
which I Present to you, because I know not if you are like
to have an Hour, which, with a good Conscience, you may
throw away in perusing it: And for the Author, I have only
to beg the continuance of your Protection to him, who is,*

MY LORD,

Your Lordships, most Obliged,

most Humble, and most

Obedient Servant,

JOHN DRYDEN.

PREFACE.

THE death of *Anthony* and *Cleopatra*, is a Subject which has been treated by the greatest Wits of our Nation, after *Shakespeare*; and by all so variously, that their Example has given me the confidence to try my self in this Bowe of *Ulysses* amongst the Crowd of Sutors; and, withal, to take my own measures, in aiming at the Mark. I doubt not but the same Motive has prevailed with all of us in this attempt; I mean the excellency of the Moral: for the chief Persons represented, were famous Patterns of unlawful Love; and their end accordingly was unfortunate. All reasonable Men have long since concluded, That the Heroe of the Poem, ought not to be a Character of perfect Virtue, for, then, he could not, without injustice, be made unhappy; nor yet altogether wicked, because he could not then be pitied: I have therefore steer'd the middle course; and have drawn the character of *Anthony* as favourably as *Plutarch*, *Appian*, and *Dion Cassius* wou'd give me leave: the like I have observ'd in *Cleopatra*. That which is wanting to work up the pity to a greater heighth, was not afforded me by the story: for the crimes of Love which they both committed, were not occasioned by any necessity, or fatal ignorance, but were wholly voluntary; since our passions are, or ought to be, within our power. The Fabrick of the Play is regular enough, as to the inferior parts of it; and the Unities of Time, Place and Action, more exactly observ'd, than, perhaps, the English Theater requires. Particularly, the Action is so much one, that it is the only of the kind without Episode, or Underplot; every Scene in the Tragedy conducing to the main design, and every Act concluding with a turn of it. The greatest error in the contrivance seems to be in the person of *Octavia*: For, though I might use the privilege of a Poet, to introduce her into *Alexandria*, yet I had not enough consider'd, that the compassion she mov'd to her self and Children, was destructive to that which I reserv'd for *Anthony* and *Cleopatra*; whose mutual love being founded upon vice, must lessen the favour of the Audience to them, when Virtue and Innocence were oppress'd by it. And, though I justified *Anthony* in some measure, by making *Octavia*'s departure, to proceed wholly from her self; yet the force of the first Machine still remain'd; and the dividing of pity, like the cutting of a River into many Channels, abated the strength of the natural Stream. But this is an Objection which none of my Criticks have urg'd against me; and therefore I might have let it pass, if I could have resolv'd to have been partial to my self. The faults my Enemies have found, are rather cavils concerning little, and not essential Decencies; which a Master of the Ceremonies may decide betwixt us. The *French* Poets, I confess, are strict Observers of these Punctilio's: They would not, for example, have suffer'd *Cleopatra* and *Octavia* to have met; or if they had met, there must only have pass'd betwixt them some cold civilities, but no eagerness of repartée, for fear of offending against the greatness of their Characters, and the modesty of their Sex. This Objection I foresaw, and at the same time contemn'd: for I judg'd it both natural and probable, that *Octavia*, proud of her new-gain'd Conquest, would search out *Cleopatra* to triumph over her; and that *Cleopatra*, thus attack'd, was not of a spirit to shun the encounter: and 'tis not unlikely, that two exasperated Rivals should use such Satyr as I have put into their mouths; for after all, though the one were a *Roman*, and the other a Queen, they were both Woman. 'Tis true, some actions, though natural, are not fit to be represented; and broad obscenities in words, ought in good manners to be avoided: expressions therefore are a modest cloathing of our thoughts, as Breeches and Petticoats are of our Bodies. If I have kept my self within the bounds of modesty, all beyond it is but nicety and affectation; which is no more but Modesty deprav'd into a Vice: they betray themselves who are too quick of apprehension in such cases, and leave all reasonable Men to imagine worse of them, than of the Poet.

Honest *Montaigne* goes yet farther : *Nous ne sommes que ceremonie; la ceremonie nous emporte, & laissons la substance des choses: Nous nous tenons aux branches, & abandonnons le tronc & le corps. Nous avons appris aux Dames de rougir, oyans seulement nommer ce qu'elles ne craignent aucunement a faire: Nous n'osons appeller a droict nos membres, & ne craignons pas de les employer a toute sorte de debauche. La ceremonie nous defend d'exprimer par paroles les choses licites & naturelles, & nous l'en croyons; la raison nous defend de n'en faire point d'illicites & mauvaises, & personne ne l'en croid.* My comfort is, that by this opinion my Enemies are but sucking Criticks, who wou'd fain be nibbling ere their Teeth are come.

Yet, in this nicety of manners does the excellency of *French* Poetry consist: their Heroes are the most civil people breathing; but their good breeding seldom extends to a word of sense: All their Wit is in their Ceremony; they want the Genius which animates our Stage; and therefore 'tis but necessary when they cannot please, that they should take care not to offend. But, as the civillest Man in the company is commonly the dullest, so these Authors, while they are afraid to make you laugh or cry, out of pure good manners, make you sleep. They are so careful not to exasperate a Critick, that they never leave him any work; so busie with the Broom, and make so clean a riddance, that there is little left either for censure or for praise: for no part of a Poem is worth our discommending, where the whole is insipid; as when we have once tasted of pall'd Wine, we stay not to examine it Glass by Glass. But while they affect to shine in trifles, they are often careless in essentials. Thus their *Hippolitus* is so scrupulous in point of decency, that he will rather expose himself to death, than accuse his Stepmother to his Father; and my Criticks I am sure will commend him for it: but we of grosser apprehensions, are apt to think that this excess of generosity, is not practicable but with Fools and Madmen. This was good manners with a vengeance; and the Audience is like to be much concern'd at the misfortunes of this admirable Heroe: but take *Hippolitus* out of his Poetick Fit, and I suppose he would think it a wiser part, to set the Saddle on the right Horse, and chuse rather to live with the reputation of a plain-spoken honest Man, than to die with the infamy of an incestuous Villain. In the mean time we may take notice, that where the Poet ought to have preserv'd the character as it was deliver'd to us by Antiquity, when he should have given us the Picture of a rough young Man, of the *Amazonian* strain, a jolly Huntsman, and both by his profession and his early rising a Mortal Enemy to Love, he has chosen to give him the turn of Gallantry, sent him to travel from *Athens* to *Paris*, taught him to make Love, and transform'd the *Hippolitus* of *Euripides* into Monsieur *Hippolite*. I should not have troubled my self thus far with French Poets, but that I find our *Chedreux* Criticks wholly form their Judgments by them. But for my part, I desire to be try'd by the Laws of my own Country; for it seems unjust to me, that the French should prescribe here, till they have conquer'd. Our little Sonnettiers who follow them, have too narrow Souls to judge of Poetry. Poets themselves are the most proper, though I conclude not the only Criticks. But till some Genius as Universal, as *Aristotle*, shall arise, who can penetrate into all Arts and Sciences, without the practice of them, I shall think it reasonable, that the Judgment of an Artificer in his own Art should be preferable to the

Hippolitus] In Racine's *Phèdre*.

opinion of another Man; at least where he is not brib'd by interest, or prejudic'd by malice: and this, I suppose, is manifest by plain induction: For, first, the Crowd cannot be presum'd to have more than a gross instinct, of what pleases or displeases them: every Man will grant me this; but then, by a particular kindness to himself, he draws his own stake first, and will be distinguish'd from the multitude, of which other Men may think him one. But, if I come closer to those who are allow'd for witty Men, either by the advantage of their quality, or by common fame, and affirm that neither are they qualified to decide Sovereignly, concerning Poetry, I shall yet have a strong party of my opinion; for most of them severally will exclude the rest, either from the number of witty Men, or at least of able Judges. But here again they are all indulgent to themselves: and every one who believes himself a Wit, that is, every Man, will pretend at the same time to a right of judging. But to press it yet farther, there are many witty Men, but few Poets; neither have all Poets a taste of Tragedy. And this is the Rock on which they are daily splitting. Poetry, which is a Picture of Nature, must generally please: but 'tis not to be understood that all parts of it must please every Man; therefore is not Tragedy to be judg'd by a witty Man, whose taste is only confin'd to Comedy. Nor is every Man who loves Tragedy a sufficient Judge of it: he must understand the excellencies of it too, or he will only prove a blind Admirer, not a Critick. From hence it comes that so many Satyrs on Poets, and censures of their Writings, fly abroad. Men of pleasant Conversation, (at least esteem'd so) and indu'd with a trifling kind of Fancy, perhaps help'd out with some smattering of Latine, are ambitious to distinguish themselves from the Herd of Gentlemen, by their Poetry;

> *Rarus enim fermè sensus communis in illâ Fortunâ.*

And is not this a wretched affectation, not to be contented with what Fortune has done for them, and sit down quietly with their Estates, but they must call their Wits in question, and needlessly expose their nakedness to publick view? Not considering that they are not to expect the same approbation from sober Men, which they have found from their flatterers after the third Bottle? If a little glittering in discourse has pass'd them on us for witty Men, where was the necessity of undeceiving the World? Would a Man who has an ill Title to an Estate, but yet is in possession of it, would he bring it of his own accord, to be try'd at *Westminster*? We who write, if we want the Talent, yet have the excuse that we do it for a poor subsistence; but what can be urg'd in their defence, who not having the Vocation of Poverty to scribble out of mere wantonness, take pains to make themselves ridiculous? *Horace* was certainly in the right, where he said, That *no Man is satisfied with his own condition*. A Poet is not pleas'd because he is not rich; and the Rich are discontented, because the Poets will not admit them of their number. Thus the case is hard with Writers: if they succeed not, they must starve; and if they do, some malicious Satyr is prepar'd to level them for daring to please without their leave. But while they are so eager to destroy the fame of others, their ambition is manifest in their concernment: some Poem of their own is to be produc'd, and the Slaves are to be laid flat with their faces on the ground, that the Monarch may appear in the greater Majesty.

Dionysius and *Nero* had the same longings, but with all their power they cou'd never bring their business well about. 'Tis true, they proclaim'd themselves Poets by sound of Trumpet; and Poets they were upon pain of death to any Man who durst call them otherwise. The Audience had a fine time on 't, you

Westminster] The Law Courts.

may imagine; they sate in a bodily fear, and look'd as demurely as they could: for 'twas a hanging matter to laugh unseasonably; and the Tyrants were suspicious, as they had reason, that their Subjects had 'em in the wind; so, every man in his own defence set as good a face upon the business as he could: 'Twas known before-hand that the Monarchs were to be Crown'd Laureats; but when the Shew was over, and an honest Man was suffer'd to depart quietly, he took out his Laughter which he had stifled; with a firm resolution never more to see an Emperor's Play, though he had been ten years a making it. In the mean time, the true Poets were they who made the best Markets, for they had Wit enough to yield the Prize with a good grace, and not contend with him who had thirty Legions: They were sure to be rewarded if they confess'd themselves bad Writers, and that was somewhat better than to be Martyrs for their Reputation. *Lucan*'s example was enough to teach them manners; and after he was put to Death, for overcoming *Nero*, the Emperor carried it without dispute for the best Poet in his Dominions: No man was ambitious of that grinning Honour; for if he heard the malicious Trumpeter proclaiming his Name before his Betters, he knew there was but one way with him. *Mecænas* took another Course, and we know he was more than a great Man, for he was witty too: but finding himself far gone in Poetry, which *Seneca* assures us was not his Talent, he thought it his best way to be well with *Virgil* and with *Horace*; that at least he might be a Poet at the second hand; and we see how happily it has succeeded with him; for his own bad Poetry is forgotten, and their Pane-gyricks of him still remain. But they who should be our Patrons, are for no such expensive ways to fame: they have much of the Poetry of *Mecænas*, but little of his Liberality. They are for persecuting *Horace* and *Virgil*, in the Persons of their Successours, (for

such is every Man, who has any part of their Soul
and Fire, though in a less degree.) Some of their
little *Zanies* yet go farther; for they are Persecutors
even of *Horace* himself, as far as they are able, by
their ignorant and vile Imitations of him; by making
an unjust use of his Authority, and turning his
Artillery against his Friends. But how would he
disdain to be Copyed by such hands! I dare answer
for him, he would be more uneasie in their Company,
than he was with *Crispinus* their Forefather in the
Holy Way; and would no more have allow'd them
a place amongst the Criticks, than he would *Demetrius*
the Mimique, and *Tigellius* the Buffoon;

> —— *Demetri, teq; Tigelli,*
> *Discipulorum inter jubeo plorare Cathedras.*

With what scorn would he look down on such miserable Translators, who make Doggrel of his Latine,
mistake his meaning, misapply his Censures, and often
contradict their own? He is fix'd as a Land-Mark to
set out the bounds of Poetry,

> —— *Saxum, antiquum ingens*
> *Limes agro positus litem ut discerneret arvis:*

But other Arms than theirs, and other Sinews are
requir'd, to raise the weight of such an Author; and
when they would toss him against their Enemies,

> *Genua labant, gelidus concrevit frigore sanguis,*
> *Tum lapis ipse, viri vacuum per inane volutus*
> *Nec spatium evasit totum, nec pertulit ictum.*

For my part, I would wish no other revenge, either
for my self or the rest of the Poets, from this Rhyming
Judge of the Twelve-penny Gallery, this Legitimate
Son of *Sternhold*, than that he would subscribe his
Name to his Censure, or (not to tax him beyond his
Learning) set his Mark: for shou'd he own himself
publickly, and come from behind the Lyons Skin,
they whom he condemns wou'd be thankful to him,

they whom he praises wou'd chuse to be Condemned;
and the Magistrates whom he has Elected, wou'd
modestly withdraw from their Employment, to avoid
the scandal of his Nomination. The sharpness of his
Satyr, next to himself, falls most heavily on his
Friends, and they ought never to forgive him for
commending them perpetually the wrong way, and
sometimes by contraries. If he have a Friend whose
hastiness in writing is his greatest fault, *Horace* wou'd
have taught him to have minc'd the matter, and to
have call'd it readiness of thought, and a flowing
Fancy; for Friendship will allow a Man to Christen an
imperfection by the Name of some Neighbour virtue:

> *Vellem in amicitiâ sic erraremus; & isti*
> *Errori, nomen virtus possuisset honestum.*

But he would never have allow'd him to have call'd
a slow Man hasty, or a hasty Writer a slow Drudge,
as *Juvenal* explains it:

> ——*Canibus pigris, scabieq; vetustâ*
> *Levibus, & siccæ lambentibus ora lucernæ*
> *Nomen erit, Pardus, Tygris, Leo; si quid adhuc est*
> *Quod fremit in terris violentius.*

Yet *Lucretius* Laughs at a foolish Lover, even for
excusing the Imperfections of his Mistress:

> *Nigra* μελίχροος *est, immunda & fœtida* ἄκοσμος.
> *Balba loqui non quit,* τραυλίζει; *muta pudens est, &c.*

But to drive it, *ad Æthiopem Cygnum* is not to be
indur'd. I leave him to interpret this by the Benefit
of his French Version on the other side, and without
farther considering him, than I have the rest of my
illiterate Censors, whom I have disdain'd to Answer,
because they are not qualified for Judges. It remains
that I acquaint the Reader, that I have endeavoured
in this Play to follow the practice of the Ancients,
who, as Mr. *Rymer* has judiciously observ'd, are and

Rymer] Thomas Rymer (1641–1713). The well-known
historiographer and famous critic, in which latter capacity

ought to be our Masters. *Horace* likewise gives it for a Rule in his Art of Poetry,

> ——*Vos exemplaria Græca*
> *Nocturnâ versate manu, versate diurnâ.*

Yet, though their Models are regular, they are too little for English Tragedy; which requires to be built in a larger Compass. I could give an instance in the *Oedipus Tyrannus*, which was the Masterpiece of *Sophocles*; but I reserve it for a more fit occasion, which I hope to have hereafter. In my Stile I have profess'd to imitate the Divine *Shakespeare*; which that I might perform more freely, I have disincumber'd my self from Rhyme. Not that I condemn my former way, but that this is more proper to my present Purpose. I hope I need not to explain my self, that I have not Copy'd my Author servilely: Words and Phrases must of necessity receive a Change in succeeding Ages: but 'tis almost a Miracle that much of his Language remains so pure; and that he who began Dramatick Poetry amongst us, untaught by any, and, as *Ben. Johnson* tells us, without Learning, should by the force of his own Genius perform so much, that in a manner he has left no Praise for any who come after him. The occasion is fair, and the Subject would be pleasant to handle the difference of Stiles betwixt him and *Fletcher*, and wherein, and how far they are both to be imitated. But since I must not be over-confident of my own performance after him, it will be prudence in me to be silent. Yet I hope I may affirm, and without vanity, that by imitating him, I have excell'd my self throughout the Play; and particularly, that I prefer the Scene betwixt *Anthony* and *Ventidius* in the first Act, to any thing which I have written in this kind.

he has until lately been much and stupidly abused. He is especially famous for having compiled the Fœdera, a collection as complete as possible of State papers connected with foreign affairs.

PROLOGUE to *Anthony* and *Cleopatra*.

What Flocks of Criticks hover here to day,
As Vultures wait on Armies for their Prey,
All gaping for the Carcass of a Play!
With Croaking Notes they bode some dire event;
And follow dying Poets by the scent.
Ours gives himself for gone; y' have watch'd your time!
He fights this day unarm'd; without his Rhyme.
And brings a Tale which often has been told;
As sad as Dido's; and almost as old.
His Heroe, whom you Wits his Bully call,
Bates of his mettle; and scarce rants at all:
He 's somewhat lewd; but a well-meaning mind;
Weeps much; fights little, but is wond'rous kind.
In short, a Pattern, and Companion fit,
For all thee keeping Tonyes of the Pit.
I cou'd name more; A Wife, and Mistress too;
Both (to be plain) too good for most of you:
The Wife well-natur'd, and the Mistress true.
    Now, Poets, if your fame has been his care;
Allow him all the Candour you can spare.
A brave Man scorns to quarrel once a day;
Like Hectors, in at every petty fray.
Let those find fault whose Wit 's so very small,
They've need to show that they can think at all:
Errours like Straws upon the surface flow;
He who would search for Pearls must dive below.
Fops may have leave to level all they can;
As Pigmies wou'd be glad to lopp a Man.
Half-Wits are Fleas; so little and so light;
We scarce cou'd know they live, but that they bite.
But, as the Rich, when tir'd with daily Feasts,
For change, become their next poor Tenants Ghests;
Drink hearty Draughts of Ale, from plain brown Bowls,
And snatch the homely Rasher from the Coals:

So you, retiring from much better Cheer,
For once, may venture to do penance here.
And since that plenteous Autumn now is past,
Whose Grapes and Peaches have Indulg'd your taste,
Take in good part from our poor Poets board,
Such rivell'd Fruits as Winter can afford.

Persons Represented.

	By
Marc Anthony,	Mr. *Hart*.
Ventidius, his General,	Mr. *Mohun*.
Dollabella, his Friend,	Mr. *Clarke*.
Alexas, the Queens Eunuch,	Mr. *Goodman*.
Serapion, Priest of *Isis*,	Mr. *Griffin*.
Another Priest,	Mr. *Coysh*.
Servants to *Anthony*.	
Cleopatra, Queen of *Egypt*,	Mrs. *Boutell*.
Octavia, *Anthony*'s Wife,	Mrs. *Corey*.

Charmion, ⎱
Iras,   ⎰ *Cleopatra*'s Maids.

Anthony's two little Daughters.

Scene Alexandria.

ALL for LOVE;

OR, THE

World well Lost.

ACT I. SCENE, *The Temple of* Isis.

Enter Serapion, Myris, *Priests of* Isis.

Serap. Portents and Prodigies are grown so frequent,
That they have lost their Name. Our fruitful *Nile*
Flow'd e're the wonted Season, with a Torrent
So unexpected, and so wondrous fierce,
That the wild Deluge overtook the haste,
Ev'n of the Hinds that watch'd it: Men and Beasts
Were borne above the tops of Trees, that grew
On th' utmost Margin of the Water-mark.
Then, with so swift an Ebb, the Floud drove backward
It slipt from underneath the Scaly Herd: 10
Here monstrous *Phocæ* panted on the Shore;
Forsaken *Dolphins* there, with their broad Tails,
Lay lashing the departing Waves: Hard by 'em,
Sea-Horses floundring in the slimy Mud,
Toss'd up their heads, and dash'd the ooze about 'em.

Enter Alexas *behind them.*

Myr. Avert these Omens, Heav'n.
Serap. Last night, between the hours of Twelve and
    One,
In a lone Isle o' th' Temple, while I walk'd,
A Whirl-wind rose, that, with a violent blast,
Shook all the *Dome*: the Doors around me clapt,   20
The Iron Wicket that defends the Vault,

11 *Phocæ*] Sea-lions.

Where the long Race of *Ptolomies* is lay'd,
Burst open, and disclos'd the mighty dead.
From out each Monument, in order plac'd,
An Armed Ghost start up: the Boy-King last
Rear'd his inglorious head. A peal of groans
Then follow'd, and a lamentable Voice
Cry'd, *Egypt* is no more. My blood ran back,
My shaking Knees against each other knock'd;
On the cold Pavement, down I fell intranc'd,   30
And so unfinish'd left the horrid Scene.
    Alexas shewing himself. And, Dream'd you this? or,
        Did invent the Story?
To frighten our *Egyptian* Boys withal,
And train 'em up betimes in fear of Priesthood?
    Serap. My Lord, I saw you not,
Nor meant my words should reach your Ears; but
    what
I utter'd was most true.
    Alex. A foolish Dream,
Bred from the fumes of indigested Feasts,
And holy Luxury.   40
    Serap. I know my duty:
This goes no farther.
    Alex. 'Tis not fit it should.
Nor would the times now bear it, were it true.
All Southern, from yon Hills, the *Roman* Camp
Hangs o'er us black and threatning, like a Storm
Just breaking on our Heads.
    Serap. Our faint *Ægyptians* pray for *Antony*;
But in their Servile Hearts they own *Octavius.*
    Myr. Why then does *Antony* dream out his hours,
And tempts not Fortune for a noble Day,   51
Which might redeem what *Actium* lost?
    Alex. He thinks 'tis past recovery.
    Serap. Yet the Foe
Seems not to press the Siege.

52 *Actium*] 31 B.C. where Antony, fleeing after Cleopatra, sustained a signal defeat.

Alex. O, there's the wonder.
Mecænas and *Agrippa*, who can most
With *Cæsar* are his Foes. His Wife *Octavia*,
Driv'n from his House, solicites her Revenge;
And *Dolabella*, who was once his Friend,   60
Upon some private grudge, now seeks his ruine:
Yet still War seems on either side to sleep.

Serap. 'Tis strange that *Antony*, for some days past,
Has not beheld the face of *Cleopatra*;
But here, in *Isis* Temple, lives retir'd,
And makes his Heart a Prey to black despair.

Alex. 'Tis true; and we much fear he hopes by absence
To cure his mind of Love.

Serap. If he be vanquish'd,
Or make his peace, *Egypt* is doom'd to be   70
A *Roman* Province; and our plenteous Harvests
Must then redeem the scarceness of their Soil.
While *Antony* stood firm, our *Alexandria*
Rival'd proud *Rome* (Dominions other Seat)
And fortune striding, like a vast *Colossus*,
Cou'd fix an equal foot of Empire here.

Alex. Had I my wish, these Tyrants of all Nature
Who Lord it o'er Mankind, should perish, perish,
Each by the others Sword; but, since our Will
Is lamely follow'd by our pow'r, we must   80
Depend on one; with him to rise or fall.

Serap. How stands the Queen affected?

Alex. O, she dotes,
She dotes, *Serapion*, on this vanquish'd Man,
And winds her self about his mighty ruins;
Whom would she yet forsake, yet yield him up,
This hunted Prey, to his pursuers hands,
She might preserve us all; but 'tis in vain——
This changes my designs, this blasts my Counsels,
And makes me use all means to keep him here,   90
Whom I could wish divided from her Arms
Far as the Earth's deep Center. Well, you know

The state of things; no more of your ill Omens,
And black Prognosticks; labour to confirm
The Peoples Hearts.

   Enter Ventidius, *talking aside with a Gentleman of*
        Antony's.

  Serap. These *Romans* will o'rehear us.
But, Who's that Stranger? By his Warlike port,
His fierce demeanor, and erected look,
He's of no vulgar note.

  Alex. O 'tis *Ventidius,*   100
Our Emp'rors great Lieutenant in the East,
Who first show'd *Rome,* that *Parthia* could be Con-
    quer'd.
When *Antony* return'd from *Syria* last,
He left this Man to guard the *Roman* Frontiers.

  Serap. You seem to know him well.

  Alex. Too well. I saw him in *Cilicia* first,
When *Cleopatra* there met *Antony*:
A mortal Foe he was to us, and *Ægypt.*
But, let me witness to the worth I hate,
A braver *Roman* never drew a Sword.   110
Firm to his Prince; but, as a Friend, not Slave.
He ne'r was of his Pleasures; but presides
O're all his cooler hours and morning counsels:
In short, the plainness, fierceness, rugged virtue
Of an old true-stampt *Roman* lives in him.
His coming bodes I know not what of ill
To our affairs. Withdraw, to mark him better;
And I'll acquaint you, why I sought you here,
And what's our present work.

       [*They withdraw to a corner of the Stage; and*
          Ventidius, *with the other, comes forwards to*
          the front.

  Ventidius. Not see him, say you?   120
I say, I must and will.

  Gent. He has commanded,
On pain of Death, none should approach his Presence.

Ven. I bring him news will raise his drooping
  Spirits,
Give him new life.

Gent. He sees not *Cleopatra.*

Ven. Would he had never seen her.

Gent. He Eats not, Drinks not, Sleeps not, has no
  use
Of any thing, but Thought; or, if he Talks,
'Tis to himself, and then 'tis perfect Raving: 130
Then he defies the World, and bids it pass;
Sometimes he gnaws his Lip, and Curses loud
The Boy *Octavius*; then he draws his Mouth
Into a scornful Smile, and cries, Take all,
The World's not worth my care.

Ven. Just, just his nature.
Virtue's his path; but sometimes 'tis too narrow
For his vast Soul; and then he starts out wide,
And bounds into a Vice that bears him far
From his first course, and plunges him in ills: 140
But, when his danger makes him find his fault,
Quick to observe, and full of sharp remorse,
He censures eagerly his own misdeeds,
Judging himself with Malice to himself,
And not forgiving what as Man he did,
Because his other parts are more than Man.
He must not thus be lost.

[*Alexas and the Priests come forward.*

Alex. You have your full Instructions, now advance;
Proclaim your Orders loudly.

Serap. Romans, *Ægyptians*, hear the Queen's Com-
  mand.   150
Thus *Cleopatra* bids, Let Labor cease,
To Pomp and Triumphs give this happy day,
That gave the World a Lord: 'tis *Antony*'s.
Live, *Antony*; and *Cleopatra* live.
Be this the general voice sent up to Heav'n,
And every publick place repeat this eccho.

Ven. aside. Fine Pageantry!

Serap. Set out before your doors
The Images of all your sleeping Fathers,
With Laurels crown'd; with Laurels wreath your
　　posts,　　　　　　　　　　　　　　　160
And strow with Flow'rs the Pavement; Let the Priests
Do present Sacrifice; pour out the Wine,
And call the Gods to joyn with you in gladness.

Ven. Curse on the Tongue that bids this general joy.
Can they be friends of *Antony*, who Revel
When *Antony*'s in danger? Hide, for shame,
You *Romans*, your Great Grandsires Images,
For fear their Souls should animate their Marbles,
To blush at their degenerate Progeny.　　　169

Alex. A Love which knows no bounds to *Antony*,
Would mark the Day with Honors; when all Heaven
Labour'd for him, when each propitious Star
Stood wakeful in his Orb, to watch that Hour,
And shed his better influence. Her own Birth-day
Our Queen neglected, like a vulgar Fate,
That pass'd obscurely by.

Ven. Would it had slept,
Divided far from his; till some remote
And future Age had call'd it out, to ruin
Some other Prince, not him.　　　　　　　180

Alex. Your Emperor,
Thô grown unkind, would be more gentle, than
T' upbraid my Queen for loving him too well.

Ven. Does the mute Sacrifice upbraid the Priest?
He knows him not his Executioner.
O, she has deck'd his ruin with her Love,
Led him in Golden Bands to gaudy slaughter,
And made perdition pleasing: She has left him
The blank of what he was;
I tell thee, Eunuch, she has unmann'd him:　　190
Can any *Roman* see, and know him now,
Thus alter'd from the Lord of half Mankind,
Unbent, unsinew'd, made a Womans Toy,
Shrunk from the vast extent of all his Honours,

And crampt within a corner of the World?
  O, *Antony*!
Thou bravest Soldier, and thou best of Friends!
Bounteous as Nature; next to Nature's God!
Could'st thou but make new Worlds, so wouldst thou
    give 'em,
As Bounty were thy Being, Rough in Battle,   200
As the first *Romans*, when they went to War;
Yet, after Victory, more pitiful,
Than all their Praying Virgins left at home!
  Alex. Would you could add to those more shining
    Virtues,
His Truth to her who loves him.
  Ven. Would I could not.
But, Wherefore waste I precious hours with thee?
Thou art her Darling mischief, her chief Engin,
Antony's other Fate. Go, tell thy Queen,
Ventidius is arriv'd, to end her Charms.   210
Let your *Ægyptian* Timbrels play alone;
Nor mix Effeminate Sounds with *Roman* Trumpets.
You dare not fight for *Antony*; go Pray,
And keep your Cowards-Holy-day in Temples.
               [*Exeunt* Alex. Serap.

    Re-enter the Gentleman of M. Antony.

  2 *Gent.* The Emperor approaches, and commands,
On pain of death that none presume to stay.
  1 *Gent.* I dare not disobey him.
              [*Going out with the other.*
  Vent. Well, I dare.
But, I'll observe him first unseen, and find   219
Which way his humor drives: the rest I'le venture.
                [*Withdraws.*

  Enter Antony, *walking with a disturb'd Motion,*
        before he speaks.

  Antony. They tell me 'tis my Birth-day, and I'le
    keep it
With double pomp of sadness.

'Tis what the Day deserves, which gave me breath.
Why was I rais'd the Meteor of the World,
Hung in the Skies, and blazing as I travell'd,
Till all my fires were spent; and then cast downward
To be trode out by *Cæsar*?

  Ven. aside. On my Soul,   •
'Tis mournful, wondrous mournful!

  Anto. Count thy Gains.   230
Now, *Antony*, Wouldst thou be born for this?
Glutton of Fortune, thy devouring youth
Has starv'd thy wanting Age.

  Ven. How Sorrow shakes him!   [*aside.*
So, now the Tempest tears him up by th' Roots,
And on the ground extends the noble Ruin.

                         Ant. having thrown himself down.
Lye there, thou shadow of an Emperor;
The place thou pressest on thy Mother-earth
Is all thy Empire now: now it contains thee;
Some few days hence, and then 'twill be too large, 240
When thou'rt contracted in thy narrow Urn,
Shrunk to a few cold Ashes; then *Octavia*,
(For *Cleopatra* will not live to see it)
Octavia then will have thee all her own,
And bear thee in her Widow'd hand to *Cæsar*;
Cæsar will weep, the Crocodile will weep,
To see his Rival of the Universe
Lie still and peaceful there. I'le think no more on't.
Give me some Musick; look that it be sad:
I'le sooth my Melancholy till I swell,   250
And burst my self with sighing——   *Soft Musick.*
'Tis somewhat to my humor. Stay, I fancy
I'm now turn'd wild, a Commoner of Nature;
Of all forsaken, and forsaking all;
Live in a shady Forest's *Sylvan* Scene,
Stretch'd at my length beneath some blasted Oke;
I lean my head upon the Mossy Bark,
And look just of a piece, as I grew from it:
My uncomb'd Locks, matted like *Misleto*,

Hang o're my hoary Face; a murm'ring Brook   260
Runs at my foot.

   Ven. Methinks I fancy
My self there too.

   Ant. The Herd come jumping by me,
And fearless, quench their thirst, while I look on,
And take me for their fellow-Citizen,
More of this Image, more; it lulls my thoughts.

[Soft Musick again.

   Ven. I must disturb him; I can hold no longer.

[Stands before him.

   Ant. starting up. Art thou *Ventidius*?

   Ven. Are you *Antony*?   270
I'm liker what I was, than you to him
I left you last.

   Ant. I'm angry.

   Ven. So am I.

   Ant. I would be private: leave me.

   Ven. Sir, I love you.
And therefore will not leave you.

   Ant. Will not leave me?
Where have you learnt that Answer? Who am I?

   Ven. My Emperor; the Man I love next Heaven:
If I said more, I think 'twere scarce a Sin;   281
Y'are all that 's good, and good-like.

   Ant. All that 's wretched.
You will not leave me then?

   Ven. 'Twas too presuming
To say I would not; but I dare not leave you:
And, 'tis unkind in you to chide me hence
So soon, when I so far have come to see you.

   Ant. Now thou hast seen me, art thou satisfy'd?
For, if a Friend, thou hast beheld enough;   290
And, if a Foe, too much.

   Ven. weeping. Look, Emperor, this is no common
     Dew.
I have not wept this Forty years; but now
My Mother comes afresh into my Eyes;

I cannot help her softness.

Ant. By Heav'n, he weeps, poor good old Man, he
    weeps!
The big round drops course one another down
The furrows of his Cheeks. Stop 'em, *Ventidius*,
Or I shall blush to death: they set my shame,
That caus'd 'em, full before me.   300

Ven. I'll do my best.

Ant. Sure there's contagion in the tears of Friends:
See, I have caught it too. Believe me, 'tis not
For my own griefs, but thine——Nay, Father.

Ven. Emperor.

Ant. Emperor! Why, that's the style of Victory,
The Conqu'ring Soldier, red with unfelt wounds,
Salutes his General so: but never more
Shall that sound reach my Ears.

Ven. I warrant you.   310

Ant. Actium, Actium! Oh——

Ven. It sits too near you.

Ant. Here, here it lies; a lump of Lead by day,
And, in my short distracted nightly slumbers,
The Hag that rides my Dreams——

Ven. Out with it; give it vent.

Ant. Urge not my shame.
I lost a Battel.

Ven. So has *Julius* done.

Ant. Thou favour'st me, and speak'st not half thou
    think'st,   320
For *Julius* fought it out, and lost it fairly:
But *Antony*——

Ven. Nay, stop not.

Ant. Antony.
(Well, thou wilt have it) like a Coward fled,
Fled while his Soldiers fought; fled first, *Ventidius*.
Thou long'st to curse me, and I give thee leave.
I know thou com'st prepar'd to rail.

Ven. I did.   329

Ant. I'll help thee——I have been a Man, *Ventidius*.

Ven. Yes, and a brave one; but——
Ant. I know thy meaning.
But, I have lost my Reason, have disgrac'd
The name of Soldier, with inglorious ease.
In the full Vintage of my flowing honours,
Sate still, and saw it prest by other hands.
Fortune came smiling to my youth, and woo'd it,
And purple greatness met my ripen'd years.
When first I came to Empire, I was borne
On Tides of People, crouding to my Triumphs;   340
The wish of Nations; and the willing World
Receiv'd me as its pledge of future peace;
I was so great, so happy, so belov'd,
Fate could not ruine me; till I took pains
And work'd against my Fortune, chid her from me,
And turn'd her loose; yet still she came again.
My careless days, and my luxurious nights,
At length have weary'd her, and now she 's gone,
Gone, gone, divorc'd for ever. Help me, Soldier,
To curse this Madman, this industrious Fool,   350
Who labour'd to be wretched: prithee curse me.
    Ven. No.
    Ant. Why?
    Ven. You are too sensible already
Of what y' have done, too conscious of your failings,
And, like a Scorpion, whipt by others first
To fury, sting your self in mad revenge.
I would bring Balm and pour it in your Wounds,
Cure your distemper'd mind, and heal your fortunes.
    Ant. I know thou would'st.   360
    Ven. I will.
    Ant. Ha, ha, ha, ha.
    Ven. You Laugh.
    Ant. I do, to see officious love
Give Cordials to the dead.
    Ven. You would be lost then?
    Ant. I am.
    Ven. I say, you are not. Try your fortune.

313   C

Ant. I have to th' utmost. Dost thou think me
    desperate
Without just cause? No, when I found all lost   370
Beyond repair, I hid me from the World,
And learnt to scorn it here; which now I do
So heartily, I think it is not worth
The cost of keeping.

Ven. *Cæsar* thinks not so:
He'll thank you for the gift he could not take.
You would be kill'd, like *Tully*, would you? do,
Hold out your Throat to *Cæsar*, and dye tamely.

Ant. No, I can kill my self; and so resolve.

Ven. I can die with you too, when time shall serve;
But Fortune calls upon us now to live,   381
To Fight, to Conquer.

Ant. Sure thou Dream'st, *Ventidius.*

Ven. No, 'tis you Dream; you sleep away your hours
In desperate sloth, miscall'd *Philosophy.*
Up, up, for Honor's sake; twelve Legions wait you,
And long to call you Chief: by painful Journeys,
I led 'em, patient, both of heat and hunger,
Down from the *Parthian* Marches, to the *Nile.*
'Twill do you good to see their Sun-burnt Faces,   390
Their skar'd Cheeks and chopt hands; there's virtue
    in 'em,
They'll sell those mangled Limbs at dearer Rates
Than yon trim Bands can buy.

Ant. Where left you them?

Ven. I said, in lower *Syria.*

Ant. Bring 'em hither;
There may be life in these.

Ven. They will not come.

Ant. Why did'st thou mock my hopes with pro-
    mis'd aids

377 *Tully*] Cicero, having sat on the fence too long,
was killed by order of Octavius, but on the demand of
Antony! Throughout the play Dryden refers to Octavius
as Caesar, since he was the reigning Caesar.

To double my despair ? They're mutinous.   400
  Ven. Most firm and loyal.
  Ant. Yet they will not March
To succour me. Oh trifler!
  Ven. They petition
You would make hast to head 'em.
  Ant. I'm besieg'd.
  Ven. There's but one way shut up : How came I
hither ?
  Ant. I will not stir.
  Ven. They would perhaps desire
A better reason.   410
  Ant. I have never us'd
My Soldiers to demand a reason of
My actions. Why did they refuse to March?
  Ven. They said, they would not fight for *Cleopatra.*
  Ant. What was 't they said ?
  Ven. They said they would not fight for *Cleopatra.*
Why should they fight, indeed, to make her Conquer,
And make you more a Slave ? to gain you Kingdoms,
Which, for a Kiss, at your next Midnight Feast,
You'll sell to her ? then she new names her Jewels, 420
And calls this Diamond such or such a Tax,
Each Pendant in her ear shall be a Province.
  Ant. Ventidius, I allow your Tongue free licence
On all my other faults; but, on your life,
No word of *Cleopatra* : She deserves
More Worlds than I can lose.
  Ven. Behold, you Pow'rs,
To whom you have intrusted Humankind;
See *Europe, Africk, Asia,* put in balance,
And all weigh'd down by one light worthless Woman !
I think the Gods are *Antony's,* and give   431
Like Prodigals, this neather World away,
To none but wastful hands.
  Ant. You grow presumptuous.
  Ven. I take the priviledge of plain love to speak.
  Ant. Plain love ! plain arrogance, plain insolence:

Thy Men are Cowards; thou an envious Traitor;
Who, under seeming honesty, hast vented
The burden of thy rank o'reflowing Gall.
O that thou wert my equal; great in Arms   440
As the first *Cæsar* was, that I might kill thee
Without a Stain to Honour!

   Ven. You may kill me;
You have done more already, call'd me Traytor.

   Ant. Art thou not one?

   Ven. For showing you your self,
Which none else durst have done; but had I been
That name, which I disdain to speak again,
I needed not have sought your abject fortunes,
Come to partake your fate, to dye with you.   450
What hindred me t' have led my Conqu'ring Eagles
To fill *Octavius*'s Bands? I could have been
A Traytor then, a glorious happy Traytor,
And not have been so call'd.

   Ant. Forgive me, Soldier:
I've been too passionate.

   Ven. You thought me false;
Thought my old Age betray'd you: kill me, Sir;
Pray kill me; yet you need not, your unkindness
Has left your Sword no work.   460

   Ant. I did not think so;
I said it in my rage: prithee forgive me:
Why did'st thou tempt my Anger, by discovery
Of what I would not hear?

   Ven. No Prince but you,
Could merit that sincerity I us'd,
Nor durst another Man have ventur'd it;
But you, e're Love misled your wandring Eyes,
Were sure the chief and best of Human Race,
Fram'd in the very pride and boast of Nature,   470
So perfect, that the Gods who form'd you, wonder'd
At their own skill, and cry'd, A lucky hit
Has mended our design. Their envy hindred,
Else you had been Immortal, and a pattern,

When Heav'n would work for ostentation sake,
To copy out again.

    Ant. But *Cleopatra*——
Go on; for I can bear it now.

    Ven. No more.

    Ant. Thou dar'st not trust my Passion; but thou
      may'st: 480
Thou only lov'st; the rest have flatter'd me.

    Ven. Heav'ns blessing on your heart for that kind
      word.
May I believe you love me? speak again.

    Ant. Indeed I do. Speak this, and this, and this.
                           [*Hugging him.*
Thy praises were unjust; but I'll deserve 'em,
And yet mend all. Do with me what thou wilt;
Lead me to victory, thou know'st the way.

    Ven. And, Will you leave this——

    Ant. Prithee do not curse her,
And I will leave her; though, Heav'n knows, I love
Beyond Life, Conquest, Empire; all, but Honor, 491
But I will leave her.

    Ven. That's my Royal Master.
And, Shall we Fight?

    Ant. I warrant thee, old Soldier,
Thou shalt behold me once again in Iron,
And at the head of our old Troops, that beat
The *Parthians,* cry aloud, Come follow me.

    Ven. O now I hear my Emperor! in that word
Octavius fell. Gods, let me see that day,   500
And if I have Ten years behind, take all;
I'll thank you for th' exchange.

    Ant. Oh *Cleopatra*!

    Ven. Again?

    Ant. I've done: in that last Sigh she went.
Cæsar shall know what 'tis to force a Lover,
From all he holds most dear.

    Ven. Methinks you breathe
Another Soul: Your looks are more Divine;

You speak a Heroe, and you move a God.   510

Ant. O, thou hast fir'd me; my Soul 's up in Arms,
And Mans each part about me: once again,
That noble eagerness of Fight has seiz'd me;
That eagerness with which I darted upward
To *Cassius*'s Camp: In vain the steepy Hill,
Oppos'd my way; in vain a War of Spears
Sung round my head ; and planted all my shield :
I won the Trenches, while my formost Men
Lagg'd on the Plain below.

Ven. Ye Gods, ye Gods,   520
For such another hour.

Ant. Come on, my Soldier!
Our Hearts and Arms are still the same: I long
Once more to meet our Foes; that Thou and I,
Like Time and Death, marching before our Troops,
May taste fate to 'em; Mowe 'em out a passage,
And entring where the foremost Squadrons yield,
Begin the noble Harvest of the Field.

[*Exeunt.*

A C T I I.

Cleopatra, *Iras*, and *Alexas*.

Cleop. What shall I do, or whither shall I turn?
Ventidius has o'rcome, and he will go.

Alex. He goes to Fight for you.

Cleo. Then he would see me e're he went to fight:
Flatter me not: if once he goes, he 's lost:
And all my hopes destroy'd.

Alex. Does this weak passion
Become a Mighty Queen?

Cleo. I am no Queen;

515 *Cassius*'s Camp] The reference is to the battle at
Philippi, 42 B.C., during the civil war after the murder of
Julius.

Is this to be a Queen, to be besieg'd 10
By yon insulting *Roman*; and to wait
Each hour the Victor's Chain? These ills are small;
For *Antony* is lost, and I can Mourn
For nothing else but him. Now come, *Octavius*,
I have no more to lose; prepare thy Bands;
I'm fit to be a Captive: *Antony*
Has taught my mind the fortune of a Slave.
  Iras. Call Reason to assist you.
  Cleo. I have none. 19
And none would have: my Love's a noble madness
Which shows the cause deserv'd it. Moderate sorrow
Fits vulgar Love; and for a vulgar Man:
But I have lov'd with such transcendent passion,
I soar'd, at first, quite out of Reasons view,
And now am lost above it——No, I'm proud
'Tis thus, would *Antony* could see me now;
Think you he would not sigh? though he must leave
    me,
Sure he would sigh; for he is noble-natur'd,
And bears a tender heart: I know him well.
Ah, no, I know him not; I knew him once, 30
But now 'tis past.
  Iras. Let it be past with you:
Forget him, Madam.
  Cleo. Never, never, *Iras*.
He once was mine; and once, though now 'tis gone,
Leaves a faint Image of possession still.
  Alex. Think him unconstant, cruel, and ungrateful.
  Cleo. I cannot: if I could, those thoughts were vain;
Faithless, ungrateful, cruel, though he be,
I still must love him. 40

Enter Charmion.

Now, What news my *Charmion*?
Will he be kind? and Will he not forsake me?
Am I to live, or dye? nay, Do I live?
Or am I dead? for when he gave his answer,

Fate took the word, and then I liv'd, or dy'd.

   Char. I found him, Madam——

   Cleo. A long Speech preparing?
If thou bring'st comfort, hast, and give it me;
For never was more need.

   Iras. I know he loves you.   50

   Cleo. Had he been kind, her Eyes had told me so,
Before her Tongue could speak it: now she studies,
To soften what he said; but give me death,
Just as he sent it, *Charmion*, undisguis'd,
And in the words he spoke.

   Char. I found him then
Incompass'd round, I think, with Iron Statues,
So mute, so motionless his Soldiers stood,
While awfully he cast his Eyes about,
And ev'ry Leaders hopes or fears survey'd: 60
Methought he look'd resolv'd, and yet not pleas'd.
When he beheld me strugling in the croud,
He blush'd, and bad, make way.

   Alex. There 's comfort yet.

   Char. Ventidius fixt his Eyes upon my passage,
Severely, as he meant to frown me back,
And sullenly gave place: I told my message,
Just as you gave it, broken and disorder'd;
I numbred in it all your sighs and tears,
And while I mov'd your pitiful request,   70
That you but only beg'd a last farewel,
He fetch an inward groan, and ev'ry time
I nam'd you, sigh'd, as if his heart were breaking,
But shun'd my Eyes, and guiltily look'd down;
He seem'd not now that awful *Antony*
Who shook an Arm'd Assembly with his Nod,
But making show as he would rub his Eyes,
Disguis'd and blotted out a falling tear.

   Cleo. Did he then weep? and, Was I worth a tear?
If what thou hast to say be not as pleasing,   80
Tell me no more, but let me die contented.

   Char. He bid me say, He knew himself so well,

He could deny you nothing, if he saw you;
And therefore——

   Cleo. Thou would say, he wou'd not see me?

   Charm. And therefore beg'd you not to use a power,
Which he could ill resist; yet he should ever
Respect you as he ought.

   Cleo. Is that a word
For *Antony* to use to *Cleopatra*?   90
Oh that faint word, Respect! how I disdain it!
Disdain my self, for loving after it!
He should have kept that word for cold *Octavia*.
Respect is for a Wife: Am I that thing,
That dull insipid lump, without desires,
And without pow'r to give 'em?

   Alex. You misjudge;
You see through Love, and that deludes your sight:
As, what is strait, seems crooked through the Water;
But I, who bear my reason undisturb'd,   100
Can see this *Antony*, this dreaded Man,
A fearful slave, who fain would run away,
And shuns his Master's Eyes: if you pursue him,
My life on 't, he still drags a chain along,
That needs must clog his flight.

   Cleo. Could I believe thee!——

   Alex. By ev'ry circumstance I know he Loves.
True, he 's hard prest, by Interest and by Honour;
Yet he but doubts, and parlies, and casts out
Many a long lookt for succour.   110

   Cleo. He sends word,
He fears to see my face.

   Alex. And would you more?
He shows his weakness who declines the Combat;
And you must urge your fortune. Could he speak
More plainly? To my Ears, the Message sounds
Come to my rescue, *Cleopatra*, come;
Come, free me from *Ventidius*; from my Tyrant:
See me, and give me a pretence to leave him.
I hear his Trumpets. This way he must pass.   120

Please you, retire a while; I'll work him first,
That he may bend more easie.

   Cleo. You shall rule me;
But all, I fear, in vain.   [*Exit with* Char. *and* Iras.

   Alex. I fear so too!
Though I conceal'd my thoughts, to make her bold:
But, 'tis our utmost means, and Fate befriend it.
                               [*Withdraws.*

Enter Lictors *with* Fasces; *one bearing the Eagle: then Enter*
    Antony *with* Ventidius, *follow'd by other Commanders.*

   Ant. Octavius is the Minion of blind Chance,
But holds from Virtue nothing.

   Ven. Has he courage?   130

   Ant. But just enough to season him from Coward.
O, 'tis the coldest youth upon a Charge,
The most deliberate fighter! if he ventures
(As in *Illyria* once they say he did)
To storm a Town 'tis when he cannot chuse,
When all the World have fixt their Eyes upon him;
And then he lives on that for seven years after,
But, at a close revenge he never fails.

   Ven. I heard, you challeng'd him.

   Ant. I did, *Ventidius*.   140
What think'st thou was his answer? 'twas so tame,—
He said he had more ways than one to die;
I had not.

   Ven. Poor!

   Ant. He has more ways than one;
But he would chuse 'em all before that one.

   Ven. He first would chuse an Ague, or a Fever:

   Ant. No: it must be an Ague, not a Fever;
He has not warmth enough to die by that.

   Ven. Or old Age, and a Bed.   150

   Ant. Ay, there's his choice.
He would live, like a Lamp, to the last wink,

   134 *Illyria*] During the pacification, and securing of the
frontiers after this civil war.

And crawl upon the utmost verge of life:
O *Hercules*! Why should a Man like this,
Who dares not trust his fate for one great action,
Be all the care of Heaven? Why should he Lord it
O're Fourscore thousand Men, of whom, each one
Is braver than himself?

Ven. You conquer'd for him:
Philippi knows it: there you shar'd with him   160
That Empire, which your Sword made all your own.

Ant. Fool that I was, upon my Eagles Wings
I bore this Wren, till I was tir'd with soaring,
And now he mounts above me.
Good Heav'ns, Is this, is this the Man who braves me?
Who bids my age make way: drives me before him,
To the World's ridge, and sweeps me off like rubbish?

Ven. Sir, we lose time; the Troops are mounted all.

Ant. Then give the word to March:
I long to leave this Prison of a Town,   170
To joyn thy Legions; and, in open Field,
Once more to shew my Face. Lead, my Deliverer.

Enter Alex.

Alex. Great Emperor,
In mighty Arms renown'd above Mankind,
But, in soft pity to th' opprest, a God:
This message sends the mournful *Cleopatra*
To her departing Lord.

Ven. Smooth Sycophant!

Alex. A thousand Wishes, and ten thousand Prayers,
Millions of Blessings wait you to the Wars,   180
Millions of Sighs and Tears she sends you too,
And would have sent
As many dear embraces to your Arms,
As many parting Kisses to your Lips;
But those, she fears, have weary'd you already.

Ven. aside. False Crocodyle!

Alex. And yet she begs not now, you would not
   leave her,

That were a wish too mighty for her hopes,
Too presuming for her low Fortune, and your ebbing
      Love,
That were a wish for her more prosperous days,   190
Her blooming Beauty, and your growing kindness.

   Ant. aside. Well, I must Man it out; What would
     the Queen?

   Alex. First, to these Noble Warriors, who attend,
Your daring Courage in the chase of Fame,
(Too daring, and too dang'rous for her Quiet)
She humbly recommends all she holds dear,
All her own Cares and Fears, the care of you.

   Ven. Yes, witness *Actium.*

   Ant. Let him speak, *Ventidius.*

   Alex. You, when his matchless Valour bears him
     forward,   200
With Ardor too Heroick, on his Foes,
Fall down, as she would do, before his Feet;
Lye in his way, and stop the paths of Death;
Tell him, this God is not invulnerable,
That absent *Cleopatra* bleeds in him;
And, that you may remember her Petition,
She begs you wear these Trifles, as a pawn,
Which, at your wisht return, she will redeem
             [*Gives Jewels to the Commanders.*
With all the Wealth of *Ægypt*:
This, to the great *Ventidius* she presents,   210
Whom she can never count her Enemy,
Because he loves her Lord.

   Ven. Tell her I'll none on 't;
I'm not asham'd of honest Poverty:
Not all the Diamonds of the East can bribe
Ventidius from his Faith. I hope to see
These, and the rest of all her sparkling store,
Where they shall more deservingly be plac'd.

   Ant. And who must wear 'em then?

   Ven. The wrong'd *Octavia.*   220

   Ant. You might have spar'd that word.

Ven. And she that Bribe.

Ant. But have I no remembrance?

Alex. Yes, a dear one:

Your Slave, the Queen——

Ant. My Mistress.

Alex. Then your Mistress,

Your Mistress would, she says, have sent her Soul,
But that you had long since; she humbly begs
This Ruby Bracelet, set with bleeding Hearts,   230
(The emblems of her own) may bind your Arm.

                         [*Presenting a Bracelet.*

Ven. Now, my best Lord, in Honor's name, I ask you,
For Manhood's sake, and for your own dear safety,
Touch not these poison'd Gifts,
Infected by the Sender, touch 'em not,
Miriads of bluest Plagues lye underneath 'em,
And more than Aconite has dipt the Silk.

Ant. Nay, now you grow too Cynical, *Ventidius.*
A Lady's Favours may be worn with Honor.
What, to refuse her Bracelet! On my Soul,   240
When I lye pensive in my Tent alone,
'Twill pass the wakeful hours of Winter nights,
To tell these pretty Beads upon my Arm,
To count for every one a soft embrace,
A melting Kiss at such and such a time;
And now and then the fury of her Love.
When——And what harm 's in this?

Alex. None, none my Lord,

But what 's to her, that now 'tis past for ever.

Ant. going to tye it. We Soldiers are so awkward——
help me tye it.   250

Alex. In faith, my Lord, we Courtiers too are
awkward

In these Affairs: so are all Men indeed;
Ev'n I, who am not one. But shall I speak?

Ant. Yes, freely.

Alex. Then, my Lord, fair hands alone
Are fit to tye it; She, who sent it, can.

Ven. Hell, Death; this Eunuch Pandar ruins you.
You will not see her?

    [*Alexas whispers an Attendant, who goes out.*

Ant. But to take my leave.

Ven. Then I have wash'd an *Æthiope*. Y'are undone;
Y'are in the Toils; y'are taken; y'are destroy'd : 261
Her Eyes do *Cæsar*'s Work.

Ant. You fear too soon.
I'm constant to my self: I know my strength;
And yet she shall not think me barbarous, neither.
Born in the depths of *Africk*: I'm a *Roman*,
Bred to the Rules of soft Humanity.
A guest, and kindly us'd, should bid farewel.

Ven. You do not know
How weak you are to her, how much an Infant: 270
You are not proof against a Smile or Glance;
A Sigh will quite disarm you.

Ant. See, she comes!
Now you shall find your error. Gods, I Thank you:
I form'd the danger greater than it was,
And, now 'tis near, 'tis lessen'd.

Ven. Mark the end yet.

   Enter Cleopatra, Charmion, *and* Iras.

Ant. Well, Madam, we are met.

Cleo. Is this a Meeting?
Then, we must part?   280

Ant. We must.

Cleo. Who says we must?

Ant. Our own hard fates.

Cleo. We make those Fates our selves.

Ant. Yes, we have made 'em; we have lov'd each other
Into our mutual Ruin.

Cleo. The Gods have seen my Joys with envious Eyes;
I have no Friends in Heaven; and all the World,
(As 'twere the bus'ness of Mankind to part us)

Is arm'd against my Love: ev'n you your self   290
Joyn with the rest; you, you are arm'd against me.
   Ant. I will be justify'd in all I do
To late Posterity, and therefore hear me.
If I mix a Lye
With any Truth, reproach me freely with it;
Else, favor me with silence.
   Cleo. You command me,
And I am dumb.
   Ven. I like this well: he shews Authority.
   Ant. That I derive my ruin   300
From you alone——
   Cleo. O Heav'ns! I ruin you!
   Ant. You promis'd me your silence, and you break it
E're I have scarce begun.
   Cleo. Well, I obey you.
   Ant. When I beheld you first, it was in *Ægypt*,
E're *Cæsar* saw your Eyes; you gave me love,
And were too young to know it; that I setled
Your Father in his Throne, was for your sake,
I left the acknowledgment for time to ripen.   310
Cæsar stept in, and with a greedy hand
Pluck'd the green Fruit, e'er the first blush of Red
Yet cleaving to the bough. He was my Lord,
And was, beside, too great for me to Rival,
But, I deserv'd you first, though he enjoy'd you.
When, after, I beheld you in *Cilicia*,
An Enemy to *Rome*, I pardon'd you.
   Cleo. I clear'd my self——
   Ant. Again you break your Promise.
I lov'd you still, and took your weak excuses,   320
Took you into my Bosom, stain'd by *Cæsar*,
And not half mine: I went to *Ægypt* with you,
And hid me from the bus'ness of the World,
Shut out enquiring Nations from my sight,
To give whole years to you.
   Ven. Yes, to your shame be 't spoken.   [*aside.*
   Ant. How I lov'd

Witness ye Days and Nights, and all your Hours,
That Danc'd away with Down upon your Feet,
As all your bus'ness were to count my Passion.   330
One day past by, and nothing saw but Love;
Another came, and still 'twas only Love:
The Suns were weary'd out with looking on,
And I untir'd with Loving.
I saw you ev'ry day, and all the day;
And ev'ry day was still but as the first:
So eager was I still to see you more.

     Ven. 'Tis all too true.

     Ant. Fulvia, my Wife, grew jealous,
As she indeed had reason; rais'd a War   340
In *Italy* to call me back.

     Ven. But yet
You went not.

     Ant. While within your Arms I lay,
The World fell mouldring from my Hands each Hour,
And left me scarce a grasp (I thank your love for 't).

     Ven. Well push'd: that last was home.

     Cleop. Yet may I speak?

     Ant. If I have urg'd a falshood, yes, else, not.
Your silence says I have not. *Fulvia* dy'd;   350
(Pardon, you gods, with my unkindness dy'd)
To set the World at Peace, I took *Octavia,*
This *Cæsar*'s Sister; in her pride of youth
And flow'r of Beauty did I wed that Lady,
Whom blushing I must praise, because I left her.
You call'd; my Love obey'd the fatal Summons:
This rais'd the *Roman* Arms; the Cause was yours,
I would have fought by Land, where I was stronger;
You hindred it: yet, when I fought at Sea,
Forsook me fighting; and (Oh stain to Honor!   360
Oh lasting shame!) I knew not that I fled;
But fled to follow you.

     Ven. What haste she made to hoist her purple Sails!
And to appear magnificent in flight,
Drew half our strength away.

    Ant. All this you caus'd.
And, Would you multiply more ruins on me?
This honest Man, my best, my only Friend,
Has gather'd up the Shipwreck of my Fortunes;
Twelve Legions I have left, my last recruits,   370
And you have watch'd the news, and bring your eyes
To seise them too. If you have ought to answer,
Now speak, you have free leave.
    Alex. aside. She stands confounded:
Despair is in her Eyes.
    Ven. Now lay a sigh i' th' way, to stop his passage:
Prepare a Tear, and bid it for his Legions;
'Tis like they shall be sold.
    Cleo. How shall I plead my cause, when you, my
       Judge
Already have condemn'd me? Shall I bring   380
The Love you bore me for my Advocate?
That now is turn'd against me, that destroys me;
For, love once past, is, at the best, forgotten;
But oftner sours to hate: 'twill please my Lord
To ruine me, and therefore I'll be guilty.
But, could I once have thought it would have pleas'd
     you,
That you would pry, with narrow searching Eyes
Into my faults, severe to my destruction:
And watching all advantages with care,
That serve to make me wretched? Speak, my Lord,
For I end here. Though I deserve this usage,   391
Was it like you to give it?
    Ant. O you wrong me,
To think I sought this parting, or desir'd
To accuse you more than what will clear my self,
And justifie this breach.
    Cleo. Thus low I thank you.
And since my innocence will not offend,
I shall not blush to own it.
    Ven. After this   400
I think she'll blush at nothing.

Cleo. You seem griev'd,
(And therein you are kind) that *Cæsar* first
Enjoy'd my love, though you deserv'd it better:
I grieve for that, my Lord, much more than you;
For, had I first been yours, it would have sav'd
My second choice: I never had been his,
And ne'r had been but yours. But *Cæsar* first,
You say, possess'd my love. Not so, my Lord;
He first possess'd my Person; you my Love: 410
Cæsar lov'd me; but I lov'd *Antony*.
If I endur'd him after, 'twas because
I judg'd it due to the first name of Men;
And, half constrain'd, I gave, as to a Tyrant,
What he would take by force.

    Ven. O Syren! Syren!
Yet grant that all the love she boasts were true,
Has she not ruin'd you? I still urge that,
The fatal consequence.

    Cleo. The consequence indeed,   420
For I dare challenge him, my greatest Foe,
To say it was design'd: 'tis true, I lov'd you,
And kept you far from an uneasie Wife,
(Such *Fulvia* was.)
Yes, but he'll say, you left *Octavia* for me;——
And, Can you blame me to receive that love,
Which quitted such desert, for worthless me?
How often have I wish'd some other *Cæsar*,
Great as the first, and as the second young,
Would court my Love to be refus'd for you!   430

    Ven. Words, words; but *Actium*, Sir, remember
    Actium.

    Cleo. Ev'n there, I dare his Malice. True, I
    Counsel'd
To fight at Sea; but I betray'd you not.
I fled; but not to the Enemy. 'Twas fear;
Would I had been a Man, not to have fear'd,
For none would then have envy'd me your friendship,
Who envy me your Love.

Ant. We're both unhappy:
If nothing else, yet our ill fortune parts us.
Speak; Would you have me perish, by my stay? 440

   Cleo. If as a friend you ask my Judgment, go;
If as a Lover, stay. If you must perish:
'Tis a hard word; but stay.

   Ven. See now th' effects of her so boasted love!
She strives to drag you down to ruine with her:
But, could she 'scape without you, oh how soon
Would she let go her hold, and haste to shore,
And never look behind!

   Cleo. Then judge my love by this.
>   [*Giving* Antony *a Writing.*

Could I have borne 450
A life or death, a happiness or woe
From yours divided, this had giv'n me means.

   Ant. By *Hercules*, the Writing of *Octavius*!
I know it well; 'tis that prescribing hand,
Young as it was, that led the way to mine,
And left me but the second place in Murder.——
See, see, *Ventidius*! here he offers *Ægypt*,
And joyns all *Syria* to it as a present,
So, in requital, she forsake my fortunes,
And joyn her Arms with his. 460

   Cleo. And yet you leave me!
You leave me, *Antony*; and yet I love you.
Indeed I do: I have refus'd a Kingdom,
That's a Trifle:
For I could part with life; with any thing,
But only you. O let me die, but with you!
Is that a hard request?

   Ant. Next living with you,
'Tis all that Heav'n can give.

   Alex. aside. He melts; We conquer. 470

   Cleo. No: you shall go: your Int'rest calls you
      hence;
Yes, your dear interest pulls too strong, for these
Weak Arms to hold you here.—— [*Takes his hand.*

Go; leave me, Soldier;
(For you're no more a Lover:) leave me dying:
Push me all pale and panting from your Bosome,
And, when your March begins, let one run after
Breathless almost for Joy; and cry, she's dead:
The Soldiers shout; you then perhaps may sigh,
And muster all your *Roman* Gravity;   480
Ventidius chides; and strait your Brow clears up,
As I had never been.

   Ant. Gods, 'tis too much; too much for Man to
     bear!

   Cleo. What is 't for me then,
A weak forsaken Woman? and a Lover?——
Here let me breath my last: envy me not
This minute in your Arms: I'll die apace:
As fast as e'er I can; and end your trouble.

   Ant. Dye! Rather let me perish: loos'nd Nature
Leap from its hinges. Sink the props of Heav'n,   490
And fall the Skies to crush the neather World.
My Eyes, my Soul; my all!——   [*Embraces her.*

   Ven. And what's this Toy
In ballance with your Fortune, Honor, Fame?

   Ant. What is 't, *Ventidius?* it out-weighs 'em all;
Why, we have more than Conquer'd *Cæsar* now:
My Queen's not only Innocent, but Loves me.
This, this is she who drags me down to ruin!
But, could she 'scape without me, with what haste
Would she let slip her hold, and make to shore,   500
And never look behind!
Down on thy knees, Blasphemer as thou art,
And ask forgiveness of wrong'd Innocence.

   Ven. I'll rather die, than take it. Will you go?

   Ant. Go! Whither? go from all that's excellent!
Faith, Honour, Virtue, all good things forbid,
That I should go from her, who sets my love
Above the price of Kingdoms. Give, you Gods,
Give to your Boy, your *Cæsar,*
This Rattle of a Globe to play withal,

This Gu-gau World, and put him cheaply off:
I'll not be pleas'd with less than *Cleopatra*.

    Cleo. She's wholly yours. My heart's so full of joy,
That I shall do some wild extravagance
Of Love in publick; and the foolish World,
Which knows not tenderness, will think me Mad.

    Ven. O Women! Women! Women! all the Gods
Have not such pow'r of doing good to Man,
As you of doing harm.   [*Exit.*

    Ant. Our Men are Arm'd.   520
Unbar the Gate that looks to *Cæsar*'s Camp;
I would revenge the Treachery he meant me:
And long security makes Conquest easie.
I'm eager to return before I go;
For, all the pleasures I have known, beat thick
On my remembrance: how I long for Night!
That both the sweets of mutual love may try,
And once Triumph o'er *Cæsar* e're we die.

                           [*Exeunt.*

ACT III.

At one door, Enter Cleopatra, Charmion, Iras, *and*
Alexas, *a Train of* Ægyptians: *at the other,* Antony
and Romans. *The entrance on both sides is prepar'd
by Musick; the Trumpets first sounding on Antony's
part: then answer'd by Timbrels, &c. on Cleopatra's.*
Charmion *and* Iras *hold a Laurel Wreath betwixt them.
A Dance of* Ægyptians. *After the Ceremony,* Cleopatra
Crowns Antony.

    Ant. I thought how those white arms would fold
      me in,
And strain me close, and melt me into love;
So pleas'd with that sweet Image, I sprung forwards,
And added all my strength to every blow.

    Cleo. Come to me, come my Soldier, to my Arms,
You've been too long away from my embraces;

But, when I have you fast, and all my own,
With broken murmurs, and with amorous sighs,
I'll say, you were unkind, and punish you,
And mark you red with many an eager kiss.   10

    Ant. My Brighter *Venus*!

    Cleo. O my greater *Mars*!

    Ant. Thou joinst us well, my Love!
Suppose me come from the *Phlegræan* Plains,
Where gasping Gyants lay, cleft by my Sword:
And Mountain tops par'd off each other blow,
To bury those I slew: receive me, Goddess:
Let *Cæsar* spread his subtle Nets, like Vulcan,
In thy embraces I would be beheld
By Heav'n and Earth at once: 20
And make their envy what they meant their sport.
Let those who took us blush; I would love on
With awful State, regardless of their frowns,
As their superior God.
There's no satiety of Love, in thee;
Enjoy'd, thou still art new; perpetual Spring
Is in thy arms; the ripen'd fruit but falls,
And blossoms rise to fill its empty place;
And I grow rich by giving.   29

        Enter Ventidius, *and stands apart.*

    Alex. O, now the danger's past, your General comes.
He joyns not in your joys, nor minds your Triumphs;
But, with contracted brows, looks frowning on,
As envying your Success.

    Ant. Now, on my Soul, he loves me; truly loves me;
He never flatter'd me in any vice,
But awes me with his virtue: ev'n this minute
Methinks he has a right of chiding me.
Lead to the Temple: I'll avoid his presence;
It checks too strong upon me.   [*Exeunt the rest.*
As Antony *is going,* Ventidius *pulls him by the Robe.*

14 *Phlegræan*] Phlegra was where the battle of the gods
and giants took place.

Ven. Emperor.   40
Ant. looking back. 'Tis the old argument; I pr'ythee
    spare me.
Ven. But this one hearing, Emperor.
Ant. Let go
My Robe; or, by my Father *Hercules*——
    Ven. By *Hercules* his Father, that's yet greater,
I bring you somewhat you would wish to know.
    Ant. Thou see'st we are observ'd; attend me here,
And I'll return.   [*Exit.*
    Ven. I'm waning in his favour, yet I love him;
I love this Man, who runs to meet his ruin;   50
And, sure the Gods, like me, are fond of him:
His Virtues lye so mingled with his Crimes,
As would confound their choice to punish one,
And not reward the other.

Enter Antony.

    Ant. We can conquer,
You see, without your aid.
We have dislodg'd their Troops,
They look on us at distance, and, like Curs
Scap'd from the Lions paws, they bay far off,
And lick their wounds, and faintly threaten War.   60
Five thousand *Romans* with their faces upward,
Lye breathless on the Plain.
    Ven. 'Tis well: and he
Who lost 'em, could have spar'd Ten thousand more.
Yet if, by this advantage, you could gain
An easier Peace, while *Cæsar* doubts the Chance
Of Arms!——
    Ant. O think not on 't, *Ventidius*;
The Boy pursues my ruin, he'll no peace:
His malice is considerate in advantage;   70
O, he's the coolest Murderer, so stanch,
He kills, and keeps his temper.

44 *Hercules*] Antonius claimed descent from Anton, the
son of Hercules.

Ven. Have you no friend
In all his Army, who has power to move him;
Mecænas, or *Agrippa* might do much.

Ant. They're both too deep in *Cæsar's* interests.
We'll work it out by dint of Sword, or perish.

Ven. Fain I would find some other.

Ant. Thank thy love.
Some four or five such Victories as this,   80
Will save thy farther pains.

Ven. Expect no more; *Cæsar* is on his Guard:
I know, Sir, you have conquer'd against odds;
But still you draw Supplies from one poor Town,
And of *Ægyptians*: He has all the World,
And, at his back, Nations come pouring in,
To fill the gaps you make. Pray think again.

Ant. Why dost thou drive me from my self, to search
For Foreign aids? to hunt my memory,
And range all o'er a wast and barren place   90
To find a Friend? The wretched have no Friends——
Yet I had one, the bravest Youth of *Rome,*
Whom *Cæsar* loves beyond the Love of Women;
He could resolve his mind, as Fire does Wax,
From that hard rugged Image, melt him down,
And mould him in what softer form he pleas'd.

Ven. Him would I see; that Man of all the world:
Just such a one we want.

Ant. He lov'd me too.
I was his Soul; he liv'd not but in me: 100
We were so clos'd within each others Breasts,
The Rivets were not found that join'd us first.
That does not reach us yet: we were so mixt,
As meeting Streams, both to our selves were lost;
We were one Mass; we could not give or take,
But from the same; for he was I, I he.

Ven. aside. He moves as I would wish him.

Ant. After this,
I need not tell his Name: 'twas *Dollabella.*

Ven. He 's now in *Cæsar*'s Camp.   110

Ant. No matter where,
Since he 's no longer mine. He took unkindly
That I forbad him *Cleopatra*'s sight;
Because I fear'd he lov'd her: he confess'd
He had a warmth, which, for my sake, he stifled;
For 'twere impossible that two, so one,
Should not have lov'd the same. When he departed,
He took no leave; and that confirm'd my thoughts.

Ven. It argues that he lov'd you more than her,
Else he had staid; but he perceiv'd you jealous,   120
And would not grieve his Friend: I know he loves you.

Ant. I should have seen him then ere now.

Ven. Perhaps
He has thus long been lab'ring for your Peace.

Ant. Would he were here.

Ven. Would you believe he lov'd you?
I read your Answer in your Eyes; you would.
Not to conceal it longer, he has sent
A Messenger from *Cæsar*'s Camp, with Letters.

Ant. Let him appear.   130

Ven. I'll bring him instantly.
                    [*Exit* Ventidius, *and Re-enters immediately
                              with* Dollabella.

Ant. 'Tis he himself, himself, by holy Friendship!
                    [*Runs to embrace him.*
Art thou return'd at last, my better half?
Come, give me all my self.
Let me not live,
If the young Bridegroom, longing for his Night,
Was ever half so fond.

Dolla. I must be silent; for my Soul is busie
About a noble Work: she 's new come home,
Like a long absent Man, and wanders o'er   140
Each Room, a Stranger to her own, to look
If all be safe.

Ant. Thou hast what 's left of me.
For I am now so sunk from what I was,

Thou find'st me at my lowest Water-mark.
The Rivers that ran in, and rais'd my Fortunes,
Are all dry'd up, or take another course:
What I have left is from my native Spring;
I've still a Heart that swells, in scorn of Fate,
And lifts me to my Banks.   150

  Dolla. Still you are Lord of all the World to me.

  Ant. Why, then I yet am so; for thou art all.
If I had any Joy when thou wert absent,
I grudg'd it to my self; methought I robb'd
Thee of thy part. But, Oh my *Dollabella*!
Thou hast beheld me other than I am.
Hast thou not seen my morning Chambers fill'd
With Scepter'd Slaves, who waited to salute me:
With Eastern Monarchs, who forgot the Sun,
To worship my uprising? Menial Kings   160
Ran coursing up and down my Palace-yard,
Stood silent in my Presence, watch'd my Eyes,
And, at my least Command, all started out
Like Racers to the Goal.

  Dolla. Slaves to your Fortune.

  Ant. Fortune is *Cæsar*'s now; and what am I?

  Ven. What you have made your self; I will not
    flatter.

  Ant. Is this friendly done?

  Dolla. Yes, when his end is so, I must join with him;
Indeed I must, and yet you must not chide: 170
Why am I else your Friend?

  Ant. Take heed, young Man,
How thou upbraid'st my Love: The Queen has Eyes,
And thou too hast a Soul. Canst thou remember
When, swell'd with hatred, thou beheld'st her first
As Accessary to thy Brothers Death?

  Dolla. Spare my Remembrance; 'twas a guilty day,
And still the blush hangs here.

  Ant. To clear her self,
For sending him no Aid, she came from *Egypt*.   180
Her Gally down the Silver *Cydnos* row'd,

The Tackling Silk, the Streamers wav'd with Gold,
The gentle Winds were lodg'd in Purple Sails:
Her Nymphs, like *Nereids*, round her Couch, were
    plac'd;
Where she, another Sea-born *Venus*, lay.
  Dolla. No more: I would not hear it.
  Ant. O, you must!
She lay, and leant her Cheek upon her Hand,
And cast a Look so languishingly sweet,
As if, secure of all Beholders Hearts,   190
Neglecting she could take 'em: Boys, like *Cupids*,
Stood fanning, with their painted Wings, the Winds
That plaid about her Face: But if she smil'd,
A darting Glory seem'd to blaze abroad:
That Mens desiring Eyes were never weary'd;
But hung upon the Object: To soft Flutes
The Silver Oars kept Time; and while they plaid,
The Hearing gave new Pleasure to the Sight;
And both to Thought: 'twas Heav'n or somewhat
    more;
For she so charm'd all Hearts, that gazing Crowds
Stood panting on the shore, and wanted Breath   201
To give their welcome Voice.
Then, *Dollabella*, where was then thy Soul?
Was not thy Fury quite disarm'd with Wonder?
Didst thou not shrink behind me from those Eyes,
And whisper in my Ears? Oh, tell her not
That I accus'd her with my Brothers Death!
  Dolla. And should my Weakness be a Plea for yours?
Mine was an Age when Love might be excus'd,
When kindly warmth, and when my springing youth
Made it a Debt to Nature. Yours——   211
  Ven. Speak boldly.
Yours, he would say, in your declining Age,
When no more heat was left but what you forc'd,
When all the Sap was needful for the Trunk,
When it went down, then you constrain'd the Course,
And robb'd from Nature, to supply Desire;

In you (I would not use so harsh a Word)
But 'tis plain Dotage.

   Ant. Ha!   220

   Dolla. 'Twas urg'd too home.
But yet the loss was private that I made;
'Twas but my self I lost: I lost no Legions;
I had no World to lose, no Peoples Love.

   Ant. This from a Friend?

   Dolla. Yes, *Anthony,* a true one;
A Friend so tender, that each Word I speak
Stabs my own Heart, before it reach your Ear.
O, judge me not less kind because I chide:
To *Cæsar* I excuse you.   230

   Ant. O ye Gods!
Have I then liv'd to be excus'd to *Cæsar?*

   Dolla. As to your Equal.

   Ant. Well, he's but my Equal:
While I wear this, he never shall be more.

   Dolla. I bring Conditions from him.

   Ant. Are they Noble?
Methinks thou shouldst not bring 'em else; yet he
Is full of deep dissembling; knows no Honour,
Divided from his Int'rest. Fate mistook him;   240
For Nature meant him for an Usurer,
He's fit indeed to buy, not conquer Kingdoms.

   Ven. Then, granting this,
What Pow'r was theirs who wrought so hard a Temper
To honourable Terms!

   Ant. It was my *Dollabella,* or some God.

   Dolla. Nor I; nor yet *Mecænas,* nor *Agrippa:*
They were your Enemies; and I a Friend
Too weak alone; yet 'twas a *Roman*'s Deed.

   Ant. 'Twas like a *Roman* done: show me that Man
Who has preserv'd my Life, my Love, my Honour;
Let me but see his Face.   252

   Ven. That task is mine,
And, Heav'n thou know'st how pleasing. [*Exit Vent.*

   Dolla. You'll remember

To whom you stand oblig'd?

   Ant. When I forget it,
Be thou unkind, and that 's my greatest curse.
My Queen shall thank him too.

   Dolla. I fear she will not.   260

   Ant. But she shall do 't: the Queen, my *Dollabella*!
Hast thou not still some grudgings of thy Fever?

   Dolla. I would not see her lost.

   Ant. When I forsake her,
Leave me, my better Stars; for she has truth
Beyond her beauty. *Cæsar* tempted her,
At no less price than Kingdoms, to betray me;
But she resisted all: and yet thou chid'st me
For loving her too well. Could I do so?

   Dolla. Yes, there 's my reason.   270

Re-enter Ventidius, *with* Octavia, *leading* Antony's
two little Daughters.

   Ant. Where?——*Octavia* there!   (*Starting back.*)

   Ven. What, is she poyson to you? a Disease?
Look on her, view her well; and those she brings:
Are they all Strangers to your eyes? has Nature
No secret Call, no whisper they are yours?

   Dolla. For shame, my Lord, if not for Love,
   receive 'em
With kinder Eyes. If you confess a Man,
Meet 'em, embrace 'em, bid 'em welcome to you.
Your Arms should open, ev'n without your knowledge,
To clasp 'em in; your Feet should turn to Wings,
To bear you to 'em; and your Eyes dart out,   281
And aim a kiss ere you could reach the Lips.

   Ant. I stood amaz'd to think how they came hither.

   Vent. I sent for 'em; I brought 'em in, unknown
To *Cleopatra*'s Guards.

   Dolla. Yet are you cold?

   Octav. Thus long I have attended for my welcome;
Which, as a Stranger, sure I might expect,
Who am I?

Ant. *Cæsar*'s Sister.   290

Octav. That's unkind!

Had I been nothing more than *Cæsar*'s Sister,
Know, I had still remain'd in *Cæsar*'s Camp;
But your *Octavia*, your much injur'd Wife,
Tho' banish'd from your Bed, driv'n from your House,
In spight of *Cæsar*'s Sister, still is yours.
'Tis true, I have a heart disdains your Coldness,
And prompts me not to seek what you should offer;
But a Wife's Virtue still surmounts that Pride:
I come to claim you as my own; to show   300
My Duty first, to ask, nay beg, your kindness:
Your hand, my Lord; 'tis mine, and I will have it.

> [*Taking his hand.*

Ven. Do, take it, thou deserv'st it.

Dolla. On my Soul,
And so she does: she's neither too submissive,
Nor yet too haughty; but so just a mean,
Shows, as it ought, a Wife and *Roman* too.

Ant. I fear, *Octavia*, you have begg'd my Life.

Octav. Begg'd it, my Lord?

Ant. Yes, begg'd it, my Ambassadress,   310
Poorly and basely begg'd it of your Brother.

Octav. Poorly and basely I could never beg;
Nor could my Brother grant.

Ant. Shall I, who, to my kneeling Slave, could say,
Rise up, and be a King; shall I fall down
And cry, Forgive me, *Cæsar*? shall I set
A Man, my Equal, in the place of *Jove*,
As he could give me being? No; that word,
Forgive, would choak me up,
And die upon my Tongue.   320

Dolla. You shall not need it.

Ant. I will not need it. Come, you've all betray'd
       me:
My Friend too! To receive some vile Conditions.
My Wife has bought me, with her Prayers and Tears;
And now I must become her branded Slave:

In every peevish Mood she will upbraid
The Life she gave: if I but look awry,
She cries, I'll tell my Brother.

    Octav. My hard Fortune
Subjects me still to your unkind mistakes.   330
But the Conditions I have brought are such
You need not blush to take: I love your Honour,
Because 'tis mine; it never shall be said
Octavia's Husband was her Brothers Slave.
Sir, you are Free; Free, ev'n from her you loath;
For, tho' my Brother bargains for your Love,
Makes me the Price and Cement of your Peace,
I have a Soul like yours; I cannot take
Your Love as Alms, nor beg what I deserve.
I'll tell my Brother we are reconcil'd;   340
He shall draw back his Troops, and you shall march
To rule the East: I may be dropt at *Athens*;
No matter where, I never will complain,
But only keep the barren Name of Wife,
And rid you of the trouble.

    Ven. Was ever such a strife of sullen Honour!
Both scorn'd to be oblig'd.

    Dolla. Oh, she has toucht him in the tender'st part;
See how he reddens with despight and shame
To be out-done in Generosity!   350

    Ven. See how he winks! how he dries up a Tear,
That fain would fall!

    Ant. Octavia, I have heard you, and must praise
The greatness of your Soul;
But cannot yield to what you have propos'd:
For I can ne'er be conquer'd but by Love;
And you do all for Duty. You would free me,
And would be dropt at *Athens*; was't not so?

    Octav. It was, my Lord.

    Ant. Then I must be oblig'd   360
To one who Loves me not, who, to her self,
May call me thankless and ungrateful Man;
I'll not endure it, no.

Ven. I'm glad it pinches there.

Octav. Would you triumph o'er poor *Octavia's*
     Virtue?
That Pride was all I had to bear me up;
That you might think you ow'd me for your Life,
And ow'd it to my Duty, not my Love.
I have been injur'd, and my haughty Soul
Could brook but ill the Man who slights my Bed.

    Ant. Therefore you Love me not.   371

    Octav. Therefore, my Lord,
I should not love you.

    Ant. Therefore you wou'd leave me?

    Octav. And therefore I should leave you——if I
     could.

    Dolla. Her Soul's too great, after such injuries,
To say she Loves; and yet she lets you see it.
Her modesty and silence plead her Cause.

    Ant. Oh, *Dollabella,* which way shall I turn?
I find a secret yielding in my Soul;   380
But *Cleopatra,* who would die with me,
Must she be left? Pity pleads for *Octavia;*
But does it not plead more for *Cleopatra?*

    Ven. Justice and Pity both plead for *Octavia;*
For *Cleopatra,* neither.
One would be ruin'd with you; but she first
Had ruin'd you: the other, you have ruin'd,
And yet she would preserve you.
In every thing their Merits are unequal.

    Ant. Oh, my distracted Soul!   390

    Octav. Sweet Heav'n compose it.
Come, come, my Lord, if I can pardon you,
Methinks you should accept it. Look on these;
Are they not yours? Or stand they thus neglected
As they are mine? Go to him, Children, go;
Kneel to him, take him by the hand, speak to
     him;
For you may speak, and he may own you too,
Without a Blush; and so he cannot all

His Children: go, I say, and pull him to me,
And pull him to your selves, from that bad Woman.
You, *Agrippina*, hang upon his Arms;   401
And you, *Antonia*, clasp about his Waste:
If he will shake you off, if he will dash you
Against the Pavement, you must bear it, Children;
For you are mine, and I was born to suffer.

> [*Here the Children go to him,* &c.

Ven. Was ever sight so moving! Emperor!
Dolla. Friend!
Octav. Husband!
Both Childr. Father!
Ant. I am vanquish'd: take me,   410
Octavia; take me, Children; share me all.

> (*Embracing them.*)

I've been a thriftless Debtor to your Loves,
And run out much, in Riot, from your Stock;
But all shall be amended.
Octav. O blest hour!
Dolla. O happy Change!
Ven. My joy stops at my tongue;
But it has found two Channels here for one,
And Bubbles out above.
Ant. to Octav. This is thy Triumph; lead me where
    thou wilt;   420
Ev'n to thy Brothers Camp.
Octav. All there are yours.

Enter Alexas *hastily.*

Alex. The Queen, my Mistress, Sir, and yours——
Ant. 'Tis past. *Octavia*, you shall stay this night;
    To morrow,
Cæsar and we are one.

> [*Ex. leading* Octavia, Doll. *and the Children follow.*

Ven. There's News for you; run,
My officious Eunuch,
Be sure to be the first; haste forward:
Haste, my dear Eunuch, haste.   [*Exit.*

Alex. This downright fighting Fool, this thick-
    scull'd Hero,   430
This blunt unthinking Instrument of Death,
With plain dull Virtue, has out-gone my Wit:
Pleasure forsook my early'st Infancy,
The Luxury of others robb'd my Cradle,
And ravish'd thence the Promise of a Man:
Cast out from Nature, disinherited
Of what her meanest Children claim by kind;
Yet, Greatness kept me from Contempt: that 's gone.
Had *Cleopatra* follow'd my advice,
Then he had been betray'd, who now forsakes.   440
She dies for love; but she has known its joys:
Gods, is this just, that I, who knows no joys,
Must die, because she loves?

    Enter Cleopatra, Charmion, Iras, Train.

Oh, Madam, I have seen what blasts my Eyes!
Octavia's here!
    Cleop. Peace with that Raven's note.
I know it too; and now am in
The Pangs of Death.
    Alex. You are no more a Queen;
Egypt is lost.   450
    Cleop. What tell'st thou me of *Egypt*?
My Life, my Soul is lost! *Octavia* has him!
O fatal Name to *Cleopatra*'s love!
My kisses, my embraces now are hers;
While I——But thou hast seen my Rival; speak,
Does she deserve this Blessing? Is she fair,
Bright as a Goddess? and is all perfection
Confin'd to her? It is. Poor I was made
Of that course matter which, when she was finish'd,
The Gods threw by, for rubbish.   460
    Alex. She 's indeed a very Miracle.
    Cleop. Death to my hopes, a Miracle!
    Alex. bowing. A Miracle;
I mean of Goodness; for in Beauty, Madam,

You make all Wonders cease.

    Cleop. I was too rash:
Take this in part of recompence. But, Oh,

                            [*Giving a Ring.*

I fear thou flatter'st me.

    Char. She comes! she 's here!

    Iras. Flie, Madam, *Cæsar's* Sister!   470

    Cleop. Were she the Sister of the Thund'rer *Jove*,
And bore her Brother's Lightning in her Eyes,
Thus would I face my Rival.

        [*Meets* Octav. *with* Ventid. Octav. *bears up to
           her. Their Trains come up on either side.*

    Octav. I need not ask if you are *Cleopatra*,
Your haughty Carriage——

    Cleop. Shows I am a Queen:
Nor need I ask you who you are.

    Octav. A *Roman*:
A Name that makes, and can unmake a Queen.

    Cleop. Your Lord, the Man who serves me, is a
    Roman.   480

    Octav. He was a *Roman*, till he lost that Name
To be a Slave in *Egypt*; but I come
To free him thence.

    Cleop. Peace, peace, my Lover's *Juno*.
When he grew weary of that Houshold-Clog,
He chose my easier Bonds.

    Octav. I wonder not
Your Bonds are easie; you have long been practis'd
In that lascivious Art; he 's not the first
For whom you spread your snares: let *Cæsar* witness.

    Cleop. I lov'd not *Cæsar*; 'twas but gratitude   491
I paid his Love: the worst your Malice can,
Is but to say the greatest of Mankind
Has been my Slave. The next, but far above him,
In my Esteem, is he whom Law calls yours,
But whom his Love made mine.

    Oct. coming up close to her. I would view nearer
That Face, which has so long usurp'd my right,

To find th' inevitable Charms, that catch
Mankind so sure, that ruin'd my dear Lord. 500

Cleop. O, you do well to search; for had you known
But half these Charms, you had not lost his heart.

Octav. Far be their knowledge from a *Roman* Lady,
Far from a modest Wife. Shame of our Sex,
Dost thou not Blush, to own those black Endearments
That make sin pleasing?

Cleop. You may Blush, who want 'em:
If bounteous Nature, if indulgent Heav'n
Have giv'n me Charms to please the bravest Man;
Should I not thank 'em? should I be asham'd, 510
And not be Proud? I am, that he has lov'd me;
And, when I love not him, Heav'n change this Face
For one like that.

Octav. Thou lov'st him not so well.

Cleop. I Love him better, and deserve him more.

Octav. You do not; cannot: you have been his
ruine.
Who made him cheap at *Rome*, but *Cleopatra*?
Who made him scorn'd abroad, but *Cleopatra*?
At *Actium*, who betray'd him? *Cleopatra*.
Who made his Children Orphans? and poor me 520
A wretched Widow? only *Cleopatra*.

Cleop. Yet she who loves him best is *Cleopatra*.
If you have suffer'd, I have suffer'd more.
You bear the specious Title of a Wife,
To gild your Cause, and draw the pitying World
To favour it: the World contemns poor me;
For I have lost my Honour, lost my Fame,
And stain'd the Glory of my Royal House,
And all to bear the branded Name of Mistress.
There wants but Life, and that too I would lose 530
For him I love.

Octav. Be 't so then; take thy Wish. [*Exit cum suis.*

Cleop. And 'tis my Wish,
Now he is lost for whom alone I liv'd.
My sight grows dim, and every Object dances.

And swims before me, in the maze of Death.
My Spirits, while they were oppos'd, kept up;
They could not sink beneath a Rivals scorn:
But now she 's gone they faint.
   Alex. Mine have had leisure   540
To recollect their Strength, and furnish Counsel,
To ruine her; who else must ruine you.
   Cleop. Vain Promiser!
Lead me, my *Charmion*; nay, your hand too, *Iras*:
My Grief has weight enough to sink you both.
Conduct me to some Solitary Chamber,
And draw the Curtains round;
Then leave me to my self, to take alone
My fill of Grief:
   There I till Death will his unkindness weep: 550
As harmless Infants moan themselves asleep.
                         [*Exeunt.*

ACT IV.

Antony, Dollabella.

   Dolla. Why would you shift it from your self, on
    me?
Can you not tell her you must part?
   Ant I cannot,
I could pull out an Eye, and bid it go,
And t' other should not weep. Oh, *Dollabella*,
How many Deaths are in this word *Depart*!
I dare not trust my tongue to tell her so:
One Look of hers, would thaw me into Tears,
And I should melt till I were lost agen.
   Dolla. Then let *Ventidius*;   10
He 's rough by Nature.
   Ant. Oh, he 'll speak too harshly;
He 'll kill her with the News: Thou, only thou.
   Dolla. Nature has cast me in so soft a Mould,
That but to hear a Story feign'd for Pleasure

Of some sad Lovers Death, moistens my Eyes,
And robs me of my Manhood.—I should speak
So faintly; with such fear to grieve her Heart,
She'd not believe it earnest.

   Ant. Therefore; therefore   20
Thou only, thou art fit: think thy self me,
And when thou speak'st (but let it first be long)
Take off the edge from every Sharper sound,
And let our parting be as gently made
As other Loves begin: wilt thou do this?

   Dolla. What you have said, so sinks into my Soul,
That, if I must speak, I shall speak just so.

   Ant. I leave you then to your sad task: Farewel.
I sent her word to meet you.

                      (Goes to the door, and comes back.)
I forgot;   30
Let her be told, I'll make her peace with mine:
Her Crown and Dignity shall be preserv'd,
If I have pow'r with *Cæsar.*——O, be sure
To think on that.

   Dolla. Fear not, I will remember.

        [*Antony goes again to the door, and comes back.*

   Ant. And tell her, too, how much I was constrain'd;
I did not this, but with extreamest force:
Desire her not to hate my Memory,
For I still cherish hers;——insist on that.

   Dolla. Trust me, I'll not forget it.   40

   Ant. Then that's all.

                      (Goes out, and returns again.)
Wilt thou forgive my fondness this once more?
Tell her, tho' we shall never meet again,
If I should hear she took another Love,
The News would break my Heart.—Now I must go;
For every time I have return'd, I feel
My Soul more tender; and my next Command
Would be to bid her stay, and ruine both.   [*Exit.*

   Dolla. Men are but Children of a larger growth,
Our Appetites as apt to change as theirs,   50

And full as craving too, and full as vain;
And yet the Soul, shut up in her dark Room,
Viewing so clear abroad, at home sees nothing;
But, like a Mole in Earth, busie and blind,
Works all her folly up, and casts it outward
To the Worlds open view: thus I discover'd,
And blam'd the Love of ruin'd *Antony*;
Yet wish that I were he, to be so ruin'd.

     Enter Ventidius *above.*

 Ven. Alone? and Talking to himself? concern'd too?
Perhaps my Guess is right; he lov'd her once,   60
And may pursue it still.
 Dolla. O Friendship! Friendship!
Ill canst thou answer this; and Reason, worse:
Unfaithful in th' Attempt; hopeless to win;
And, if I win, undone: mere madness all.
And yet th' occasion 's fair. What injury,
To him, to wear the Robe which he throws by?
 Ven. None, none at all. This happens as I wish,
To ruine her yet more with *Antony.*

  Enter Cleopatra, *talking with* Alexas, Charmion,
     Iras *on the other side.*

 Dolla. She comes! What Charms have sorrow on
   that Face!   70
Sorrow seems pleas'd to dwell with so much sweetness;
Yet, now and then, a Melancholy smile
Breaks loose, like Lightning, in a Winter's night,
And shows a moments day.
 Ven. If she should love him too! Her Eunuch there!
That *Porcpisce* bodes ill weather. Draw, draw nearer,
Sweet Devil, that I may hear.
 Alex. Believe me; try

    [Dollabella *goes over to* Charmion *and*
     Iras; *seems to talk with them.*

To make him jealous; jealousie is like   79
A polish Glass held to the lips when Life 's in doubt:

   76 *Porcpisce*] Porcupine.

If there be Breath, 'twill catch the damp and show it.

Cleop. I grant you Jealousie's a Proof of Love,
But 'tis a weak and unavailing Med'cine;
It puts out the Disease, and makes it show,
But has no pow'r to cure.

Alex. 'Tis your last Remedy, and strongest too:
And then this *Dollabella,* who so fit
To practice on? He's handsome, valiant, young,
And looks as he were laid for Nature's bait
To catch weak Womens Eyes.   90
He stands already more than half suspected
Of loving you: the least kind word, or glance,
You give this Youth, will kindle him with Love:
Then, like a burning Vessel set adrift,
You'll send him down amain before the Wind,
To fire the Heart of jealous *Antony.*

Cleop. Can I do this? Ah no; my Love's so true,
That I can neither hide it where it is,
Nor show it where it is not. Nature meant me
A Wife, a silly harmless houshold Dove,   100
Fond without Art; and kind without Deceit;
But Fortune, that has made a Mistress of me,
Hast thrust me out to the wide World, unfurnish'd
Of falshood to be happy.

Alex. Force your self.
Th' event will be, your Lover will return
Doubly desirous to possess the good
Which once he fear'd to lose.

Cleop. I must Attempt it;
But Oh with what regret!   110
            [*Exit* Alex. (*She comes up to* Dollabella.)

Ven. So, now the Scene draws near; they're in my reach.

Cleop. to Dol. Discoursing with my Women! Might not I
Share in your Entertainment?

Char. You have been
The Subject of it, Madam.

Cleop. How; and how?

Iras. Such praises of your Beauty!

Cleop. Mere Poetry.

Your *Roman* Wits, your *Gallus* and *Tibullus*,

Have taught you this from *Citheris* and *Delia*.   120

Dolla. Those *Roman* Wits have never been in *Egypt*,

Citheris and *Delia* else had been unsung:

I, who have seen——had I been born a Poet,

Should chuse a nobler Name.

Cleop. You flatter me.

But, 'tis your Nation's vice: all of your Country

Are flatterers, and all false. Your Friend's like you.

I'm sure he sent you not to speak these words.

Dolla. No, Madam; yet he sent me——

Cleop. Well, he sent you——   130

Dolla. Of a less pleasing Errand.

Cleop. How less pleasing?

Less to yourself, or me?

Dolla. Madam, to both;

For you must mourn, and I must grieve to cause it.

Cleop. You, *Charmion*, and your Fellow, stand at

   distance.

   (*Aside.*) Hold up, my Spirits.—Well, now your

   mournful matter;

For I'm prepar'd, perhaps can Guess it too.

Dolla. I wish you would; for 'tis a thankless office

To tell ill News: and I, of all your Sex,   140

Most fear displeasing you.

Cleop. Of all your Sex,

I soonest could forgive you, if you should.

Ven. Most delicate advances! Woman! Woman!

Dear damn'd, inconstant Sex!

Cleop. In the first place,

I am to be forsaken; is 't not so?

Dolla. I wish I could not Answer to that Question.

Cleop. Then pass it o'er, because it troubles you:

I should have been more griev'd another time.   15c

Next, I'm to lose my Kingdom.——Farewel, *Egypt*.

Yet, is there any more?

Dolla. Madam, I fear

Your too deep Sense of Grief has turn'd your Reason.

 Cleop. No, no, I'm not run mad; I can bear Fortune:

And Love may be expell'd by other Love

As Poysons are by Poysons.

 Dolla. You o'erjoy me, Madam,

To find your Griefs so moderately borne.

You've heard the worst; all are not false, like him.

 Cleop. No; Heav'n forbid they should.   161

 Dolla. Some Men are constant.

 Cleop. And Constancy deserves Reward, that's certain.

 Dolla. Deserves it not; but give it leave to hope.

 Ven. I'll swear thou hast my leave. I have enough:

But how to manage this! Well, I'll consider. [*Exit.*

 Dolla. I came prepar'd,

To tell you heavy News; News, which I thought,

Would fright the Blood from your pale Cheeks to hear: 170

But you have met it with a Cheerfulness

That makes my Task more easie; and my Tongue,

Which on anothers Message was employ'd,

Would gladly speak its own.

 Cleop. Hold, *Dollabella.*

First tell me, were you chosen by my Lord?

Or sought you this Employment?

 Dolla. He pick'd me out ; and, as his Bosom-Friend,

He Charg'd me with his words.

 Cleop. The Message then

I know was tender, and each Accent smooth,   180

To mollifie that rugged word *Depart.*

 Dolla. Oh, you mistake: he chose the harshest words,

With fiery Eyes, and with contracted Brows,

He Coyn'd his Face in the severest stamp:

And fury shook his Fabrick like an Earthquake;

He heav'd for vent, and burst like bellowing *Ætna,*

In Sounds scarce humane, " Hence, away for ever :
" Let her be gone, the blot of my renown,
" And bane of all my hopes :
  [*All the time of this Speech,* Cleop. *seems more*
    and more concern'd, till she sinks quite down.
" Let her be driv'n as far as Men can think 190
" From Mans commerce : She'll poyson to the Center."
 Cleop. Oh, I can bear no more !
 Dolla. Help, help : Oh Wretch ! Oh cursed, cursed
  Wretch !
What have I done?
 Char. Help, chafe her Temples, *Iras.*
 Iras. Bend, bend her forward quickly.
 Char. Heav'n be prais'd,
She comes again.
 Cleop. Oh, let him not approach me.
Why have you brought me back to this loath'd Being,
Th' abode of Falshood, violated Vows, 201
And injur'd Love? For Pity, let me go ;
For, if there be a place of long repose,
I'm sure I want it. My disdainful Lord
Can never break that quiet ; not awake
The sleeping Soul, with hollowing in my Tomb
Such words as fright her hence, Unkind, unkind.
 Dolla. kneeling. Believe me, 'tis against my self I
  speak,
That sure deserves Belief ; I injur'd him :
My Friend ne'er spoke those words. Oh, had you
  seen 210
How often he came back, and every time
With something more obliging and more kind,
To add to what he said ; what dear Farewels ;
How almost vanquisht by his Love he parted,
And lean'd to what unwillingly he left :
I, Traitor as I was, for love of you,
(But what can you not do, who made me false !)
I forg'd that Lye ; for whose forgiveness kneels
This self-accus'd, self-punish'd Criminal.

Cleop. With how much ease believe we what we
    wish!   220

Rise, *Dollabella*; if you have been Guilty,
I have contributed, and too much Love
Has made me Guilty too.
Th' advance of kindness which I made, was feign'd,
To call back fleeting Love by Jealousie;
But 'twould not last. Oh, rather let me lose
Than so ignobly trifle with his heart.

Dolla. I find your Breast fenc'd round from humane
    reach,
Transparent as a Rock of solid Chrystal;
Seen through, but never pierc'd. My Friend, my
    Friend!   230
What endless Treasure hast thou thrown away,
And scatter'd, like an Infant, in the Ocean,
Vain sums of Wealth which none can gather
    thence.

Cleop. Could you not beg
An hours Admittance to his private Ear?
Like one who wanders through long barren Wilds,
And yet foreknows no Hospitable Inn
Is near to succour Hunger,
Eats his fill, before his painful March:
So would I feed a while my famish'd Eyes   240
Before we part; for I have far to go,
If Death be far, and never must return.

Ventidius, *with* Octavia, *behind.*

Ven. From hence you may discover——Oh, sweet,
    sweet!
Would you indeed? the pretty hand in Earnest?
                                    [*Takes her hand.*
Dolla. I will, for this Reward.——Draw it not back,
'Tis all I e'er will beg.

Ven. They turn upon us.

Octav. What quick Eyes has Guilt!

Ven. Seem not to have observ'd 'em, and go on.

They Enter.

Dolla. Saw you the Emperor, *Ventidius*? 250
Ven. No.
I sought him; but I heard that he was private,
None with him, but *Hipparchus* his Freedman.
Dolla. Know you his bus'ness?
Ven. Giving him Instructions,
And Letters, to his Brother *Cæsar.*
Dolla. Well,
He must be found.   [*Exeunt* Dol. *and* Cleop.
Octav. Most glorious impudence!
Ven. She look'd methought 260
As she would say, Take your old Man, *Octavia*;
Thank you, I'm better here.
Well, but what use
Make we of this Discovery?
Octav. Let it die.
Ven. I pity *Dollabella*; but she's dangerous:
Her Eyes have pow'r beyond *Thessalian* Charms
To draw the Moon from Heav'n; for Eloquence,
The Sea-green Syrens taught her Voice their flatt'ry;
And, while she speaks, Night steals upon the Day, 270
Unmark'd of those that hear: Then she's so charming,
Age buds at sight of her, and swells to youth:
The holy Priests gaze on her when she smiles;
And with heav'd hands forgetting Gravity,
They bless her wanton Eyes: Even I who hate her,
With a malignant joy behold such Beauty;
And, while I Curse, desire it. *Anthony*
Must needs have some remains of Passion still,
Which may ferment into a worse Relapse,
If now not fully cur'd. I know, this minute, 280
With *Cæsar* he's endeavouring her Peace.
Octav. You have prevail'd:—but for a farther pur-
        pose   [*Walks off.*
I'll prove how he will relish this Discovery.
What, make a Strumpet's peace! it swells my Heart:

It must not, sha' not be.

Ven. His Guards appear.
Let me begin, and you shall second me.

Enter Antony.

Ant. Octavia, I was looking you, my Love:
What, are your Letters ready? I have giv'n
My last Instructions.   290

Octav. Mine, my Lord, are written.

Ant. Ventidius!   [*Drawing him aside.*

Ven. My Lord?

Ant. A word in private.
When saw you *Dollabella?*

Ven. Now, my Lord,
He parted hence; and *Cleopatra* with him.

Ant. Speak softly. 'Twas by my Command he went,
To bear my last farewel.

Ven. aloud. It look'd indeed   300
Like your farewel.

Ant. More softly.——My farewel?
What secret meaning have you in those words
Of my Farewel? He did it by my Order.

Ven. aloud. Then he obey'd your Order. I suppose
You bid him do it with all Gentleness,
All kindness, and all——love.

Ant. How she mourn'd,
The poor forsaken Creature!

Ven. She took it as she ought; she bore your parting
As she did *Cæsar*'s, as she would anothers,   311
Were a new Love to come.

Ant. aloud. Thou dost belye her;
Most basely, and maliciously belye her.

Ven. I thought not to displease you; I have done.

Octav. coming up. You seem disturb'd, my Lord.

Ant. A very trifle.
Retire, my Love.

Ven. It was indeed a trifle.
He sent——   320

    Ant. angrily. No more. Look how thou disobey'st
    me;
Thy Life shall answer it.
    Octav. Then 'tis no trifle.
    Ven. to Octav. 'Tis less; a very nothing: you too
    saw it,
As well as I, and therefore 'tis no Secret.
    Ant. She saw it!
    Ven. Yes: she saw young *Dollabella*——
    Ant. Young *Dollabella*!
    Ven. Young, I think him young,
And handsom too; and so do others think him.   330
But what of that? He went by your Command,
Indeed 'tis probable, with some kind Message;
For she receiv'd it graciously; she smil'd:
And then he grew familiar with her Hand,
Squeez'd it, and worry'd it with ravenous Kisses;
She blush'd, and sigh'd, and smil'd, and blush'd
    again;
At last she took occasion to Talk softly,
And brought her Cheek up close, and lean'd on his:
At which, he whisper'd Kisses back on hers;
And then she cry'd aloud, That Constancy   340
Should be rewarded.
    Octav. This I saw and heard.
    Ant. What Woman was it, whom you heard and
    saw
So playful with my Friend!
Not *Cleopatra*?
    Ven. Ev'n she, my Lord!
    Ant. My *Cleopatra*?
    Ven. Your *Cleopatra*;
Dollabella's Cleopatra?
Every Man's *Cleopatra*.   350
    Ant. Thou ly'st.
    Ven. I do not lye, my Lord.
Is this so strange? should Mistresses be left,
And not provide against a time of Change?

You know she 's not much us'd to lonely Nights.

   Ant. I'll think no more on 't.

I know 'tis false, and see the Plot betwixt you.
You needed not have gone this way, *Octavia.*
What harms it you that *Cleopatra*'s just?
She 's mine no more. I see; and I forgive: 360
Urge it no farther, Love.

   Octav. Are you concern'd
That she 's found false?

   Ant. I should be, were it so;
For, tho' 'tis past, I would not that the World
Should Tax my former Choice: That I lov'd one
Of so light Note; but I forgive you both.

   Ven. What has my Age deserv'd, that you should
     think
I would abuse your Ears with Perjury?
If Heav'n be true, she 's false.   370

   Ant. Tho' Heav'n and Earth
Should witness it, I'll not believe her tainted.

   Ven. I'll bring you then a Witness
From Hell to prove her so. Nay, go not back;
       [*Seeing* Alexas *just entring, and starting back.*
For stay you must and shall.

   Alex. What means my Lord?

   Ven. To make you do what most you hate; speak
     truth.
You are of *Cleopatra*'s private Counsel,
Of her Bed-Counsel, her lascivious hours;
Are conscious of each Nightly change she makes, 380
And watch her, as *Chaldeans* do the Moon,
Can tell what Signs she passes through, what day.

   Alex. My Noble Lord.

   Ven. My most Illustrious Pandar,
No fine set Speech, no Cadence, to turn'd Periods,
But a plain home-spun Truth, is what I ask:
I did, my self, o'erhear your Queen make love

   381 *Chaldeans*] who were the great astronomers and
astrologers of the ancient world.

To *Dollabella*. Speak; for I will know,
By your Confession, what more past betwixt 'em;
How near the bus'ness draws to your Employment;
And when the happy hour.   391

   Ant. Speak truth, *Alexas*, whether it offend
Or please *Ventidius*, care not: justifie
Thy injur'd Queen from Malice: dare his worst.

   Oct. aside. See how he gives him Courage! how he
     ears
To find her false! and shuts his Eyes to truth,
Willing to be misled!

   Alex. As far as love may plead for Woman's frailty,
Urg'd by desert and greatness of the Lover;
So far (Divine *Octavia*!) may my Queen   400
Stand ev'n excus'd to you, for loving him,
Who is your Lord: so far, from brave *Ventidius*,
May her past Actions hope a fair Report.

   Ant. 'Tis well, and truly spoken: mark, *Ventidius*.

   Alex. To you, most Noble Emperor, her strong
     Passion
Stands not excus'd, but wholly justifi'd.
Her Beauty's Charms alone, without her Crown,
From *Ind* and *Meroe* drew the distant Vows
Of sighing Kings; and at her Feet were laid
The Scepters of the Earth, expos'd on heaps,   410
To choose where she would Reign:
She thought a *Roman* only could deserve her;
And, of all *Romans*, only *Antony*.
And, to be less than Wife to you, disdain'd
Their lawful Passion.

   Ant. 'Tis but Truth.

   Alex. And yet, tho' Love, and your unmatch'd
     Desert,
Have drawn her from the due regard of Honor,
At last, Heav'n open'd her unwilling Eyes
To see the wrongs she offer'd fair *Octavia*,   420
Whose holy Bed she lawlessly usurpt.
The sad Effects of this improsperous War,

Confirm'd those pious Thoughts.

Ven. aside. O, wheel you there?

Observe him now; the Man begins to mend,
And Talk substantial Reason. Fear not, Eunuch,
The Emperor has giv'n thee leave to speak.

Alex. Else had I never dar'd t' offend his Ears
With what the last necessity has urg'd
On my forsaken Mistress; yet I must not   430
Presume to say her Heart is wholly alter'd.

Ant. No, dare not for thy Life, I Charge thee dare not,
Pronounce that fatal word.

Octav. aside. Must I bear this? good Heav'n, afford me patience.

Ven. On, sweet Eunuch; my dear half Man, proceed.

Alex. Yet _Dollabella_
Has lov'd her long, he, next my God-like Lord,
Deserves her best; and should she meet his Passion,
Rejected, as she is, by him she lov'd——

Ant. Hence, from my sight; for I can bear no more:
Let Furies drag thee quick to Hell; each torturing hand   441
Do thou employ, till _Cleopatra_ comes,
Then joyn thou too, and help to torture her.

[_Exit_ Alexas, _thrust out by_ Antony.

Octav. 'Tis not well,
Indeed, my Lord, 'tis much unkind to me,
To show this Passion, this extreme Concernment
For an abandon'd, faithless Prostitute.

Ant. _Octavia_, leave me: I am much disorder'd.
Leave me, I say.

Octav. My Lord?   450

Ant. I bid you leave me.

Ven. Obey him, Madam: best withdraw a while,
And see how this will work.

Octav. Wherein have I offended you, my Lord,
That I am bid to leave you? Am I false,

Or infamous? Am I a *Cleopatra*?
Were I she,
Base as she is, you would not bid me leave you;
But hang upon my Neck, take slight Excuses,
And fawn upon my Falshood.   460
   Ant. 'Tis too much,
Too much, *Octavia*; I am prest with Sorrows
Too heavy to be borne, and you add more:
I would retire, and recollect what's left
Of Man within, to aid me.
   Octav. You would mourn
In private, for your Love, who has betray'd you;
You did but half return to me: your kindness
Linger'd behind with her. I hear, my Lord,
You make Conditions for her,   470
And would include her Treaty. Wondrous proofs
Of Love to me!
   Ant. Are you my Friend, *Ventidius*?
Or are you turn'd a *Dollabella* too,
And let this Fury loose?
   Ven. Oh, be advis'd,
Sweet Madam, and retire.
   Octav. Yes, I will go; but never to return.
You shall no more be haunted with this Fury.
My Lord, my Lord, Love will not always last,   480
When urg'd with long unkindness, and disdain;
Take her again whom you prefer to me;
She stays but to be call'd. Poor cozen'd Man!
Let a feign'd parting give her back your Heart,
Which a feign'd Love first got; for injur'd me,
Tho' my just Sense of wrongs forbid my stay,
My Duty shall be yours.
To the dear Pledges of our former Love,
My tenderness and care shall be transferr'd,
And they shall Cheer, by Turns, my Widow'd Nights:
So, take my last farewel; for I despair   491
To have you whole, and scorn to take you half.
                              [Exit.

Ven. I combat Heav'n, which blasts my best
    Designs:
My last Attempt must be to win her back;
But Oh, I fear in vain.   [*Exit.*

    Ant. Why was I fram'd with this plain honest
      Heart,
Which knows not to disguise its Griefs, and Weakness,
But bears its workings outward to the World?
I should have kept the mighty Anguish in,
And forc'd a Smile at *Cleopatra*'s falshood: 500
Octavia had believ'd it, and had staid;
But I am made a shallow-forded Stream,
Seen to the Bottom: all my clearness scorn'd,
And all my Faults expos'd!——See, where he comes

Enter Dollabella.

Who has prophan'd the Sacred Name of Friend,
And worn it into Vileness!
With how secure a Brow, and specious Form
He gilds the secret Villain! Sure that Face
Was meant for Honesty; but Heav'n mis-match'd it,
And furnish'd Treason out with Natures Pomp,   510
To make its work more easie.

    Dolla. O, my Friend!

    Ant. Well, *Dollabella*, you perform'd my Message?

    Dolla. I did, unwillingly.

    Ant. Unwillingly?
Was it so hard for you to bear our parting?
You should have wisht it.

    Dolla. Why?

    Ant. Because you love me.
And she receiv'd my Message, with as true,   520
With as unfeign'd a Sorrow, as you brought it?

    Dolla. She loves you, ev'n to madness.

    Ant. Oh, I know it.
You, *Dollabella*, do not better know
How much she loves me. And should I
Forsake this Beauty? This all-perfect Creature?

Dolla. I could not, were she mine.

Ant. And yet you first
Perswaded me: how come you alter'd since?

Dolla. I said at first I was not fit to go;   530
I could not hear her sighs, and see her tears,
But Pity must prevail: and so, perhaps,
It may again with you; for I have promis'd
That she should take her last farewel: and, see,
She comes to claim my word.

Enter Cleopatra.

Ant. False *Dollabella*!

Dolla. What's false, my Lord?

Ant. Why, *Dollabella*'s false;
And *Cleopatra*'s false; both false and faithless.
Draw near, you well-joyn'd wickedness, you Serpents,
Whom I have, in my kindly Bosom, warm'd   541
Till I am stung to Death.

Dolla. My Lord, have I
Deserv'd to be thus us'd?

Cleop. Can Heav'n prepare
A newer Torment? Can it find a Curse
Beyond our Separation?

Ant. Yes, if Fate
Be just, much greater; Heav'n should be ingenious
In punishing such Crimes. The rowling Stone,   550
And gnawing Vulture, were slight Pains, invented
When *Jove* was young, and no Examples known
Of mighty Ills; but you have ripen'd sin
To such a monstrous growth, 'twill pose the Gods
To find an equal Torture. Two, two such,
Oh there's no farther Name, two such——to me,
To me, who lock'd my Soul within your Breasts,
Had no Desires, no Joys, no Life, but you;
When half the Globe was mine, I gave it you
In Dowry with my Heart; I had no use,   560

552 When *Jove* was young] The references are to
Sisyphus and Prometheus.

No fruit of all, but you: a Friend and Mistress
Was what the World could give. Oh, *Cleopatra*!
Oh, *Dollabella*! how could you betray
This tender Heart, which with an Infant-fondness
Lay lull'd betwixt your Bosoms, and there slept
Secure of injur'd Faith?

 Dolla. If she has wrong'd you,
Heav'n, Hell, and You revenge it.

 Ant. If she wrong'd me,
Thou wouldst evade thy part of Guilt; but swear   570
Thou lov'st not her.

 Dolla. Not so as I love you.

 Ant. Not so! Swear, swear, I say, thou dost not
  love her.

 Dolla. No more than Friendship will allow.

 Ant. No more?
Friendship allows thee nothing: thou art perjur'd.——
And yet thou didst not swear thou lov'dst her not;
But not so much, no more. Oh trifling Hypocrite,
Who dar'st not own to her thou dost not love,
Nor own to me thou dost! *Ventidius* heard it;   580
Octavia saw it.

 Cleop. They are Enemies.

 Ant. Alexas is not so: he, he confest it.
He, who, next Hell, best knew it, he avow'd it.
(*To Dol.*) Why do I seek a Proof beyond your self?
You whom I sent to bear my last Farewel,
Return'd to plead her stay.

 Dolla. What shall I Answer?
If to have lov'd be guilt, then I have sinn'd;
But if to have repented of that Love   590
Can wash away my Crime, I have repented.
Yet, if I have offended past forgiveness,
Let not her suffer: she is innocent.

 Cleop. Ah, what will not a Woman do who loves!
What means will she refuse, to keep that Heart
Where all her joys are plac'd! 'Twas I encourag'd,
'Twas I blew up the Fire that scorch'd his Soul,

To make you jealous; and by that regain you.
But all in vain; I could not Counterfeit:
In spight of all the Dams, my Love broke o'er,   600
And drown'd my Heart again: Fate took th' occasion;
And thus one minutes feigning has destroy'd
My whole Life's truth.

   Ant. Thin Cobweb Arts of Falshood;
Seen, and broke through at first.

   Dolla. Forgive your Mistress.

   Cleop. Forgive your Friend.

   Ant. You have convinc'd your selves,
You plead each others Cause: What Witness have you,
That you but meant to raise my Jealousie?   610

   Cleop. Our selves, and Heav'n.

   Ant. Guilt witnesses for Guilt. Hence, Love and
     Friendship;
You have no longer place in human Breasts,
These two have driv'n you out: avoid my sight;
I would not kill the Man whom I lov'd;
And cannot hurt the Woman; but avoid me,
I do not know how long I can be tame;
For, if I stay one minute more to think
How I am wrong'd, my Justice and Revenge
Will cry so loud within me, that my Pity   620
Will not be heard for either.

   Dolla. Heav'n has but
Our sorrow for our sins; and then delights
To pardon erring Man: sweet Mercy seems
Its darling Attribute, which limits Justice;
As if there were Degrees in Infinite;
And Infinite would rather want perfection
Than punish to extent.

   Ant. I can forgive
A Foe; but not a Mistress, and a Friend: 630
Treason is there in its most horrid shape,
Where trust is greatest: and the Soul resign'd
Is stabb'd by its own Guards: I'll hear no more;
Hence from my sight for ever.

Cleop. How? for ever,
I cannot go one moment from your sight,
And must I go for ever?
My Joys, my only Joys are center'd here:
What place have I to go to? my own Kingdom?
That I have lost for you: or to the *Romans*?   640
They hate me for your sake: or must I wander
The wide World o'er, a helpless, banish'd Woman,
Banish'd for love of you; banish'd from you?
Ay, there's the Banishment! Oh hear me; hear me,
With strictest Justice: For I beg no favour:
And if I have offended you: then kill me,
But do not banish me.

   Ant. I must not hear you.
I have a Fool within me takes your part;
But Honour stops my Ears.   650

   Cleop. For pity hear me!
Wou'd you cast off a Slave who follow'd you,
Who crouch'd beneath your Spurn?——He has no
   pity!
See, if he gives one tear to my Departure;
One look, one kind farewel: Oh Iron heart!
Let all the Gods look down, and judge betwixt us,
If he did ever love!

   Ant No more: *Alexas*!

   Dolla. A perjur'd Villain!

   Ant. to Cleop. Your *Alexas*; yours.   660

   Cleop. O 'twas his Plot: his ruinous Design
T' ingage you in my love by jealousie.
Hear him; confront him with me; let him speak.

   Ant. I have; I have.

   Cleop. And if he clear me not——

   Ant. Your Creature! one who hangs upon your
   Smiles!
Watches your Eye to say or to unsay
Whate'er you please! I am not to be mov'd.

   Cleop. Then must we part? Farewel, my cruel
   Lord

Th' appearance is against me; and I go   670
Unjustifi'd, for ever from your sight.
How I have lov'd, you know; how yet I love,
My only Comfort is, I know my self:
I love you more, ev'n now you are unkind,
Than when you lov'd me most; so well, so truly,
I'll never strive against it; but die pleas'd
To think you once were mine.
   Ant. Good Heav'n, they weep at parting.
Must I weep too? that calls 'em innocent.
I must not weep; and yet I must, to think   680
That I must not forgive——
Live; but live wretched, 'tis but just you shou'd,
Who made me so: Live from each others sight:
Let me not hear you meet: Set all the Earth,
And all the Seas, betwixt your sunder'd Loves:
View nothing common but the Sun and Skys:
Now, all take several ways;
   And each your own sad fate with mine deplore;
   That you were false, and I could trust no more.
                          [*Exeunt severally.*

ACT V.

Cleopatra, Charmion, Iras.

   Char. Be juster, Heav'n: such Virtue punish'd
     thus,
Will make us think that Chance rules all above,
And shuffles, with a Random hand, the Lots
Which Man is forc'd to draw.
   Cleop. I cou'd tear out these Eyes, that gain'd his
     Heart,
And had not pow'r to keep it. O the Curse
Of doting on, ev'n when I find it Dotage!
Bear witness, Gods, you heard him bid me go;
You whom he mock'd with imprecating Vows

Of promis'd Faith——I'll die, I will not bear it.   10
You may hold me.——

[She pulls out her Dagger, and they hold her.

But I can keep my Breath; I can die inward,
And choak this Love.

Enter Alexas.

Iras. Help, O *Alexas* help!
The Queen grows desperate, her Soul struggles in her,
With all the Agonies of Love and Rage,
And strives to force its Passage.

    Cleop. Let me go.
Art thou there, Traitor!——O,
O, for a little Breath, to vent my Rage!   20
Give, give me way, and let me loose upon him.

    Alex. Yes, I deserve it, for my ill-tim'd truth.
Was it for me to prop
The Ruins of a falling Majesty?
To place my self beneath the mighty flaw,
Thus to be crush'd, and pounded into Atoms,
By its o'erwhelming weight? 'Tis too presuming
For Subjects, to preserve that wilful pow'r
Which Courts its own Destruction.

    Cleop. I wou'd reason   30
More calmly with you. Did not you o'er-rule,
And force my plain, direct, and open Love
Into these crooked paths of Jealousie?
Now, what's th' event? *Octavia* is remov'd;
But *Cleopatra*'s banish'd. Thou, thou, Villain,
Has push'd my Boat, to open Sea; to prove,
At my sad Cost, if thou canst steer it back.
It cannot be; I'm lost too far; I'm ruin'd:
Hence, thou Impostor, Traitor, Monster, Devil.——
I can no more: thou, and my Griefs, have sunk   40
Me down so low, that I want voice to Curse thee.

    Alex. Suppose from Shipwrack'd Seaman near the
      shore,
Dropping and faint, with climbing up the Cliff,

If, from above, some Charitable hand
Pull him to safety, hazarding himself
To draw the others weight; wou'd he look back
And Curse him for his Pains? The Case is yours;
But one step more, and you have gain'd the heighth.

 Cleop. Sunk, never more to rise.

 Alex. *Octavia*'s gone, and *Dollabella* banish'd. 50
Believe me, Madam, *Antony* is yours.
His Heart was never lost; but started off
To Jealousie, Love's last retreat and covert:
Where it lies hid in Shades, watchful in silence,
And list'ning for the Sound that calls it back,
Some other, any Man, ('tis so advanc'd)
May perfect this unfinish'd work, which I
(Unhappy only to my self) have left
So easie to his hand.

 Cleop. Look well thou do't; else—— 60

 Alex. Else, what your silence threatens——*Antony*
Is mounted up the *Pharos*; from whose Turret,
He stands surveying our *Egyptian* Gallies,
Engag'd with *Cæsar*'s Fleet: now Death, or Conquest.
If the first happen, Fate acquits my Promise:
If we o'ercome, the Conqueror is yours.

A distant shout within.

 Char. Have comfort, Madam: did you mark that
  Shout?

Second Shout nearer.

 Iras. Hark; they redouble it.

 Alex. 'Tis from the Port.
The loudness shows it near: good News, kind
  Heavens. 70

 Cleop. *Osiris* make it so.

Enter Serapion.

 Serap. Where, where's the Queen?

 Alex. How frightfully the holy Coward stares!
As if not yet recover'd of th' Assault,
When all his Gods, and what's more dear to him,

His Offerings were at stake.

 Serap. O horror, horror!
Egypt has been; our latest hour is come:
The Queen of Nations from her ancient Seat,
Is Sunk for ever in the dark Abyss: 80
Time has unrowl'd her Glories to the last,
And now clos'd up the Volume.

 Cleop. Be more plain:
Say, whence thou com'st, (though Fate is in thy Face,
Which from thy haggard Eyes looks wildly out,
And threatens ere thou speak'st.)

 Serap. I came from *Pharos*;
From viewing (spare me and imagine it)
Our Lands last hope, your Navy.——

 Cleop. Vanquish'd?   90

 Serap. No.
They fought not.

 Cleop. Then they fled.

 Serap. Nor that. I saw,
With *Antony*, your well appointed Fleet
Row out; and thrice he wav'd his hand on high,
And thrice with cheerful Crys they shouted back:
'Twas then, false Fortune, like a fawning Strumpet,
About to leave the Bankrupt Prodigal,
With a dissembling Smile would kiss at parting, 100
And flatter to the last; the well-tim'd Oars
Now dipt from every Bank, now smoothly run
To meet the Foe; and soon indeed they met,
But not as Foes. In few, we saw their Caps
On either side thrown up; the *Egyptian* Gallies
(Receiv'd like Friends) past through, and fell behind
The *Roman* rear: and now, they all come forward,
And ride within the Port.

 Cleop. Enough, *Serapion*:
I've heard my doom. This needed not, you Gods:
When I lost *Antony*, your work was done; 111
'Tis but superfluous malice. Where's my Lord?
How bears he this last blow?

Serap. His fury cannot be express'd by words:
Thrice he Attempted headlong to have faln
Full on his Foes, and aim'd at *Cæsar*'s Galley:
With-held, he raves on you; Crys, He's betray'd.
Should he now find you——
    Alex. Shun him, seek your safety,
Till you can clear your Innocence.   120
    Cleop. I'll stay.
    Alex. You must not, haste you to your Monument,
While I make speed to *Cæsar*.
    Cleop. Cæsar ! No,
I have no business with him.
    Alex. I can work him
To spare your Life, and let this Madman perish.
    Cleop. Base fawning Wretch! wouldst thou betray
      him too?
Hence from my sight, I will not hear a Traytor;
'Twas thy Design brought all this ruine on us;   130
Serapion, thou art honest; Counsel me:
But haste, each moment's precious.
    Serap. Retire; you must not yet see *Antony*.
He who began this mischief,
'Tis just he tempt the Danger: let him clear you;
And, since he offer'd you his servile tongue,
To gain a poor precarious Life from *Cæsar*,
Let him expose that fawning Eloquence,
And speak to *Antony*.
    Alex. O Heavens! I dare not,   140
I meet my certain Death.
    Cleop. Slave, thou deserv'st it.
Not that I fear my Lord, will I avoid him;
I know him Noble: when he banish'd me,
And thought me false, he scorn'd to take my
    Life;
But I'll be justifi'd, and then die with him.
    Alex. O pity me, and let me follow you.
    Cleop. To Death, if thou stir hence. Speak, if thou
    canst.

Now for thy Life, which basely thou wou'dst save;
While mine I prize at this. Come, good *Serapion.* 150
    [*Exeunt* Cleop. Serap. Char. Iras.

 Alex. O that I less cou'd fear to lose this Being,
Which, like a Snow-ball, in my Coward hand,
The more 'tis grasp'd, the faster melts away.
Poor Reason! what a wretched Aid art thou!
For still in spight of thee,
These two long Lovers, Soul and Body, dread
Their final Separation. Let me think:
What can I say, to save my self from Death?
No matter what becomes of *Cleopatra.*

 Ant. within. Which way? where?   160

 Ven. within. This leads to th' Monument.

 Alex. Ah me! I hear him; yet I'm unprepar'd:
My gift of lying's gone;
And this Court-Devil, which I so oft have rais'd,
Forsakes me at my need. I dare not stay;
Yet cannot far go hence.   [*Exit.*

    Enter Antony *and* Ventidius.

 Ant. O happy *Cæsar!* Thou hast Men to lead:
Think not 'tis thou hast conquer'd *Antony*;
But *Rome* has conquer'd *Egypt.* I'm betray'd.

 Ven. Curse on this treach'rous Train!   170
Their Soil and Heav'n infect 'em all with Baseness:
And their young Souls come tainted to the World
With the first breath they draw.

 Ant. Th' Original Villain sure no God created;
He was a Bastard of the Sun, by *Nile.*
Ap'd into Man: with all his Mother's Mud
Crusted about his Soul.

 Ven. The Nation is
One Universal Traitor; and their Queen
The very Spirit and Extract of 'em all.   180

 Ant. Is there yet left
A possibility of Aid from Valour?
Is there one God unsworn to my Destruction?

The least unmortgag'd hope? for, if there be,
Methinks I cannot fall beneath the Fate
Of such a Boy as *Cæsar*.
The World's one half is yet in *Antony*;
And, from each Limb of it that 's hew'd away,
The Soul comes back to me.
    Ven. There yet remain   190
Three Legions in the Town. The last Assault
Lopt off the rest: if Death be your Design,
(As I must wish it now) these are sufficient
To make a heap about us of dead Foes,
An honest Pile for burial.
    Ant. They're enough.
We'll not divide our Stars; but side by side
Fight emulous: and with malicious Eyes
Survey each other's Acts: so every Death
Thou giv'st, I'll take on me, as a just Debt,   200
And pay thee back a Soul.
    Ven. Now you shall see I love you. Not a word
Of chiding more. By my few hours of Life,
I am so pleas'd with this brave *Roman* Fate,
That I wou'd not be *Cæsar*, to out-live you.
When we put off this Flesh, and mount together,
I shall be shown to all th' Etherial crowd;
Lo, this is he who dy'd with *Antony*.
    Ant. Who knows but we may pierce through all
        their Troops,
And reach my Veterans yet? 'Tis worth the tempting,
T' o'er-leap this Gulph of Fate,   211
And leave our wand'ring Destinies behind.

Enter Alexas, *trembling.*

    Ven. See, see, that Villain;
See *Cleopatra* stampt upon that Face,
With all her cunning, all her Arts of Falshood!
How she looks out through those dissembling Eyes!
How he sets his Count'nance for deceit;
And promises a Lye, before he speaks!

Let me dispatch him first.   *(Drawing.)*

   Alex. O, spare me, spare me.   220

   Ant. Hold; he's not worth your killing. On thy Life,
(Which thou mayst keep, because I scorn to take it)
No Syllable to justifie thy Queen;
Save thy base tongue its Office.

   Alex. Sir she's gone,
Where she shall never be molested more
By Love, or you.

   Ant. Fled to her *Dollabella*!
Die, Traitor, I revoke my Promise, die.
                  (Going to kill him.)

   Alex. O hold, she is not fled.   230

   Ant. She is: my Eyes
Are open to her Falshood; my whole Life
Has been a Golden dream, of Love and Friendship.
But, now I wake, I'm like a Merchant, rows'd
From soft repose, to see his Vessel sinking,
And all his Wealth cast o'er. Ingrateful Woman!
Who follow'd me, but as the Swallow Summer,
Hatching her young ones in my kindly Beams,
Singing her flatt'ries to my morning wake;
But, now my Winter comes, she spreads her wings,
And seeks the Spring of *Cæsar*.   241

   Alex. Think not so: in all things, mixt with yours.
Her Fortunes have,
Had she betray'd her Naval force to *Rome*,
How easily might she have gone to *Cæsar*,
Secure by such a Bribe!

   Ven. She sent it first,
To be more welcome after.

   Ant. 'Tis too plain;
Else wou'd she have appear'd, to clear her self.   250

   Alex. Too fatally she has; she could not bear
To be accus'd by you; but shut her self
Within her Monument: look'd down, and sigh'd;
While, from her unchang'd face, the silent tears

Dropt, as they had not leave, but stole their
  parting.
Some undistinguish'd words she inly murmur'd;
At last, she rais'd her Eyes; and, with such Looks
As dying *Lucrece* cast,——

  Ant. My heart forbodes.——

  Ven. All for the best: go on.   260

  Alex. She snatch'd her Ponyard,
And, ere we cou'd prevent the fatal Blow,
Plung'd it within her Breast: then turn'd to me,
Go, bear my Lord (said she) my last Farewel;
And ask him if he yet suspect my Faith.
More she was saying, but Death rush'd betwixt.
She half pronounc'd your Name with her last Breath,
And bury'd half within her.

  Ven. Heav'n be prais'd.

  Ant. Then art thou innocent, my poor dear Love?
And art thou dead?   271
O those two words! their Sound shou'd be divided:
Hadst thou been false, and dy'd; or hadst thou
  liv'd,
And hadst been true——. But Innocence and Death!
This shows not well above. Then what am I,
The Murderer of this Truth, this Innocence!
Thoughts cannot form themselves in words so horrid
As can express my Guilt!

  Ven. Is 't come to this? The Gods have been too
  gracious:
And thus you thank 'em for 't.   280

  Ant. to Alex. Why stay'st thou here?
Is it for thee to spy upon my Soul,
And see its inward mourning? Get thee hence;
Thou art not worthy to behold, what now
Becomes a *Roman* Emperor to perform.

  Alex. Aside. He loves her still:
His grief betrays it. Good! The joy to find
She 's yet alive, compleats the Reconcilement.
I've sav'd my self, and her. But, Oh! the *Romans*!

Fate comes too fast upon my Wit.   290
Hunts me too hard, and meets me at each double.
                                            [*Exit.*

   Ven. Wou'd she had dy'd a little sooner tho',
Before *Octavia* went; you might have treated:
Now 'twill look tame, and wou'd not be receiv'd.
Come, rouze your self, and lets die warm together.

   Ant. I will not fight; there 's no more work for War.
The bus'ness of my angry hours is done.

   Ven. Cæsar is at your Gates.

   Ant. Why, let him enter;
He 's welcome now.   300

   Ven. What Lethargy has crept into your Soul?

   Ant. 'Tis but a scorn of Life, and just desire
To free my self from Bondage.

   Ven. Do it bravely.

   Ant. I will; but not by fighting. O, *Ventidius*!
What shou'd I fight for now? My Queen is dead.
I was but great for her; my Pow'r, my Empire,
Were but my Merchandise to buy her Love;
And conquer'd Kings, my Factors. Now she 's dead,
Let *Cæsar* take the World,——   310
An Empty Circle, since the Jewel 's gone
Which made it worth my strife: my Being 's nauseous;
For all the Bribes of Life are gone away.

   Ven. Wou'd you be taken?

   Ant. Yes, I wou'd be taken;
But, as a *Roman* ought, dead, my *Ventidius*:
For I'll convey my Soul from *Cæsar*'s reach,
And lay down life my self. 'Tis time the World
Shou'd have a Lord, and know whom to obey.
We two have kept its Homage in suspense,   320
And bent the Globe on whose each side we trod,
Till it was dinted inwards: Let him walk
Alone upon 't; I'm weary of my part.
My Torch is out; and the World stands before me
Like a black Desart, at the approach of Night:
I'll lay me down, and stray no farther on.

Ven. I cou'd be griev'd,
But that I'll not out-live you: choose your Death;
For, I have seen him in such various shapes,
I care not which I take: I'm only troubled   330
The Life I bear, is worn to such a Rag,
'Tis scarce worth giving. I cou'd wish indeed
We threw it from us with a better Grace;
That, like two Lyons taken in the Toils,
We might at last thrust out our paws, and wound
The Hunters that inclose us.
    Ant. I have thought on 't.
Ventidius, you must live.
    Ven. I must not Sir.   339
    Ant. Wilt thou not live, to speak some good of me?
To stand by my fair Fame, and guard th' approaches
From the ill Tongues of Men?
    Ven. Who shall guard mine,
For living after you?
    Ant. Say, I command it.
    Ven. If we die well, our Deaths will speak them-
        selves,
And need no living Witness.
    Ant. Thou hast lov'd me,
And fain I wou'd reward thee: I must die;
Kill me, and take the Merit of my Death   350
To make thee Friends with *Cæsar.*
    Ven. Thank your kindness.
You said I lov'd you; and, in recompence,
You bid me turn a Traitor: did I think
You wou'd have us'd me thus? that I shou'd die
With a hard thought of you?
    Ant. Forgive me, *Roman.*
Since I have heard of *Cleopatra's* Death,
My Reason bears no rule upon my Tongue,
But lets my thoughts break all at Random out: 360
I've thought better; do not deny me twice.
    Ven. By Heav'n, I will not.
Let it not be t' out-live you.

Ant. Kill me first,
And then die thou; for 'tis but just thou serve
Thy Friend, before thy self.

   Ven. Give me your hand.
We soon shall meet again. Now farewel, Emperor.
                              (*Embrace.*)
Methinks that word 's too cold to be my last:
Since Death sweeps distinctions, Farewel, Friend. 370
That 's all.——
I will not make a bus'ness of a trifle:
And yet I cannot look on you, and kill you;
Pray turn your Face.

   Ant. I do: strike home sure.

   Ven. Home, as my Sword will reach.
                             (*Kills himself.*)

   Ant. O, thou mistak'st;
That wound was none of thine: give it me back:
Thou robb'st me of my Death.

   Ven. I do indeed; 380
But, think 'tis the first time I e'er deceiv'd you;
If that may plead my Pardon. And you, Gods,
Forgive me, if you will; for I die perjur'd,
Rather then kill my Friend.   (*Dies.*)

   Ant. Farewel. Ever my Leader, ev'n in Death!
My Queen and thou have got the start of me,
And I'm the lag of Honour.——Gone so soon?
Is Death no more? He us'd him carelessly,
With a familiar kindness: ere he knock'd,
Ran to the Door, and took him in his Arms, 390
As who shou'd say, Y' are welcome at all hours,
A Friend need give no warning. Books had spoil'd
    him;
For all the Learn'd are Cowards by Profession.
'Tis not worth
My farther thought: for Death, for ought I know,
Is but to think no more. Here 's to be satisfi'd.
                         (*Falls on his Sword.*)
I've mist my heart. O unperforming hand!

Thou never cou'dst have err'd in a worse time.
My Fortune jades me to the last; and Death,
Like a great Man, takes state, and makes me wait 400
For my Admittance——.   (*Trampling within.*)
Some perhaps from *Cæsar*:
If he shou'd find me living, and suspect
That I plaid booty with my Life! I'll mend
My work, ere they can reach me.

                              (*Rises upon his Knees.*)

          Enter Cleopatra, Charmion, Iras.

     Cleop. Where is my Lord? where is he?
     Char. There he lies,
And dead *Ventidius* by him.
     Cleop. My fears were Prophets; I am come too late.
O that accurs'd *Alexas*!   (*Runs to him.*)
     Ant. Art thou living?   411
Or am I dead before I knew? and thou
The first kind Ghost that meets me?
     Cleop. Help me Seat him.
Send quickly, send for help.

                              (*They place him in a Chair.*)

     Ant. I am answer'd.
We live both. Sit thee down, my *Cleopatra*:
I'll make the most I can of Life, to stay
A moment more with thee.
     Cleop. How is it with you?   420
     Ant. 'Tis as with a Man
Removing in a hurry; all pack'd up,
But one dear Jewel that his haste forgot;
And he, for that returns upon the spur:
So I come back, for thee.
     Cleop. Too long, you Heav'ns, you have been cruel
          to me;
Now show your mended Faith, and give me back
His fleeting Life.
     Ant. It will not be, my Love.

I keep my Soul by force. 430
Say but thou art not false.

    Cleop. 'Tis now too late
To say I'm true: I'll prove it, and die with you.
Unknown to me, *Alexas* feign'd my Death:
Which, when I knew, I hasted to prevent
This fatal consequence. My Fleet betray'd
Both you and me.

    Ant. And *Dollabella.*——

    Cleop. Scarce esteem'd before he lov'd; but hated
now.

    Ant. Enough: my Life 's not long enough for more.
Thou sayst thou wilt come after: I believe thee; 441
For I can now believe whate'er thou sayst,
That we may part more kindly.

    Cleop. I will come:
Doubt not, my Life, I'll come, and quickly too:
Cæsar shall triumph o'er no part of thee.

    Ant. But grieve not, while thou stay'st
My last disastrous Times:
Think we have had a clear and glorious day;
And Heav'n did kindly to delay the Storm 450
Just till our close of Ev'ning. Ten years love,
And not a moment lost, but all improv'd
To th' utmost Joys: What Ages have we liv'd?
And now to die each others; and, so dying,
While hand in hand we walk in Groves below,
Whole Troops of Lovers Ghosts shall flock about us,
And all the Train be ours.

    Cleop. Your words are like the Notes of dying
Swans,
Too sweet to last. Were there so many hours
For your unkindness, and not one for Love? 460

    Ant. No, not a minute.——This one kiss——more
worth
Than all I leave to *Cæsar.*   (*Dies.*)

    Cleop. O, tell me so again,
And take Ten thousand kisses, for that word.

My Lord, my Lord: speak, if you yet have being;
Sigh to me, if you cannot speak; or cast
One look: Do any thing that shows you live.
 Iras. He's gone too far, to hear you;
And this you see, a Lump of sensless Clay,
The leavings of a Soul.   470
 Char. Remember Madam,
He charg'd you not to grieve.
 Cleop. And I'll obey him.
I have not lov'd a *Roman* not to know
What should become his Wife; his Wife, my *Char-*
  mion;
For 'tis to that high Title I aspire,
And now I'll not die less. Let dull *Octavia*
Survive, to mourn him dead: my Nobler Fate
Shall knit our Spousals with a tie too strong
For *Roman* Laws to break.   480
 Iras. Will you then die?
 Cleop. Why shou'dst thou make that Question?
 Iras. *Cæsar* is most merciful.
 Cleop. Let him be so
To those that want his Mercy: my poor Lord
Made no such Cov'nant with him to spare me
When he was dead. Yield me to *Cæsar's* pride?
What, to be led in Triumph through the Streets,
A Spectacle to base *Plebeian* Eyes;
While some dejected Friend of *Antony's*,   490
Close in a Corner, shakes his Head, and mutters
A Secret Curse on her who ruin'd him?
I'll none of that.
 Char. Whatever you resolve,
I'll follow ev'n to Death.
 Iras. I only fear'd
For you; but more shou'd fear to live without you.
 Cleop. Why, now 'tis as it shou'd be. Quick, my
  Friends,
Dispatch; ere this, the Town's in *Cæsar's* hands:
My Lord looks down concern'd, and fears my stay,

Lest I shou'd be surpriz'd;   501
Keep him not waiting for his Love too long.
You, _Charmion_, bring my Crown and richest Jewels,
With 'em, the Wreath of Victory I made
(Vain Augury!) for him who now lies dead;
You, _Iras_, bring the Cure of all our Ills.
    Iras. The Aspicks, Madam?
    Cleop. Must I bid you twice?

                                    [_Exeunt_ Char. _and_ Iras.
'Tis sweet to die, when they wou'd force life on me
To rush into the dark aboad of Death,   510
And seize him first; if he be like my Love,
He is not frightful sure.
We're now alone, in secresie and silence;
And is not this like Lovers? I may kiss
These pale, cold Lips; _Octavia_ does not see me;
And, Oh! 'tis better far to have him thus,
Than see him in her Arms.——O welcome, welcome.

                                    [_Enter_ Charmion, Iras.

    Char. What must be done?
    Cleop. Short Ceremony, Friends:
But yet it must be decent. First, this Laurel   520
Shall Crown my Hero's Head: he fell not basely,
Nor left his Shield behind him. Only thou
Cou'dst triumph o'er thy self; and thou alone
Wert worthy so to triumph.
    Char. To what end
These Ensigns of your Pomp and Royalty?
    Cleop. Dull, that thou art! why, 'tis to meet my
        Love;
As when I saw him first, on _Cydnos_ bank,
All sparkling, like a Goddess; so adorn'd,
I'll find him once again: my second Spousals   530
Shall match my first, in Glory. Haste, haste, both,
And dress the Bride of _Antony_.
    Char. 'Tis done.
    Cleop. Now seat me by my Lord. I claim this place;

For I must Conquer *Cæsar* too, like him,
And win my share o'th' World. Hail, you dear
    Relicks
Of my Immortal Love!
O let no Impious hand remove you hence;
But rest for ever here: let *Egypt* give
His Death that Peace, which it deny'd his Life.   540
Reach me the Casket.

    Iras. Underneath the fruit the Aspick lies.

    Cleop. putting aside the leaves. Welcom, thou kind
    Deceiver!

Thou best of Thieves; who, with an easie key,
Do'st open Life, and unperceiv'd by us,
Ev'n steal us from our selves: discharging so
Death's dreadful Office, better than himself,
Touching our Limbs so gently into slumber,
That Death stands by, deceiv'd by his own Image,
And thinks himself but Sleep.   550

    Serap. within. The Queen, where is she?

The Town is yielded, *Cæsar*'s at the Gates.

    Cleop. He comes too late to invade the Rights of
    Death.

Haste, bare my Arm, and rouze the Serpents fury.

            [Holds out her Arm and draws it back.

Coward Flesh——
Would'st thou conspire with *Cæsar*, to betray me,
As thou wert none of mine? I'll force thee to 't,
And not be sent by him,
But bring my Self, my Soul to *Antony.*

       [Turns aside, and then shows her Arm bloody.

Take hence; the work is done.   560

    Serap. within. Break ope the Door,
And guard the Traitor well.

    Char. The next is ours.

    Iras. Now, *Charmion*, to be worthy
Of your great Queen and Mistress.

              [They apply the Aspicks.

    Cleop. Already, Death, I feel thee in my Veins;

I go with such a will to find my Lord,
That we shall quickly meet.
A heavy numbness creeps through every Limb,
And now 'tis at my Head: my Eye-lids fall,   570
And my dear Love is vanish'd in a Mist.
Where shall I find him, where? O turn me to him,
And lay me on his Breast.——*Cæsar*, thy worst;
Now part us, if thou canst.

> (*Dies.*) Iras *sinks down at her feet, and dies;*
> Charmion *stands behind her Chair, as
> dressing her Head.*

Enter Serapion, *two Priests,* Alexas *bound,* Egyptians.

2. Priests. Behold, *Serapion*, what havock Death has
made!

Serap. 'Twas what I fear'd.
Charmion, is this well done?

Char. Yes, 'tis well done, and like a Queen, the last
Of her great Race: I follow her.   (*Sinks down; Dies.*)

Alexas. 'Tis true,   580
She has done well: much better thus to die,
Than live to make a Holy-day in *Rome*.

Serap. See, see how the Lovers sit in State together,
As they were giving Laws to half Mankind.
Th' impression of a Smile left in her Face,
Shows she dy'd pleas'd with him for whom she liv'd
And went to Charm him in another World.
Cæsar's just entring; grief has now no leisure.
Secure that Villain, as our pledge of safety
To grace th' Imperial Triumph. Sleep, blest Pair,
Secure from humane Chance, long Ages out,   591
While all the Storms of Fate fly o'er your Tomb;
> And Fame, to late Posterity, shall tell,
> No Lovers liv'd so great, or dy'd so well.

Epilogue.

Poets, like Disputants, when Reasons fail,
Have one sure Refuge left and that's to rail;
Fop, Coxcomb, Fool, are thunder'd through the Pit;
And this is all their Equipage of Wit.
We wonder how the Devil this diff'rence grows,
Betwixt our Fools in Verse, and yours in Prose?
For, 'Faith, the quarrel rightly understood,
'Tis Civil War with their own Flesh and Blood.
The Thread-bare Author hates the gawdy Coat;
And swears at the Gilt Coach, but swears a foot: 10
For 'tis observ'd of every Scribling Man,
He grows a Fop as fast as e'er he can;
Prunes up, and asks his Oracle the Glass,
If Pink or Purple best become his Face.
For our poor Wretch, he neither rails nor prays; ⎫
Nor likes your Wit just as you like his Plays;   ⎬
He has not yet so much of Mr. Bays.   ⎭
He does his best; and, if he cannot please,
Wou'd quietly sue out his Writ of Ease.
Yet, if he might his own Grand Jury call,   20
By the Fair Sex he begs to stand or fall.
Let Cæsar's Pow'r the Mens ambition move,
But grace you him who lost the World for Love.
Yet if some antiquated Lady say,
The last Age is not Copy'd in his Play;
Heav'n help the Man who for that Face must drudge,
Which only has the wrinkles of a Judge.
Let not the Young and Beauteous joyn with those;
For shou'd you raise such numerous Hosts of Foes,
Young Wits and Sparks he to his aid must call;   30
'Tis more than one Man's work to please you all.

FINIS.

Venice Preserv'd,

OR,

A Plot Discover'd.

A

TRAGEDY.

As it is Acted at the

DUKE'S THEATRE.

Written by *THOMAS OTWAY.*

LONDON,

Printed for *Jos. Hindmarsh* at the Sign of the
Black Bull, over against the Royal
Exchange in *Cornhill.* 1682.

EPISTLE DEDICATORY

To Her GRACE the

DUTCHESS

OF

PORTSMOUTH.

MADAM,

Were it possible for me to let the World know how entirely your Graces Goodness has devoted a poor man to your service; were there words enough in speech to express the mighty sense I have of your great bounty towards me; surely I should write and talk of it for ever: But your Grace has given me so large a Theam, and laid so very vast a foundation, that Imagination wants stock to build upon it. I am as one dumb when I would speak of it, and when I strive to write, I want a scale of thought sufficient to comprehend the height of it. Forgive me then, Madam, if (as a poor Peasant once made a Present of an Apple to an Emperour) I bring this small Tribute, the humble growth of my little Garden, and lay it at your feet. Believe it is paid you with the utmost gratitude, believe that so long as I have thought to remember, how very much I owe your generous Nature, I will ever have a heart that shall be gratefull for it too: Your Grace, next Heaven,

Dutchess of Portsmouth] Louise de Kéroualle (1649–1734), mistress of Charles II, who created her Duchess of Portsmouth 1673. The young Prince referred to in the dedication was born in 1672, and was the ancestor of the Dukes of Richmond.

*deserves it amply from me; That gave me life, but on a hard
condition, till your extended favour taught me to prize the
gift, and took the heavy burthen it was clogg'd with from
me: I mean hard Fortune: When I had enemies, that with
malitious power kept back and shaded me from those Royal
Beams, whose warmth is all I have, or hope to live by; Your
noble pity and compassion found me, where I was far cast
backward from my blessing; down in the rear of Fortune,
call'd me up, plac'd me in the shine, and I have felt its
comfort. You have in that restor'd me to my native Right,
for a steady Faith, and Loyalty to my Prince, was all the
Inheritance my Father left me, and however hardly my ill
Fortune deal with me, 'tis what I prize so well that I ne'r
pawn'd it yet, and hope I ne'r shall part with it. Nature
and Fortune were certainly in league when you were born,
and as the first took care to give you beauty enough to enslave
the hearts of all the World, so the other resolv'd to doe its
merit Justice, that none but a Monarch, fit to rule that
World, should e'r possess it, and in it he had an Empire.
The Young Prince you have given him, by his blooming
Vertues, early declares the mighty stock he came from; and
as you have taken all the pious care of a dear Mother and a
prudent Guardian to give him a noble and generous education;
may it succeed according to his merits and your wishes:
May he grow up to be a Bulwark to his illustrious Father,
and a Patron to his Loyal Subjects, with Wisedom and
Learning to assist him, whenever call'd to his Councils, to
defend his right against the encroachments of Republicans in
his Senates, to cherish such men as shall be able to vindicate
the Royal Cause, that good and fit servants to the Crown,
may never be lost for want of a Protectour. May He have
courage and conduct, fit to fight his Battels abroad, and
terrifie his Rebells at home; and that all these may be yet
more sure, may He never, during the Spring-time of his years,
when those growing Vertues ought with care to be cherish'd,
in order to their ripening; may he never meet with vitious
Natures, or the tongues of faithless, sordid, insipid Flatterers,
to blast 'em: To conclude; may He be as great as the hand*

*of Fortune (with his Honour) shall be able to make him:
And may your Grace, who are so good a Mistress, and so
noble a Patroness, never meet with a less gratefull Servant,
than,*

Madam,
        Your Graces entirely
                Devoted Creature,
                        Thomas Otway.

PROLOGUE.

In these distracted times, when each man dreads
The bloudy stratagems of busie heads;
When we have fear'd three years we know not what,
Till Witnesses begin to die o' th' rot,
What made our Poet meddle with a Plot?
Was't that he fansy'd, for the very sake
And name of Plot, his trifling Play might take?
For there's not in't one Inch-board Evidence,
But 'tis, he says, to reason plain and sense,
And that he thinks a plausible defence.　　　　　10
Were Truth by Sense and Reason to be tri'd,
Sure all our Swearers might be laid aside:
No, of such Tools our Author has no need,
To make his Plot, or may his Play succeed;
He, of black Bills, has no prodigious Tales,
Or Spanish Pilgrims cast a-shore in Wales,
Here's not one murther'd Magistrate at least,
Kept rank like Ven'son for a City feast,
Grown four days stiff, the better to prepare
And fit his plyant limbs to ride in Chair:　　　　　20
Yet here's an Army rais'd, though under ground,
But no man seen, nor one Commission found;
Here is a Traitour too, that's very old,
Turbulent, subtle, mischeivous and bold,
Bloudy, revengefull, and to crown his part,
Loves fumbling with a Wench, with all his heart;
Till after having many changes pass'd,
In spight of Age (thanks Heaven) is hang'd at last:

1 *distracted times*] viz. of the Popish Plot.

17 *Magistrate*] Sir Edmund Berry Godfrey, who was murdered on Primrose Hill between October 12 and 15, 1678.

23 *Traitour*] Antony Ashley Cooper, Lord Shaftesbury. Antonio in this play.

Next is a Senatour that keeps a Whore,
In Venice *none a higher office bore;*   30
To lewdness every night the Letcher ran,
Shew me, all London, *such another man,*
Match him at Mother Creswolds *if you can.*
Oh Poland, Poland! *had it been thy lot,*
T' have heard in time of this Venetian Plot,
Thou surely chosen hadst one King from thence,
And honour'd them as thou hast England *since.*

33 Creswold] A notorious bawd; usually Creswell.
34 Poland] Shaftesbury had hopes of being elected King of Poland.

Personæ Dramatis.

Duke of *Venice*	Mr. *D. Williams.*
Priuli, Father to *Belvidera,* a Senatour,	Mr. *Boman.*
Antonio, A fine Speaker in the Senate,	Mr. *Leigh.*
Jaffeir,	Mr. *Betterton.*
Pierre,	Mr. *Smith.*
Renault,	Mr. *Wilshire.*
Bedamar,	Mr. *Gillo.*
Spinosa,	Mr. *Percival.*
Theodore,	
Eliot,	
Revillido, } Conspiratours,	
Durand,	
Mezzana,	
Bramveil,	
Ternon,	
Brabe,	
Belvidera,	Mrs. *Barry.*
Aquilina,	Mrs. *Currer.*

Two Women, Attendants on *Belvidera.*
Two Women, Servants to *Aquilina.*
The Council of Ten.
Officer.
Guards.
Friar.
Executioner and Rable.

VENICE PRESERV'D,

OR

A Plot Discover'd.

ACT I. SCENE I.

Enter Priuli *and* Jaffeir.

Priu. No more! I'le hear no more; begone and
    leave.
Jaff. Not hear me! by my sufferings but you shall!
My Lord, my Lord; I'm not that abject wretch
You think me: Patience! where's the distance throws
Me back so far, but I may boldly speak
In right, though proud oppression will not hear mee!
    Priu. Have you not wrong'd me?
    Jaff. Could my Nature e're
Have brook'd Injustice or the doing wrongs,
I need not now thus low have bent my self,   10
To gain a Hearing from a Cruel father!
Wrong'd you?
    Priu. Yes! wrong'd me, in the nicest point:
The Honour of my House; you have done me wrong;
You may remember: (For I now will speak,
And urge its baseness:) When you first came home
From Travell, with such hopes, as made you lookt on
By all men's Eyes, a Youth of expectation;
Pleas'd with your growing Virtue, I receiv'd you;
Courted, and sought to raise you to your Merits: 20
My House, my Table, nay my Fortune too,
My very self, was yours; you might have us'd me
To your best service; like an open friend,
I treated, trusted you, and thought you mine;
When in requital of my best Endeavours,

You treacherously practis'd to undo me,
Seduc'd the weakness of my Age's Darling,
My only Child, and stole her from my bosome:
Oh *Belvidera*!

Jaff. 'Tis to me you owe her,   30
Childless you had been else, and in the Grave,
Your name Extinct, nor no more *Priuli* heard of.
You may remember, scarce five years are past,
Since in your Brigandine you sail'd to see
The *Adriatick* wedded by our Duke,
And I was with you: Your unskilfull Pilot
Dash't us upon a Rock; when to your Boat
You made for safety; entred first your self;
The affrighted *Belvidera* following next,
As she stood trembling on the Vessel side,   40
Was by a Wave washt off into the Deep,
When instantly I plung'd into the Sea,
And Buffeting the Billows to her rescue,
Redeem'd her Life with half the loss of mine,
Like a rich Conquest in one hand I bore her,
And with the other dasht the sawcy Waves,
That throng'd and prest to rob me of my prize:
I brought her, gave her to your despairing Arms:
Indeed you thank't me; but a nobler gratitude
Rose in her soul: for from that hour she lov'd me,
Till for her Life she paid me with her self.   51

Priu. You stole her from me, like a Theif you stole
       her,
At dead of night; that cursed hour you chose
To rifle me of all my Heart held dear.
May all your Joys in her prove false like mine;
A steril Fortune, and a barren Bed,
Attend you both: Continual discord make
Your Days and Nights bitter and grievous: Still
May the hard hand of a vexatious Need
Oppress, and grind you; till at last you find   60
The Curse of Disobedience all your Portion.

Jaff. Half of your Curse you have bestow'd in vain

Heav'n has already crown'd our faithfull Loves
With a young Boy, sweet as his mothers Beauty:
May he live to prove more Gentle than his Grandsire,
And happier than his Father!
    Priu. Rather live
To bait thee for his bread, and din your ears
With hungry Cries: Whilst his unhappy Mother
Sits down and weeps in bitterness of want.   7c
    Jaff. You talk as if it would please you.
    Priu. 'Twould by Heav'n.
Once she was dear indeed; the Drops that fell
From my sad heart, when she forgot her Duty,
The fountain of my Life was not so pretious:
But she is gone, and if I am a man
I will forget her.
    Jaff. Would I were in my Grave.
    Priu. And she too with thee;
For, living here, you're but my curs'd Remembrancers
I once was happy.   81
    Jaff. You use me thus, because you know my soul
Is fond of *Belvidera*: You perceive
My Life feeds on her, therefore thus you treat me;
Oh! could my Soul ever have known satiety:
Were I that Theif, the doer of such wrongs
As you upbraid me with; what hinders me,
But I might send her back to you with Contumely,
And court my fortune where she wou'd be kinder!
    Priu. You dare not do 't.——   90
    Jaff. Indeed, my Lord, I dare not.
My heart that awes me is too much my Master:
Three years are past since first our Vows were
        plighted,
During which time, the World must bear me witness,
I have treated *Belvidera* like your Daughter,
The Daughter of a Senator of *Venice*;
Distinction, Place, Attendance and Observance,
Due to her Birth, she always has commanded;
Out of my little Fortune I have done this;

Because (though hopeless e're to win your Nature)
The World might see, I lov'd her for her self,   101
Not as the Heiress of the great *Priuli*.——

  Priu. No more!

  Jaff. Yes! all, and then adieu for ever.
There 's not a Wretch that lives on common Charity
But 's happier than me: for I have known
The Luscious Sweets of Plenty; every night
Have slept with soft content about my head,
And never waked but to a joyfull morning,
Yet now must fall like a full Ear of Corn,   110
Whose blossom scap'd, yet 's withered in the ripening.

  Priu. Home and be humble, study to retrench;
Discharge the lazy Vermin of thy Hall,
Those Pageants of thy Folly,
Reduce the glittering Trappings of thy Wife
To humble Weeds, fit for thy little state;
Then to some suburb Cottage both retire;
Drudge, to feed loathsome life: Get Brats, and
    Starve——
Home, home, I say.——   [*Exit* Priuli.

  Jaff. Yes, if my heart would let me—   120
This proud, this swelling heart: Home I would go,
But that my Dores are hatefull to my eyes,
Fill'd and damm'd up with gaping Creditors,
Watchfull as Fowlers when their Game will spring;
I have now not 50 Ducats in the World,
Yet still I am in love, and pleas'd with Ruin.
Oh *Belvidera*! oh she 's my Wife——
And we will bear our wayward Fate together,
But ne're know Comfort more.

Enter Pierre.

  Pierr. My Friend, good morrow!   130
How fares the honest Partner of my Heart?
What, melancholy! not a word to spare me?

  Jaff. I'm thinking *Pierre*, how that damn'd starving
    Quality

Call'd Honesty, got footing in the World.

Pierr. Why, pow'rfull Villainy first set it up,
For its own ease and safety: Honest men
Are the soft easy Cushions on which Knaves
Repose and fatten: Were all mankind Villains,
They'd starve each other; Lawyers wou'd want
    practice,
Cut-Throats Rewards: Each man would kill his
    Brother   140
Himself, none would be paid or hang'd for Murder:
Honesty was a Cheat invented first
To bind the Hands of bold deserving Rogues,
That Fools and Cowards might sit safe in Power,
And lord it uncontroul'd above their Betters.

Jaff. Then Honesty is but a Notion.

Pierr. Nothing else,
Like wit, much talkt of, not to be defin'd:
He that pretends to most too, has least share in 't;
'Tis a ragged Virtue: Honesty! no more on 't.   150

Jaff. Sure thou art Honest?

Pierr. So indeed men think me.
But they're mistaken *Jaffeir*: I am a Rogue
As well as they;
A fine gay bold fac'd Villain, as thou seest me;
'Tis true, I pay my debts when they'r contracted;
I steal from no man; would not cut a Throat
To gain admission to a great man's purse,
Or a Whores bed; I'de not betray my Friend,
To get his Place or Fortune: I scorn to flatter   160
A Blown-up Fool above me, or Crush the wretch
    beneath me,
Yet, *Jaffeir*, for all this, I am a Villain!

Jaff. A Villain——

Pierr. Yes a most notorious Villain:
To see the suffring's of my fellow Creatures,
And own my self a Man: To see our Senators
Cheat the deluded people with a shew
Of Liberty, which yet they ne'r must taste of;

They say, by them our hands are free from Fetters,
Yet whom they please they lay in basest bonds; 170
Bring whom they please to Infamy and Sorrow;
Drive us like Wracks down the rough Tide of Power,
Whilst no hold 's left to save us from Destruction;
All that bear this are Villains; and I one,
Not to rouse up at the great Call of Nature,
And check the Growth of these Domestick spoilers,
That makes us slaves and tells us 'tis our Charter.

   Jaff. Oh *Aquilina*! Friend, to lose such Beauty,
The Dearest Purchase of thy noble Labours;
She was thy Right by Conquest, as by Love. 180

   Pierr. Oh *Jaffeir*! I'de so fixt my heart upon her,
That wheresoe're I fram'd a Scheme of Life
For time to come, she was my only Joy
With which I wish't to sweeten future Cares;
I fancy'd pleasures, none but one that loves
And dotes as I did can Imagine like 'em:
When in the Extremity of all these Hopes,
In the most Charming hour of Expectation,
Then when our Eager Wishes soar the highest,
Ready to stoop and grasp the lovely Game, 190
A Haggard Owl, a Worthless Kite of Prey,
With his foul wings sayl'd in and spoyl'd my Quarry.

   Jaff. I know the Wretch, and scorn him as thou
hat'st him.

   Pierr. Curse on the Common Good that 's so
protected,
Where every slave that heaps up wealth enough
To do much Wrong, becomes a Lord of Right:
I, who beleiv'd no Ill could e're come near me,
Found in the Embraces of my *Aquilina*
A Wretched old but itching Senator;
A wealthy Fool, that had bought out my Title, 200
A Rogue, that uses Beauty like a Lambskin,
Barely to keep him warm: That filthy Cuckoo too
Was in my absence crept into my Nest,
And spoyling all my Brood of noble Pleasure.

Jaff. Didst thou not chace him thence?
Pierr. I did, and drove
The rank old bearded *Hirco* stinking home:
The matter was complain'd of in the Senate,
I summon'd to appear, and censur'd basely,
For violating something they call *priviledge*——   210
This was the Recompence of my service:
Would I'd been rather beaten by a Coward!
A Souldier's Mistress *Jaffeir*'s his Religion,
When that 's prophan'd, all other Tyes are broken,
That even dissolves all former bonds of service,
And from that hour I think my self as free
To be the Foe as e're the Friend of *Venice*——
Nay, Dear Revenge, when e're thou call'st I am ready.
Jaff. I think no safety can be here for Virtue,
And grieve my friend as much as thou to live   220
In such a wretched State as this of *Venice*;
Where all agree to spoil the Publick Good,
And Villains fatten with the brave man's Labours.
Pierr. We have neither safety, Unity, nor Peace,
For the foundation 's lost of Common Good;
Justice is lame as well as blind amongst us;
The Laws (corrupted to their ends that make 'em)
Serve but for Instruments of some new Tyranny,
That every day starts up to enslave us deeper:
Now could this glorious Cause but find out friends
To do it right! oh *Jaffeir*! then might'st thou   231
Not wear these seals of Woe upon thy Face,
The proud *Priuli* should be taught humanity,
And learn to value such a son as thou art.
I dare not speak! But my heart bleeds this moment!
Jaff. Curst be the Cause, though I thy friend be part on 't:
Let me partake the troubles of thy bosom,
For I am us'd to misery, and perhaps
May find a way to sweeten 't to thy spirit.

207 *Hirco*] Goat, lecher.

Pierr. Too soon it will reach thy knowledg—— 240

Jaff. Then from thee

Let it proceed.   There's Virtue in thy Friendship
Would make the saddest Tale of sorrow pleasing,
Strengthen my Constancy, and welcome Ruin.

Pierr. Then thou art ruin'd!

Jaff. That I long since knew,

I and ill Fortune have been long Acquaintance.

Pierr. I past this very moment by thy dores,
And found them guarded by a Troop of Villains;
The sons of public Rapine were destroying: 250
They told me, by the sentence of the Law
They had Commission to seize all thy fortune,
Nay more, *Priuli*'s cruel hand hath sign'd it.
Here stood a Ruffian with a horrid face
Lording it o're a pile of massy Plate,
Tumbled into a heap for publick sale:
There was another making villainous jests
At thy undoing; he had ta'ne possession
Of all thy antient most domestick Ornaments,
Rich hangings, intermixt and wrought with gold;
The very bed, which on thy wedding night 261
Receiv'd thee to the Arms of *Belvidera*,
The scene of all thy Joys, was violated
By the course hands of filthy Dungeon Villains,
And thrown amongst the common Lumber.

Jaff. Now thank Heav'n——

Pierr. Thank Heav'n! for what?

Jaff. That I am not worth a Ducat.

Pierr. Curse thy dull Stars, and the worse Fate of
     Venice, 269

Where Brothers, Friends, and Fathers, all are false;
Where there's no trust, no truth; where Innocence
Stoop's under vile Oppression; and Vice lords it:
Hadst thou but seen, as I did, how at last
Thy Beauteous *Belvidera*, like a Wretch
That's doom'd to Banishment, came weeping forth,
Shining through Tears, like *April* Sun's in showers

That labour to orecome the Cloud that loads 'm,
Whilst two young Virgins, on whose Arms she lean'd,
Kindly lookt up, and at her Grief grew sad,
As if they catch't the Sorrows that fell from her: 280
Even the lewd Rabble that were gather'd round
To see the sight, stood mute when they beheld her;
Govern'd their roaring throats and grumbled pity:
I cou'd have hugg'd the greazy Rogues: They pleas'd
   me.

Jaff. I thank thee for this story from my soul,
Since now I know the worst that can befall me:
Ah *Pierre*! I have a Heart, that could have borne
The roughest Wrong my Fortune could have done
   me:
But when I think what *Belvidera* feels,
The bitterness her tender spirit tasts of,   290
I own my self a Coward: Bear my weakness,
If throwing thus my Arms about thy Neck,
I play the Boy, and blubber in thy bosome.
Oh! I shall drown thee with my Sorrows!

   Pierr. Burn!

First burn, and Level *Venice* to thy Ruin,
What starve like Beggars Brats in frosty weather,
Under a Hedge, and whine our selves to Death!
Thou, or thy Cause, shall never want assistance,
Whilst I have blood or Fortune fit to serve thee;   300
Command my heart: Thou art every way its master.

   Jaff. No: there's a secret Pride in bravely dying.

   Pierr. Rats die in Holes and Corners, Dogs run
   mad;
Man knows a braver Remedy for sorrow:
Revenge! the Attribute of Gods, they stampt it
With their great Image on our Natures; dye!
Consider well the Cause that calls upon thee:
And if thou art base enough, dye then: Remember
Thy *Belvidera* suffers: *Belvidera*!
Dye—Damn first—what be decently interr'd   310
In a Church-yard, and mingle thy brave dust

With stinking Rogues that rot in dirty winding sheets,
Surfeit-slain Fools, the common Dung o 'th Soyl.
   Jaff. Oh!
   Pierr. Well said, out with 't, Swear a little——
   Jaff. Swear!
By Sea and Air! by Earth, by Heaven and Hell,
I will revenge my *Belvidera's* Tears!
Heark thee my Friend—*Priuli*—is—a Senator!
   Pierr. A Dog!   320
   Jaff. Agreed.
   Pierr. Shoot him.
   Jaff. With all my heart.
No more: Where shall we meet at Night?
   Pierr. I'l tell thee;
On the *Ryalto* every Night at Twelve
I take my Evening's walk of Meditation,
There we two will meet, and talk of pretious
Mischief——
   Jaff. Farewell.   330
   Pierr. At Twelve.
   Jaff. At any hour, my plagues
Will keep me waking.   [*Ex. Pierr.*
Tell me why, good Heav'n,
Thou mad'st me what I am, with all the Spirit,
Aspiring thoughts and Elegant desires
That fill the happiest Man? Ah! rather why
Did'st thou not form me sordid as my Fate,
Base minded, dull, and fit to carry Burdens?
Why have I sence to know the Curse that 's on me?
Is this just dealing, Nature? *Belvidera*!   341
                           [*Enter* Belvidera.

Poor *Belvidera*!
   Belvid. Lead me, lead me my Virgins!
To that kind Voice. My Lord, my Love, my Refuge!
Happy my Eyes, when they behold thy Face:
My heavy heart will leave its doleful beating
At sight of thee, and bound with sprightful joys.
Oh smile, as when our Loves were in their Spring,

And cheer my fainting Soul.

Jaff. As when our Loves   350
Were in their Spring? has then my Fortune chang'd?
Art thou not *Belvidera*, still the same,
Kind, good, and tender, as my Arms first found thee?
If thou art alter'd, where shall I have harbour?
Where ease my loaded Heart? Oh! where complain?

 Belv. Does this appear like Change, or Love
  decaying?
When thus I throw my self into thy bosom,
With all the resolution of a strong Truth:
Beat's not my heart, as 'twou'd alarm thine
To a new Charge of bliss; I joy more in thee,   360
Than did thy Mother when she hugg'd thee first,
And bless'd the Gods for all her Travel past.

 Jaff. Can there in Woman be such glorious Faith?
Sure all ill stories of thy Sex are false;
Oh Woman! lovely Woman! Nature made thee
To temper Man: We had been Brutes without you,
Angels are Painted fair, to look like you;
There's in you all that we believe of Heav'n,
Amazing Brightness, Purity and Truth,
Eternal Joy, and everlasting Love.   370

 Belv. If Love be Treasure, wee'l be wondrous rich:
I have so much, my heart will surely break with 't;
Vow's cannot express it, when I wou'd declare
How great's my Joy, I am dumb with the big thought;
I swell, and sigh, and labour with my longing.
Oh lead me to some Desart wide and wild,
Barren as our Misfortunes, where my Soul
May have its vent: Where I may tell aloud
To the high Heaven's, and every list'ning Planet,
With what a boundless stock my bosom 's fraught;
Where I may throw my eager Arms about thee,   381
Give loose to Love with kisses, kindling Joy,
And let off all the Fire that 's in my Heart.

 Jaff. Oh *Belvidera*! double I am a Begger,
Undone by Fortune, and in debt to thee;

Want! worldly Want! that hungry meager Fiend
Is at my heels, and chaces me in view;
Can'st thou bear Cold and Hunger? Can these Limbs,
Fram'd for the tender Offices of Love,
Endure the bitter Gripes of smarting Poverty?   390
When banisht by our miseries abroad,
(As suddenly we shall be) to seek out
(In some far Climate where our Names are strangers)
For charitable succour; wilt thou then,
When in a Bed of straw we shrink together,
And the bleak winds shall whistle round our heads;
Wilt thou then talk thus to me? Wilt thou then
Hush my Cares thus, and shelter me with Love?

   Belv. Oh I will love thee, even in Madness love thee:
Tho my distracted Senses should forsake me,   400
I'd find some intervals, when my poor heart
Should swage it self and be let loose to thine.
Though the bare Earth be all our Resting-place,
It's Roots our food, some Clift our Habitation,
I'l make this Arm a Pillow for thy Head;
As thou sighing ly'st, and swell'd with sorrow,
Creep to thy Bosom, pou'r the balm of Love
Into thy Soul, and kiss thee to thy Rest;
Then praise our God, and watch thee 'till the Morning.

   Jaff. Hear this you Heaven's, and wonder how you made her!   410
Reign, reign ye Monarchs that divide the World,
Busy Rebellion ner'e will let you know
Tranquility and Happiness like mine;
Like gawdy Ships, th' obsequious Billows fall
And rise again, to lift you in your Pride;
They wait but for a storm and then devour you:
I, in my private Bark, already wreck't,
Like a poor Merchant driven on unknown Land,
That had by chance packt up his choicest Treasure

In one dear Casket, and sav'd only that: 420
   Since I must wander further on the shore,
   Thus hug my little, but my precious store;
   Resolv'd to scorn, and trust my Fate no more.
                                        [*Exeunt.*

ACT II.

Enter Pierre *and* Aquilina.

Aquil. By all thy Wrongs, thou art dearer to my
      Arms
Than all the Wealth of *Venice*: Prithee stay,
And let us love to night.
   Peirr. No: There's Fool,
There's Fool about thee: When a Woman sells
Her Flesh to Fools, her Beauty's lost to me;
They leave a Taint, a sully where th'ave past,
There's such a baneful Quality about 'em,
Even spoyls Complexions with their own Nauseous-
      ness,
They infect all they touch; I cannot think   10
Of tasting any thing a Fool has pall'd.
   Aquil. I loath and scorn that Fool thou mean'st,
      as much
Or more than thou can'st; But the Beast has Gold
That makes him necessary: Power too,
To qualifie my Character, and poise me
Equal with peevish Virtue, that beholds
My Liberty with Envy: In their Hearts
Are loose as I am; But an ugly Power
Sits in their Faces, and frights Pleasures from 'em.
   Pierr. Much good may't do you, Madam, with
      your Senator.   20
   Aquil. My Senator! why, can'st thou think that
      Wretch
E're fill'd thy *Aquilina*'s Arms with Pleasure?
Think'st thou, because I sometimes give him leave

313   F

To soyle himself at what he is unfit for;
Because I force my self to endure and suffer him,
Think'st thou I love him? No, by all the Joys
Thou ever gav'st me, his Presence is my Pennance;
The worst thing an old Man can be 's a Lover,
A meer *Memento Mori* to poor woman.
I never lay by his decrepit side,   30
But all that night I ponder'd on my Grave.

   Pierr. Would he were well sent thither.

   Aquil. That's my wish too:
For then, my *Pierre*, I might have cause with pleasure
To play the Hypocrite: Oh! how I could weep
Over the dying Dotard, and kiss him too,
In hopes to smother him quite; then, when the time
Was come to pay my Sorrows at his Funeral,
For he has already made me Heir to Treasures,
Would make me out-act a real Widows whining: 40
How could I frame my face to fit my mourning!
With wringing hands attend him to his Grave,
Fall swooning on his Hearse: Take mad possession,
Even of the Dismal Vault, where he lay bury'd,
There like the *Ephesian* Matron dwell, till Thou,
My lovely Soldier, comest to my Deliverance;
Then throwing up my Veil, with open Armes
And laughing Eyes, run to new dawning Joy.

   Pierr. No more! I have Friends to meet me here
     to night,
And must be private. As you prize my Friendship 50
Keep up your Coxcomb: Let him not pry nor listen,
Nor fisk about the House as I have seen him,
Like a tame mumping Squirrel with a bell on;
Currs will be abroad to bite him, if you do.

   Aquil. What Friends to meet? may I not be of your
     Council?

   Pierr. How! a Woman ask Questions out of Bed?

45 *Ephesian* Matron] A reference to the famous story
in the *Satyricon* of Petronius.   Chapman based his *The
Widdowe's Tears* on this.

Go to your Senator, ask him what passes
Amongst his Brethren, hee'l hide nothing from you;
But pump not me for Politicks. No more!
Give order that whoever in my name   60
Comes here, receive Admittance: so good night.

   Aquil. Must we ne're meet again! Embrace no
    more!
Is Love so soon and utterly forgotten!

   Pierr. As you hence-forward treat your Fool, I'le
    think on 't.

   Aquil. Curst be all Fools, and doubly curst my self,
The worst of Fools—I die if he forsakes me;
And now to keep him, Heav'n or Hell instruct me.

                          [Exeunt.

SCENE *The Ryalto.*

Enter Jaffeir.

   Jaff. I am here, and thus, the Shades of Night
    around me,
I look as if all Hell were in my Heart,
And I in Hell. Nay, surely 'tis so with me;—   70
For every step I tread, methinks some Fiend
Knocks at my Breast, and bids it not be quiet:
I've heard, how desperate Wretches, like my self,
Have wander'd out at this dead time of Night
To meet the Foe of Mankind in his walk:
Sure I am so Curst, that, tho' of Heav'n forsaken,
No Minister of Darkness cares to Tempt me.
Hell! Hell! why sleepest thou?

Enter Pierre.

   Pierr. Sure I have stay'd too long:
The Clock has struck, and I may lose my Proselyte.
Speak, who goes there?   81

   Jaff. A Dog, that comes to howl
At yonder Moon: What 's he that asks the Question?

   Pierr. A Friend to Dogs, for they are honest
    Creatures,

And ne're betray their Masters; never Fawn
On any that they love not: Well met, Friend:
Jaffeir!

   Jaff. The same. Oh *Peirre!* Thou art come in
season,
I was just going to Pray.

   Pierr. Ah that 's Mechanick,   90
Priests make a Trade on 't, and yet starve by it too:
No Praying, it spoils Business, and time 's precious;
Where 's *Belvidera?*

   Jaff. For a Day or two
I've lodg'd her privately, 'till I see farther
What Fortune will do with me? Prithee, Friend,
If thou would'st have me fit to hear good Council,
Speak not of *Belvidera*—

   Pierr. Speak not of her.

   Jaff. Oh no!   100

   Pierr. Nor name her. May be I wish her well.

   Jaff. Who well?

   Pierr. Thy Wife, thy lovely *Belvidera,*
I hope a man may wish his Friends Wife well,
And no harm done!

   Jaff. Y' are merry *Pierre!*

   Pierr. I am so:
Thou shalt smile too, and *Belvidera* smile;
We'll all rejoyce, here 's something to buy Pins,
Marriage is Chargeable.   110

   Jaff. I but half wisht
To see the Devil, and he 's here already.
Well!
What must this buy, Rebellion, Murder, Treason?
Tell me which way I must be damn'd for this.

   Pierr. When last we parted, we had no qualms like
these,
But entertain'd each others thoughts like Men,
Whose Souls were well acquainted. Is the World
Reform'd since our last meeting? What new miracles
Have happen'd? Has *Priuli*'s heart relented?   120

Can he be honest?

Jaff. Kind Heav'n! let heavy Curses
Gall his old Age; Cramps, Aches, rack his Bones;
And bitterest disquiet wring his Heart;
Oh let him live 'till Life become his burden!
Let him groan under 't long, linger an Age
In the worst Agonies and Pangs of Death,
And find its ease, but late.

Pierr. Nay, could'st thou not
As well, my Friend, have stretcht the Curse to all
The Senate round, as to one single Villain?   131

Jaff. But Curses stick not: Could I kill with
       Cursing,
By Heav'n I know not thirty Heads in *Venice*
Should not be blasted; Senators should rot
Like Dogs on Dunghills; but their Wives and Daugh-
       ters
Dye of their own diseases.   Oh for a Curse
To kill with!

Pierr. Daggers, Daggers, are much better!

Jaff. Ha!

Pierr. Daggers.   140

Jaff. But where are they?

Pierr. Oh, a Thousand
May be dispos'd in honest hands in *Venice*.

Jaff. Thou talk'st in Clouds.

Pierr. But yet a Heart half wrong'd
As thine has bin, would find the meaning, *Jaffeir*.

Jaff. A thousand Daggers, all in honest hands;
And have not I a Friend will stick one here?

Pier. Yes, if I thought thou wert not to be cherisht
To a nobler purpose, I'd be that Friend.   150
But thou hast better Friends, Friends, whom thy
       Wrongs
Have made thy Friends; Friends, worthy to be
       call'd so;
I'l trust thee with a secret: There are Spirits
This hour at work.   But as thou art a Man,

Whom I have pickt and chosen from the World,
Swear, that thou wilt be true to what I utter,
And when I have told thee, that which only Gods
And Men like Gods are privy to, then swear,
No Chance or Change shall wrest it from thy Bosom.

    Jaff. When thou would'st bind me, is there need
    of Oaths?   160
(Green-sickness Girls lose Maiden-heads with such
    Counters)
For thou art so near my heart, that thou may'st see
Its bottom, sound its strength, and firmness to thee:
Is Coward, Fool, or Villian, in my face?
If I seem none of these, I dare believe
Thou would'st not use me in a little Cause,
For I am fit for Honour's toughest task;
Nor ever yet found fooling was my Province;
And for a villainous inglorious enterprize,
I know thy heart so well, I dare lay mine   170
Before thee, set it to what Point thou wilt.

    Pierr. Nay, It 's a Cause thou wilt be fond of *Jaffeir.*
For it is founded on the noblest Basis,
Our Liberties, our natural Inheritance;
There 's no Religion, no Hypocrisie in 't;
Wee'l do the Business, and ne'r fast and pray for 't:
Openly act a deed, the World shall gaze
With wonder at, and envy when it is done.

    Jaff. For Liberty!

    Pierr. For Liberty my Friend: 180
Thou shalt be freed from base *Priuli*'s Tyranny,
And thy sequestred Fortunes heal'd again.
I shall be freed from opprobrious Wrongs,
That press me now, and bend my Spirit downward:
All *Venice* free, and every growing Merit
Succeed to its just Right: Fools shall be pull'd
From Wisdoms Seat; those baleful unclean Birds,
Those Lazy-Owls, who (perch'd near Fortunes Top)
Sit only watchful with their heavy Wings
To cuff down new fledg'd Virtues, that would rise   190

To nobler heights, and make the Grove harmonious.
  Jaff. What can I do?
  Pierr. Cans't thou not kill a Senator?
  Jaff. Were there one wise or honest, I could kill him
For herding with that nest of Fools and Knaves;
By all my Wrongs, thou talk'st as if revenge
Were to be had, and the brave Story warms me.
  Pierr. Swear then!
  Jaff. I do, by all those glittering Stars,
And yond great Ruling Planet of the Night!   200
By all good Pow'rs above, and ill below!
By Love and Friendship, dearer than my Life!
No Pow'r or Death shall make me false to thee.
  Pierr. Here we embrace, and I'l unlock my Heart.
A Councel's held hard by, where the destruction
Of this great Empire's hatching: There I'l lead thee!
But be a Man, for thou art to mix with Men
Fit to disturb the Peace of all the World,
And rule it when it's wildest——
  Jaff. I give thee thanks   210
For this kind warning: Yes, I will be a Man,
And charge thee, *Pierre*, when er'e thou see'st my fears
Betray me less, to rip this Heart of mine
Out of my Breast, and shew it for a Cowards.
Come, let's begone, for from this hour I chase
All little thoughts, all tender humane Follies
Out of my bosom: Vengeance shall have room:
Revenge!
  Pierr. And Liberty!
  Jaff. Revenge! Revenge——   [*Exeunt.* 220

   The Scene *changes to* Aquilina's *house, the Greek*
             Curtezan.
          Enter Renault.

  Renault. Why was my choice Ambition, the first
    ground
A Wretch can build on? it's indeed at distance
A good Prospect, tempting to the View,

The Height delights us, and the Mountain Top
Looks beautiful, because it 's nigh to Heav'n,
But we ne're think how sandy 's the Foundation,
What Storm will batter, and what Tempest shake us!
Who 's there?

Enter Spinosa.

Spino. Renault, good morrow! for by this time
I think the Scale of Night has turn'd the ballance, 230
And weighs up Morning: Has the Clock struck
    Twelve?

Rena. Yes, Clocks will go as they are set: But Man,
Irregular Man 's ne're constant, never certain:
I've spent at least three pretious hours of darkness
In waiting dull attendance; 'tis the Curse
Of diligent Virtue to be mixt like mine,
With giddy Tempers, Souls but half resolv'd.

Spin. Hell seize that Soul amongst us, it can frighten.

Rena. What 's then the cause that I am here alone?
Why are we not together? 240

Enter Eliot.

O Sir, welcome!
You are an *Englishman*: When Treason 's hatching
One might have thought you'd not have been behind
    hand.
In what Whore's lap have you been lolling?
Give but an *Englishman* his Whore and ease,
Beef and a Sea-coal fire, he 's yours for ever.

Eliot. Frenchman, you are sawcy.

Rena. How!

Enter Bedamore *the Embassador*, Theodore, Brainveil,
    Durand, Brabe, Revellido, Mezzana, Ternon,
    Retrosi, *Conspirators.*

Bedam. At difference, fy.
Is this a time for quarrels? Thieves and Rogues 250
Fall out and brawl: Should Men of your high calling,
Men separated by the Choice of Providence,
From the gross heap of Mankind, and set here

In this great assembly as in one great Jewel,
T' adorn the bravest purpose it er'e smil'd on;
Should you like Boys wrangle for trifles?

   Ren. Boys!

   Beda. Renault, thy Hand!

   Ren. I thought I'd given my Heart
Long since to every Man that mingles here;   260
But grieve to find it trusted with such Tempers,
That can't forgive my froward Age its weakness.

   Beda. Eliot, thou once had'st Vertue, I have seen
Thy stubborn Temper bend with godlike Goodness,
Not half thus courted: 'Tis thy Nations Glory,
To hugg the Foe that offers brave Alliance.
Once more embrace, my Friends—wee'l all embrace—
United thus, we are the mighty Engin
Must twist this rooted Empire from its Basis!
Totters it not already?   270

   Eliot. Would it were tumbling.

   Bed. Nay it shall down: This Night we Seal its
   ruine.

Enter Pierre.

Oh *Pierre*! thou art welcome!
Come to my breast, for by its hopes thou look'st
Lovelily dreadful, and the Fate of *Venice*
Seems on thy Sword already. Oh my *Mars*!
The Poets that first feign'd a God of War
Sure prophesy'd of thee.

   Pierr. Friends! was not *Brutus*,
(I mean that *Brutus*, who in open Senate   280
Stabb'd the first *Cæsar* that usurp'd the World)
A Gallant Man?

   Rena. Yes, and *Cateline* too;
Tho story wrong his Fame: for he conspir'd
To prop the reeling Glory of his Country:
His Cause was good.

   Beda. And ours as much above it,
As *Renault* thou art Superior to *Cethegus*,

Or *Pierre* to *Cassius*.

 Pierr. Then to what we aim at   290
When do we start? or must we talk for ever?

 Beda. No *Pierre*, the Deed's near Birth : Fate seems
   to have set
The Business up, and given it to our care,
I hope there's not a heart nor hand amongst us
But is firm and ready.

 All. All!
Wee'l die with *Bedamore*.

 Beda. Oh Men,
Matchless, as will your Glory be hereafter.
The Game is for a Matchless Prize, if won;   300
If lost, disgraceful Ruine.

 Ren. What can lose it?
The publick Stock's a Beggar; one *Venetian*
Trusts not another : Look into their Stores
Of general safety; Empty Magazines,
A tatter'd Fleet, a murmuring unpaid Army,
Bankrupt Nobility, a harrast Commonalty,
A Factious, giddy, and divided Senate,
Is all the strength of *Venice* : Let's destroy it;
Let's fill their Magazines with Arms to awe them, 310
Man out their Fleet, and make their Trade maintain
  it;
Let loose the murmuring Army on their Masters,
To pay themselves with plunder; Lop their Nobles
To the base Roots, whence most of 'em first sprung;
Enslave the Rowt, whom smarting will make humble,
Turn out their droning Senate, and possess
That Seat of Empire which our Souls were fram'd for.

 Pierr. Ten thousand men are Armed at your Nod,
Commanded all by Leaders fit to guide
A Battle for the freedom of the World;   320
This wretched State has starv'd them in its service,

289 *Cassius*] Seventeenth-century conspirators liked to
assume some Roman name. See Marvell's satire ' On
the Death of Tom May '.

And by your bounty quicken'd, they 're resolv'd
To serve your Glory, and revenge their own!
Th' have all their different Quarters in this City
Watch for th' Alarm, and grumble 'tis so tardy.

   Beda. I doubt not Friend, but thy unweary'd
      diligence
Has still kept waking, and it shall have ease;
After this Night it is resolv'd we meet
Nomore, 'till *Venice* own us for her Lords.

   Pierr. How lovely the *Adriatique* Whore,   330
Drest in her Flames, will shine! devouring Flames!
Such as shall burn her to the watery bottom
And hiss in her Foundation.

   Beda. Now if any
Amongst us that owns this glorious Cause,
Have friends or Interest, hee'd wish to save,
Let it be told, the general Doom is Seal'd;
But I'de forgo the Hopes of a Worlds Empire,
Rather than wound the Bowels of my Friend.

   Pierr. I must confess you there have toucht my
      weakness,   340
I have a Friend; hear it, such a Friend!
My heart was ner'e shut to him: Nay, I'l tell you,
He knows the very Business of this Hour;
But he rejoyces in the Cause, and loves it,
W' have chang'd a Vow to live and die together,
And He 's at hand to ratify it here.

   Ren. How! all betray'd?

   Pierr. No—I've dealt nobly with you;
I've brought my All into the publick Stock;
I had but one Friend, and him I'l share amongst
     you!   350
Receive and Cherish him: Or if, when seen
And searcht, you find him worthless, as my Tongue
Has lodg'd this Secret in his faithful Breast,
To ease your fears I wear a Dagger here
Shall rip it out again, and give you rest.
Come forth, thou only Good I er'e could boast of.

Enter Jaffeir *with a Dagger.*

Beda. His Presence bears the show of Manly Vertue.
Jaff. I know you'l wonder all, that thus uncall'd,
I dare approach this place of fatal Councels;
But I am amongst you, and by Heav'n it glads me,
To see so many Vertues thus united,   361
To restore Justice and dethrone Oppression.
Command this Sword, if you would have it quiet,
Into this Breast; but if you think it worthy
To cut the Throats of reverend Rogues in Robes,
Send me into the curs'd assembl'd Senate;
It shrinks not, tho I meet a Father there;
Would you behold this City Flaming? Here 's
A hand shall bear a lighted Torch at noon
To the Arsenal, and set its Gates on fire.   370
Ren. You talk this well, Sir.
Jaff. Nay—by Heav'n I'l do this.
Come, come, I read distrust in all your faces,
You fear me a Villain, and indeed it 's odd
To hear a stranger talk thus at first meeting,
Of matters, that have been so well debated;
But I come ripe with Wrongs as you with Councels;
I hate this Senate, am a Foe to *Venice*;
A Friend to none, but Men resolv'd like me,
To push on Mischief: Oh did you but know me,
I need not talk thus!   381
Beda. *Pierre*! I must embrace him,
My heart beats to this Man as if it knew him.
Rena. I never lov'd these huggers:
Jaff. Still I see
The cause delights me not. Your Friends survey
  me,
As I were dang'rous—but I come Arm'd
Against all doubts, and to your trust will give
A Pledge, worth more than all the World can pay
  for.
My *Belvidera*! Ho! my *Belvidera*!   390

Bed. What wonder next?

Jaff. Let me entreat you,
As I have henceforth hopes to call ye friends,
That all but the Ambassador, this
Grave Guide of Councels, with my friend that owns
    me,
Withdraw a while to spare a Womans blushes.
            [*Ex. all but* Bed. Rena. Jaff. Pierr.

Beda. *Pierre*, whither will this Ceremony lead us?

Jaff. My *Belvidera*! *Belvidera*!

Belvid. Who?   [*Enter* Belvidera.
Who calls so lowd at this late peacefull hour?   400
That Voice was wont to come in gentler whispers,
And fill my Ears with the soft breath of Love:
Thou hourly Image of my Thoughts, where art
    thou?

Jaff. Indeed 'tis late.

Belv. Oh! I have slept, and dreamt,
And dreamt again: Where hast thou been thou
    Loyterer?
Tho my Eyes clos'd, my Arms have still been open'd;
Stretcht every way betwixt my broken slumbers,
To search if thou wert come to crown my Rest;
There's no repose without thee: Oh the day,   410
Too soon will break, and wake us to our sorrow;
Come, come to bed, and bid thy Cares good Night.

Jaff. Oh *Belvidera*! we must change the Scene
In which the past Delights of Life were tasted:
The poor sleep little, we must learn to watch
Our labours late, and early every Morning,
Mid'st winter Frosts, then clad and fed with sparing,
Rise to our toils, and drudge away the day.

Belv. Alas! where am I! whither is't you lead me!
Methinks I read distraction in your face!   420
Something less gentle than the Fate you tell me:
You shake and tremble too! your blood runs cold!
Heaven's guard my Love, and bless his heart with
    Patience.

Jaff. That I have Patience, let our Fate bear
    witness,
Who has ordain'd it so, that thou and I
(Thou the divinest Good man e're possest,
And I the wretched'st of the Race of Man)
This very hour, without one tear, must part.

    Belv. Part! must we part? Oh! am I then forsaken?
Will my Love cast me off? have my misfortunes   430
Offended him so highly, that hee'l leave me?
Why dragg you from me? whither are you going?
My Dear! my Life! my Love!

    Jaff. Oh Friends!

    Belv. Speak to me.

    Jaff. Take her from my heart,
Shee'l gain such hold else, I shall ner'e get loose.
I charge thee take her, but with tender'st care,
Relieve her Troubles and asswage her sorrows.

    Ren. Rise, Madam! and Command amongst your
    Servants!   440

    Jaff. To you, Sirs, and your Honours, I bequeath
    her,
And with her this, when I prove unworthy—
        [*Gives a dagger.*
You know the rest:—Then strike it to her heart;
And tell her, he, who three whole happy years
Lay in her Arms, and each kind Night repeated
The passionate Vows of still encreasing Love,
Sent that Reward for all her Truth and Sufferings.

    Belv. Nay, take my Life, since he has sold it cheaply;
Or send me to some distant Clime your slave,
But let it be far off, least my complainings   450
Should reach his guilty Ears, and shake his peace.

    Jaff. No *Belvidera*, I've contriv'd thy honour,
Trust to my Faith, and be but Fortune kind
To me, as I'l preserve that faith unbroken,
When next we meet, I'l lift thee to a height,
Shall gather all the gazing World about thee,
To wonder what strange Virtue plac'd thee there.

But if we ner'e meet more——
   Belv. Oh thou unkind one,
Never meet more! have I deserv'd this from you? 460
Look on me, tell me, tell me, speak thou dear deceiver,
Why am I separated from thy Love?
If I am false, accuse me; but if true,
Don't, prithee don't in poverty forsake me.
But pitty the sad heart, that's torn with parting.
Yet hear me! yet recall me——
                     [Ex. Ren. Bed. *and* Belv.
   Jaff. Oh my Eyes!
Look not that way, but turn your selves awhile
Into my heart, and be wean'd all together.
My Friend, where art thou?   470
   Pierr. Here, my Honour's Brother.
   Jaff. Is *Belvidera* gone?
   Pierr. *Renault* has lead her
Back to her own Apartment: but, by Heav'n!
Thou must not see her more till our work's over.
   Jaff. No:
   Pierr. Not for your life.
   Jaff. Oh *Pierre,* wert thou but she,
How I could pull thee down into my heart,
Gaze on thee till my Eye-strings crackt with Love,
Till all my sinews with its fire extended,   481
Fixt me upon the Rack of ardent longing;
Then swelling, sighing, raging to be blest,
Come like a panting Turtle to thy Breast,
On thy soft Bosom, hovering, bill and play,
Confess the cause why last I fled away;
   'Own 'twas a fault, but swear to give it or'e,
   And never follow false Ambition more.
                         [Ex. Ambo.

ACT III.

Enter Aquilina *and her* Maid.

Aquil. Tell him I am gone to bed: Tell him I am not at home; tell him I've better Company with me, or any thing; tell him in short I will not see him, the eternal troublesome vexatious Fool: He's worse Company than an ignorant Physitian—I'l not be disturb'd at these unseasonable hours.

Maid. But Madam! He's here already, just enter'd the doors.　　　　　　　　　　　　　　　　　　　　8

Aquil. Turn him out agen, you unnecessary, useless, giddy-brain'd Asse! if he will not begone, set the house a fire and burn us both: I had rather meet a Toad in my dish than that old hideous Animal in my Chamber to Night.　　　　　　　　　[*Enter* Antonio.

Anto. *Nacky, Nacky, Nacky*—how dost do *Nacky?* Hurry durry. I am come little *Nacky*; past eleven a Clock, a late hour; time in all Conscience to go to bed *Nacky*—*Nacky* did I say? Ay *Nacky*; *Aquilina, lina, lina, quilina, quilina, quilina, Aquilina, Naquilina, Naquilina, Acky, Acky, Nacky, Nacky,* Queen *Nacky*—come let's to bed—you Fubbs, you Pugg you—you little Puss—Purree Tuzzey—I am a Senator.　　　　21

Aquil. You are Fool, I am sure.

Anto. May be so too sweet-heart. Never the worse Senator for all that. Come *Nacky, Nacky,* lets have a Game at Rump, *Nacky.*

Aquil. You would do well Signior to be trouble-some here no longer, but leave to my self, be sober and go home, Sir.

Anto. Home *Madona*!

Aquil. Ay home, Sir. Who am I?　　　　　　　30

Anto. *Madona*, as I take it you are my—you are—thou art my little *Nicky Nacky*—that's all!

Aquil. I find you are resolv'd to be troublesome,

and so to make short of the matter in few words, I hate you, detest you, loath you, I am weary of you, sick of you—hang you, you are an Old, silly, Impertinent, impotent, sollicitous Coxcomb, Crazy in your head, and lazy in your Body, love to be medling with every thing, and if you had not Money, you are good for nothing. 40

Anto. Good for nothing! Hurry durry, I'l try that presently. Sixty one years Old, and good for nothing; that's brave. [*To the Maid.*] Come come come Mistress fiddle-faddle, turn you out for a season; go turn out I say, it is our will and pleasure to be private some moments—out, out when you are bid too— [*Puts her out and locks the door.*] Good for nothing you say.

Aquil. Why what are you good for? 49

Anto. In the first place, Madam, I am Old, and consequently very wise, very wise, *Madona*, d'e mark that? in the second place take notice, if you please, that I am a Senator, and when I think fit can make Speeches *Madona*. Hurry durry, I can make a Speech in the Senate-house now and then—wou'd make your hair stand an end, *Madona*.

Aquil. What care I for your Speeches in the Senate-house, if you wou'd be silent here, I should thank you.

Anto. Why, I can make Speeches to thee too, my lovely *Madona*; for Example—my cruel fair one, 60 [*Takes out a Purse of Gold, and at every pawse shakes it.* Since it is my Fate, that you should with your Servant angry prove; tho late at Night—I hope 'tis not too late with this to gain reception for my Love—there's for thee my little *Nicky Nacky*—take it, here take it— I say take it, or I'l throw it at your head—how now rebel!

Aquil. Truly, my Illustrious Senator, I must confess your Honour is at present most profoundly eloquent indeed. 69

Anto. Very well: Come, now let's sit down and

think upon 't a little—come sit I say—sit down by me
a little my *Nicky Nacky*, hah—[*Sits down*] Hurry durry
—good for nothing—

Aquil. No Sir, if you please I can know my distance
and stand.

Anto. Stand: How? *Nacky*, up and I down! Nay
then let me exclaim with the Poet.

> *Shew me a Case more pitiful who can,*
> *A standing Woman, and a falling Man.*

Hurry durry—not sit down—*see this ye Gods*——   80
You won't sit down?

Aquil. No Sir.

Anto. Then look you now, suppose me a Bull, **a**
Basan-Bull, the Bull of Bulls, or any Bull. Thus up
I get and with my brows thus bent—I broo, I say I
broo, I broo, I broo. You won't sit down will you?
—I broo—   [*Bellows like a Bull, and drives her about.*

Aquil. Well, Sir, I must endure this.   [*She sits down.*
Now your honour has been a Bull, pray what Beast
will your Worship please to be next?   90

Anto. Now I'l be a Senator agen, and thy Lover
little *Nicky Nacky*! [*He sits by her.*] Ah toad, toad,
toad, toad! spit in my Face a little, *Nacky*—spit in
my Face prithee, spit in my Face, never so little:
spit but a little bit—spit, spit, spit, spit, when you
are bid I say; do, prithee spit—now, now, now,
spit: what you won't spit, will you? Then I'l be a
Dog.

Aquil. A Dog my Lord?

Anto. Ay a Dog—and I'l give thee this to'ther purse
to let me be a Dog—and to use me like a Dog a little.
Hurry durry—I will—here 'tis.—   [*Gives the Purse.*

Aquil. Well, with all my heart. But let me beseech
your Dogship to play your trick's over as fast as you
can, that you may come to stinking the sooner, and
be turn'd out of dores as you deserve.   106

Anto. Ay, ay—no matter for that—that [*He gets*

under the Table] shan't move me—Now, bough waugh waugh, bough waugh—— [*Barks like a Dog.*

Aquil. Hold, hold, hold Sir, I beseech you: what is 't you do? If Curs bite, they must be kickt, Sir. Do you see, kickt thus. 112

Anto. Ay with all my heart: do kick, kick on, now I am under the Table, kick agen—kick harder—harder yet, bough waugh waugh, waugh, bough—'odd, I'le have a snap at thy shins—bough waugh wough, waugh, bough—'odd she kicks bravely.—

Aquil. Nay then I'l go another way to work with you: and I think here's an Instrument fit for the purpose. [*Fetches a Whip and Bell.*] What bite your Mistress, sirrah! out, out of dores, you Dog, to kennel and behang'd—bite your Mistress by the Legs, you rogue.—— [*She Whips him.*

Anto. Nay prithee *Nacky*, now thou art too loving: Hurry durry, 'odd I'l be a Dog no longer. 125

Aquil. Nay none of your fawning and grinning: But be gone, or here's the discipline: What bite your Mistress by the Legs you mungril? out of dores—hout hout, to kennel sirra! go.

Anto. This is very barbarous usage *Nacky*, very barbarous: look you, I will not go—I will not stir from the dore, that I resolve—hurry durry, what shut me out? [*She Whips him out.*

Aquil. Ay, and if you come here any more to night I'l have my Foot-men lug you, you Curr: What bite your poor Mistress *Nacky*, sirrah! 136

Enter Maid.

Maid. Heav'ns Madam! Whats the matter?
[*He howls at the dore like a Dog.*
Aquil. Call my Foot-men hither presently.

Enter two Foot-men.

Maid. They are here already Madam, the house is all alarm'd with a strange noise, that no body knows what to make of. 141

Aquil. Go all of you and turn that troublesome
Beast in the next room out of my house—If I ever see
him within these walls again, without my leave for
his Admittance, you sneaking Rogues—I'l have you
poison'd all, poison'd, like Rats: every Corner of the
house shall stink of one of you: Go, and learn hereafter to know my pleasure. So now for my *Pierre*:

> *Thus when Godlike Lover was displeas'd;*
> *We Sacrifice our Fool and he's appeas'd.*   150

[Exeunt.

SCENE *The Second.*

Enter Belvidera.

Belvid. I'm Sacrific'd! I am sold! betray'd to
  shame!
Inevitable Ruin has inclos'd me!
No sooner was I to my bed repair'd,
To weigh, and (weeping) ponder my condition,
But the old hoary Wretch, to whose false Care
My Peace and Honour was intrusted, came
(Like *Tarquin*) gastely with infernal Lust.
Oh thou *Roman Lucrece*! thou could'st find friends to
  vindicate thy Wrong;
I never had but one, and he's prov'd false;
He that should guard my Virtue, has betray'd it; 160
Left me! undone me! Oh that I could hate him!
Where shall I go! Oh whither whither wander?

Enter Jaffeir.

Jaff. Can *Belvidera* want a resting place
When these poor Arms are open to receive her?
Oh 'tis in vain to struggle with Desires
Strong as my Love to thee; for every moment
I am from thy sight, the Heart within my Bosom
Moans like a tender Infant in its Cradle
Whose Nurse had left it; Come, and with the Songs
Of gentle Love perswade it to its peace.   170

Belvid. I fear the stubborn Wanderer will not own
  me,

'Tis grown a Rebel to be rul'd no longer,
Scorns the Indulgent Bosom that first lull'd it,
And like a Disobedient Child disdains
The soft Authority of *Belvidera*.

    Jaff. There was a time——
    Belv. Yes, yes, there was a time,
When *Belvidera's* tears, her crys, and sorrows,
Were not despis'd; when if she chanc'd to sigh,
Or look but sad;—there was indeed a time   180
When *Jaffeir* would have ta'ne her in his Arms,
Eas'd her declining Head upon his Breast,
And never left her 'till he found the Cause.
But let her now weep Seas,
Cry, 'till she rend the Earth; sigh 'till she burst
Her heart asunder; still he bears it all;
Deaf as the Wind, and as the Rocks unshaken.

    Jaff. Have I been deaf? am I that Rock unmov'd?
Against whose root, Tears beat and sighes are sent!
In vain have I beheld thy Sorrows calmly!   190
Witness against me Heav'ns, have I done this?
Then bear me in a Whirlwind back agen,
And let that angry dear one ne're forgive me!
Oh thou too rashly censur'st of my Love!
Could'st thou but think how I have spent this night,
Dark and alone, no pillow to my Head,
Rest in my Eyes, nor quiet in my Heart,
Thou would'st not *Belvidera*, sure thou would'st not
Talk to me thus, but like a pitying Angel
Spreading thy wings come settle on my breast,   200
And hatch warm comfort there e're sorrows freeze it.

    Belv. Why, then poor Mourner, in what baleful
      Corner
Hast thou been talking with that Witch the Night?
On what cold stone hast thou been stretcht along,
Gathering the grumbling Winds about thy Head,
To mix with theirs the Accents of thy Woes!
Oh now I find the Cause my Love forsakes me!
I am no longer fit to bear a share

In his Concernments: My weak female Virtue
Must not be trusted; 'Tis too frail and tender.   210
   Jaff. Oh *Porcia*! *Porcia*! What a Soul was thine?
   Belv. That *Porcia* was a Woman, and when *Brutus*
Big with the fate of *Rome*, (Heav'n guard thy safety!)
Conceal'd from her the Labours of his Mind,
She let him see, her Blood was great as his,
Flow'd from a Spring as noble, and a Heart
Fit to partake his Troubles, as his Love:
Fetch, fetch that Dagger back, the dreadful dower
Thou gav'st last night in parting with me; strike it
Here to my heart; and as the Blood flows from it,
Judge if it run not pure as *Cato*'s Daughter's.   221
   Jaff. Thou art too good, and I indeed unworthy,
Unworthy so much Virtue: Teach me how
I may deserve such matchless Love as thine,
And see with what attention I'l obey thee.
   Belv. Do not despise me: that's the All I ask.
   Jaff. Despise thee! Hear me——
   Belv. Oh thy charming Tongue
Is but too well acquainted with my weakness,   229
Knows, let it name but Love, my melting heart
Dissolves withing my Breast; 'till with clos'd Eyes
I reel into thy Arms, and all's forgotten.
   Jaff. What shall I do?
   Belv. Tell me! be just, and tell me
Why dwells that busy Cloud upon thy face?
Why am I made a stranger? why that sigh,
And I not know the Cause? Why when the World
Is wrapt in Rest, why chooses then my Love
To wander up and down in horrid darkness,
Loathing his bed, and these desiring Arms?   240
Why are these Eyes Blood-shot, with tedious watch-
    ing?
Why starts he now? and looks as if he wisht
His Fate were finisht? 'Tell me, ease my fears;
Least when we next time meet, I want the power
To search into the sickness of thy Mind,

But talk as wildly then as thou look'st now.
   Jaff. Oh *Belvidera*!
   Belv. Why was I last night deliver'd to a Villain?
   Jaff. Hah, a Villain!
   Belv. Yes! to a Villain! Why at such an hour
Meets that assembly all made up of Wretches   251
That look as Hell had drawn 'em into League?
Why, I in this hand, and in that a Dagger,
Was I deliver'd with such dreadful Ceremonies?
" *To you, Sirs, and to your Honour I bequeath her,*
" *And with her this: When e're I prove unworthy,*
" *You know the rest, then strike it to her Heart?* "
Oh! why 's that *rest* conceal'd from me? must I
Be made the hostage of a hellish Trust?
For such I know I am; that 's all my value!   260
But by the Love and Loyalty I owe thee,
I'l free thee from the Bondage of these Slaves,
Strait to the Senate, tell 'em all I know,
All that I think, all that my fears inform me!
   Jaff. Is this the *Roman* Virtue! this the Blood
That boasts its purity with *Cato*'s Daughter!
Would she have e're betray'd her *Brutus*?
   Belv. No:
For *Brutus* trusted her: Wer't thou so kind,
What would not *Belvidera* suffer for thee?   270
   Jaff. I shall undo my self, and tell thee all.
   Belv. Look not upon me, as I am a Woman,
But as a Bone, thy Wife, thy Friend; who long
Has had admission to thy heart, and there
Study'd the Virtues of thy gallant Nature;
Thy Constancy, thy Courage and thy Truth,
Have been my daily lesson: I have learnt them,
Am bold as thou, can suffer or despise
The worst of Fates for thee; and with thee share
    them.
   Jaff. Oh you divinest Powers! look down and hear
My Prayers! instruct me to reward this Virtue!   281
Yet think a little, e're thou tempt me further:

Think I have a Tale to tell, will shake thy Nature,
Melt all this boasted Constancy thou talk'st of
Into vile tears and despicable sorrows:
Then if thou shoud'st betray me!

Belv. Shall I swear?

Jaff. No: do not swear: I would not violate
Thy tender Nature with so rude a Bond:
But as thou hop'st to see me live my days,   290
And love thee long, lock this within thy Breast;
I've bound my self by all the strictest Sacraments,
Divine and humane——

Belv. Speak!——

Jaff. To kill thy Father——

Belv. My Father!

Jaff. Nay the Throats of the whole Senate
Shall bleed, my *Belvidera*: He amongst us
That spares his Father, Brother, or his Friend,   299
Is Damn'd: How rich and beauteous will the face
Of Ruin look, when these wide streets run blood;
I and the glorious Partner's of my Fortune
Shouting, and striding o're the prostrate Dead;
Still to new waste; whilst thou, far off in safety
Smiling, shalt see the wonders of our daring;
And when night comes, with Praise and Love receive
   me.

Belv. Oh!

Jaff. Have a care, and shrink not even in thought!
For if thou do'st——

Belv. I know it, thou wilt kill me.   310
Do, strike thy Sword into this bosom: Lay me
Dead on the Earth, and then thou wilt be safe:
Murder my Father! tho his Cruel Nature
Has persecuted me to my undoing,
Driven me to basest wants; Can I behold him
With smiles of Vengeance, butcher'd in his Age?
The sacred Fountain of my life destroy'd?
And canst thou shed the blood that gave me being?
Nay, be a Traitor too, and sell thy Country;

Can thy great Heart descend so vilely low,   320
Mix with hired Slaves, Bravoes, and Common
    stabbers,
Nose-slitters, Ally-lurking Villians! joyn
With such a Crew, and take a Ruffian's Wages,
To cut the Throats of Wretches as they sleep?

    Jaff. Thou wrong'st me, *Belvidera*! I've engag'd
With Men of Souls: fit to reform the ills
Of all Mankind: There's not a Heart amongst them,
But's as stout as Death, yet honest as the Nature
Of Man first made, e're Fraud and Vice were
    fashions.

    Belv. What's he, to whose curst hands last night
    thou gav'st me?   330
Was that well done? Oh! I could tell a story
Would rowse thy Lyon Heart out of its Den,
And make it rage with terrifying fury.

    Jaff. Speak on I charge thee!

    Belv. Oh my Love! if e're
Thy *Belvidera*'s Peace deserv'd thy Care,
Remove me from this place: Last night, last night!

    Jaff. Distract me not, but give me all the Truth.

    Belv. No sooner wer't thou gone, and I alone,
Left in the pow'r of that old Son of Mischief;   340
No sooner was I lain on my sad Bed,
But that vile Wretch approacht me; loose, unbutton'd,
Ready for violation: Then my Heart
Throbb'd with its fears: Oh how I wept and sigh'd,
And shrunk and trembled; wish'd in vain for him
That should protect me. Thou alas! wert gone!

    Jaff. Patience! sweet Heav'n, 'till I make vengeance
    sure.

    Belv. He drew the hideous Dagger forth thou
    gav'st him,
And with upbraiding smiles he said, *behold it*;
This is the pledge of a false Husbands love: 350
And in my Arms then prest, and wou'd have clasp'd
    me;

But with my Cries I scar'd his Coward heart,
'Till he withdrew, and mutter'd vows to Hell.
These are thy Friends! with these thy Life, thy
    Honour,
Thy Love, all 's stak't, and all will go to ruine.

    Jaff. No more: I charge thee keep this secret close;
Clear up thy sorrows, look as if thy wrongs
Were all forgot, and treat him like a Friend,
As no complaint were made. No more, retire,
Retire my Life, and doubt not of my Honour;   360
I'l heal its failings, and deserve thy Love.

    Belv. Oh should I part with thee, I fear thou wilt
In Anger leave me, and return no more:

    Jaff. Return no more! I would not live without
    thee
Another Night to purchase the Creation.

    Belv. When shall we meet again?

    Jaff. Anon at Twelve!
I'l steal my self to thy expecting Arms,
Come like a Travell'd Dove and bring thee Peace.

    Belv. Indeed!   370

    Jaff. By all our loves!

    Belv. 'Tis hard to part:
But sure no falsehood e're lookt so fairly.
Farewell—Remember Twelve.   [*Ex.* Belvid.

    Jaff. Let Heav'n forget me
When I remember not thy Truth, thy Love.
How curst is my Condition, toss'd and justl'd,
From every Corner; Fortune's Common Fool,
The jest of Rogues, an Instrumental Ass
For Villains to lay loads of Shame upon,   380
And drive about just for their ease and scorn.

        Enter Pierre.

    Pierr. Jaffeir!

    Jaff. Who calls!

    Pierr. A Friend, that could have wisht
T'have found thee otherwise imploy'd: what, hunt

A Wife on the dull soil! sure a stanch Husband
Of all Hounds is the dullest? wilt thou never,
Never be wean'd from Caudles and Confections?
What feminine Tale hast thou been listening to,
Of unayr'd shirts; Catharrs and Tooth Ach got 390
By thin-sol'd shoos? Damnation! that a Fellow
Chosen to be a Sharer in the Destruction
Of a whole People, should sneak thus in Corners
To ease his fulsom Lusts, and Fool his Mind.

Jaff. May not a Man then trifle out an hour
With a kind Woman and not wrong his calling?

Pierr. Not in a Cause like ours.

Jaff. Then Friend our Cause
Is in a damn'd condition: for I'l tell thee,
That Canker-worm call'd *Letchery* has toucht it, 400
'Tis tainted vilely: would'st thou think it, *Renault*,
(That mortify'd old wither'd Winter Rogue)
Loves simple Fornication like a Priest,
I found him out for watering at my Wife:
He visited her last night like a kind Guardian:
Faith she has some Temptations, that 's the truth on 't.

Pierr. He durst not wrong his Trust!

Jaff. 'Twas something late tho
To take the freedome of a Ladies Chamber.

Pierr. Was she in bed? 410

Jaff. Yes, faith, in Virgin sheets
White as her bosom, *Pierre*, disht neatly up,
Might tempt a weaker appetite to taste.
Oh how the old Fox stunk I warrant thee
When the rank fit was on him.

Pierr. Patience guide me!
He us'd no violence?

Jaff. No, no! out on 't, violence!
Play'd with her neck; brusht her with his Gray-beard,
Struggl'd and towz'd, tickl'd her 'till she squeak'd a
little 420
May be, or so—but not a jot of violence——

Pierr. Damn him.

Jaff. Ay, so say I: but hush, no more on 't;
All hitherto is well, and I believe
My self no Monster yet: Tho no Man knows
What Fate he 's born to? sure 'tis near the hour
We all should meet for our concluding Orders:
Will the Ambassador be here in person?

   Pierr. No: he has sent Commission to that Villain,
     Renault,
To give the Executing Charge;   430
I'd have thee be a Man if possible
And keep thy temper; for a brave Revenge
Ne're comes too late.

   Jaff. Fear not, I am cool as Patience:
Had he compleated my dishonour, rather
Then hazard the Success our hopes are ripe for,
I'd bear it all with mortifying Vertue.

   Pierr. He 's yonder coming this way through the
     Hall,
His thoughts seem full.

   Jaff. Prithee retire, and leave me   440
With him alone: I'l put him to some tryal,
See how his rotten part will bear the touching.

   Pierr. Be careful then.   [*Ex.* Pierre.

   Jaff. Nay never doubt, but trust me.
What, be a Devil! take a Damning Oath
For shedding native blood! can there be a sin
In merciful repentance? Oh this Villain.

Enter Renault.

   Renault. Perverse! and peevish! what a slave is
     Man!
To let his itching flesh thus get the better of him!
Dispatch the Tool her Husband—that were well. 450
Who 's there?

   Jaff. A Man.

   Ren. My Friend, my near Ally!
The hostage of your faith, my beauteous Charge, is
     very well.

Jaff. Sir, are you sure of that?
Stands she in perfect health? beats her pulse even?
Neither too hot nor cold?

   Ren. What means that question?

   Jaff. Oh Women have fantastick Constitutions,
Inconstant as their Wishes, always wavering,   460
And ne're fixt; was it not boldly done
Even at first sight to trust the Thing I lov'd
(A tempting Treasure too!) with Youth so fierce
And vigorous as thine? but thou art honest.

   Ren. Who dares accuse me?

   Jaff. Curst be him that doubts
Thy virtue, I have try'd it, and declare,
Were I to choose a Guardian of my Honour
I'd put it into thy keeping: for I know thee.

   Ren. Know me!   470

   Jaff. Ay know thee: There's no falsehood in thee.
Thou look'st just as thou art: Let us embrace.
Now would'st thou cut my Throat or I cut thine?

   Ren. You dare not do 't.

   Jaff. You lye Sir.

   Ren. How!

   Jaff. No more.
'Tis a base World, and must reform, that 's all.

Enter Spinosa, Theodore, Eliot, Revellido, Durand
     Brainveil, *and the rest of the Conspirators.*

   Ren. Spinosa! Theodore!

   Spin. The same.   480

   Ren. You are welcome!

   Spin. You are trembling, Sir.

   Ren. 'Tis a cold Night indeed, I am Aged,
Full of decay and natural infirmities; [Pierre *re-enters.*
We shall be warm, my Friend, I hope to morrow.

   Pierr. 'Twas not well done, thou shou'dst have
    stroakt him and not have gall'd him.

   Jaff. Damn him, let him chew on 't.
Heav'n! where am I? beset with cursed Fiends,

That wait to Damn me: What a Devil's man,
When he forgets his nature—hush my heart.   490

   Ren. My Friends, 'tis late: are we assembled all?
Where's *Theodore*?

   Theo. At hand.

   Ren. Spinosa.

   Spin. Here.

   Ren. Brainveil.

   Brain. I am ready.

   Ren. Durand and *Brabe.*

   Dur. Command us,
We are both prepar'd!   500

   Ren. Mezzana, Revellido,
Ternon Retrosi; Oh you are Men I find
Fit to behold your Fate, and meet her Summons,
To morrow's rising Sun must see you all
Deckt in your honours! are the Souldiers ready?

   Omn. All, all.

   Ren. You, *Durand*, with your thousand must possess
St. *Marks*; You, Captain, know your charge already;
'Tis to secure the Ducal Palace: you
Brabe with a hundred more must gain the *Secque.*   510
With the like number *Brainveil* to the *Procuralle.*
Be all this done with the least tumult possible,
'Till in each place you post sufficient guards:
Then sheath your Swords in every breast you meet.

   Jaff. Oh reverend Cruelty: Damn'd bloody
     Villain!

   Ren. During this Execution, *Durand*, you
Must in the mid'st keep your Battalia fast,
And *Theodore* be sure to plant the Canon
That may Command the streets; whilst *Revellido,*
Mezzana, Ternon and *Retrosi*, Guard you.   520
(This done!) weel give the General Alarm,
Apply Petards, and force the Ars'nal Gates;
Then fire the City round in several places,
Or with our Canon (if it dare resist)

Batter't to Ruin. But above all I charge you
Shed blood enough, spare neither Sex nor Age,
Name nor Condition; if there live a Senator
After to morrow, tho the dullest Rogue
That er'e said nothing, we have lost our ends;
If possible, lets kill the very Name   530
Of Senator, and bury it in blood.
    Jaff. Merciless, horrid slave!—Ay, blood enough!
Shed blood enough, old *Renault*: how thou charm'st
    me!
    Ren. But one thing more, and then farewell till
    Fate
Join us again, or separate us ever:
First, let 's embrace, Heav'n knows who next shall
    thus
Wing ye together: But let 's all remember
We wear no common Cause upon our Swords,
Let each Man think that on his single Virtue
Depends the Good and Fame of all the rest;   540
Eternal Honour or perpetual Infamy.
Let's remember, through what dreadful hazards
Propitious Fortune hitherto has led us,
How often on the brink of some discovery
Have we stood tottering, and yet still kept our ground
So well, the busiest searchers ne'r could follow
Those subtle Tracks which puzzled all suspition:
You droop Sir.
    Jaff. No: with a most profound attention
I've heard it all, and wonder at thy vertue.   550
    Ren. Though there be yet few hours 'twixt them
    and Ruin,
Are not the Senate lull'd in full security,
Quiet and satisfy'd, as Fools are always!
Never did so profound repose forerun
Calamity so great: Nay our good Fortune
Has blinded the most piercing of Mankind:
Strengthen'd the fearfull'st, charm'd the most sus-
    pectful,

Confounded the most subtle: for we live,
We live my Friends, and quickly shall our Life
Prove fatal to these Tyrants: Let's consider   560
That we destroy Oppression, Avarice,
A People nurst up equally with Vices
And loathsome Lusts, which Nature most abhors,
And such as without shame she cannot suffer.

   Jaff. Oh *Belvidera*, take me to thy Arms
And shew me where's my Peace, for I've lost it.
                       [*Ex.* Jaff.

   Ren. Without the least remorse then let's resolve
With Fire and Sword t' exterminate these Tyrants,
And when we shall behold those curst Tribunals, 569
Stain'd by the Tears and sufferings of the Innocent,
Burning with flames rather from Heav'n than ours,
The raging furious and unpitying Souldier
Pulling his reeking Dagger from the bosoms
Of gasping Wretches; Death in every Quarter,
With all that sad disorder can produce,
To make a Spectacle of horror: Then,
Then let's call to mind, my dearest Friends,
That there's nothing pure upon the Earth,
That the most valu'd things have most allays,
And that in change of all those vile Enormities, 580
Under whose weight this wretched Country labours,
The Means are only in our hands to Crown them.

   Pierr. And may those Powers above that are
        propitious
To gallant minds record this Cause, and bless it.

   Ren. Thus happy, thus secure of all we wish for,
Should there my Friends be found amongst us one
False to this glorious Enterprize, what Fate,
What Vengeance were enough for such a Villian?

   Eliot. Death here without repentance, Hell here-
        after.

   Ren. Let that be my lott, if as here I stand   590
Lifted by Fate amongst her darling Sons,
Tho I had one only Brother, dear by all

The strictest ties of Nature; tho one hour
Had given us birth, one Fortune féd our wants,
One only love, and that but of each other,
Still fill'd our minds: Could I have such a Friend
Joyn'd in this Cause, and had but ground to fear
Meant foul play; may this right hand drop from me,
If I'd not hazard all my future peace,
And stabb him to the heart before you: who   600
Would not do less? Would'st not thou *Pierre* the same?

  Pierr. You have singled me, Sir, out for this hard
      question,
As if 'twere started only for my sake!
Am I the thing you fear? Here, here's my bosom,
Search it with all your Swords! am I a Traytor?

  Ren. No: but I fear your late commended Friend
Is little less: Come Sirs, 'tis now no time
To trifle with our safety. Where's this *Jaffeir*?

  Spino. He left the room just now in strange disorder.

  Ren. Nay, there is danger in him: I observ'd him,
During the time I took for Explanation,   611
He was transported from most deep attention
To a confusion which he could not smother.
His looks grew full of sadness and surprize,
All which betray'd a wavering Spirit in him,
That labour'd with reluctancy and sorrow;
What's requisite for safety must be done
With speedy Execution: he remains
Yet in our power: I for my own part wear
A Dagger.   620

  Pierr. Well.

  Ren. And I could wish it!

  Pierr. Where?

  Ren. Bury'd in his heart.

  Pierr. Away! w' are yet all friends;
No more of this, 'twill Breed ill blood amongst us.

  Spin. Let us all draw our Swords, and search the
      house,
Pull him from the dark hole where he sits brooding

O're his cold fears, and each man kill his share of him.
 Pierr. Who talks of killing? who's he'll shed the blood 630
That's dear to me? is 't you? or you? or you Sir?
What not one speak? how you stand gaping all
On your grave Oracle, your wooden God there;
Yet not a word: Then Sir I'l tell you a secret,
Suspition's but at best a Cowards Virtue! [To *Ren.*
 Ren. A Coward— [*Handles his Sword.*
 Pierr. Put, put up thy Sword, old Man,
Thy hand shakes at it; come let's heal this breach,
I am too hot: we yet may live Friends.
 Spino. 'Till we are safe, our Friendship cannot be so.
 Pierr. Again: who's that? 641
 Spino. 'Twas I.
 Theo. And I.
 Revell. And I.
 Eliot. And all.
 Ren. Who are on my side?
 Spino. Every honest Sword,
Let's die like men and not be sold like Slaves.
 Pierr. One such word more, by Heav'n I'l to the Senate
And hang ye all, like Dogs in Clusters, 650
Why peep your Coward Swords half out their shells?
Why do you not all brandish them like mine?
You fear to die, and yet dare talk of Killing?
 Ren. Go to the Senate and betray us, hasten,
Secure thy wretched life, we fear to die
Less than thou dar'st be honest.
 Pierr. That's rank falsehood,
Fear'st not thou death? fy, there's a knavish itch
In that salt blood, an utter foe to smarting.
Had *Jaffeir*'s Wife prov'd kind, he had still been true.
Foh—how that stinks? 661
Thou dy! thou kill my Friend! or thou, or thou,
Or thou, with that lean wither'd wretched Face!
Away! disperse all to your several Charges,

And meet to morrow where your honour calls you,
I'l bring that man, whose blood you so much thirst for,
And you shall see him venture for you fairly—
Hence, hence, I say.   [*Ex.* Renault *angrily.*
    Spino. I fear we have been to blame,
And done too much.   670
    Theo. 'Twas too farr urg'd against the man you
        lov'd.
    Rev. Here, take our Swords and crush 'em with
        your feet.
    Spino. Forgive us, gallant Friend.
    Pierr. Nay, now y' have found
The way to melt and cast me as you will:
I'll fetch this Friend and give him to your mercy:
Nay he shall dye if you will take him from me,
For your repose I'll quit my hearts Jewel;
But would not have him torn away by Villains
And spitefull villany.   680
    Spino. No; may you both
For ever live and fill the world with fame!
    Pierr. Now you are too kind. Whence rose all this
        discord?
Oh what a dangerous precipice have we scap'd!
How near a fall was all we had long been building!
What an eternal blot had stain'd our glories,
If one the bravest and the best of men
Had fallen a Sacrifice to rash suspicion!
Butcher'd by those whose Cause he came to cherish:
Oh could you know him all as I have known him,
How good he is, how just, how true, how brave, 691
You wou'd not leave this place till you had seen him;
Humbled your selves before him, kiss'd his feet,
And gain'd remission for the worst of follies;
    Come but to morrow all your doubts shall end, ⎫
    And to your Loves me better recommend,   ⎬
    That I've preserv'd your Fame, and, sav'd my Friend. ⎭
                                    [*Exeunt omnes.*
        The end of the third Act.

ACT IV.

Enter Jaffeir *and* Belvidera.

Jaff. Where dost thou lead me? Every step I move,
Methinks I tread upon some mangled Limb
Of a rack'd Friend: Oh my dear charming ruine!
Where are we wandring?
 Bel. To eternal Honour;
To doe a deed shall Chronicle thy name,
Among the glorious Legends of those few
That have sav'd sinking Nations: thy Renown
Shall be the future Song of all the Virgins,
Who by thy piety have been preserv'd   10
From horrid violation: Every Street
Shall be adorn'd with Statues to thy honour,
And at thy feet this great Inscription written,
 Remember him that prop'd the fall of Venice.
 Jaff. Rather, Remember him, who after all
The sacred Bonds of Oaths and holyer Friendship
In fond compassion to a Womans tears
Forgot his Manhood, Vertue, truth and Honour,
To sacrifice the Bosom that reliev'd him.
Why wilt thou damn me?   20
 Bel. Oh inconstant man!
How will you promise? how will you deceive?
Do, return back, re-place me in my Bondage,
Tell all thy Friends how dangerously thou lovst me;
And let thy Dagger doe its bloudy office.
Oh that kind Dagger, *Jaffeir*, how twill look
Stuck through my heart, drench'd in my bloud to
 th' hilts!
Whilst these poor dying eyes shall with their tears
No more torment thee, then thou wilt be free:
Or if thou think'st it nobler, Let me live   30
Till I am a Victim to the hatefull lust
Of that Infernal Devil, that old Fiend

That 's Damn'd himself and wou'd undoe Mankind:
Last night, my Love!
   Jaff. Name, name it not again.
It shews a beastly Image to my fancy;
Will wake me into madness.   Oh the Villain!
That durst approach such purity as thine
On terms so vile: Destruction, swift destruction
Fall on my Coward-head, and make my Name   40
The common scorn of Fools if I forgive him;
If I forgive him, If I not revenge
With utmost rage, and most unstaying fury,
Thy sufferings thou dear darling of my life, Love.
   Bel. Delay no longer then, but to the Senate;
And tell the dismalst story e'r was utter'd,
Tell 'em what bloudshed, rapines, desolations,
Have been prepar'd, how near 's the fatal hour!
Save thy poor Country, save the Reverend bloud
Of all its Nobles, which to morrows Dawn   50
Must else see shed: Save the poor tender lives
Of all those little Infants which the Swords
Of murtherers are whetting for this moment;
Think thou already hearst their dying screams,
Think that thou seest their sad distracted Mothers
Kneeling before thy feet, and begging pity
With torn dishevel'd hair and streaming eyes,
Their naked mangled breasts besmeared with bloud,
And even the Milk with which their fondled Babes,
Softly they hush'd, dropping in anguish from 'em.
Think thou seest this, and then consult thy heart. 61
   Jaff. Oh!
   Bel. Think too, If thou lose this present minute,
What miseries the next day bring upon thee.
Imagine all the horrours of that night
Murther and Rapine, Waste and Desolation,
Confusedly ranging.   Think what then may prove
My Lot! the Ravisher may then come safe,
And midst the terrour of the publick ruine
Doe a damn'd deed; perhaps to lay a Train   70

May catch thy life; then where will be revenge,
The dear revenge that 's due to such a wrong?

   Jaff. By all Heavens powers Prophetick truth
    dwells in thee,
For every word thou speak'st strikes through my
    heart
Like a new light, and shows it how 't has wander'd;
Just what th' hast made me, take me, *Belvidera*,
And lead me to the place where I'm to say
This bitter Lesson, where I must betray
My truth, my vertue, constancy and friends:
Must I betray my friends? Ah take me quickly,   80
Secure me well before that thought 's renew'd;
If I relapse once more, all 's lost for ever.

   Bel. Hast thou a friend more dear than *Belvidera*?

   Jaff. No, th' art my Soul it self, wealth, friendship,
    honour,
All present joys, and earnest of all future,
Are summ'd in thee: methinks when in thy armes
Thus leaning on thy breast, one minute 's more
Than a long thousand years of vulgar hours.
Why was such happiness not given me pure?
Why dash'd with cruel wrongs, and bitter wantings?
Come, lead me forward now like a tame Lamb   91
To Sacrifice, thus in his fatal Garlands,
Deck'd fine and pleas'd, The wanton skips and plays,
   Trots by the enticing flattering Priestess side,
   And much transported with his little pride,
   Forgets his dear Companions of the plain
   Till by Her, bound, Hee 's on the Altar layn
   Yet then too hardly bleats, such pleasure 's in the pain.

        Enter Officer *and* 6 Guards

   Offic. Stand who goes there?

   Bel. Friends.   100

   Jaff. Friends, *Belvidera*! hide me from my Friends,
By Heaven I'd rather see the face of Hell,
Than meet the man I love.

Offic. But what friends are you?

Bel. Friends to the Senate and the State of *Venice.*

Offic. My orders are to seize on all I find
At this late hour, and bring 'em to the Council,
Who now are sitting.

Jaff. Sir, you shall be obey'd.
Hold, Brutes, stand off, none of your paws upon me.
Now the Lot 's cast, and Fate doe what thou wilt. 111

> [*Exeunt guarded.*

SCENE *The Senate-house,*

Where appear sitting, the Duke of Venice, Priuli, Antonio,
And Eight other Senators.

Duke. Antony, *Priuli,* Senators of *Venice,*
Speak; why are we assembled here this night?
What have you to inform us of, concerns
The State of *Venice,* honour, or its safety?

Priu. Could words express the story I have to tell
   you,
Fathers, these tears were useless, these sad tears
That fall from my old eyes; but there is cause
We all should weep; tear off these purple Robes,
And wrap our selves in Sack-cloth, sitting down 120
On the sad Earth, and cry aloud to Heaven.
Heaven knows if yet there be an hour to come
E'r *Venice* be no more!

*All Sent*ʳᵉ How!

Priu. Nay we stand
Upon the Very brink of gaping ruine;
Within this City 's form'd a dark Conspiracy,
To massacre us all, our Wives and Children,
Kindred and Friends, our Palaces and Temples
To lay in Ashes: nay the hour too, fixt; 130
The Swords, for ought I know, drawn even this
   moment,
And the wild Waste begun: from unknown hands
I had this warning: but if we are men

Let's not be tamely butcher'd, but doe something
That may inform the world in after Ages,
Our Virtue was not ruin'd though we were.

[A noise without.

Room, room, make room for some Prisoners—
  2 Senat. Let's raise the City.

Enter Officer *and* Guard.

  Priu. Speak there, what disturbance?
  Offic. Two Prisoners have the Guard seiz'd in the
    Streets,   140
Who say they come to inform this Reverend Senate
About the present danger.

Enter Jaffeir *and* Belvidera *guarded.*

  All. Give 'em entrance—
Well, who are you?
  Jaff. A Villain.
  Anto. Short and pithy.
The man speaks well.
  Jaff. Would every man that hears me
Would deal so honestly, and own his title.   149
  Duke. 'Tis rumour'd that a Plot has been contriv'd
Against this State; that you have a share in 't too.
If you are a Villain, to redeem your honour,
Unfold the truth and be restor'd with Mercy.
  Jaff. Think not that I to save my life come hither,
I know its value better; but in pity
To all those wretches whose unhappy dooms
Are fix'd and seal'd.   You see me here before you,
The sworn and Covenanted foe of *Venice.*
But use me as my dealings may deserve
And I may prove a friend.   160
  Duke. The Slave Capitulates,
Give him the Tortures.
  Jaff. That you dare not doe,
Your fears won't let you, nor the longing Itch
To hear a story which you dread the truth of.
Truth which the fear of smart shall ne'r get from me.

Cowards are scar'd with threatnings. Boys are whipt
Into confessions: but a Steady mind
Acts of its self, ne'r asks the body Counsell.
Give him the Tortures ! Name but such a thing   170
Again; by Heaven I'll shut these lips for ever;
Not all your Racks, your Engines or your Wheels
Shall force a groan away——that you may guess at.

   Anto. A bloudy minded fellow I'll warrant;
A damn'd bloudy minded fellow.

   Duke. Name your Conditions.

   Jaff. For my self full pardon,
Besides the lives of two and twenty friends

                                [Delivers a list.
Whose names are here inroll'd: Nay, let their Crimes
Be ne'r so monstrous, I must have the Oaths   180
And sacred promise of this Reverend Council,
That in a full Assembly of the Senate
The thing I ask be ratifi'd. Swear this,
And I'll unfold the secrets of your danger.

   All. Wee'l swear.

   Duke. Propose the Oath.

   Jaff. By all the hopes
Ye have of Peace and Happiness hereafter,
Swear.

   All. We all swear.   190

   Jaff. To grant me what I've ask'd,
Ye swear,

   All. We swear.

   Jaff. And as ye keep the Oath,
May you and your posterity be blest
Or curst for ever.

   All. Else be curst for ever.

   Jaff. Then here 's the list, and with 't the full dis-
     close of all that threatens you.

                           [Delivers another paper.
Now Fate thou hast caught me.   199

   Anto. Why what a dreadfull Catalogue of Cut-
throats is here ! I'll warrant you not one of these

fellows but has a face like a Lion. I dare not so
much as reade their names over.

Duke. Give orders that all diligent search be made
To seize these men, their characters are publick,
The paper intimates their Rendevouz
To be at the house of a fam'd Grecian Curtezan
Call'd *Aquilina*; see that place secur'd.

    Anto. What my Nicky Nacky, Hurry Durry, Nicky
    Nacky in the Plot——I'll make a Speech. Most
    noble Senators,   211
What headlong apprehension drives you on,
Right noble, wise and truly solid Senators,
To violate the Laws and right of Nations?
The Lady is a Lady of renown.
'Tis true, she holds a house of fair Reception,
And though I say 't my self, as many more
Can say as well as I.

    2 *Senat.* My Lord, long Speeches
Are frivolous here, when dangers are so near us;
We all well know your Interest in that Lady,   221
The world talks loud on 't.

    Anto. Verily I have done,
I say no more.

    Duke. But since he has declar'd
Himself concern'd, Pray, Captain, take great caution
To treat the fair one, as becomes her Character,
And let her Bed-chamber be search'd with decency.
You, *Jaffeir*, must with patience bear till morning, to
    be our
Prisoner.   230

    Jaff. Would the Chains of death
Had bound me fast e'r I had known this minute,
I've done a deed will make my Story hereafter
Quoted in competition with all ill ones:
The History of my wickedness shall run
Down through the low traditions of the vulgar,
And Boys be thought to tell the tale of *Jaffeir*.

    Duke. Captain, withdraw your Prisoner.

Jaff. Sir, if possible,
Lead me where my own thoughts themselves may
    lose me,   240
Where I may doze out what I've left of life,
Forget my self and this days guilt and falsehood.
Cruel remembrance how shall I appease thee!
                         [*Ex. guarded.*

            Noise without.

More Traitors; room, room, make room there.
    Duke. How's this, Guards?
Where are our Guards? shut up the Gates, the Treason's already at our Dores.

           Enter Officer.

    Offic. My Lords, more Traitors:
Seiz'd in the very act of Consultation;
Furnish'd with Arms and Instruments of mischief,
Bring in the prisoners.   251

  Enter Pierre, Renault, Theodore, Elliot, Revillido
    and other Conspirators, in fetters, guarded.

    Pierr. You, my Lords and Fathers,
(As you are pleas'd to call your selves) of *Venice*;
If you sit here to guide the course of justice,
Why these disgracefull chains upon the limbs
That have so often labour'd in your service?
Are these the wreaths of triumphs ye bestow
On those that bring you Conquests home and Honours?
    Duke. Go on, you shall be heard, Sir.
    Anto. And be hang'd too, I hope.   260
    Pierr. Are these the Trophies I've deserv'd for
    fighting
Your Battels with confederated Powers,
When winds and Seas conspir'd to overthrow you?
And brought the Fleets of *Spain* to your own Harbours,
When you, great Duke, shrunk trembling in your
    Palace,
And saw your Wife, th' Adriatick, plough'd
Like a lew'd Whore by bolder Prows than yours

Stept not I forth, and taught your loose Venetians
The task of honour and the way to greatness,
Rais'd you from your capitulating fears   270
To stipulate the terms of su'd for peace,
And this my recompence? If I am a Traitor
Produce my charge; or shew the wretch that's base
      enough
And brave enough to tell me I am a Traitor.

   Duke. Know you one *Jaffeir*?

                             [*All the conspirators murmur.*

   Pierr. Yes, and know his Vertue.
His Justice, Truth, his general Worth and Sufferings
From a hard father taught me first to love him.

Enter Jaffeir *guarded.*

   Duke. See him brought forth.

   Pierr. My friend too bound? nay then   280
Our Fate has conquer'd us, and we must fall,
Why droops the man whose welfare's so much mine
They're but one thing? these Reverend Tyrants,
   Jaffeir,
Call us all Traitors, art thou one, my Brother?

   Jaff. To thee I am the falsest, veryest slave
That e'r betray'd a generous trusting friend,
And gave up honour to be sure of ruine.
All our fair hopes which morning was to have crown'd
Has this curst tongue o'rthrown.

   Pierr. So, then all's over: 290
Venice has lost her freedom; I my life;
No more, farewell.

   Duke. Say; will you make confession
Of your vile deeds and trust the Senates mercy?

   Pierr. Curst be your Senate: Curst your Constitu-
   tion:
The Curse of growing factions and division
Still vex your Councils, shake your publick safety,
And make the Robes of Government, you wear,
Hatefull to you, as these base Chains to me.

Duke. Pardon or death? 300
Pierr. Death, honourable death,
Renault. Death's the best thing we ask or you can give.
All Conspir. No shamefull bonds, but honourable death.
Duke. Break up the Council: Captain, guard your prisoners.
Jaffeir, y'are free, but these must wait for judgment.
[*Ex. all the Senators.*

Pierr. Come, where's my Dungeon? lead me to my straw:
It will not be the first time I've lodg'd hard
To doe your Senate service.
Jaff. Hold one moment.
Pierr. Who's he disputes the Judgment of the Senate? 310
Presumptuous Rebel——on—— [*Strikes* Jaff.
Jaff. By Heaven you stir not.
I must be heard, I must have leave to speak:
Thou hast disgrac'd me, *Pierre*, by a vile blow:
Had not a dagger done thee nobler justice?
But use me as thou wilt, thou canst not wrong me,
For I am fallen beneath the basest injuries;
Yet look upon me with an eye of mercy,
With pity and with charity behold me; 319
Shut not thy heart against a friend's repentance,
But as there dwells a God-like nature in thee
Listen with mildness to my supplications.
Pierr. What whining Monk art thou? what holy cheat
That wou'dst encroach upon my credulous ears
And cant'st thus vilely? hence. I know thee not,
Dissemble and be nasty: leave me, Hippocrite.
Jaff. Not know me, *Pierre*?
Pierr. No, know thee not: what art thou?
Jaff. Jaffeir, thy friend, thy once lov'd, valu'd friend, 329

Though now deservedly scorn'd, and us'd most hardly.

   Pierr. Thou *Jaffeir*! Thou my once lov'd, valu'd
     friend!

By Heavens thou ly'st; the man, so call'd, my friend,
Was generous, honest, faithfull, just and valiant,
Noble in mind, and in his person lovely,
Dear to my eyes and tender to my heart:
But thou a wretched base, false, worthless Coward,
Poor even in Soul, and loathsome in thy aspect,
All eyes must shun thee, and all hearts detest thee.
Prithee avoid, nor longer cling thus round me,   339
Like something banefull, that my nature's chill'd at.

   Jaff. I have not wrong'd thee, by these tears I have
     not.

But still am honest, true, and hope too, valiant;
My mind still full of thee: therefore still noble,
Let not thy eyes then shun me, nor thy heart
Detest me utterly: Oh look upon me
Look back and see my sad sincere submission!
How my heart swells, as even 'twould burst my
     bosom;
Fond of its Gaol, and labouring to be at thee!
What shall I doe? what say to make thee hear me?

   Pierr. Hast thou not wrong'd me? dar'st thou call
     thy self   350

Jaffeir, that once lov'd, valued friend of mine,
And swear thou hast not wrong'd me? whence these
     chains?
Whence the vile death, which I may meet this
     moment?
Whence this dishonour, but from thee, thou false one?

   Jaff. All's true, yet grant one thing, and I've done
     asking.

   Pierr. What's that?

   Jaff. To take thy life on such conditions

The Council have propos'd: Thou and thy friends
May yet live long, and to be better treated.   359

   Pierr. Life! ask my life! confess! record my self

A villain for the privilege to breathe,
And carry up and down this cursed City
A discontented and repining spirit,
Burthensome to it self a few years longer,
To lose, it may be, at last in a lewd quarrel
For some new friend, treacherous and false as thou art!
No, this vile world and I have long been jangling,
And cannot part on better terms than now,
When onely men like thee are fit to live in 't.

Jaff. By all that 's just——   370

Pierr. Swear by some other powers,
For thou hast broke that sacred Oath too lately.

Jaff. Then by that hell I merit, I'll not leave thee,
Till to thy self at least, thou'rt reconcil'd,
However thy resentments deal with me.

Pierr. Not leave me!

Jaff. No, thou shalt not force me from thee,
Use me reproachfully, and like a slave,
Tread on me, buffet me, heap wrongs on wrongs
On my poor head; I'll bear it all with patience, 380
Shall weary out thy most unfriendly cruelty,
Ly at thy feet and kiss 'em though they spurn me,
Till, wounded by my sufferings, thou relent,
And raise me to thy armes with dear forgiveness.

Pierr. Art thou not——

Jaff. What?

Pierr. A Traitor?

Jaff. Yes.

Pierr. A Villain?

Jaff. Granted.   390

Pierr. A Coward, a most scandalous Coward,
Spiritless, void of honour, one who has sold
Thy everlasting Fame, for shameless life?

Jaff. All, all, and more, much more: my faults are
    Numberless.

Pierr. And wouldst thou have me live on terms like
    thine?
Base as thou art false——

Jaff. No, 'tis to me that's granted,
The safety of thy life was all I aim'd at,
In recompence for faith, and trust so broken.   399

Pierr. I scorn it more because preserv'd by thee,
And as when first my foolish heart took pity
On thy misfortunes, sought thee in thy miseries,
Reliev'd thy wants, and rais'd thee from thy State
Of wretchedness in which thy fate had plung'd thee,
To rank thee in my list of noble friends;
All I receiv'd in surety for thy truth,
Were unregarded oaths; and this, this dagger,
Given with a worthless pledge, thou since hast stoln,
So I restore it back to thee again,   409
Swearing by all those powers which thou hast violated,
Never from this curs'd hour to hold communion,
Friendship or interest with thee, though our years
Were to exceed those limited the world.
Take it—farewell—for now I owe thee nothing.

Jaff. Say thou wilt live then.

Pierr. For my life, dispose it
Just as thou wilt, because tis what I'm tir'd with.

Jaff. Oh, *Pierre*!

Pierr. No more.

Jaff. My eyes won't lose the sight of thee,   420
But languish after thine, and ake with gazing.

Pierr. Leave me——Nay, then thus, thus, I throw
thee from me.
And curses, great as is thy falsehood, catch thee.

Jaff. Amen.
He's gone, my father, friend, preserver,
And here's the portion he has left me.

                    [*Holds the dagger up.*
This dagger, well remember'd, with this dagger
I gave a solemn vow of dire importance,
Parted with this and *Belvidera* together;   429
Have a care, Mem'ry, drive that thought no farther;
No, I'll esteem it as a friend's last legacy,
Treasure it up in this wretched bosom,

Where it may grow acquainted with my heart,
That when they meet, they start not from each other;
So; now for thinking: A blow, call'd Traitor, Villain,
Coward, dishonourable coward, fogh!
Oh for a long sound sleep, and so forget it!
Down, busie Devil——.

Enter Belvidera.

  Bel. Whither shall I fly?
Where hide me and my miseries together?   440
Where's now the Roman Constancy I boasted?
Sunk into trembling fears and desperation!
Not daring now to look up to that dear face
Which us'd to smile even on my faults, but down
Bending these miserable eyes to earth,
Must move in penance, and implore much Mercy.
  Jaff. Mercy, kind Heaven has surely endless stores
Hoarded for thee of blessings yet untasted;
Let wretches loaded hard with guilt as I am,
Bow the weight and groan beneath the burthen, 450
Creep with a remnant of that strength th' have left,
Before the footstool of that Heaven th' have injur'd.
Oh *Belvidera*! I'm the wretchedst creature
E'r crawl'd on earth; now if thou hast Vertue help
  me,
Take me into thy Armes, and speak the words of
  peace
To my divided Soul, that wars within me,
And raises every Sense to my confusion;
By Heav'n I am tottering on the very brink
Of Peace; and thou art all the hold I've left. 459
  Bel. Alass! I know thy sorrows are most mighty;
I know th' hast cause to mourn; to mourn, my *Jaffeir*,
With endless cries, and never ceasing wailings,
Th' hast lost—
  Jaff. Oh I have lost what can't be counted;
My friend too, *Belvidera*, that dear friend,
Who, next to thee, was all my health rejoyc'd in.

Has us'd me like a slave; shamefully us'd me;
'Twould break thy pitying heart to hear the story,
What shall I doe? resentment, indignation,   469
Love, pity, fear and mem'ry, how I've wrong'd him,
Distract my quiet with the very thought on 't,
And tear my heart to pieces in my bosome.

Bel. What has he done?

Jaff. Thou'dst hate me, should I tell thee.

Bel. Why?

Jaff. Oh he has us'd me! yet by Heaven I bear it;
He has us'd me, *Belvidera*, but first swear
That when I've told thee, thou'lt not loath me utterly,
Though vilest blots and stains appear upon me;
But still at least with charitable goodness,   480
Be near me in the pangs of my affliction,
Not scorn me, *Belvidera*, as he has done.

Bel. Have I then e'r been false that now I am
    doubted?
Speak, whats the cause I am grown into distrust,
Why thought unfit to hear my Love's complainings?

Jaff. Oh!

Bel. Tell me.

Jaff. Bear my failings, for they are many,
Oh my dear Angel! in that friend I've lost
All my Soul's peace; for every thought of him   490
Strikes my Sense hard, and deads it in my brains;
Wouldst thou believe it?

Bel. Speak.

Jaff. Before we parted,
E'r yet his Guards had led him to his prison,
Full of severest sorrows for his suff'rings,
With eyes o'rflowing and a bleeding heart,
Humbling my self almost beneath my nature;
As at his feet I kneel'd, and su'd for mercy,
Forgetting all our friendship, all the dearness,   500
In which w' have liv'd so many years together,
With a reproachfull hand, he dash'd a blow,
He struck me, *Belvidera*, by Heaven, he struck me,

Buffeted, call'd me Traitor, Villain, Coward;
Am I a Coward? am I a Villain? tell me:
Th'art the best Judge, and mad'st me, if I am so.
Damnation; Coward!

Bel. Oh! forgive him, *Jaffeir.*
And if his sufferings wound thy heart already,
What will they doe to morrow?   510

Jaff. Hah!

Bel. To morrow,
When thou shalt see him stretch'd in all the Agonies
Of a tormenting and a shamefull death,
His bleeding bowels, and his broken limbs,
Insulted o'r by a vile butchering villain;
What will thy heart doe then? Oh sure 't will stream
Like my eyes now.

Jaff. What means thy dreadfull story?   519
Death, and to morrow? broken limbs and bowels?
Insulted o'r by a vile butchering Villain?
By all my fears I shall start out to madness,
With barely guessing if the truth's hid longer.

Bel. The faithless Senators, 'tis they've decree'd it:
They say according to our friends request,
They shall have death, and not ignoble bondage:
Declare their promis'd mercy all as forfeited,
False to their oaths, and deaf to intercession;
Warrants are pass'd for publick death to morrow. 529

Jaff. Death! doom'd to die! condemn'd unheard!
    unpleaded!

Bel. Nay, cruel'st racks and torments are preparing,
To force confessions from their dying pangs;
Oh do not look so terribly upon me,
How your lips shake, and all your face disorder'd!
What means my Love?

Jaff. Leave me, I charge thee leave me—strong
    temptations
Wake in my heart.

Bel. For what?

Jaff. No more, but leave me.

Bel. Why?   540

Jaff. Oh! by Heaven I love thee with that fondness
I would not have thee stay a moment longer,
Near these curst hands: are they not cold upon thee?

Bel. No, everlasting comfort's in thy armes,

[Pulls the dagger half out of his bosom and puts it back agen.

To lean thus on thy breast is softer ease
Than downy pillows deck'd with leaves of roses.

Jaff. Alas thou thinkest not of the thorns 'tis fill'd
    with,
Fly e'r they call thee: there's a lurking serpent
Ready to leap and sting thee to thy heart:
Art thou not terrifi'd?   550

Bel. No.

Jaff. Call to mind
What thou hast done, and whither thou hast brought
    me.

Bel. Hah!

Jaff. Where's my friend? my friend, thou smiling
    mischief?
Nay, shrink not, now 'tis too late, thou shouldst have
    fled
When thy Guilt first had cause, for dire revenge
Is up and raging for my friend. He groans,
Hark how he groans, his screams are in my ears
Already; see, th' have fixt him on the wheel,   560
And now they tear him—Murther! perjur'd Senate!
Murther—Oh!—hark thee, Traitress, thou hast done
    this;
Thanks to thy tears and false perswading love,
                              [Fumbling for his Dagger.
How her eyes speak! Oh thou bewitching creature!
Madness cannot hurt thee: Come, thou little trembler,
Creep, even into my heart, and there lie safe;
'Tis thy own Cittadel——hah——yet stand off,
Heaven must have Justice, and my broken vows
Will sink me else beneath its reaching mercy;

    548 *call*] Perhaps gall.

I'll wink and then 'tis done—— 570
    Bel. What means the Lord
Of me, my life and love, what's in thy bosom,
Thou graspst at so? nay, why am I thus treated?
                [Draws the dagger, offers to stab her.
What wilt thou doe? Ah, do not kill me, *Jaffeir*,
Pity these panting breasts, and trembling limbs,
That us'd to clasp thee when thy looks were milder,
That yet hang heavy on my unpurg'd Soul,
And plunge it not into eternal darkness.
    Jaff. No, *Belvidera*, when we parted last
I gave this dagger with thee as in trust 580
To be thy portion, if I e'r prov'd false.
On such condition was my truth believ'd:
But now 'tis forfeited and must be paid for.
                [Offers to stab her again.
    Bel. Oh, mercy!   *[Kneeling.*
    Jaff. Nay, no struggling.
    Bell. Now then kill me
              [Leaps upon his neck and kisses him.
While thus I cling about thy cruel neck,
Kiss thy revengefull lips and die in joys
Greater than any I can guess hereafter. 589
    Jaff. I am, I am a Coward; witness 't, Heaven,
Witness it, Earth, and every being Witness;
'Tis but one blow: yet by immortal Love,
I cannot longer bear a thought to harm thee,
          [He throws away the dagger and embraces her.
The Seal of providence is sure upon thee.
And thou wert born for yet unheard of wonders:
Oh thou wert either born to save or damn me!
By all the power that's given thee o'r my soul,
By thy resistless tears and conquering smiles,
By the victorious love that still waits on thee;
Fly to thy cruel Father: save my friend, 600
Or all our future Quiet's lost for ever:

576 *milder . . .*] There appears to be a line or lines
missing here, probably about unabsolved sins.

Fall at his feet, cling round his reverend knees;
Speak to him with thy Eyes, and with thy tears,
Melt his hard heart, and wake dead nature in him,
Crush him in th' Arms, and torture him with thy
    softness:

     Nor, till thy Prayers are granted, set him free,
     But conquer him, as thou hast vanquish'd me.

                              [*Ex. ambo.*

      The end of the fourth Act.

ACT V.

      Enter Priuli *solus.*

  Priu. Why, cruel Heaven, have my unhappy days
Been lengthen'd to this sad one? Oh! dishonour
And deathless infamy is fall'n upon me.
Was it my fault? Am I a traitour? No.
But then, my onely child, my daughter, wedded;
There my best bloud runs foul, and a disease
Incurable has seiz'd upon my memory,
To make it rot and stink to after ages.
Curst be the fatal minute when I got her;
Or woud that I'd been any thing but man,   10
And rais'd an issue which wou'd ne'r have wrong'd
    me.
The miserablest Creatures (man excepted)
Are not the less esteem'd, though their posterity
Degenerate from the vertues of their fathers;
The vilest Beasts are happy in their off-springs,
While onely man gets traitours, whores and villains.
Curst be the names, and some swift blow from Fate
Lay his head deep, where mine may be forgotten.

     Enter Belvidera *in a long mourning Veil.*

  Bel. He's there, my father, my inhumane father,
That, for three years, has left an onely child   20

Expos'd to all the outrages of Fate,
And cruel ruine——oh !——
 Priu. What child of sorrow
Art thou that com'st thus wrapt in weeds of sadness,
And mov'st as if thy steps were towards a grave?
 Bel. A wretch, who from the very top of happiness
Am fallen into the lowest depths of misery,
And want your pitying hand to raise me up again.
 Priu. Indeed thou talk'st as thou hadst tasted
  sorrows ;
Would I could help thee.   30
 Bel. 'Tis greatly in your power,
The world too, speaks you charitable, and I,
Who ne'r ask'd almes before, in that dear hope
Am come a begging to you, Sir.
 Priu. For what?
 Bel. Oh, well regard me, is this voice a strange one?
Consider too, when beggars once pretend
A case like mine, no little will content 'em.
 Priu. What wouldst thou beg for?
 Bel. Pity and forgiveness ;   [*Throws up her Veil.*
By the kind tender names of child and father, 41
Hear my complaints and take me to your love.
 Priu. My daughter?
 Bel. Yes, your daughter, by a mother
Vertuous and noble, faithfull to your honour,
Obedient to your will, kind to your wishes,
Dear to your armes ; by all the joys she gave you,
When in her blooming years she was your treasure,
Look kindly on me ; in my face behold
The lineaments of hers y' have kiss'd so often, 50
Pleading the cause of your poor cast-off Child.
 Priu. Thou art my daughter.
 Bel. Yes——And y' have oft told me
With smiles of love and chaste paternal kisses,
I'd much resemblance of my mother.
 Priu. Oh !
Hadst thou inherited her matchless vertues

I'd been too bless'd.

    Bel. Nay, do not call to memory
My disobedience, but let pity enter   60
Into your heart, and quite deface the impression;
For could you think how mine's perplext, what sadness
Fears and despairs distract the peace within me,
Oh, you woud take me in your dear, dear Armes,
Hover with strong compassion o'r your young one,
To shelter me with a protecting wing,
From the black gather'd storm, that's just, just breaking.

    Priu. Don't talk thus.

    Bel. Yes, I must, and you must hear too.
I have a husband.   70

    Priu. Damn him.

    Bel. Oh, do not curse him!
He would not speak so hard a word towards you
On any terms, oh! e'r he deal with me.

    Priu. Hah! what means my child?

    Bel. Oh there's but this short moment
'Twixt me and Fate, yet send me not with curses
Down to my grave, afford me one kind blessing
Before we part: just take me in your armes
And recommend me with a prayer to Heaven,   80
That I may dye in peace, and when I'm dead——

    Priu. How my Soul's catcht?

    Bel. Lay me, I beg you, lay me
By the dear ashes of my tender mother.
She would have pitied me, had fate yet spared her.

    Priu. By Heaven, my aking heart forebodes much mischief,
Tell me thy story, for I'm still thy father.

    Bel. No, I'm contented.

    Priu. Speak.

    Bel. No matter.   90

    Priu. Tell me.
By yon blest Heaven, my heart runs o'r with fondness.

Bel. Oh!

Priu. Utter't.

Bel. Oh my husband, my dear husband
Carries a dagger in his once kind bosome
To peirce the heart of your poor *Belvidera.*

Priu. Kill thee?

Bel. Yes, kill me, when he pass'd his faith
And covenant, against your State and Senate,   100
He gave me up as hostage for his truth,
With me a dagger and a dire commission,
When e'r he fail'd to plunge it through this bosome.
I learnt the danger, chose the hour of love
T' attempt his heart, and bring it back to honour,
Great love prevail'd and bless'd me with success,
He came, confest, betray'd his dearest friends
For promis'd mercy; now they're doom'd to suffer,
Gall'd with remembrance of what then was sworn,
If they are lost, he vows t' appease the Gods   110
With this poor life, and make my bloud th' attone-
      ment.

Priu. Heavens!

Bel. Think you saw what pass'd at our last parting;
Think you beheld him like a raging lion,
Pacing the earth and tearing up his steps,
Fate in his eyes, and roaring with the pain
Of burning fury; think you saw his one hand
Fix't on my throat, while the extended other
Grasp'd a keen threatning dagger, oh 'twas thus,
We last embrac'd, when, trembling with revenge, 120
He dragg'd me to the ground, and at my bosome
Presented horrid death, cried out, my friends,
Where are my friends? swore, wept, rag'd, threaten'd,
      lov'd,
For he yet lov'd, and that dear love preserv'd me,
To this last tryal of a father's pity.
I fear not death, but cannot bear a thought
That that dear hand should do th' unfriendly office;
If I was ever then your care, now hear me;

Fly to the Senate, save the promis'd lives
Of his dear friends, e'r mine be made the sacrifice.

   Priu. Oh, my hearts comfort!   131
   Bel. Will you not, my father?
Weep not but answer me.
   Priu. By Heaven, I will.
Not one of 'em but what shall be immortal.
Canst thou forgive me all my follies past,
I'll henceforth be indeed a father; never,
Never more thus expose, but cherish thee,
Dear as the vital warmth that feeds my life,
Dear as these eyes that weep in fondness o'r thee,
Peace to thy heart.   Farewel.   141
   Bel. Go, and remember,
'Tis *Belvidera*'s life her father pleads for.

                                        [*Ex. severally.*
                     Enter Antonio.

Hum, hum, hah,
Seignior *Priuli*, my Lord *Priuli*, my Lord, my Lord,
my Lord: Now, we Lords love to call one another
by our Titles.   My Lord, my Lord, my Lord——Pox
on him, I am a Lord as well as he, And so let him
fiddle—I'll warrant him he's gone to the Senate-
house, and I'll be there too, soon enough for somebody.   Odd—here's a tickling speech about the
Plot, I'll prove there's a Plot with a Vengeance—
would I had it without book; let me see—   153
   Most Reverend Senatours,
That there is a Plot, surely by this time, no man that
hath eyes or understanding in his head will presume
to doubt, 'tis as plain as the light in the Cowcumber
—no—hold there—Cowcumber does not come in
yet—'tis as plain as the light in the Sun, or as the
man in the Moon, even at noon day; It is indeed a
Pumpkin-Plot, which, just as it was mellow, we have
gathered, and now we have gathered it, prepar'd and
dress'd it, shall we throw it like a pickled Cowcumber
out at the window? no: that it is not onely a bloudy,

horrid, execrable, damnable and audacious Plot, but
it is, as I may so say, a sawcy Plot: and we all know,
most Reverend Fathers, that what is sawce for a
Goose is sawce for a Gander: Therefore, I say, as
those bloud-thirsty Ganders of the conspiracy would
have destroyed us Geese of the Senate, let us make
haste to destroy them, so I humbly move for hanging
—hah, hurry durry—I think this will doe, thô I was
something out, at first, about the Sun and the Cowcumber.   174

Enter Aquilina.

Aquil. Good morrow, Senatour.

Anto. Nacky, my dear Nacky, morrow, Nacky, odd
I am very brisk, very merry, very pert, very jovial—
ha a a aa—kiss me, Nacky; how dost thou doe, my little
Tory rory Strumpet, kiss me, I say, hussy kiss me.

Aquil. Kiss me, Nacky! hang you, Sir Coxcomb,
hang you, Sir.   181

Anto. Hayty tayty, is it so indeed, with all my heart,
faith—*Hey then up go we*, faith—*hey then up go we*, dum
dum derum dump.   [*Sings.*

Aquil. Seignior.

Anto. Madona.

Aquil. Do you intend to die in your bed——?

Anto. About threescore years hence, much may be
done, my dear.

Aquil. You'll be hang'd, Seignior.   190

Anto. Hang'd, sweet heart, prithee be quiet, hang'd
quoth-a, that's a merry conceit, with all my heart,
why thou jok'st, Nacky, thou art given to joking, I'll
swear; well, I protest, Nacky, nay, I must protest,
and will protest that I love joking dearly, man. And
I love thee for joking, and I'll kiss thee for joking,
and towse thee for joking, and odd, I have a devilish
mind to take thee aside about that business for joking
too, odd I have, and *Hey then up go we*, dum dum
derum dump.   [*Sings.* 200

Aquil. See you this, Sir?   [*Draws a dagger.*

Anto. O Laud, a dagger! Oh Laud! it is naturally
my aversion, I cannot endure the sight on 't, hide it,
for Heavens sake, I cannot look that way till it be
gone—hide it, hide it, oh, oh, hide it!

Aquil. Yes, in your heart, I'll hide it.

Anto. My heart; what, hide a dagger in my heart's
bloud!

Aquil. Yes, in thy heart, thy throat, thou pamper'd
Devil;

Thou hast help'd to spoil my peace, and I'll have
vengeance

On thy curst life, for all the bloody Senate,   210

The perjur'd faithless Senate: Where 's my Lord,

My happiness, my love, my God, my Hero,

Doom'd by thy accursed tongue, amongst the rest,

T' a shamefull wrack? By all the rage that 's in me

I'll be whole years in murthering thee.

Anto. Why, Nacky,

Wherefore so passionate? what have I done? what 's
the matter, my dear Nacky? am not I thy Love, thy
Happiness, thy Lord, thy Hero, thy Senatour, and
every thing in the world, Nacky?   220

Aquil. Thou! thinkst thou, thou art fit to meet my
joys;

To bear the eager clasps of my embraces?

Give me my *Pierre*, or——

Anto. Why, he 's to be hang'd, little Nacky,

Trust up for Treason, and so forth, Child.

Aquil. Thou ly'st, stop down thy throat that hellish
sentence,

Or 'tis thy last: swear that my Love shall live,

Or thou art dead.

Anto. Ah h h h.

Aquil. Swear to recall his doom,   230

Swear at my feet, and tremble at my fury.

Anto. I do, now if she would but kick a little bit,
one kick now Ah h h h.

Aquil. Swear, or——

Anto. I doe, by these dear fragrant foots
And little toes, sweet as, e e e e my Nacky Nacky
   Nacky.

Aquil. How!

Anto. Nothing but untie thy shoe-string a little
   faith and troth,
That 's all, that 's all, as I hope to live, Nacky, that 's
   all.

Aquil. Nay, then——   240

Anto. Hold, hold, thy Love, thy Lord, thy Hero
Shall be preserv'd and safe.

Aquil. Or may this Poniard
Rust in thy heart.

Anto. With all my soul.

Aquil. Farewell——   *[Ex.* Aquil.

Anto. Adieu.   Why what a bloudy-minded invete-
rate, termagant, Strumpet have I been plagu'd with!
oh h h yet more! nay then I die, I die—I am dead
already.   *[Stretches himself out.* 250

Enter Jaffeir.

Jaff. Final destruction seize on all the world:
Bend down, ye Heavens, and shutting round this
   earth,
Crush the Vile Globe into its first confusion;
Scorch it, with Elemental flames, to one curst Cindar,
And all us little creepers in 't, call'd men,
Burn, burn to nothing: but let *Venice* burn
Hotter than all the rest: Here kindle Hell
Ne'r to extinguish, and let souls hereafter
Groan here, in all those pains which mine feels now.

Enter Belvidera.

Bel. My Life——   *[Meeting him.* 260

Jaff. My Plague——   *[Turning from her.*

Bel. Nay then I see my ruine,
If I must die!

Jaff. No, Death 's this day too busie,

Thy Father's ill time'd Mercy came too late,
I thank thee for thy labours thô and him too,
But all my poor betray'd unhappy friends
Have Summons to prepare for Fate's black hour;
And yet I live.

   Bel. Then be the next my doom.   270
I see thou hast pass'd my sentence in thy heart,
And I'll no longer weep or plead against it,
But with the humblest, most obedient patience
Meet thy dear hands, and kiss 'em when they wound
     me;
Indeed I am willing, but I beg thee doe it
With some remorse, and when thou giv'st the blow,
View me with eyes of a relenting love,
And shew me pity, for 'twill sweeten Justice.

   Jaff. Shew pity to thee?

   Bel. Yes, and when thy hands,   280
Charg'd with my fate, come trembling to the deed,
As thou hast done a thousand thousand dear times,
To this poor breast, when kinder rage has brought
     thee,
When our sting'd hearts have leap'd to meet each
     other,
And melting kisses seal'd our lips together,
When joyes have left me gasping in thy armes,
So let my death come now, and I'll not shrink from 't.

   Jaff. Nay, *Belvidera*, do not fear my cruelty,
Nor let the thoughts of death perplex thy fancy,
But answer me to what I shall demand   290
With a firm temper and unshaken spirit.

   Bel. I will when I've done weeping——

   Jaff. Fie, no more on 't——
How long is 't since the miserable day
We wedded first——

   Bel. Oh h h.

   Jaff. Nay, keep in thy tears,
Lest they unman me too.

   Bel. Heaven knows I cannot;

The words you utter sound so very sadly   300
These streams will follow—

Jaff. Come, I'll kiss 'em dry then.

Bel. But, was 't a miserable day?

Jaff. A curs 'd one.

Bel. I thought it otherwise, and you've oft sworn
In the transporting hours of warmest love
When sure you spoke the truth, you've sworn you
          bless'd it.

Jaff. Twas a rash oath.

Bel. Then why am I not curs'd too?

Jaff. No, *Belvidera*; by th' eternal truth,   310
I doat with too much fondness.

Bel. Still so kind?
Still then do you love me?

Jaff. Nature, in her workings,
Inclines not with more ardour to Creation,
Than I doe now towards thee; man ne'r was bless'd,
Since the first pair first met, as I have been.

Bel. Then sure you will not curse me.

Jaff. No, I'll bless thee.
I came on purpose, *Belvidera*, to bless thee.   320
'Tis now, I think, three years w' have liv'd together.

Bel. And may no fatal minute ever part us,
Till, reverend grown, for age and love, we go
Down to one Grave, as our last bed, together,
There sleep in peace till an eternal morning.

Jaff. When will that be?   [*Sighing.*

Bel. I hope long Ages hence.

Jaff. Have I not hitherto (I beg thee tell me
Thy very fears) us'd thee with tender'st love?
Did e'r my Soul rise up in wrath against thee?   330
Did I e'r frown when *Belvidera* smil'd,
Or, by the least unfriendly word, betray
A bating passion? have I ever wrong'd thee?

Bel. No.

Jaff. Has my heart, or have my eyes e'r wandred
To any other woman?

Bel. Never, never—I were the worst of false ones
    should I accuse thee.
I own I've been too happy, bless'd above
My Sexes Charter.

    Jaff. Did I not say I came to bless thee?   340
    Bel. Yes.
    Jaff. Then hear me, bounteous Heaven,
Pour down your blessings on this beauteous head,
Where everlasting sweets are always springing.
With a continual giving hand, let peace,
Honour and safety always hover round her,
Feed her with plenty, let her eyes ne'r see
A sight of sorrow, nor her heart know mourning,
Crown all her days with joy, her nights with rest,
Harmless as her own thoughts, and prop her vertue,
To bear the loss of one that too much lov'd,   351
And comfort her with patience in our parting.

    Bel. How, parting, parting!
    Jaff. Yes, for ever parting,
I have sworn, *Belvidera*; by yon Heaven,
That best can tell how much I lose to leave thee,
We part this hour for ever.

    Bel. Oh, call back
Your cruel blessings, stay with me and curse me!
    Jaff. No, 'Tis resolv'd.   360
    Bel. Then hear me too, just Heaven,
Pour down your curses on this wretched head
With never-ceasing Vengeance, let despair,
Danger or infamy, nay all surround me,
Starve me with wantings, let my eyes ne'r see
A sight of comfort, nor my heart know peace,
But dash my days with sorrow, nights with horrours
Wild as my own thoughts now, and let loose fury
To make me mad enough for what I lose,
If I must lose him; if I must, I will not.   370
Oh turn and hear me!

    Jaff. Now hold, heart, or never.
    Bel. By all the tender days we have liv'd together,

By all our charming nights, and joyes that crown'd
 'em,
Pity my sad condition, speak, but speak.

 Jaff. Oh h h.

 Bel. By these armes that now cling round thy neck,
By this dear kiss and by ten thousand more,
By these poor streaming eyes——

 Jaff. Murther! unhold me: 380
By th' immortal destiny that doom'd me
        [Draws his Dagger.
To this curs'd minute, I'll not live one longer,
Resolve to let me go or see me fall——

 Bel. Hold, Sir, be patient.

 Jaff. Hark, the dismal Bell *[Passing-bell towles.*
Towles out for death, I must attend its call too,
For my poor friend, my dying *Pierre* expects me,
He sent a message to require I'd see him
Before he dy'd, and take his last forgiveness.
Farewell for ever.   390

 Bel. Leave thy dagger with me.
Bequeath me something—Not one kiss at parting?
Oh my poor heart, when wilt thou break?
     [Going out looks back at her.

 Jaff. Yet stay,
We have a Child, as yet, a tender Infant.
Be a kind mother to him when I am gone,
Breed him in vertue and the paths of Honour,
But let him never know his father's story;
I charge thee guard him from the wrongs my Fate
May doe his future fortune or his name. 400
Now——nearer yet—— *[Approaching each other.*
Oh that my armes were rivetted
Thus round thee ever! But my friends, my oath!
This and no more.   *[Kisses her.*

 Bel. Another, sure another,
For that poor little one you've ta'n care of,
I'll giv't him truly.

 Jaff. So, now farewell.

Bel. For ever?   409

Jaff. Heaven knows for ever; all good Angels guard
thee.   [*Exit.*

Bel. All ill ones sure had charge of me this moment,
Curst be my days, and doubly curst my nights,
Which I must now mourn out in widdow'd tears;
Blasted be every herb and fruit and tree,
Curst be the rain that falls upon the earth,
And may the general Curse reach man and beast;
Oh give me daggers, fire or water,
How I could bleed, how burn, how drown the waves
Huzzing and booming round my sinking head,
Till I descended to the peacefull bottome!   420
Oh there 's all quiet, here all rage and fury,
The Air 's too thin, and pierces my weak brain,
I long for thick substantial sleep: Hell, Hell,
Burst from the Centre, rage and roar aloud,
If thou art half so hot, so mad as I am.

Enter Priuli *and* Servants.

Who 's there?   [*They seize her.*

Priu. Run, seize and bring her safely home,
Guard her as you would life: Alas poor creature!

Bel. What? to my husband then conduct me
quickly,
Are all things ready? shall we dye most gloriously?
Say not a word of this to my old father,   431
Murmuring streams, soft shades, and springing
flowers,
Lutes, Laurells, Seas of Milk, and ships of Amber. [*Ex.*

*Scene opening discovers a Scaffold and a Wheel prepar'd for
the executing of* Pierre, *then enter Officers,* Pierre *and
Guards, a Friar, executioner and a great Rabble.*

Offic. Room room there——stand all by, make
room for the Prisoner.

Pierr. My friend not come yet?

433 This passage was ridiculed by Gay in *The What-D'Ye-
Call-It.*

Father. Why are you so obstinate?

Pierr. Why you so troublesome, that a poor wretch
    cannot dye in peace?

But you, like Ravens will be croaking round him——

    Fath. Yet, Heaven——

    Pierr. I tell thee Heaven and I are friends,   440

I ne'r broke Peace with 't yet, by cruel murthers,

Rapine, or perjury, or vile deceiving,

But liv'd in moral Justice towards all men,

Nor am a foe to the most strong believers:

How e'r my own short-sighted Faith confine me.

    Fath. But an all-seeing Judge——

    Pierr. You say my conscience

Must be mine accuser: I have search'd that Con-
    science,

And find no records there of crimes that scare me.

    Fath. 'Tis strange you should want faith.   450

    Pierr. You want to lead

My Reason blindfold, like a hamper'd Lion,

Check'd of its nobler vigour then, when baited,

Down to obedient tameness, make it couch,

And shew strange tricks which you call signs of Faith.

So silly Souls are gull'd and you get money.

Away, no more: Captain, I would hereafter

This fellow write no lyes of my conversion,

Because he has crept upon my troubled hours.

Enter Jaffeir.

    Jaff. Hold: Eyes, be dry;   460

Heart, strengthen me to bear

This hideous sight, and humble me, take

The last forgiveness of a dying friend,

Betray'd by my vile falsehood, to his ruine.

Oh *Pierre*!

    Pierr. Yet nearer.

    Jaff. Crawling on my knees,

And prostrate on the earth, let me approach thee,

How shall I look up to thy injur'd face,

That always us'd to smile, with friendship, on me?
It darts an air of so much manly virtue,   471
That I, methinks, look little in thy sight,
And stripes are fitter for me than embraces.

    Pierr. Dear to my Armes, though thou hast undone
      my fame,
I cannot forget to love thee: prithee, *Jaffeir*,
Forgive that filthy blow my passion dealt thee;
I am now preparing for the land of peace,
And fain would have the charitable wishes
Of all good men, like thee, to bless my journy.   479

    Jaff. Good! I am the vilest creature, worse than e'r
Suffer'd the shamefull Fate thou art going to taste of,
Why was I sent for to be us'd thus kindly?
Call, call me villain, as I am, describe
The foul complexion of my hatefull deeds,
Lead me to the Rack, and stretch me in thy stead,
I've crimes enough to give it its full load,
And doe it credit: Thou wilt but spoil the use on 't,
And honest men hereafter bear its figure
About 'em, as a charm from treacherous friendship.

    Offic. The time grows short, your friends are dead
      already.   490

    Jaff. Dead!

    Pierr. Yes, dead, *Jaffeir*, they've all dy'd like men too,
Worthy their Character.

    Jaff. And what must I doe?

    Pierr. Oh, *Jaffeir*!

    Jaff. Speak, aloud thy burthen'd Soul,
And tell thy troubles to thy tortur'd friend.

    Pierr. Friend! Could'st thou yet be a Friend, a
      generous friend,
I might hope Comfort from thy noble sorrows,
Heav'n knows I want a Friend.   500

    Jaff. And I a kind one,
That would not thus scorn my repenting Vertue,
Or think when he is to dye, my thoughts are idle.

    Pierr. No! live, I charge thee, *Jaffeir*.

Jaff. Yes, I will live,
But it shall be to see thy fall reveng'd
At such a rate, as *Venice* long shall groan for.
    Pierr. Wilt thou?
    Jaff. I will, by Heav'n.
    Pierr. Then still thou 'rt noble,   510
And I forgive thee, oh—yet—shall I trust thee?
    Jaff. No : I've been false already.
    Pierr. Dost thou love me?
    Jaff. Rip up my heart, and satisfie thy doubtings.
    Pierr. Curse on this weakness.   [*He weeps.*
    Jaff. Tears! Amazement! Tears!
I never saw thee melted thus before ;
And know there 's something lab'ring in thy bosom
That must have vent : Though I'm a Villain, tell me.
    Pierr. Seest thou that Engine?   520
                              [*Pointing to the Wheel.*
    Jaff. Why?
    Pierr. Is 't fit a Souldier, who has liv'd with Honour,
Fought Nations Quarrels, and bin Crown'd with
    Conquest,
Be expos'd a common Carcass on a Wheel?
    Jaff. Hah!
    Pierr. Speak! is 't fitting?
    Jaff. Fitting?
    Pierr. Yes, Is 't fitting?
    Jaff. What 's to be done?
    Pierr. I'd have thee undertake   530
Something that 's Noble, to preserve my Memory
From the disgrace that 's ready to attaint it.
    Offic. The day grows late, Sir.
    Pierr. I'll make haste! oh *Jaffeir*,
Though thou'st betray'd me, doe me some way
    Justice.
    Jaff. No more of that : Thy wishes shall be satisfi'd,
I have a Wife, and she shall bleed, my Child too
Yield up his little Throat, and all t' appease thee—
                  [*Going away* Pierr. *holds him.*

Pierr. No———this———no more!

[*He whispers* Jaffeir.

Jaff. Hah! is 't then so?   540
Pierr. Most certainly.
Jaff. I 'll do 't.
Pierr. Remember.
Offic. Sir.
Pierr. Come, now I'm ready.
Captain, you should be a Gentleman of honour,

[*He and* Jaffeir *ascend the Scaffold.*

Keep off the Rabble, that I may have room
To entertain my Fate, and dye with Decency.
Come! [*Takes off his Gown. Executioner prepares to
bind him.*

Fath. Son!   550
Pierr. Hence, Tempter.
Offic. Stand off, Priest.
Pierr. I thank you, Sir,
You'll think on 't.   [*To* Jaffeir.
Jaff. 'Twon't grow stale before to morrow.
Pierr. Now, *Jaffeir*! now I am going, Now;—

[*Executioner having bound him.*

Jaff. Have at thee,
Thou honest heart, then———here———   [*Stabs him.*
And this is well too.   [*Then stabs himself.*
Fath. Damnable Deed!   560
Pierr. Now thou hast indeed been faithful.
This was done Nobly———We have deceiv'd the Senate.
Jaff. Bravely.
Pierr. Ha ha ha———oh oh———   [*Dies.*
Jaff. Now, ye curs'd Rulers,
Thus of the blood y' have shed I make Libation,
And sprinkl't mingling: May it rest upon you,
And all your Race: Be henceforth Peace a stranger
Within your Walls; let Plagues and Famine waste
Your Generations—oh poor *Belvidera*!   570
Sir, I have a Wife, bear this in safety to her.
A Token that with my dying breath I blest *her*,

And the dear little Infant left behind me.
I am sick——I'm quiet——   [*Jaff. dyes.*
  Offic. Bear this news to the Senate,
And guard their Bodies till there 's farther order:
Heav'n grant I dye so well—   [*Scene shuts upon them.*

Soft Musick. Enter Belvidera *distracted, led by two of her
    Women,* Priuli *and Servants.*

  Priu. Strengthen her heart with Patience, pitying
    Heav'n.
  Belv. Come come come come come. Nay, come
    to bed!
Prithee my Love. The Winds! hark how they
    whistle!   580
And the Rain beats: oh how the weather shrinks me!
You are angry now, who cares? pish, no indeed.
Choose then, I say you shall not go, you shall not;
Whip your ill nature; get you gone then! oh,
                  [*Jaffeir's Ghost rises.*
Are you return'd? See, Father, here he 's come
    agen,
Am I to blame to love him! oh thou dear one.
                     [*Ghost sinks.*
Why do you fly me? are you angry still then?
Jaffeir! where art thou? Father, why do you doe
    thus?
Stand off, don't hide him from me. He 's here some-
    where.
Stand off I say! what gone? remember 't, Tyrant!
I may revenge my self for this trick one day.   591
              [*Enter Officer and others.*
I'll do 't——I'll do 't. *Renault* 's a nasty fellow.
Hang him, hang him, hang him.
  Priu. News, what news?   [*Offic. whispers* Priuli.
  Offic. Most sad, Sir.
Jaffeir upon the Scaffold, to prevent
A shamefull death, stab'd *Pierre*, and next himself:
Both fell together.

Priu. Daughter.

> [*The Ghosts of* Jaff. *and* Pierr. *rise together both bloody.*

Bel. Hah, look there!   600
My Husband bloody, and his friend too! Murther!
Who has done this? speak to me thou sad Vision,

> [*Ghosts sink.*

On these poor trembling Knees I beg it, Vanisht——
Here they went down; Oh I'll dig, dig the Den up.
You shan't delude me thus.   Hoa, *Jaffeir, Jaffeir.*
Peep up and give me but a look.   I have him!
I've got him, Father: Oh now how I'll smuggle him!
My Love! my Dear! my Blessing! help me, help me!
They have hold on me, and drag me to the bottom.
Nay—now they pull so hard——farewell— [*She dyes.*

Maid. She's dead.   611
Breathless and dead.

Priu. Then guard me from the sight on't:
Lead me into some place that's fit for mourning;
Where the free Air, Light and the chearfull Sun
May never enter: Hang it round with Black;
Set up one Taper that may last a day
As long as I've to live: And there all leave me.

> *Sparing no Tears when you this Tale relate,*
> *But bid all Cruel Fathers dread my Fate.*   620

> Curtain falls, *Ex. omnes.*

FINIS

EPILOGUE,

The Text is done, and now for Application,
And when that's ended pass your Approbation.
Though the Conspiracy 's prevented here,
Methinks I see another hatching there;
And there's a certain Faction fain would sway, ⎫
If they had strength enough and damn this Play, ⎬
But this the Author bad me boldly say: ⎭
If any take his plainness in ill part,
He's glad on't from the bottome of his heart;
Poets in honour of the Truth shou'd write,   10
With the same Spirit brave men for it fight;
And though against him causeless hatreds rise, ⎫
And dayly where he goes of late, he spies ⎬
The scowles of sullen and revengefull eyes; ⎭
'Tis what he knows with much contempt to bear,
And serves a cause too good to let him fear:
He fears no poison from an incens'd Drabb,
No Russian's five-foot-sword, nor Rascal's stab;
Nor any other snares of mischief laid,
Not a Rose-alley Cudgel-Ambuscade,   20
From any private cause where malice reigns,
Or general Pique all Block-heads have to brains:
Nothing shall daunt his Pen when Truth does call,
No not the * Picture-mangler at Guild-hall.
The Rebel-Tribe, of which that Vermin 's one,
Have now set forward and their course begun;
And while that Prince's figure they deface,
   As they before had massacred his Name,
Durst their base fears but look him in the face,

   * The Rascal that cut the Duke of York's Picture.

   20 Ambuscade] Dryden had been cudgelled in Rose Alley
by Rochester's orders.
   28 Name] He had been implicated in the Plot.

They'd use his Person as they've us'd his Fame; 30
A face, in which such lineaments they reade
Of that great Martyr's, whose rich bloud they shed,
That their rebellious hate they still retain,
And in his Son would murther Him again:
With indignation then, let each brave heart,
Rouse and unite to take his injur'd part;
Till Royal Love and Goodness call him home,
And Songs of Triumph meet him as he come;
Till Heaven his Honour and our Peace restore,
And Villains never wrong his Vertue more. 40

32 *Martyr*] Charles I.
37 Charles II had sent him into Scotland.

Oroonoko :

A

TRAGEDY

As it is Acted at the

𝕿𝕳𝖊𝖆𝖙𝖗𝖊-𝕽𝖔𝖞𝖆𝖑,

By His MAJESTY'S SERVANTS.

Written by *THO. SOVTHERNE.*

---- Quo fata trahunt, virtus secura sequetur. Lucan.

Virtus recludens immeritis mori
Cœlum, negatâ tentat iter viâ

Hor. Od. 2. lib. 3.

LONDON:

Printed for *H. Playford* in the *Temple-Change. B. Tooke*
at the *Middle-Temple-Gate.* And *S. Buckley* at the
Dolphin against St. *Dunstan's* Church in *Fleetstreet.*
MDCXCVI.

To His GRACE

WILLIAM

Duke of Devonshire, &c.

Lord Steward of His Majesty's Houshold,
Knight of the Most Noble Order of the
Garter, and One of His Majesty's Most
Honourable Privy Council.

MY LORD,

The Best part of the Fortune of my last Play (*The
Innocent Adultery*) was, that it gave me an Opportunity
of making my self known to Your Grace. You were
pleased to countenance the Advances which I had
been a great while directing and aiming at You, and
have since encourag'd me into an Industry, which,
I hope, will allow me in this Play to own (which is
the only way I can) the great Obligations I have
to You.

I stand engag'd to Mrs. *Behn* for the Occasion of
a most Passionate Distress in my Last Play; and in
a Conscience that I had not made her a sufficient
Acknowledgment, I have run further into her Debt
for *Oroonoko*, with a Design to oblige me to be honest;
and that every one may find me out for Ingratitude,
when I don't say all that's fit for me upon that
Subject. She had a great Command of the Stage;
and I have often wonder'd that she would bury her

Devonshire]William Cavendish (1640–1707), first Duke.
He was one of the seven who signed the invitation to
William of Orange. It was he who built Chatsworth,
employing Verrio, Thornhill, and Grinling Gibbons as
decorators.

Favourite Hero in a *Novel*, when she might have
reviv'd him in the *Scene*. She thought either that no
Actor could represent him; or she could not bear him
represented: And I believe the last, when I remember
what I have heard from a Friend of hers, That she
always told his Story, more feelingly, than she writ
it. Whatever happen'd to him at *Surinam*, he has
mended his Condition in *England*. He was born here
under Your Grace's Influence; and that has carried
his Fortune farther into the World, than all the
Poetical Stars that I could have sollicited for his
Success. It was Your Opinion, *My Lord*, that directed
me to Mr. *Verbruggen*; and it was his Care to maintain
Your Opinion, that directed the Town to me, the
Better Part of it, the People of Quality; whose Favours
as I am proud of, I shall always be industrious to
preserve.

My Lord, I know the Respect and Reverence which
in this Address I ought to appear in before You,
who are so intimate with the Ancients, so general
a Knower of the several Species of Poetry, and so
Just a Judge in the Trials of this kind. You have an
Absolute Power to Arraign and Convict, but a prevailing Inclination to Pardon and Save; and from
the Humanity of Your Temper, and the true Knowledge of the Difficulties of succeeding this way, never
aggravate or insist upon Faults

> ——*Quas aut incuria fudit,*
> *Aut humana parùm cavit Natura.*——
>
> Hor. Art. Poet.

to our Condemnation, where they are Venial, and
not against the Principles of the Art we pretend to.
Horace, who found it so, says,

> ——*Gratia Regum*
> *Pieriis tentata modis.*

The Favour of Great Men is the Poets Inheritance,

and all Ages have allow'd 'em to put in their Claim;
I only wish that I had Merit enough to prefer me to
Your Grace: That I might deserve in some measure
that Patronage which You are pleased to bestow on
me: That I were a *Horace* for such a *Mecænas*: That
I could describe what I admire; and tell the World
what I really think, That as You possess those In-
finite Advantages of Nature and Fortune in so
Eminent a degree; that as You so far excel in the
Perfections of Body and Mind, You were design'd
and fashion'd a Prince, to be the Honour of the
Nation, and the Grace and Ornament of the Court.
Sir, In the Fulness of Happiness and Blessings which
You enjoy, I can only bring in my Wishes for the
Continuance of 'em; they shall constantly be devoted
to you, with all the Services of,

MY LORD,

Your Grace's most Obliged, most
Thankful, and most Humble Servant,

THO. SOUTHERNE.

PROLOGUE to *Oroonoko*.

Sent by **an Unknown Hand**.   And Spoken by **Mr.**
Powell.

As when in Hostile Times two Neighbouring States
Strive by themselves, and their Confederates;
The War at first is made with awkard Skill,
And Soldiers clumsily each other kill:
Till time at length their untaught Fury tames,
And into Rules their heedless Rage reclaims:
Then every Science by degrees is made
Subservient to the Man-destroying Trade:
Wit, Wisdom, Reading, Observation, Art;
A well-turn'd Head to guide a Generous Heart.
So it may prove with our Contending Stages,
If you will kindly but supply their Wages:
Which you with ease may furnish, by retrenching
Your Superfluities of Wine and Wenching.
Who'd grudge to spare from Riot and hard Drinking,
To lay it out on means to mend his thinking?
To follow such Advice you shou'd have leisure,
Since what refines your Sense, refines your Pleasure:
Women grown tame by Use each Fool can get,
But Cuckolds all are made by Men of Wit.
To Virgin Favours Fools have no pretence:
For Maidenheads were made for Men of Sense.
'Tis not enough to have a Horse well bred,
To shew his Mettle, he must be well fed:
Nor is it all in Provender and Breed,
He must be try'd and strain'd, to mend his speed:
A Favour'd Poet, like a Pamper'd Horse,
Will strain his Eye-balls out to win the Course.
Do you but in your Wisdoms vote it fit
To yield due Succors to this War of Wit,
The Buskin with more grace shall tread the Stage,
Love sigh in softer Strains, Heroes less Rage:

Satyr shall show a Triple Row of Teeth,
And Comedy shall laugh your Fops to death:
Wit shall refine, and Pegasus shall foam,
And soar in search of Ancient Greece and Rome.
And since the Nation's in the Conquering Fit,
As you by Arms, we'll vanquish France in Wit:
The Work were over, cou'd our Poets write
With half the Spirit that our Soldiers fight.

Persons Represented.

MEN.

	BY
Oroonoko,	*Mr. Verbruggen.*
Aboan,	*Mr. Powell.*
Lieutenant-Governor of *Surinam*,	*Mr. Williams.*
Blanford,	*Mr. Harland.*
Stanmore,	*Mr. Horden.*
Jack Stanmore,	*Mr. Mills.*
Capt. Driver,	*Mr. Ben. Johnson.*
Daniel, *Son to Widow* Lackitt,	*Mr. Mich. Lee.*
Hottman,	*Mr. Sympson.*

Planters, Indians, Negroes, Men, Women, and Children.

WOMEN.

	BY
Imoinda,	*Mrs. Rogers.*
Widow Lackitt,	*Mrs. Knight.*
Charlot Welldon, *in Man's Cloaths*,	*Mrs. Verbruggen.*
Lucy Welldon, *her Sister*,	*Mrs. Lucas.*

The SCENE *Surinam*, a Colony in the *West-Indies*; at the Time of the Action of this Tragedy, in the Possession of the *English*.

O R O O N O K O.

ACT I. SCENE I.

Enter Welldon *following* Lucia.

Luc. What will this come to? What can it end in? You have persuaded me to leave dear *England*, and dearer *London*, the place of the World most worth living in, to follow you a Husband-hunting into *America*: I thought Husbands grew in these Plantations.

Well. Why so they do, as thick as Oranges, ripening one under another. Week after week they drop into some Woman's mouth: 'Tis but a little patience, spreading your Apron in expectation, and one of 'em will fall into your Lap at last.   11

Luc. Ay, so you say indeed.

Well. But you have left dear *London*, you say: Pray what have you left in *London* that was very dear to you, that had not left you before?

Luc. Speak for your self, Sister.

Well. Nay, I'll keep you in countenance. The Young Fellows, you know, the dearest part of the Town, and without whom *London* had been a Wilderness to you and me, had forsaken us a great while.   20

Luc. Forsaken us! I don't know that they ever had us.

Well. Forsaken us the worst way, Child; that is, did not think us worth having; they neglected us, no longer design'd upon us, they were tir'd of us. Women in *London* are like the Rich Silks, they are out of fashion a great while before they wear out——

Luc. The Devil take the Fashion, I say.   28

Well. You may tumble 'em over and over at their first coming up, and never disparage their Price;

but they fall upon wearing immediately, lower and lower in their value, till they come to the Broker at last.

Luc. Ay, ay, that's the Merchant they deal with. The Men would have us at their own scandalous Rates: Their Plenty makes 'em wanton; and in a little time, I suppose, they won't know what they would have of the Women themselves.   38

Well. O, yes, they know what they wou'd have. They wou'd have a Woman give the Town a Pattern of her Person and Beauty, and not stay in it so long to have the whole Piece worn out. They wou'd have the Good Face only discover'd, and not the Folly that commonly goes along with it. They say there is a vast Stock of Beauty in the Nation, but a great part of it lies in unprofitable hands; therefore for the good of the Publick, they wou'd have a Draught made once a Quarter, send the decaying Beauties for Breeders into the Countrey, to make room for New Faces to appear, to countenance the Pleasures of the Town.

Luc. 'Tis very hard, the Men must be young as long as they live, and poor Women be thought decaying and unfit for the Town at One or Two and twenty. I'm sure we were not Seven Years in *London*. 54

Well. Not half the time taken notice of, Sister. The Two or Three last Years we could make nothing of it, even in a Vizard-Masque; not in a Vizard-Masque, that has cheated many a man into an old acquaintance. Our Faces began to be as familiar to the Men of Intrigue, as their Duns, and as much avoided. We durst not appear in Publick Places, and were almost grudg'd a Gallery in the Churches: Even there they had their Jests upon us, and cry'd, She's in the right on't, good Gentlewoman, since no man considers her Body, she does very well indeed to take care of her Soul. 66

Luc. Such unmannerly fellows there will always be.

Well. Then, you may remember, we were reduc'd

to the last necessity, the necessity of making silly
Visits to our civil Acquaintance, to bring us into
tolerable Company. Nay, the young Inns-of-Court
Beaus, of but one Term's standing in the Fashion,
who knew no body, but as they were shewn 'em by
the Orange-Women, had Nicknames for us: How
often have they laugh'd out, There goes my Landlady;
Is not she come to let Lodgings yet?   76

Luc. Young Coxcombs that knew no better.

Well. And that we must have come to. For your
part, what Trade cou'd you set up in? You wou'd
never arrive at the Trust and Credit of a Guinea-
Bawd: You wou'd have too much Business of your
own, ever to mind other Peoples.   82

Luc. That is true indeed.

Well. Then, as a certain sign that there was nothing
more to be hop'd for, the Maids at the Chocolate-
Houses found us out, and laugh'd at us: Our *Billet-
doux* lay there neglected for Waste-Paper: We were
cry'd down so low we cou'd not pass upon the City;
and became so notorious in our galloping way, from
one end of the Town to t'other, that at last we cou'd
hardly compass a competent change of Petticoats to
disguize us to the Hackney-Coachmen: And then it
was near walking a-foot indeed.   93

Luc. Nay, that I began to be afraid of.

Well. To prevent which, with what Youth and
Beauty was left, some Experience, and the small
Remainder of Fifteen hundred Pounds apiece, which
amounted to bare Two hundred between us both, I
persuaded you to bring your Person for a Venture to
the *Indies.* Every thing has succeeded in our Voyage:
I pass for your Brother: One of the Richest Planters
here happening to dye just as we landed, I have
claim'd Kindred with him: So, without making his
Will, he has left us the Credit of his Relation to trade
upon: We pass for his Cousins, coming here to
Surinam chiefly upon his Invitation: We live in

Reputation; have the best Acquaintance of the place; and we shall see our account in 't, I warrant you.

Luc. I must rely upon you——   109

Enter Widow Lackitt.

Wid. Mr. *Welldon*, your Servant. Your Servant, Mrs. *Lucy.* I am an Ill Visitor, but 'tis not too late, I hope, to bid you welcome to this side of the world.
[Salutes Lucy.

Well. Gad so, I beg your Pardon, Widow, I shou'd have done the Civilities of my House before: but, as you say, 'tis not too late, I hope——
[Going to kiss her.

Wid. What! You think now this was a civil way of begging a Kiss; and by my Troth, if it were, I see no harm in 't; 'tis a pitiful Favour indeed that is not worth asking for: Tho' I have known a Woman speak plainer before now, and not understood neither.

Well. Not under my Roof. Have at you, Widow.—

Wid. Why, that's well said, spoke like a Younger Brother, that deserves to have a Widow.——   123
[He kisses her.

You're a Younger Brother, I know, by your kissing.

Well. How so, pray?

Wid. Why, you kiss as if you expected to be paid for 't. You have Birdlime upon your Lips. You stick so close, there's no getting rid of you.

Well. I am a-kin to a Younger Brother.

Wid. So much the better: We Widows are commonly the better for Younger Brothers.   131

Luc. Better, or worse, most of you. But you won't be much better for him, I can tell you.——   *[aside.*

Well. I was a Younger Brother; but an Uncle of my Mother's has maliciously left me an Estate, and, I'm afraid, spoil'd my Fortune.

Wid. No, no; an Estate will never spoil your Fortune. I have a good Estate my self, thank Heaven, and a kind Husband that left it behind him.

Well. Thank Heaven, that took him away from it, Widow, and left you behind him.   141

Wid. Nay, Heav'ns Will must be done; he's in a better place.

Well. A better place for you, no doubt on't: Now you may look about you; chuse for your self, Mrs. *Lackitt,* that's your business; for I know you design to marry again.

Wid. O dear! Not I, I protest and swear; I don't design it: But I won't swear neither; one does not know what may happen to tempt one.   150

Well. Why, a lusty young Fellow may happen to tempt you.

Wid. Nay, I'll do nothing rashly: I'll resolve against nothing. The Devil, they say, is very busy upon these occasions; especially with the Widows. But if I am to be tempted, it must be with a Young Man, I promise you.—Mrs. *Lucy,* Your Brother is a very pleasant Gentleman: I came about Business to him, but he turns every thing into Merriment.   159

Well. Business, Mrs. *Lackitt.* Then, I know, you wou'd have me to your self. Pray leave us together, Sister. [*Exit Luc.*] What am I drawing upon my self here?   [*aside.*

Wid. You have taken a very pretty House here; every thing so neat about you already. I hear you are laying out for a Plantation.

Well. Why, yes truly, I like the Countrey, and wou'd buy a Plantation, if I cou'd, reasonably.

Wid. O! by all means, reasonably.

Well. If I cou'd have one to my mind, I wou'd think of settling among you.   171

Wid. O! you can't do better. Indeed we can't pretend to have so good company for you, as you had in *England*; but we shall make very much of you. For my own part, I assure you, I shall think my self very happy to be more particularly known to you.

Well. Dear Mrs. *Lackitt*, you do me too much
Honour.   179

Wid. Then as to a Plantation, Mr. *Welldon*, you
know I have several to dispose of. Mr. *Lackitt*, I
thank him, has left me, though I say it, the Richest
Widow upon the place; therefore I may afford to
use you better than other people can. You shall have
one upon any reasonable terms.

Well. That's a fair Offer indeed.

Wid. You shall find me as easy as any body you
can have to do with, I assure you. Pray try me, I
wou'd have you try me, Mr. *Welldon*. Well, I like
that Name of yours exceedingly, Mr. *Welldon*.   190

Well. My Name!

Wid. O exceedingly! If any thing cou'd persuade
me to alter my own Name, I verily believe nothing
in the world wou'd do it so soon, as to be call'd
Mrs. *Welldon*.

Well. Why, indeed *Welldon* does sound something
better than *Lackitt*.

Wid. O! a great deal better. Not that there is so
much in a Name neither. But I don't know, there is
something: I shou'd like mightily to be call'd Mrs.
Welldon.   201

Well. I'm glad you like my Name.

Wid. Of all things. But then there's the misfortune; one can't change ones Name, without changing
ones Condition.

Well. You'l hardly think it worth that, I believe.

Wid. Think it worth what, Sir? Changing my
Condition? Indeed, Sir, I think it worth every thing.
But, alas! Mr. *Welldon*, I have been a Widow but
Six Months; 'tis too soon to think of changing ones
Condition yet; indeed it is: Pray don't desire it of
me: Not but that you may persuade me to any thing,
sooner than any Person in the world.——   213

Well. Who, I, Mrs. *Lackitt*?

Wid. Indeed you may, Mr. *Welldon*, sooner than

any man living. Lord, there's a great deal in saving
a Decency: I never minded it before: Well, I'm glad
you spoke first to excuse my Modesty. But what,
Modesty means nothing, and is the Virtue of a Girl,
that does not know what she would be at: A Widow
should be wiser. Now I will own to you; but I won't
confess neither; I have had a great Respect for you
a great while: I beg your Pardon, Sir, and I must
declare to you, indeed I must, if you desire to dispose
of all I have in the world, in an Honourable Way,
which I don't pretend to be any way deserving your
consideration, my Fortune and Person, if you won't
understand me without telling you so, are both at
your service. Gad so! another time——   229

Stanmore enters to 'em.

Stan. So, Mrs. *Lackitt*, your Widowhood is waneing
apace. I see which way 'tis going. *Welldon*, you're
a happy man. The Women and their Favours come
home to you.

Wid. A fiddle of favour, Mr. *Stanmore*: I am a lone
Woman, you know it, left in a great deal of Business;
and Business must be followed or lost. I have several
Stocks and Plantations upon my hands, and other
things to dispose of, which Mr. *Welldon* may have
occasion for.

Well. We were just upon the brink of a Bargain,
as you came in.   241

Stan. Let me drive it on for you.

Well. So you must, I believe, you or somebody
for me.

Stan. I'll stand by you: I understand more of this
business, than you can pretend to.

Well. I don't pretend to't; 'tis quite out of my way
indeed.

Stan. If the Widow gets you to her self, she will
certainly be too hard for you: I know her of old:
She has no Conscience in a Corner; a very *Jew* in

a bargain, and would circumcise you to get more
of you.   253

Well. Is this true, Widow?

Wid. Speak as you find, Mr. *Welldon*: I have
offer'd you very fair: Think upon 't, and let me hear of
you: The sooner the better, Mr. *Welldon.*—— [*Exit.*

Stan. I assure you, my Friend, she'll cheat you if
she can.

Well. I don't know that; but I can cheat her, if
I will.   261

Stan. Cheat her? How?

Well. I can marry her; and then I'm sure I have it
in my power to cheat her.

Stan. Can you marry her?

Well. Yes, faith, so she says: Her pretty Person
and Fortune (which, one with the other, you know,
are not contemptible) are both at my service.   268

Stan. Contemptible! very considerable, I'gad; very
desirable: Why, she's worth Ten thousand Pounds,
man; a clear Estate: No charge upon 't, but a boobily
Son: He indeed was to have half; but his Father
begot him, and she breeds him up, not to know or
have more than she has a mind to: And she has a
mind to something else, it seems.

Well. There's a great deal to be made of this.——
                                                  [*musing.*

Stan. A handsome Fortune may be made on 't;
and I advise you to 't, by all means.

Well. To marry her! an old, wanton Witch! I
hate her.   280

Stan. No matter for that: Let her go to the Devil
for you. She'll cheat her Son of a good Estate for
you: That's a Perquisite of a Widow's Portion
always.

Well. I have a design, and will follow her at least,
till I have a Pen'worth of the Plantation.

Stan. I speak as a friend, when I advise you to
marry her. For 'tis directly against the Interest of

my own Family. My Cousin *Jack* has belabour'd her
a good while that way.   290

Well. What! Honest *Jack* ! I'll not hinder him,
I'll give over the thoughts of her.

Stan. He'll make nothing on't; she does not care
for him. I'm glad you have her in your power.

Well. I may be able to serve him.

Stan. Here's a Ship come into the River; I was in
hopes it had been from *England*.

Well. From *England*!

Stan. No, I was disappointed; I long to see this
handsome Cousin of yours: The Picture you gave me
of her has charm'd me.   301

Well. You'll see whether it has flatter'd her or no,
in a little time. If she recover'd of that Illness that
was the reason of her staying behind us, I know she
will come with the first opportunity. We shall see
her, or hear of her death.

Stan. We'll hope the best. The Ships from *England*
are expected every day.

Well. What Ship is this?   309

Stan. A Rover, a Buccaneer, a Trader in Slaves:
That's the Commodity we deal in, you know. If
you have a curiosity to see our manner of marketting,
I'll wait upon you.

Well. We'll take my Sister with us.——   [*Exeunt.*

SCENE II.   *An Open Place.*

Enter Lieutenant-Governor *and* Blandford.

Gov. There's no resisting your Fortune, *Blandford*;
you draw all the Prizes.

Blan. I draw for our Lord Governor, you know;
his Fortune favours me.

Gov. I grudge him nothing this time; but if Fortune
had favour'd me in the last Sale, the Fair Slave had
been mine; *Clemene* had been mine.

Blan. Are you still in love with her?

Gov. Every day more in love with her.　　　9

Enter Capt. Driver, *teaz'd and pull'd about by Widow* Lackitt *and several Planters. Enter at another door* Welldon, Lucia, Stanmore.

Wid. Here have I six Slaves in my Lot, and not a Man among 'em; all Women and Children; what can I do with 'em, Captain? Pray consider, I am a Woman my self, and can't get my own Slaves, as some of my Neighbours do.

1 *Plan.* I have all Men in mine: Pray, Captain, let the Men and Women be mingled together, for Procreation-sake, and the good of the Plantation.

2 *Plan.* Ay, ay, a Man and a Woman, Captain, for the good of the Plantation.　　　19

Capt. Let 'em mingle together and be damn'd, what care I? Would you have me pimp for the good of the Plantation?

1 *Plan.* I am a constant Customer, Captain.

Wid. I am always Ready Money to you, Captain.

1 *Plan.* For that matter, Mistress, my Money is as ready as yours.

Wid. Pray hear me, Captain.

Capt. Look you, I have done my part by you; I have brought the number of Slaves you bargain'd for; if your Lots have not pleas'd you, you must draw again among your selves.　　　31

3 *Plan.* I am contented with my Lot.

4 *Plan.* I am very well satisfied.

3 *Plan.* We'll have no drawing again.

Capt. Do you hear, Mistress? You may hold your tongue: For my part, I expect my Money.

Wid. Captain, No body questions or scruples the Payment. But I won't hold my tongue; 'tis too much to pray and pay too: One may speak for ones own, I hope.

Capt. Well, what wou'd you say?

Wid. I say no more than I can make out.

Capt. Out with it then.

Wid. I say, things have not been so fair carry'd as they might have been. How do I know how you have juggled together in my absence? You drew the Lots before I came, I'm sure.

Capt. That's your own fault, Mistress; you might have come sooner.   49

Wid. Then here's a Prince, as they say, among the Slaves, and you set him down to go as a common Man.

Capt. Have you a mind to try what a Man he is? You'll find him no more than a common Man at your business.

Wid. Sir, You're a scurvy Fellow to talk at this rate to me. If my Husband were alive, Gadsbodykins, you wou'd not use me so.   57

Capt. Right, Mistress, I would not use you at all.

Wid. Not use me! Your Betters every Inch of you, I wou'd have you to know, wou'd be glad to use me, Sirrah. Marry come up here, who are you, I trow? You begin to think your self a Captain, forsooth, because we call you so. You forget your self as fast as you can; but I remember you; I know you for a pitiful paltry Fellow, as you are; an Upstart to Prosperity; one that is but just come acquainted with Cleanliness, and that never saw Five Shillings of your own, without deserving to be hang'd for 'em.

Gov. She has giv'n you a Broadside, Captain; You'll stand up to her.   70

Capt. Hang her, Stink-pot, I'll come no near.

Wid. By this good light, it wou'd make a Woman do a thing she never design'd; Marry again, tho' she were sure to repent it, to be reveng'd of such a——

J. Stan. What's the matter, Mrs. *Lackitt*? Can I serve you?

Wid. No, no, you can't serve me: You are for serving your self, I'm sure. Pray go about your business, I have none for you: You know I have told

you so. Lord! how can you be so troublesome? nay,
so unconscionable, to think that every Rich Widow
must throw her self away upon a Young Fellow that
has nothing? 83

Stan. Jack, You are answer'd, I suppose.

J. Stan. I'll have another pluck at her.

Wid. Mr. *Welldon*, I am a little out of order; but
pray bring your Sister to dine with me. Gad's my
life, I'm out of all patience with that pitiful Fellow:
My flesh rises at him: I can't stay in the place where
he is.——— [*Exit.* 90

Blan. Captain, You have us'd the Widow very
familiarly.

Capt. This is my way; I have no design, and therefore am not over civil. If she had ever a handsome
Daughter to wheedle her out of: Or if I cou'd make
any thing of her Booby Son.

Well. I may improve that hint, and make something of him. [*aside.*

Gov. She's very Rich. 99

Capt. I'm rich my self. She has nothing that I
want: I have no Leaks to stop. Old Women are
Fortune-Menders. I have made a good Voyage, and
wou'd reap the fruits of my labour. We plow the
deep, my Masters, but our Harvest is on shore. I'm
for a Young Woman.

Stan. Look about, Captain, there's one ripe, and
ready for the Sickle.

Capt. A Woman indeed! I will be acquainted
with her: Who is she?

Well. My Sister, Sir. 110

Capt. Wou'd I were a-kin to her: If she were my
Sister, she shou'd never go out of the Family. What
say you, Mistress? You expect I should marry you,
I suppose.

Luc. I shan't be disappointed, if you don't.

 [*turning away.*

Well. She won't break her heart, Sir.

Capt. But I mean——   [*following her.*

Well. And I mean——

   [*Going between him and* Lucia.

That you must not think of her without marrying.

Capt. I mean so too.   120

Well. Why then your meaning's out.

Capt. You're very short.

Well. I will grow, and be taller for you.

Capt. I shall grow angry, and swear.

Well. You'll catch no fish then.

Capt. I don't well know whether he designs to affront me, or no.

Stan. No, no, he's a little familiar; 'tis his way.

Capt. Say you so? Nay, I can be as familiar as he, if that be it. Well, Sir, look upon me full: What say you? How do you like me for a Brother-in-law?   131

Well. Why yes, faith, you'll do my business, [*turning him about*] If we can agree about my Sister's.

Capt. I don't know whether your Sister will like me, or not: I can't say much to her: But I have Money enough: And if you are her Brother, as you seem to be a-kin to her, I know that will recommend me to you.

Well. This is your Market for Slaves; my Sister is a Free Woman, and must not be dispos'd of in publick. You shall be welcome to my House, if you please: And, upon better acquaintance, if my Sister likes you, and I like your Offers,——   143

Capt. Very well, Sir, I'll come and see her.

Gov. Where are the Slaves, Captain? They are long a coming.

Blan. And who is this Prince that's fallen to my Lot, for the Lord Governor? Let me know something of him, that I may treat him accordingly; who is he?

Capt. He's the Devil of a Fellow, I can tell you; a Prince every Inch of him: You have paid dear enough for him, for all the good he'll do you: I was forc'd to clap him in Irons, and did not think the

Ship safe neither. You are in hostility with the *Indians*, they say; they threaten you daily: You had best have an eye upon him.

Blan. But who is he?   157

Gov. And how do you know him to be a Prince?

Capt. He is Son and Heir to the great King of *Angola*, a mischievous Monarch in those parts, who, by his good will, wou'd never let any of his Neighbours be in quiet. This Son was his General, a plaguy fighting Fellow: I have formerly had dealings with him for Slaves, which he took Prisoners, and have got pretty roundly by him: But the Wars being at an end, and nothing more to be got by the Trade of that Countrey, I made bold to bring the Prince along with me.

Gov. How could you do that?

Blan. What! steal a Prince out of his own Countrey? Impossible!   171

Capt. 'Twas hard indeed; but I did it. You must know, this *Oroonoko*——

Blan. Is that his Name?

Capt. Ay, *Oroonoko*.

Gov. *Oroonoko*.

Capt. Is naturally inquisitive about the Men and Manners of the White Nations. Because I could give him some account of the other Parts of the World, I grew very much into his favour: In return of so great an Honour, you know I cou'd do no less upon my coming away, than invite him on board me: Never having been in a Ship, he appointed his time, and I prepared my Entertainment: He came the next Evening as privately as he cou'd, with about some Twenty along with him. The Punch went round; and as many of his Attendants as wou'd be dangerous, I sent dead drunk on shore; the rest we secur'd: And so you have the Prince *Oroonoko*.   189

1 *Blan.* Gad-a-mercy, Captain, there you were with him, I'faith.

2 *Plan.* Such men as you are fit to be employ'd in Publick Affairs: The Plantation will thrive by you.

3 *Plan.* Industry shou'd be encourag'd.

Capt. There's nothing done without it, Boys. I have made my Fortune this way.

Blan. Unheard-of Villany!

Stan. Barbarous Treachery!

Blan. They applaud him for 't.   200

Gov. But, Captain, methinks you have taken a great deal of pains for this Prince *Oroonoko*; why did you part with him at the common rate of Slaves?

Capt. Why, Lieutenant-Governor, I'll tell you; I did design to carry him to *England*, to have show'd him there; but I found him troublesome upon my hands, and I'm glad I'm rid of him.——Oh, ho, here they come.

Black Slaves, Men, Women, and Children, pass across the Stage by two and two; Aboan, and others of Oroonoko's *Attendants two and two;* Oroonoko *last of all in Chains.*

Luc. Are all these Wretches Slaves?

Stan. All sold, they and their Posterity all Slaves.

Luc. O miserable Fortune!   211

Blan. Most of 'em know no better; they were born so, and only change their Masters. But a Prince, born only to Command, betray'd and sold! My heart drops blood for him.

Capt. Now, Governor, here he comes, pray observe him.

Oro. So, Sir, You have kept your Word with me.

Capt. I am a better Christian, I thank you, than to keep it with a Heathen.   221

Oro. You are a Christian, be a Christian still:
If you have any God that teaches you
To break your Word, I need not curse you more:
Let him cheat you, as you are false to me.

You faithful Followers of my better Fortune!
We have been Fellow-Soldiers in the Field;
       [*Embracing his Friends.*
Now we are Fellow-Slaves. This last farewell.
Be sure of one thing that will comfort us,
Whatever World we next are thrown upon,   230
Cannot be worse than this.
      [*All Slaves go off, but* Oroonoko.
  Capt. You see what a Bloody Pagan he is, Governor;
but I took care that none of his Followers should be
in the same Lot with him, for fear they shou'd under-
take some desperate action, to the danger of the
Colony.
  Oro. Live still in fear; it is the Villains Curse,
And will revenge my Chains: Fear ev'n me,
Who have no pow'r to hurt thee. Nature abhors,
And drives thee out from the Society   240
And Commerce of Mankind, for Breach of Faith.
Men live and prosper but in Mutual Trust,
A Confidence of one another's Truth:
That thou hast violated. I have done.
I know my Fortune, and submit to it.
  Gov. Sir, I am sorry for your Fortune, and wou'd
help it, if I cou'd.
  Blan. Take off his Chains. You know your condi-
tion; but you are fall'n into Honourable Hands:
You are the Lord Governor's Slave, who will use
you nobly: In his absence it shall be my care to
serve you.   [Blanford *applying to him.*
  Oro. I hear you, but I can believe no more.   253
  Gov. Captain, I'm afraid the world won't speak
so honourably of this action of yours, as you wou'd
have 'em.
  Capt. I have the Money. Let the world speak and
be damn'd, I care not.
  Oro. I wou'd forget my self. Be satisfied,
            [*to* Blanford.
I am above the rank of common Slaves.   260

Let that content you. The Christian there, that
    knows me,
For his own sake will not discover more.

   Capt. I have other matters to mind. You have him,
and much good may do you with your Prince. [*Exit.*

    The Planters pulling and staring at Oroonoko.

   Blan. What wou'd you have there? You stare as if
you never saw a Man before. Stand further off.
                                [*turns 'em away.*

   Oro. Let 'em stare on. I am unfortunate, but not
    asham'd
Of being so: No, let the Guilty blush,
The White Man that betray'd me: Honest Black
Disdains to change its Colour. I am ready: 270
Where must I go? Dispose me as you please.
I am not well acquainted with my Fortune,
But must learn to know it better: So I know, you say:
Degrees make all things easy.

   Blan. All things shall be easy.

   Oro. Tear off this Pomp, and let me know my self:
The slavish Habit best becomes me now.
Hard Fare, and Whips, and Chains may overpow'r
The frailer flesh, and bow my Body down.
But there 's another, Nobler Part of Me,   280
Out of your reach, which you can never tame.

   Blan. You shall find nothing of this wretchedness
You apprehend. We are not Monsters all.
You seem unwilling to disclose your self:
Therefore for fear the mentioning your Name
Should give you new disquiets, I presume
To call you *Cæsar.*

   Oro. I am my self; but call me what you please.

   Stan. A very good Name, *Cæsar.*

   Gov. And very fit for his great Character.   290

   Oro. Was *Cæsar* then a Slave?

   Gov. I think he was; to Pirates too: He was a great
Conqueror, but unfortunate in his Friends.——

Oro. His Friends were Christians?

Blan. No.

Oro. No! that's strange.

Gov. And murder'd by 'em.

Oro. I wou'd be *Cæsar* there. Yet I will live.

Blan. Live to be happier.

Oro. Do what you will with me.   300

Blan. I'll wait upon you, attend, and serve you.

                          [*Exit with* Oroonoko.

Luc. Well, if the Captain had brought this Prince's Countrey along with him, and wou'd make me Queen of it, I wou'd not have him, after doing so base a thing.

Well. He's a man to thrive in the world, Sister: He'll make you the better Jointure.

Luc. Hang him, nothing can prosper with him.

Stan. Enquire into the great Estates, and you will find most of 'em depend upon the same Title of Honesty: The men who raise 'em first are much of the Captain's Principles.   312

Well. Ay, ay, as you say, let him be damn'd for the good of his Family. Come, Sister, we are invited to dinner.

Gov. Stanmore, You dine with me.   [*Exeunt Omnes.*

A C T II.   Scene I.   *Widow* Lackitt's House.

Widow Lackitt, Welldon.

Well. This is so great a Favour, I don't know how to receive it.

Wid. O dear Sir! you know how to receive and how to return a Favour, as well as any body, I don't doubt it: 'Tis not the first you have had from our Sex, I suppose.

Well. But this is so unexpected.

Wid. Lord, how can you say so, Mr. *Welldon*? I

won't believe you. Don't I know you handsome
Gentlemen expect every thing that a Woman can
do for you? And by my troth you're in the right on 't:
I think one can't do too much for a Handsome
Gentleman; and so you shall find it.   13

Well. I shall never have such an Offer again, that 's
certain: What shall I do? I am mightily divided.——
                            [*pretending a concern.*

Wid. Divided! O dear, I hope not so, Sir. If I
marry, truly I expect to have you to my self.

Well. There 's no danger of that, Mrs. *Lackitt.* I am
divided in my thoughts. My Father upon his Death-
bed oblig'd me to see my Sister dispos'd of, before
I married my self. 'Tis that sticks upon me. They
say indeed Promises are to be broken or kept; and
I know 'tis a foolish thing to be tied to a Promise;
but I can't help it: I don't know how to get rid of it.

Wid. Is that all?   25

Well. All in all to me. The Commands of a dying
Father, you know, ought to be obey'd.

Wid. And so they may.

Well. Impossible, to do me any good.

Wid. They shan't be your hindrance. You wou'd
have a Husband for your Sister, you say: He must
be very well to pass too in the world, I suppose?   32

Well. I wou'd not throw her away.

Wid. Then marry her out of hand to the Sea-
Captain you were speaking of.

Well. I was thinking of him, but 'tis to no purpose:
She hates him.

Wid. Does she hate him? Nay, 'tis no matter, an
Impudent Rascal as he is, I wou'd not advise her to
marry him.   40

Well. Can you think of no body else?

Wid. Let me see.

Well. Ay, pray do: I shou'd be loth to part with
my good fortune in you for so small a matter as a
Sister: But you find how it is with me.

Wid. Well remembred, I'faith: Well, if I thought you wou'd like of it, I have a Husband for her: What do you think of my Son?

Well. You don't think of it your self. 49

Wid. I protest but I do: I am in earnest, if you are. He shall marry her within this half hour, if you'll give your consent to it.

Well. I give my consent! I'll answer for my Sister, she shall have him: You may be sure I shall be glad to get over the difficulty.

Wid. No more to be said then, that difficulty is over. But I vow and swear you frightned me, Mr. *Welldon.* If I had not had a Son now for your Sister, what must I have done, do you think? Were not you an ill-natur'd thing to boggle at a Promise? I cou'd break twenty for you. 61

Well. I am the more oblig'd to you: But this Son will save all.

Wid. He 's in the house; I'll go and bring him my self. [*going.*] You wou'd do well to break the business to your Sister: She 's within, I'll send her to you.——
[*going again, comes back.*

Well. Pray do.

Wid. But d'you hear? Perhaps she may stand upon her Maidenly Behaviour, and blush, and play the fool, and delay: But don't be answer'd so: What! she is not a Girl at these years: Shew your Authority, and tell her roundly, she must be married immediately. I'll manage my Son, I warrant you.—— 73
[*goes out in haste.*

Well. The Widow 's in haste, I see: I thought I had laid a rub in the road, about my Sister: But she has stept over that. She 's making way for her self as fast as she can; but little thinks where she is going: I cou'd tell her she is going to play the fool: But people don't love to hear of their faults: Besides, that is not my business at present. [*Enter Lucia.*] So, Sister, I have a Husband for you.—— 81

Luc. With all my heart: I don't know what Confinement Marriage may be to the Men, but I'm sure the Women have no liberty without it. I am for any thing that will deliver me from the care of a Reputation, which I begin to find impossible to preserve.

Well. I'll ease you of that care: You must be married immediately. 89

Luc. The sooner the better; for I am quite tir'd of setting up for a Husband. The Widow's foolish Son is the man, I suppose.

Well. I consider'd your Constitution, Sister; and finding you wou'd have occasion for a Fool, I have provided accordingly.

Luc. I don't know what occasion I may have for a Fool when I'm married: But I find none but Fools have occasion to marry.

Well. Since he is to be a Fool then, I thought it better for you to have one of his Mother's making than your own; 'twill save you the trouble. 101

Luc. I thank you; you take a great deal of pains for me: But, pray tell me, what are you doing for your self all this while?

Well. You were never true to your own secrets, and therefore I won't trust you with mine. Only remember this, I am your elder Sister, and consequently laying my Breeches aside, have as much occasion for a Husband as you can have. I have a Man in my eye, be satisfied. 110

Enter Widow Lackitt, *with her Son* Daniel.

Wid. Come, *Daniel,* hold up thy head, Child: Look like a Man: You must not take it as you have done. Gad's my life! there's nothing to be done with twirling your Hat, Man.

Dan. Why, Mother, what's to be done then?

Wid. Why look me in the face, and mind what I say to you.

Dan. Marry, who's the fool then? what shall I get by minding what you say to me?   119

Wid. Mrs. *Lucy*, the Boy is bashful, don't discourage him: Pray come a little forward, and let him salute you.

                  [*Going between* Lucia *and* Daniel.

Luc. A fine Husband I am to have truly.

                           [*to* Welldon.

Wid. Come, *Daniel*, you must be acquainted with this Gentlewoman.

Dan. Nay, I'm not proud, that is not my fault: I am presently acquainted when I know the Company; but this Gentlewoman is a stranger to me.

Wid. She is your Mistress; I have spoke a good word for you; make her a Bow, and go and kiss her.

Dan. Kiss her! Have a care what you say; I warrant she scorns your words. Such Fine Folk are not us'd to be slopt and kiss'd. Do you think I don't know that, Mother?   133

Wid. Try her, try her, Man. [Daniel *bows, she thrusts him forward.*] Why that's well done; go nearer her.

Dan. Is the Devil in the Woman? Why so I can go nearer her, if you would let a body alone. [*To his Mother.*] Cry you mercy, forsooth; my Mother is always shaming one before company: She wou'd have me as unmannerly as her self, and offer to kiss you.   [*To* Lucia.

Well. Why, won't you kiss her?   143

Dan. Why, pray, may I?

Well. Kiss her, Kiss her, Man.

Dan. Marry, and I will. [*Kisses her.*] Gadsooks! she kisses rarely! An' please you, Mistress, and seeing my Mother will have it so, I don't much care if I kiss you again, forsooth.   [*Kisses her again.*

Luc. Well, how do you like me now?   150

Dan. Like you! marry, I don't know. You have bewitch'd me, I think: I was never so in my born days before.

Wid. You must marry this Fine Woman, *Daniel.*

Dan. Hey day! marry her! I was never married in all my life. What must I do with her then, Mother?

Wid. You must live with her, eat and drink with her, go to bed with her, and sleep with her.   159

Dan. Nay, marry, if I must go to bed with her, I shall never sleep, that's certain: She'll break me of my rest, quite and clean, I tell you before-hand. As for eating and drinking with her, why I have a good stomach, and can play my part in any company. But how do you think I can go to bed to a Woman I don't know?

Well. You shall know her better.

Dan. Say you so, Sir?

Well. Kiss her again.   [Daniel *kisses* Lucy.

Dan. Nay, kissing I find will make us presently acquainted. We'll steal into a Corner to practise a little, and then I shall be able to do any thing.   172

Well. The Young Man mends apace.

Wid. Pray don't baulk him.

Dan. Mother, Mother, if you'll stay in the room by me, and promise not to leave me, I don't care for once if I venture to go to bed with her.

Wid. There's a good Child; go in and put on thy best Cloaths; pluck up a spirit; I'll stay in the room by thee. She won't hurt thee, I warrant thee.   180

Dan. Nay, as to that matter, I'm not afraid of her: I'll give her as good as she brings: I have a *Rowland* for her *Oliver*, and so you may tell her.   [*Exit.*

Wid. Mrs. *Lucy*, we shan't stay for you: You are in a readiness, I suppose.

Well. She's always ready to do what I wou'd have her, I must say that for my Sister.

Wid. 'Twill be her own another day. Mr. *Welldon*, we'll marry 'em out of hand, and then——   189

Well. And then, Mrs. *Lackitt*, look to your self.——
                              [*Exeunt.*

SCENE II.

Oroonoko *and* Blanford.

Oro. You grant I have good reason to suspect
All the professions you can make to me.

Blan. Indeed you have.

Oro. The Dog that sold me did profess as much
As you can do.——But yet I know not why,——
Whether it is because I'm fall'n so low,
And have no more to fear.——That is not it:
I am a Slave no longer than I please.
'Tis something nobler.——Being just my self,
I am inclining to think others so :   10
'Tis that prevails upon me to believe you.

Blan. You may believe me.

Oro. I do believe you.
From what I know of you, you are no Fool:
Fools only are the Knaves, and live by Tricks:
Wise men may thrive without 'em, and be honest.

Blan. They won't all take your counsel.——
                                        [*aside.*

Oro. You know my Story, and you say you are
A Friend to my Misfortunes : That 's a name
Will teach you what you owe your self and me.   20

Blan. I'll study to deserve to be your Friend.
When once our Noble Governor arrives,
With him you will not need my Interest:
He is too generous not to feel your wrongs.
But be assur'd I will employ my pow'r,
And find the means to send you home again.

Oro. I thank you, Sir.——My honest, wretched
    Friends !
Their Chains are heavy : They have hardly found
                                        [*sighing.*
So kind a Master. May I ask you, Sir,
What is become of 'em? Perhaps I shou'd not.   30
You will forgive a Stranger.

Blan. I'll enquire, and use my best endeavours,
    where they are,
To have 'em gently us'd.
  Oro. Once more I thank you.
You offer every Cordial that can keep
My Hopes alive, to wait a better day.
What Friendly Care can do, you have apply'd.
But, Oh! I have a Grief admits no Cure.
  Blan. You do not know, Sir,——
  Oro. Can you raise the dead?   40
Pursue and overtake the Wings of Time?
And bring about again the Hours, the Days,
The Years that made me happy.
  Blan. That is not to be done.
  Oro. No, there is nothing to be done for me.
               [Kneeling and kissing the Earth.
Thou God ador'd! thou ever-glorious Sun!
If she be yet on Earth, send me a Beam
Of thy All-seeing Power to light me to her.
Or if thy Sister Goddess has preferr'd
Her Beauty to the skies to be a Star;   50
O tell me where she shines, that I may stand
Whole Nights, and gaze upon her.
  Blan. I am rude, and interrupt you.
  Oro. I am troublesome:
But pray give me your Pardon. My swoll'n Heart
Bursts out its passage, and I must complain.
O! can you think of nothing dearer to me?
Dearer than Liberty, my Countrey, Friends,
Much dearer than my Life? that I have lost.
The tend'rest, best belov'd, and loving Wife.   60
  Blan. Alas! I pity you.
  Oro. Do, pity me:
Pity 's a-kin to Love; and every thought
Of that soft kind is welcome to my Soul.
I wou'd be pity'd here.
  Blan. I dare not ask more than you please to tell
    me: but if you

Think it convenient to let me know
Your Story, I dare promise you to bear
A part in your Distress, if not assist you.

 Oro. Thou honest-hearted man! I wanted such,
Just such a Friend as thou art, that would sit   71
Still as the night, and let me talk whole days
Of my *Imoinda*. O! I'll tell thee all
From first to last; and pray observe me well.

 Blan. I will most heedfully.

 Oro. There was a Stranger in my Father's Court,
Valu'd and honour'd much: He was a White,
The first I ever saw of your Complexion:
He chang'd his gods for ours, and so grew great;
Of many Virtues, and so fam'd in Arms,   80
He still commanded all my Father's Wars.
I was bred under him. One Fatal Day,
The Armies joining, he before me stept,
Receiving in his breast a Poyson'd Dart
Levell'd at me; He dy'd within my Arms.
I've tir'd you already.

 Blan. Pray go on.

 Oro. He left an only Daughter, whom he brought
An Infant to *Angola*. When I came
Back to the Court, a happy Conqueror;   90
Humanity oblig'd me to condole
With this sad Virgin for a Father's Loss,
Lost for my safety. I presented her
With all the Slaves of Battel to attone
Her Father's Ghost. But when I saw her Face,
And heard her speak, I offer'd up my self
To be the Sacrifice. She bow'd and blush'd;
I wonder'd and ador'd. The Sacred Pow'r
That had subdu'd me, then inspir'd my Tongue,
Inclin'd her Heart; and all our Talk was Love.   100

 Blan. Then you were happy.

 Oro. O! I was too happy.
I marry'd her: And though my Country's Custom
Indulg'd the Privilege of many Wives,

I swore my self never to know but her.
She grew with Child, and I grew happier still.
O my *Imoinda*! but it cou'd not last.
Her fatal Beauty reach'd my Father's Ears:
He sent for her to Court, where, cursed Court!
No Woman comes, but for his Amorous Use.   110
He raging to possess her, she was forc'd
To own her self my Wife. The furious King
Started at Incest: But grown desperate,
Not daring to enjoy what he desir'd,
In mad Revenge, which I cou'd never learn,
He Poyson'd her, or sent her far, far off,
Far from my hopes ever to see her more.

   Blan. Most barbarous of Fathers! the sad Tale
Has struck me dumb with wonder.

   Oro. I have done.   120
I'le trouble you no farther: now and then,
A Sigh will have its way; that shall be all.

                        [Enter *Stanmore*.

   Stan. Blandford, the Lieutenant Governour is gone
    to your Plantation.
He desires you wou'd bring the Royal Slave with
    you.
The sight of his fair Mistriss, he says, is an Entertain-
    ment
For a Prince; he wou'd have his opinion of her.

   Oro. Is he a Lover?

   Blan. So he says himself: he flatters a beautifull
Slave, that I have, and calls her Mistress.

   Oro. Must he then flatter her to call her Mistress?
I pity the proud Man, who thinks himself   131
Above being in love: what, tho' she be a Slave,
She may deserve him.

   Blan. You shall judge of that, when you see her,
    Sir.

   Oro. I go with you.   [*Exeunt*.

SCENE III. *A Plantation.*

[*L. Governour following* Imoinda.]

Gov. I have disturb'd you, I confess my fault,
My fair *Clemene*, but begin again,
And I will listen to your mournfull Song,
Sweet as the soft complaining Nightingales.
While every Note calls out my trembling Soul,
And leaves me silent, as the Midnight Groves,
Only to shelter you, sing, sing agen,
And let me wonder at the many ways
You have to ravish me.
  Imo. O! I can weep   10
Enough for you, and me, if that will please you.
  Gov. You must not weep: I come to dry your
    Tears,
And raise you from your Sorrow. Look upon me:
Look with the Eyes of kind indulging Love,
That I may have full cause for what I say:
I come to offer you your liberty,
And be my self the Slave. You turn away.
                              [*Following her.*
But every thing becomes you. I may take
This pretty hand: I know your Modesty
Wou'd draw it back: but you wou'd take it ill,   20
If I shou'd let it go, I know you wou'd.
You shall be gently forc'd to please your self;
That you will thank me for.
          [*She struggles, and gets her hand from him, then
            he offers to kiss her.*
Nay if you struggle with me, I must take——
  Imo. You may, my life, that I can part with freely.
                                            [*Exit.*

[*Enter* Blanford, Stanmore, Oroonoko *to him.*]
  Blan. So, Governour, we don't disturb you, I hope :
your Mistriss has left you: you were making Love,
she 's thankfull for the Honour, I suppose.

Gov. Quite insensible to all I say, and do:
When I speak to her, she sighs, or weeps,   30
But never answers me as I wou'd have her.

   Stan. There's something nearer than her Slavery,
    that touches her.

   Blan. What do her fellow Slaves say of her? cann't
    they find the cause?

   Gov. Some of 'em, who pretend to be wiser than
the rest, and hate her, I suppose, for being us'd
better than they are, will needs have it that she's
with Child.

   Blan. Poor wretch! if it be so, I pity her:
She has lost a husband, that perhaps was dear
To her, and then you cannot blame her.   40

   Oro. If it be so, indeed you cannot blame her.
                              [*Sighing.*

   Gov. No, no, it is not so: if it be so,
I still must love her: and desiring still,
I must enjoy her.

   Blan. Try what you can do with fair means, and
    wellcome.

   Gov. I'll give you ten Slaves for her.

   Blan. You know she is our Lord Governour's: but
    if I could
Dispose of her, I wou'd not now, especially to you.

   Gov. Why not to me?

   Blan. I mean against her Will. You are in love
    with her.   50
And we all know what your desires wou'd have:
Love stops at nothing but possession.
Were she within your pow'r, you do not know
How soon you wou'd be tempted to forget
The Nature of the Deed, and, may be, act
A violence, you after wou'd repent.

   Oro. 'Tis Godlike in you to protect the weak.

   Gov. Fye, fye, I wou'd not force her. Tho' she be
A Slave, her Mind is free, and shou'd consent.   59

   Oro. Such Honour will engage her to consent:

And then, if you're in love, she's worth the having.
Shall we not see this wonder?

  Gov. Have a care;
You have a Heart, and she has conquering Eyes.

  Oro. I have a Heart: but if it cou'd be false
To my first Vows, ever to love agen,
These honest Hands shou'd tear it from my Breast,
And throw the Traytor from me. O! *Imoinda*!
Living or dead, I can be only thine.

  Blan. *Imoinda* was his Wife: she's either dead,   70
Or living, dead to him: forc't from his Arms
By an inhuman Father. Another time
I'le tell you all.   [*To* Gov. *and* Stanmore.

  Stan. Hark! the Slaves have done their work;
And now begins their Evening merriment.

  Blan. The Men are all in love with fair *Clemene*
As much as you are: and the Women hate her,
From an instinct of natural jealousie.
They sing, and dance, and try their little tricks
To entertain her, and divert her sadness.   80
May be she is among 'em: shall we see?

                      [*Exeunt.*

    The Scene drawn shews the Slaves, Men, Women,
      and Children upon the Ground, some rise and
      dance, others sing the following Songs.

A S O N G.   [By an unknown hand.]

Sett by Mr. *Courtevill*, and sung by the Boy to
             Miss Cross.

I.

A Lass there lives upon the Green,
  Cou'd I her Picture draw;
A brighter Nymph was never seen,
That looks, and reigns a little Queen,
  And keeps the Swains in awe.

II.

Her Eyes are Cupid's *Darts, and Wings,*
   Her Eyebrows are his Bow;
Her Silken Hair the Silver Strings,
Which sure and swift destruction brings   90
   To all the Vale below.

III.

If Pastorella's *dawning Light*
   Can warm, and wound us so:
Her Noon will shine so piercing bright,
Each glancing beam will kill outright,
   And every Swain subdue.

A S O N G, by Mr. *Cheek.*

Sett by Mr. *Courtevill,* and sung by Mr. *Leveridge.*

I.

Bright Cynthia's *Pow'r divinely great,*
   What Heart is not obeying?
A thousand Cupids *on her wait,*
   And in her Eyes are playing.   100

II.

She seems the Queen of Love to reign,
   For She alone dispences
Such Sweets, as best can entertain
   The Gust of all the Senses.

III.

Her Face a charming prospect brings;
   Her Breath gives balmy Blisses;
I hear an Angel, when she sings,
   And taste of Heaven in Kisses.

IV.

Four Senses thus she feasts with joy,
*   From Nature's richest Treasure:*   110
Let me the other Sense employ,
*   And I shall dye with pleasure.*

During the Entertainment, the Governour, Blan-
    ford, Stanmore, Oroonoko, *enter as Spec-*
    tators; that ended, Captain Driver, Jack
    Stanmore, *and several Planters enter with*
    their Swords drawn.   [*A Bell rings.*

Capt. Where are you, Governour? make what hast
    you can
To save your self, and the whole Colony.
I bid 'em ring the Bell.
    Gov. What 's the matter?
    J. Stan. The *Indians* are come down upon us:
They have plunder'd some of the Plantations already,
And are marching this way, as fast as they can.
    Gov. What can we do against 'em?   120
    Blan. We shall be able to make a stand,
Till more Planters come in to us.
    J. Stan. There are a great many more without,
If you wou'd show your self, and put us in order.
    Gov. There 's no danger of the White Slaves, they'll
    not stir:
Blanford, and *Stanmore* come you along with me:
Some of you stay here to look after the Black Slaves.
        [*All go out but the Captain, and* 6 *Planters, who*
        *   at once seize* Oroonoko.
    1 *Plan.* Ay, ay, let us alone.
    Capt. In the first place we secure you, Sir,
As an Enemy to the Government.   130
    Oro. Are you there, Sir, you are my constant Friend.
    1 *Plan.* You will be able to do a great deal of
        mischief.
    Capt. But we shall prevent you: bring the Irons
hither. He has the malice of a Slave in him, and

wou'd be glad to be cutting his Masters Throats, I
know him. Chain his hands and feet, that he may
not run over to 'em : if they have him, they shall carry
him on their backs, that I can tell 'em.

 [*As they are chaining him,* Blanford *enters, runs to 'em.*
Blan. What are you doing there?
Capt. Securing the main chance : this is a bosom
  enemy.   140
Blan. Away you Brutes : I'll answer with my life
for his behaviour; so tell the Governour.
Capt. } Well, Sir, so we will. { *Exeunt*
Plan. }   { Capt. *and Planters.*
Oro. Give me a Sword and I'll deserve your trust.

 [*A Party of* Indians *enter, hurrying* Imoinda
  among the Slaves; another Party of Indians
  sustains 'em retreating, follow'd at a distance
  by the Governour with the Planters: Blanford,
  Oroonoko *joyn 'em.*

Blan. Hell, and the Devil! they drive away our
Slaves before our Faces. Governour, can you stand
tamely by, and suffer this? *Clemene,* Sir, your Mistress
is among 'em.
 Gov. We throw our selves away, in the attempt to
  rescue 'em.
 Oro. A Lover cannot fall more glorious,   150
Than in the cause of Love. He that deserves
His Mistress's favour wonnot stay behind :
I'le lead you on, be bold, and follow me.
  [Oroonoko *at the head of the Planters, falls upon*
   the Indians *with a great shout, beats 'em off.*

     Imoinda *enters.*

 Imo. I'm tost about by my tempestuous Fate,
And no where must have rest; *Indians,* or *English*!
Whoever has me, I am still a Slave.
No matter whose I am, since I am no more,
My Royal Masters; Since I'm his no more.

O I was happy! nay, I will be happy,
In the dear thought that I am still his Wife,   160
Tho' far divided from him.

> *[Draws off to a corner of the Stage.*

> *After a shout, enter the Governour with* Oroonoko,
> Blanford, Stanmore, *and the Planters.*

Gov. Thou glorious Man! thou something greater sure
Than *Cæsar* ever was! that single Arm
Has sav'd us all: accept our general thanks.

> *All bow to* Oroonoko.

And what we can do more to recompense
Such noble services, you shall command.
Clemene too shall thank you,——she is safe——
Look up, and bless your brave deliverer.

> *[Brings* Clemene *forward, looking down on the ground.*

Oro. Bless me indeed!
Blan. You start!   170
Oro. O all you Gods!
Who govern this great World, and bring about
Things strange, and unexpected, can it be?
Gov. What is 't you stare at so?
Oro. Answer me some of you, you who have power,
And have your Senses free: or are you all
Struck thro' with wonder too?   *[Looking still fixt on her.*
Blan. What wou'd you know?
Oro. My Soul steals from my Body thro' my Eyes:
All that is left of life, I'll gaze away,   180
And die upon the Pleasure.
Gov. This is strange!
Oro. If you but mock me with her Image here:
If she be not *Imoinda*——

> *[She looks upon him, and falls into a Swoon, he
> runs to her.*

Ha! she faints!
Nay, then it must be she: it is *Imoinda*:
My Heart confesses her, and leaps for joy,

To welcome her to her own Empire here.
I feel her all, in every part of me.
O! let me press her in my eager Arms,   190
Wake her to life, and with this kindling Kiss
Give back that Soul, she only sent to me. [*Kisses her.*

  Gov. I am amaz'd!
  Blan. I am as much as you.
  Oro. Imoinda! O! thy *Oroonoko* calls.
                [*Imoinda coming to life.*

  Imo. My *Oroonoko*! O! I can't believe
What any Man can say. But if I am
To be deceiv'd, there's something in that Name,
That Voice, that Face,   [*Staring on him.*
O! if I know my self, I cannot be mistaken.   200
          [*Runs, and embraces* Oroonoko.

  Oro. Never here;
You cannot be mistaken: I am yours,
Your *Oroonoko*, all that you wou'd have,
Your tender loving Husband.
  Imo. All indeed
That I wou'd have: my Husband! then I am
Alive, and waking to the Joys I feel:
They were so great, I cou'd not think 'em true.
But I believe all that you say to me:
For Truth it self, and everlasting Love   210
Grows in this Breast, and pleasure in these arms.
  Oro. Take, take me all: enquire into my heart,
(You know the way to every secret there)
My Heart, the sacred treasury of Love:
And if, in absence, I have mis-employ'd
A Mite from the rich store: if I have spent
A Wish, a Sigh, but what I sent to you:
May I be curst to wish, and sigh in vain,
And you not pity me.
  Imo. O! I believe,   220
And know you by my self. If these sad Eyes,
Since last we parted, have beheld the Face
Of any Comfort; or once wish'd to see

The light of any other Heaven, but you:
May I be struck this moment blind, and lose
Your blessed sight, never to find you more.

   Oro. Imoinda! O! this separation
Has made you dearer, if it can be so,
Than you were ever to me. You appear
Like a kind Star to my benighted Steps,   230
To guide me on my way to happiness:
I cannot miss it now. Governour, Friend,
You think me mad: but let me bless you all,
Who, any way, have been the Instruments
Of finding her again. *Imoinda*'s found!
And every thing, that I wou'd have in her.
           [*Embracing her in the most passionate Fondness.*
   Stan. Where's your Mistress now, Governour?
   Gov. Why, where most Men's Mistresses are forc'd
    to be sometimes,
With her Husband, it seems: but I won't lose her so.
                           [*Aside.*
   Stan. He has fought lustily for her, and deserves
    her, I'll say that for him.   240
   Blan. Sir we congratulate your happiness: I do
    most heartily.
   Gov. And all of us: but how it comes to pass——
   Oro. That will require more precious time than
    I can spare you now.
I have a thousand things to ask of her,
And she as many more to know of me.
But you have made me happier, I confess,
Acknowledge it, much happier, than I
Have words, or pow'r to tell you. Captain, you,
Ev'n you, who most have wrong'd me, I forgive.
I won't say you have betray'd me now: 250
I'll think you but the minister of Fate,
To bring me to my lov'd *Imoinda* here.

   Imo. How, how shall I receive you? how be worthy
Of such Endearments, all this tenderness?
These are the Transports of Prosperity,

When Fortune smiles upon us.

   Oro. Let the Fools, who follow Fortune, live upon
   her smiles.

All our Prosperity is plac'd in Love.

We have enough of that to make us happy.

This little spot of Earth you stand upon,   260

Is more to me, than the extended Plains

Of my great Father's Kingdom. Here I reign

In full delights, in Joys to Pow'r unknown;

Your Love my Empire, and your Heart my Throne.

                                 [Exeunt.

ACT III.

SCENE I.

[Aboan *with several Slaves,* Hottman.]

   Hott. What! to be Slaves to Cowards! Slaves to
   Rogues!

Who cann't defend themselves!

   Abo. Who is this Fellow? he talks as if he were
   acquainted

With our design: is he one of us?

                          [Aside to his own Gang.

   Slav. Not yet: but he will be glad to make one,
   I believe.

   Abo. He makes a mighty noise.

   Hott. Go, sneak in Corners; whisper out your
   Griefs,

For fear your Masters hear you: cringe and crouch

Under the bloody whip, like beaten Currs,

That lick their Wounds, and know no other cure. 10

All, wretches all! you feel their cruelty,

As much as I can feel, but dare not groan.

For my part, while I have a Life and Tongue,

I'll curse the Authors of my Slavery.

   Abo. Have you been long a Slave?

   Hott. Yes, many years.

Abo. And do you only curse?

Hott. Curse? only curse? I cannot conjure,
To raise the Spirits of other Men:
I am but one. O! for a Soul of fire,   20
To warm, and animate our common Cause,
And make a body of us: then I wou'd
Do something more than curse.

Abo. That body set on Foot, you wou'd be one,
A limb, to lend it motion.

Hott. I wou'd be the Heart of it: the Head, the
   Hand, and Heart.
Wou'd I cou'd see the day.

Abo. You will do all your self.

Hott. I wou'd do more, than I shall speak: but I
   may find a time.

Abo. The time may come to you; be ready for 't.
Methinks he talks too much: I'll know him more,   31
Before I trust him farther.

Slav. If he dares half what he says, he'll be of use
   to us.

[*Enter* Blanford *to 'em.*]

Blan. If there be any one among you here,
That did belong to *Oroonoko*, speak,
I come to him.

Abo. I did belong to him: *Aboan*, my Name.

Blan. You are the Man I want; pray, come with
   me.   [*Exeunt.*

SCENE II.

[Oroonoko *and* Imoinda.]

Oro. I do not blame my Father for his Love:
(Tho' that had been enough to ruine me)
'Twas Nature's fault, that made you like the Sun,
The reasonable worship of Mankind:
He cou'd not help his Adoration.
Age had not lock'd his Sences up so close,
But he had Eyes, that open'd to his Soul,

And took your Beauties in: he felt your pow'r,
And therefore I forgive his loving you.
But when I think on his Barbarity,   10
That cou'd expose you to so many Wrongs;
Driving you out to wretched Slavery,
Only for being mine; then I confess,
I wish I cou'd forget the Name of Son,
That I might curse the Tyrant.

    Imo. I will bless him, for I have found you here:
      Heav'n only knows
What is reserv'd for us: but if we ghess
The future by the past, our Fortune must
Be wonderfull, above the common Size
Of good or ill; it must be in extreams: 20
Extreamly happy, or extreamly wretched.

    Oro. 'Tis in our pow'r to make it happy now.

    Imo. But not to keep it so.

                [*Enter* Blanford *and* Aboan.

    Blan. My Royal Lord! I have a Present for you.

    Oro. Aboan!

    Abo. Your lowest Slave.

    Oro. My try'd and valu'd Friend.
This worthy Man always prevents my wants:
I only wish'd, and he has brought thee to me.
Thou art surpriz'd: carry thy duty there;   30
      [Aboan *goes to* Imoinda *and falls at her Feet.*
While I acknowledge mine, how shall I thank you.

    Blan. Believe me honest to your interest,
And I am more than paid. I have secur'd,
That all your Followers shall be gently us'd.
This Gentleman, your chiefest Favourite,
Shall wait upon your Person, while you stay among us.

    Oro. I owe every thing to you.

    Blan. You must not think you are in Slavery.

    Oro. I do not find I am.

    Blan. Kind Heaven has miraculously sent   40
Those Comforts, that may teach you to expect
Its farther care, in your deliverance.

Oro. I sometimes think my self, Heav'n is concern'd
For my deliverance.

Blan. It will be soon:
You may expect it. Pray, in the mean time,
Appear as chearfull as you can among us.
You have some Enemies, that represent
You dangerous, and wou'd be glad to find
A Reason, in your discontent, to fear: 50
They watch your looks. But there are honest Men,
Who are your Friends: You are secure in them.

Oro. I thank you for your caution.

Blan. I will leave you:
And be assur'd, I wish your liberty.   [*Exit.*

Abo. He speaks you very fair.

Oro. He means me fair.

Abo. If he should not, my Lord.

Oro. If, he should not.
I'll not suspect his Truth: but if I did,   60
What shall I get by doubting?

Abo. You secure, not to be disappointed: but
    besides,
There's this advantage in suspecting him:
When you put off the hopes of other men,
You will rely upon your God-like self:
And then you may be sure of liberty.

Oro. Be sure of liberty! what dost thou mean;
Advising to rely upon my self?
I think I may be sure on't: we must wait:
'Tis worth a little patience.   [*Turning to* Imoinda.

Abo. O my Lord!   71

Oro. What dost thou drive at?

Abo. Sir, another time,
You wou'd have found it sooner: but I see
Love has your Heart, and takes up all your thoughts.

Oro. And canst thou blame me?

Abo. Sir, I must not blame you.
But as our fortune stands there is a Passion
(Your pardon Royal Mistress, I must speak:)

That wou'd become you better than your Love: 80
A brave resentment; which inspir'd by you,
Might kindle, and diffuse a generous rage
Among the Slaves, to rouze and shake our Chains,
And struggle to be free.

   Oro. How can we help our selves?

   Abo. I knew you, when you wou'd have found a
     way.
How, help our selves! the very *Indians* teach us:
We need but to attempt our Liberty,
And we may carry it. We have Hands sufficient,
Double the number of our Masters force, 90
Ready to be employ'd. What hinders us
To set 'em then at work? we want but you,
To head our enterprize, and bid us strike.

   Oro. What wou'd you do?

   Abo. Cut our Oppressors Throats.

   Oro. And you wou'd have me joyn in your design
     of Murder?

   Abo. It deserves a better Name:
But be it what it will, 'tis justified
By self-defence, and natural liberty.

   Oro. I'll hear no more on 't. 100

   Abo. I am sorry for 't.

   Oro. Nor shall you think of it.

   Abo. Not think of it!

   Oro. No, I command you not.

   Abo. Remember Sir,
You are a Slave your self, and to command,
Is now anothers right. Not think of it!
Since the first moment they put on my Chains,
I've thought of nothing but the weight of 'em,
And how to throw 'em off: can yours sit easie? 110

   Oro. I have a sense of my condition,
As painfull, and as quick, as yours can be.
I feel for my *Imoinda* and my self;
Imoinda much the tenderest part of me.
But though I languish for my liberty,

I wou'd not buy it at the Christian Price
Of black Ingratitude: they shannot say,
That we deserv'd our Fortune by our Crimes.
Murder the Innocent!

   Abo. The Innocent!   120

   Oro. These men are so, whom you wou'd rise
      against:
If we are Slaves, they did not make us Slaves;
But bought us in an honest way of trade:
As we have done before 'em, bought and sold
Many a wretch, and never thought it wrong.
They paid our Price for us, and we are now
Their Property, a part of their Estate,
To manage as they please. Mistake me not,
I do not tamely say, that we should bear
All they could lay upon us: but we find   130
The load so light, so little to be felt,
(Considering they have us in their power,
And may inflict what grievances they please)
We ought not to complain.

   Abo. My Royal Lord!
You do not know the heavy Grievances,
The Toyls, the Labours, weary Drudgeries,
Which they impose; Burdens, more fit for Beasts,
For senseless Beasts to bear, than thinking Men.
Then if you saw the bloody Cruelties,   140
They execute on every slight offence;
Nay sometimes in their proud, insulting sport:
How worse than Dogs, they lash their fellow Crea-
    tures:
Your heart wou'd bleed for 'em. O cou'd you know
How many Wretches lift their Hands and Eyes
To you, for their Relief.

   Oro. I pity 'em,
And wish I cou'd with honesty do more.

   Abo. You must do more, and may, with honesty.
O Royal Sir, remember who you are,   150
A Prince, born for the good of other Men:

Whose God-like Office is to draw the Sword
Against Oppression, and set free Mankind:
And this, I'm sure, you think Oppression now.
What tho' you have not felt these miseries,
Never believe you are oblig'd to them:
They have their selfish reasons, may be, now,
For using of you well: but there will come
A time, when you must have your share of 'em.

  Oro. You see how little cause I have to think so:
Favour'd in my own Person, in my Friends;   161
Indulg'd in all that can concern my care,
In my *Imoinda's* soft Society.   [*Embracing her.*

  Abo. And therefore wou'd you lye contented down
In the forgetfulness, and arms of Love,
To get young Princes for 'em?

  Oro. Say'st thou! ha!

  Abo. Princes, the Heirs of Empire, and the last
Of your illustrious Lineage, to be born
To pamper up their Pride, and be their Slaves?   170

  Oro. *Imoinda*! save me, save me from that thought.

  Imo. There is no safety from it: I have long
Suffer'd it with a Mother's labouring pains;
And can no longer. Kill me, kill me now,
While I am blest, and happy in your love;
Rather than let me live to see you hate me:
As you must hate me; me, the only cause;
The Fountain of these flowing miseries:
Dry up this Spring of Life, this pois'nous Spring,
That swells so fast, to overwhelm us all.   180

  Oro. Shall the dear Babe, the eldest of my hopes,
Whom I begot a Prince, be born a Slave?
The treasure of this Temple was design'd
T' enrich a Kingdoms Fortune: shall it here
Be seiz'd upon by vile unhallow'd hands,
To be employ'd in uses most prophane?

  Abo. In most unworthy uses; think of that;
And while you may, prevent it. O my Lord!
Rely on nothing that they say to you.

They speak you fair, I know, and bid you wait.   190
But think what 'tis to wait on promises:
And promises of Men, who know no tye
Upon their words, against their interest:
And where's their interest in freeing you?

  Imo. O! where indeed, to lose so many Slaves?

  Abo. Nay grant this Man, you think so much your
      Friend,
Be honest, and intends all that he says:
He is but one; and in a Government,
Where, he confesses, you have Enemies,
That watch your looks: what looks can you put on,
To please these men, who are before resolv'd   201
To read 'em their own way? alas! my Lord!
If they incline to think you dangerous,
They have their knavish Arts to make you so,
And then who knows how far their cruelty
May carry their revenge?

  Imo. To every thing,
That does belong to you; your Friends, and me;
I shall be torn from you, forc't away,
Helpless, and miserable: shall I live   210
To see that day agen?

  Oro. That day shall never come.

  Abo. I know you are perswaded to believe
The Governour's arrival will prevent
These mischiefs, and bestow your liberty:
But who is sure of that? I rather fear
More mischiefs from his coming: he is young,
Luxurious, passionate, and amorous:
Such a Complexion, and made bold by power,
To countenance all he is prone to do,   220
Will know no bounds, no law against his Lusts:
If, in a fit of his Intemperance,
With a strong hand, he should resolve to seize,
And force my Royal Mistress from your Arms,
How can you help your self?

  Oro. Ha! thou hast rouz'd

The Lion in his den, he stalks abroad,
And the wide Forest trembles at his roar.
I find the danger now: my Spirits start
At the alarm, and from all quarters come   230
To Man my Heart, the Citadel of love.
Is there a power on Earth to force you from me?
And shall I not resist it? not strike first
To keep, to save you? to prevent that curse?
This is your Cause, and shall it not prevail?
O! you were born all ways to conquer me.
Now I am fashion'd to thy purpose: speak,
What Combination, what Conspiracy,
Woud'st thou engage me in? I'le undertake
All thou woud'st have me now for liberty,   240
For the great Cause of Love and Liberty.

 Abo. Now, my great Master, you appear your
  self.
And since we have you joyn'd in our design,
It cannot fail us. I have muster'd up
The choicest Slaves, Men who are sensible
Of their condition, and seem most resolv'd:
They have their several parties.

 Oro. Summon 'em,
Assemble 'em: I will come forth, and shew
My self among 'em: if they are resolv'd,   250
I'le lead their foremost resolutions.

 Abo. I have provided those will follow you.

 Oro. With this reserve in our proceeding still,
The means that lead us to our liberty,
Must not be bloody.

 Abo. You command in all.
We shall expect you, Sir.

 Oro. You shannot long.

   [*Exeunt* Oroonoko *and* Imoinda *at* **one** *Door*,
    Aboan *at another.*

SCENE III.

[Welldon *coming in before Mrs.* Lackit.]

Wid. These unmannerly *Indians* were something unseasonable, to disturb us just in the nick, Mr. *Welldon*: but I have the Parson within call still, to doe us the good turn.

Well. We had best stay a little I think, to see things settled agen, had not we? Marriage is a serious thing you know.

Wid. What do you talk of a serious thing, Mr. *Welldon*? I think you have found me sufficiently serious: I have marry'd my Son to your Sister, to pleasure you: and now I come to claim your promise to me, you tell me marriage is a serious thing.   12

Well. Why, is it not?

Wid. Fidle fadle, I know what it is: 'tis not the first time I have been marry'd, I hope: but I shall begin to think, you don't design to do fairly by me, so I shall.

Well. Why indeed, Mrs. *Lackit*, I am afraid I can't do as fairly as I wou'd by you. 'Tis what you must know, first or last; and I shou'd be the worst man in the world to conceal it any longer; therefore I must own to you, that I am marry'd already.   22

Wid. Marry'd! you don't say so I hope! how have you the Conscience to tell me such a thing to my face! have you abus'd me then, fool'd and cheated me? What do you take me for, Mr. *Welldon*? do you think I am to be serv'd at this rate? but you shan't find me the silly creature, you think me: I wou'd have you to know, I understand better things, than to ruine my Son without a valuable consideration. If I can't have you, I can keep my Money. Your Sister shan't have the catch of him, she expected: I won't part with a Shilling to 'em.   33

Well. You made the match your self, you know, you can't blame me.

Wid. Yes, yes, I can, and do blame you:
You might have told me before you were marry'd.

Well. I wou'd not have told you now; but you
follow'd me so close, I was forc'd to 't: indeed I am
marry'd in *England*; but 'tis, as if I were not; for
I have been parted from my Wife a great while:
and to do reason on both sides, we hate one another
heartily. Now I did design, and will marry you still,
if you'll have a little patience.　　　　　　44

Wid. A likely business truly.

Well. I have a Friend in *England* that I will write
to, to poyson my Wife, and then I can marry you
with a good Conscience, if you love me, as you say
you do; you'll consent to that, I'm sure.

Wid. And will he do it, do you think?　　50

Well. At the first word, or he is not the Man I
take him to be.

Wid. Well, you are a dear Devil, Mr. *Welldon*:
And wou'd you poyson your Wife for me?

Well. I wou'd do any thing for you.

Wid. Well, I am mightily oblig'd to you.
But 'twill be a great while before you can have an
answer of your Letter.

Well. 'Twill be a great while indeed.

Wid. In the mean time, Mr. *Welldon*——　　60

Well. Why in the mean time——
Here's company: we'll settle that within.
I'll follow you.　　　　　　　[*Exit* Widow.

　　　　　　[*Enter* Stanmore.]

Stan. So, Sir, you carry your business swimmingly:
You have stolen a Wedding, I hear.

Well. Ay, my Sister is marry'd: and I am very near
being run away with my self.

Stan. The Widow will have you then.

Well. You come very seasonably to my rescue:
Jack Stanmore is to be had, I hope.　　70

Stan. At half an hours warning.

Well. I must advise with you.　　　　[*Exeunt.*

SCENE IV.

[Oroonoko *with* Aboan, Hottman, *Slaves.*]

Oro. Impossible! nothing 's impossible:
We know our strength only by being try'd.
If you object the Mountains, Rivers, Woods
Unpassable, that lie before our March:
Woods we can set on fire: we swim by nature:
What can oppose us then, but we may tame?
All things submit to vertuous industry:
That we can carry with us, that is ours.

Slave. Great Sir, we have attended all you said,
With silent joy and admiration: 10
And, were we only Men, wou'd follow such,
So great a Leader, thro' the untry'd World.
But, oh! consider we have other Names,
Husbands and Fathers, and have things more dear
To us, than Life, our Children, and our Wives,
Unfit for such an expedition:
What must become of them?

Oro.   We wonnot wrong
The virtue of our Women, to believe
There is a Wife among 'em, wou'd refuse
To share her Husband's fortune. What is hard,
We must make easie to 'em in our Love: while we
         live,
And have our Limbs, we can take care for them;
Therefore I still propose to lead our march
Down to the Sea, and plant a Colony:
Where, in our native innocence, we shall live
Free, and be able to defend our selves;
Till stress of weather, or some accident
Provide a Ship for us.

Abo.   An accident! the luckiest accident presents
         it self: 30
The very Ship, that brought and made us Slaves,
Swims in the River still; I see no cause
But we may seize on that.

Oro. It shall be so:
There is a justice in it pleases me.
Do you agree to it?   [*To the Slaves.*
  Omn. We follow you.
  Oro. You do not relish it.   [*To* Hottman.
  Hott. I am afraid
You'll find it difficult, and dangerous.   40
  Abo. Are you the Man to find the danger first?
You shou'd have giv'n example. Dangerous!
I thought you had not understood the word;
You, who wou'd be the Head, the Hand, and
          Heart:
Sir, I remember you, you can talk well;
I wonnot doubt but you'll maintain your word.
  Oro. This Fellow is not right, I'll try him further.
                                      [*To* Aboan.

The danger will be certain to us all:
And Death most certain in miscarrying.
We must expect no mercy, if we fail: 50
Therefore our way must be not to expect:
We'll put it out of expectation,
By Death upon the place, or Liberty.
There is no mean, but Death or Liberty.
There's no Man here, I hope, but comes prepar'd
For all that can befall him.
  Abo. Death is all:
In most conditions of humanity
To be desir'd but to be shun'd in none:
The remedy of many; wish of some;   60
And certain end of all.
If there be one among us, who can fear
The face of Death appearing like a Friend,
As in this cause of Honour Death must be:
How will he tremble, when he sees him drest
In the wild fury of our Enemies,
In all the terrors of their cruelty?
For now if we shou'd fall into their hands,
Cou'd they invent a thousand murd'ring ways,

By racking Torments, we shou'd feel 'em all.   70
  Hott. What will become of us?
  Oro. Observe him now.
                    [To Aboan *concerning* Hottman.
I cou'd die altogether, like a Man:
As you, and you, and all of us may do:
But who can promise for his bravery
Upon the Rack? where fainting, weary life,
Hunted thro' every Limb, is forc'd to feel
An agonizing death of all its parts?
Who can bear this? resolve to be empal'd?
His Skin flead off, and roasted yet alive?   80
The quivering flesh torn from his broken Bones,
By burning Pincers? who can bear these Pains?
  Hott. They are not to be borne.
             [Discovering all the confusion of fear.
  Oro. You see him now, this Man of mighty words!
  Abo. How his Eyes roul!
  Oro. He cannot hide his fear:
I try'd him this way, and have found him out.
  Abo. I cou'd not have believ'd it. Such a Blaze,
And not a spark of Fire!
  Oro. His violence,   90
Made me suspect him first: now I'm convinc'd.
  Abo. What shall we do with him?
  Oro. He is not fit——
  Abo. Fit! hang him, he is only fit to be
Just what he is, to live and die a Slave:
The base Companion of his servile Fears.
  Oro. We are not safe with him.
  Abo. Do you think so?
  Oro. He'll certainly betray us.
  Abo. That he shan't: 100
I can take care of that: I have a way
To take him off his evidence.
  Oro. What way?
  Abo. I'll stop his mouth before you, stab him
    here,

And then let him inform.

       [Going to stab Hottman, Oroonoko *holds him.*

  Oro. Thou art not mad?

  Abo. I wou'd secure our selves.

  Oro. It shannot be this way; nay cannot be:
His Murder wou'd alarm all the rest,
Make 'em suspect us of Barbarity,   110
And, may be, fall away from our design.
We'll not set out in Blood: we have, my Friends,
This Night to furnish what we can provide,
For our security, and just defence.
If there be one among us, we suspect
Of baseness, or vile fear, it will become
Our common care, to have our Eyes on him:
I wonnot name the Man.

  Abo. You ghess at him.   *[To* Hottman.

  Oro. To morrow, early as the breaking day,   120
We rendezvous behind the Citron Grove.
That Ship secur'd, we may transport our selves
To our respective homes: my Fathers Kingdom
Shall open her wide arms to take you in,
And nurse you for her own, adopt you all,
All, who will follow me.

  Omn. All, all follow you.

  Oro. There I can give you all your liberty;
Bestow its Blessings, and secure 'em yours.
There you shall live with honour, as becomes   130
My Fellow-sufferers, and worthy Friends:
This if we do succeed: But if we fall
In our attempt, 'tis nobler still to dye,
Than drag the galling yoke of slavery.

                     [Exeunt Omnes.

ACT IV.

SCENE I.

[Welldon *and* Jack Stanmore.]

Well. You see, honest *Jack*, I have been industrious for you: you must take some pains now to serve your self.

J. Stan. Gad, Mr. *Welldon*, I have taken a great deal of pains: And if the Widow speaks honestly, faith and troth, She'll tell you what a pains-taker I am.

Well. Fie, fie, not me: I am her Husband you know:
She won't tell me what pains you have taken with her: Besides, she takes you for me.   10

J. Stan. That 's true: I forgot you had marry'd her. But if you knew all——

Well. 'Tis no matter for my knowing all: if she does——

J. Stan. Ay, ay, she does know, and more than ever she knew since she was a woman, for the time; I will be bold to say: for I have done——

Well. The Devil take you, you'll never have done.

J. Stan. As old as she is, she has a wrincle behind more than she had, I believe——   20
For I have taught her, what she never knew in her life before.

Well. What care I what wrincles she has? or what you have taught her? If you'll let me advise you, you may; if not, you may prate on, and ruine the whole design.

J. Stan. Well, well, I have done.

Well. No body, but your Cozin, and you, and I, know any thing of this matter. I have marry'd Mrs. *Lackit*; and put you to bed to her, which she knows nothing of, to serve you: in two or three days

I'll bring it about so, to resign up my claim, with her consent, quietly to you. 33

J. Stan. But how will you do it?

Well. That must be my business: in the mean time, if you should make any noise, 'twill come to her Ears, and be impossible to reconcile her.

J. Stan. Nay, as for that, I know the way to reconcile her, I warrant you.

Well. But how will you get her Money? I am marry'd to her. 41

J. Stan. That I don't know indeed.

Well. You must leave it to me, you find, all the pains I shall put you to, will be to be silent: you can hold your Tongue for two or three days?

J. Stan. Truly, not well, in a matter of this nature: I should be very unwilling to lose the reputation of this nights work, and the pleasure of telling.

Well. You must mortifie that vanity a little: you will have time enough to brag, and lie of your Manhood, when you have her in a bare-fac'd condition to disprove you. 52

J. Stan. Well, I'll try what I can do: the hopes of her Money must do it.

Well. You'll come at night again? 'tis your own business.

J. Stan. But you have the credit on 't.

Well. 'Twill be your own another day, as the Widow says. Send your Cozin to me: I want his advise. 60

J. Stan. I want to be recruited, I'm sure, a good Breakfast, and to Bed: She has rock'd my Cradle sufficiently. [*Exit.*

Well. She wou'd have a Husband; and if all be, as he says, she has no reason to complain: but there's no relying on what the Men say upon these occasions: they have the benefit of their bragging, by recommending their abilities to other Women: theirs is a trading Estate, that lives upon credit, and increases

by removing it out of one Bank into another. Now
poor Women have not these opportunities: we must
keep our stocks dead by us, at home, to be ready for
a purchase, when it comes, a Husband, let him be
never so dear, and be glad of him: or venture our
Fortunes abroad on such rotten security, that the
principal and interest, nay very often our persons
are in danger. If the Women wou'd agree (which
they never will) to call home their Effects, how many
proper Gentlemen wou'd sneak into another way of
living, for want of being responsible in this? then
Husbands wou'd be cheaper. Here comes the
Widow, she'll tell truth: she'll not bear false Witness
against her own interest, I know.   83

[Enter Widow Lackit.]

Well. Now, Mrs. *Lackit.*

Wid. Well, well, *Lackit,* or what you will now;
now I am marry'd to you: I am very well pleas'd
with what I have done, I assure you.

Well. And with what I have done too, I hope.

Wid. Ah! Mr. *Welldon!* I say nothing, but you're
a dear Man, and I did not think it had been in you.

Well. I have more in me than you imagine.   91

Wid. No, no, you can't have more than I imagine:
'tis impossible to have more: you have enough for
any Woman, in an honest way, that I will say for you.

Well. Then I find you are satisfied.

Wid. Satisfied! no indeed; I'm not to be satisfied,
with you or without you: to be satisfied, is to have
enough of you; now, 'tis a folly to lye: I shall never
think I can have enough of you. I shall be very fond
of you: wou'd you have me fond of you? What do
you do to me, to make me love you so well?   101

Well. Can't you tell what?

Wid. Go; there's no speaking to you: you bring
all the Blood of ones body into ones face, so you do:
why do you talk so?

Well. Why, how do I talk?

Wid. You know how: but a little colour becomes me,
I believe: how do I look to day?

Well. O! most lovingly, most amiably.

Wid. Nay, this can't be long a secret, I find,   110
I shall discover it by my Countenance.

Well. The Women will find you out, you look so cheerfully.

Wid. But do I, do I really look so cheerfully, so amiably? there's no such paint in the World as the natural glowing of a Complexion. Let 'em find me out, if they please, poor Creatures, I pity 'em: they envy me, I'm sure, and wou'd be glad to mend their looks upon the same occasion. The young jil-flirting Girls, forsooth, believe nobody must have a Husband, but themselves; but I wou'd have 'em to know there are other things to be taken care of, besides their green Sickness.   123

Well. Ay, sure, or the Physicians wou'd have but little practise.

Wid. Mr. *Welldon,* what must I call you: I must have some pretty fond name or other for you: what shall I call you?

Well. I thought you lik'd my own name.

Wid. Yes, yes, I like it, but I must have a nick-name for you: most Women have nick-names for their Husbands——   132

Well. Cuckold.

Wid. No, no, but 'tis very pretty before company; It looks negligent, and is the fashion, you know.

Well. To be negligent of their Husbands, it is indeed.

Wid. Nay then, I won't be in the fashion; for I can never be negligent of dear Mr. *Welldon*: and to convince you, here's something to encourage you not to be negligent of me.   141

[*Gives him a Purse and a little Casket.*

Five hundred pounds in Gold in this; and Jewels
to the value of five hundred pounds more in this.

[*Welldon opens the Casket.*

Well. Ay, marry, this will encourage me indeed.

Wid. There are comforts in marrying an elderly
Woman, Mr. *Welldon.* Now a young Woman wou'd
have fancy'd she had paid you with her person, or
had done you the favour.

Well. What do you talk of young Women? you
are as young as any of 'em, in every thing, but their
folly and ignorance.   151

Wid. And do you think me so? but I have no
reason to suspect you. Was not I seen at your house
this Morning, do you think?

Well. You may venture again: you'll come at
night, I suppose.

Wid. O dear! at night? so soon?

Well. Nay, if you think it so soon.

Wid. O! no, it is not for that Mr. *Welldon*, but——

Well. You won't come then.   160

Wid. Won't! I don't say, I won't: that is not a
          word for a Wife:
If you command me——

Well. To please your self.

Wid. I will come to please you.

Well. To please your self, own it.

Wid. Well, well, to please my self then, you're
the strangest Man in the world, nothing can 'scape
you: you'll to the bottom of every thing.

[*Enter* Daniel, Lucia *following.*]

Dan. What wou'd you have? what do you follow
me for?   170

Luc. Why, mayn't I follow you? I must follow
you now all the World over.

Dan. Hold you, hold you there: not so far by
a mile or two; I have enough of your Company
already, byrlady; and something to spare: you may

go home to your Brother, an you will, I have no
farther to do with you.

Wid. Why, *Daniel*, Child, thou art not out of thy
wits sure, art thou?

Dan. Nay, marry, I don't know; but I am very
near it, I believe: 180
I am alter'd for the worse mightily since you saw me;
And she has been the cause of it there.

Wid. How so, Child?

Dan. I told you before what wou'd come on't, of
putting me to bed to a strange Woman: but you wou'd
not be said nay.

Wid. She is your Wife now, Child, you must love
her.

Dan. Why, so I did, at first.

Wid. But you must love her always.   190

Dan. Always! I lov'd her as long as I cou'd,
Mother, and as long as loving was good, I believe,
for I find now I don't care a fig for her.

Luc. Why, you lubberly, slovenly, misbegotten
Blockhead——

Wid. Nay, Mistress *Lucy*, say any thing else, and
spare not: but as to his begetting, that touches me,
he is as honestly begotten, tho' I say it, that he is the
worse agen.

Luc. I see all good nature is thrown away upon
you——   201

Wid. It was so with his Father before him: he
takes after him.

Luc. And therefore I will use you, as you deserve,
you Tony.

Wid. Indeed he deserves bad enough; but don't
call him out of his name, his name is *Daniel*, you know.

Dan. She may call me Hermophrodite, if she will,
For I hardly know whether I'm a Boy or a Girl.

Well. A Boy, I warrant thee, as long as thou liv'st.

Dan. Let her call me what she pleases, Mother,
'Tis not her Tongue that I am afraid of.   212

Luc. I will make such a Beast of thee, such a Cuckold!

Wid. O, pray, no, I hope; do nothing rashly, Mrs. *Lucy.*

Luc. Such a Cuckold will I make of thee!

Dan. I had rather be a Cuckold, than what you wou'd make of me in a week, I'm sure: I have no more Manhood left in me already, than there is, saving the mark, in one of my Mothers old under Petticoats here.   222

Wid. Sirrah, Sirrah, meddle with your Wife's Petticoats, and let your Mother's alone, you ungracious Bird, you.   [*Beats him.*

Dan. Why is the Devil in the Woman? what have I said now?

Do you know, if you were ask'd, I trow? but you are all of a bundle; ev'n hang together; he that unties you, makes a Rod for his own tail; and so he will find it, that has any thing to do with you.   230

Wid. Ay, Rogue enough, you shall find it: I have a Rod for your Tail still.

Dan. No, Wife and I care not.

Wid. I'll swinge you into better manners, you Booby.   [*Beats him off,* Exit.

Well. You have consummated our project upon him.

Luc. Nay, if I have a limb of the Fortune, I care not who has the whole body of the Fool.

Well. That you shall, and a large one, I promise you.   241

Luc. Have you heard the news? they talk of an English Ship in the River.

Well. I have heard on't; and am preparing to receive it, as fast as I can.

Luc. There's something the matter too with the Slaves,

Some disturbance or other; I don't know what 'tis.

Well. So much the better still:

We fish in troubled waters:
We shall have fewer Eyes upon us.   250
Pray, go you home, and be ready to assist me in your
    part of the design.
    Luc. I can't fail in mine.   [*Exit.*
    Well. The Widow has furnish'd me, I thank her,
    to carry it on.
Now I have got a Wife, 'tis high time to think of
    getting a Husband.
I carry my fortune about me;
A thousand Pounds in Gold and Jewels.
Let me see——
'Twill be a considerable trust:
And I think, I shall lay it out to advantage.

        [*Enter* Stanmore.]

    Stan. So *Welldon*, *Jack* has told me his success; and
his hopes of marrying the Widow by your means.   261
    Well. I have strain'd a point, *Stanmore*, upon your
    account,
To be serviceable to your Family.
    Stan. I take it upon my account; and am very
    much oblig'd to you.
But here we are all in an uproar.
    Well. So they say, what's the matter?
    Stan. A Mutiny among the Slaves:
Oroonoko is at the head of 'em,
Our Governour is gone out with his rascally Militia
    against 'em,
What it may come to no body knows.   270
    Well. For my part, I shall do as well as the rest:
but I'm concern'd for my Sister, and Cozen, whom
I expect in the Ship from *England*.
    Stan. There's no danger of 'em.
    Well. I have a thousand pounds here, in Gold and
Jewels, for my Cozens use, that I wou'd more parti-
cularly take care of: 'tis too great a summ to venture
at home; and I wou'd not have her wrong'd of it:

therefore, to secure it, I think my best way will be, to put it into your keeping.   280

Stan. You have a very good opinion of my honesty.
    [*Takes the Purse and Casket.*

Well. I have indeed, if any thing shou'd happen to me, in this bustle, as no body is secure of accidents, I know you will take my Cozen into your protection and care.

Stan. You may be sure on 't.

Well. If you hear she is dead, as she may be, then I desire you to accept of the Thousand Pound, as a Legacy, and Token of my Friendship; my Sister is provided for.   290

Stan. Why, you amaze me: but you are never the nearer dying, I hope, for makeing your Will?

Well. Not a jot; but I love to be before-hand with Fortune.

If she comes safe; this is not a place for a single Woman, you know;

Pray see her marryed as soon as you can.

Stan. If she be as handsom as her Picture, I can promise her a Husband.

Well. If you like her, when you see her, I wish nothing so much as to have you marry her your self.   300

Stan. From what I have heard of her, and my Engagements to you, it must be her Fault, if I don't: I hope to have her from your own Hand.

Well. And I hope to give her to you, for all this.

Stan. Ay, ay, hang these melancholy Reflections. Your Generosity has engag'd all my Services.

Well. I always thought you worth making a Friend.

Stan. You shan't find your good Opinion thrown away upon me: I am in your Debt, and shall think so as long as I live.   [*Exeunt.*   310

SCENE II.

Enter on one side of the Stage Oroonoko, Aboan, *with the*
Slaves, Imoinda *with a Bow and Quiver, the Women, some*
leading, others carrying their Children upon their Backs.

Oro. The Women, with their Children, fall behind.
Imoinda you must not expose your self:
Retire, my Love: I almost fear for you.

Imo. I fear no Danger: Life, or Death, I will
Enjoy with you.

Oro. My Person is your Guard.

Abo. Now, Sir, blame your self: if you had not
prevented my cutting his Throat, that Coward there
had not discover'd us; He comes now to upbraid you.

Enter on the other side Governour, *talking to* Hottman,
with his Rabble.

Gov. This is the very thing I would have wisht.   10
Your honest Service to the Government [*To* Hottman.
Shall be rewarded with your Liberty.

Abo. His honest Service! call it what it is,
His Villany, the Service of his Fear:
If he pretends to honest Services,
Let him stand out, and meet me, like a Man.
                                        [*Advancing.*

Oro. Hold, you: And you who come against us, hold;
I charge you in a general good to all,
And wish I cou'd command you, to prevent
The bloody Havock of the murdering Sword.   20
I wou'd not urge Destruction uncompell'd:
But if you follow Fate, you find it here.
The Bounds are set, the Limits of our Lives:
Between us lyes the gaping Gulph of Death,
To swallow all: who first advances——
                            [*Enter the Capt. with his Crew.*

Capt. Here, here, here they are, Governour:
What! seize upon my Ship!
Come, Boys, fall on—— [*Advancing first,* **Oroonoko** *kills him.*

Oro. Thou art fall'n indeed. Thy own Blood be
    upon thee.

Gov. Rest it there: he did deserve his Death.   30
Take him away.   *[the Body remov'd.*
You see, Sir, you and those mistaken Men
Must be our Witnesses, we do not come
As Enemies, and thirsting for your Blood.
If we desir'd your Ruin, the Revenge
Of our Companions Death, had pusht it on.
But that we over-look, in a Regard
To common Safety, and the publick Good.

Oro. Regard that publick good: draw off your Men,
And leave us to our Fortune: We're resolv'd.   40

Gov. Resolv'd, on what? your Resolutions
Are broken, overturn'd, prevented, lost:
What Fortune now can you raise out of 'em?
Nay, grant we shou'd draw off, what can you do?
Where can you move? What more can you resolve?
Unless it be to throw your selves away.
Famine must eat you up, if you go on.
You see, our Numbers cou'd with Ease compel
What we request: And what do we request?
Only to save your selves?   50
        [The Women with their Children gathering about
           the Men.

Oro. I'le hear no more.

Women. Hear him, hear him. He takes no care of us.

Gov. To those poor wretches who have been
    seduc'd,
And led away, to all, and every one,
We offer a full Pardon——

Oro. Then fall on.   *[Preparing to Engage.*

Gov. Lay hold upon't, before it be too late,
Pardon and Mercy.
       [The Women clinging about the Men, they leave
          Oroonoko, and fall upon their Faces crying
          out for Pardon.

Slaves. Pardon, Mercy, Pardon.

Oro. Let 'em go all: now, Governour, I see,   60
I own the Folly of my Enterprise,
The Rashness of this Action, and must blush
Quite thro' this Vail of Night, a whitely Shame,
To think I cou'd design to make those free,
Who were by Nature Slaves; Wretches design'd
To be their Masters Dogs, and lick their Feet.
Whip, whip 'em to the Knowledge of your Gods,
Your Christian Gods, who suffer you to be
Unjust, dishonest, cowardly, and base,
And give 'em your Excuse for being so.   70
I wou'd not live on the same Earth with Creatures,
That only have the Faces of their Kind:
Why shou'd they look like Men, who are not so?
When they put off their Noble Natures, for
The groveling qualities of down-cast Beasts,
I wish they had their Tails.

Abo. Then we shou'd know 'em.

Oro. We were too few before for Victory:
We're still enow to dye.   [*To* Imoinda, Aboan.

Blanford *Enters.*

Gov. Live, Royal Sir;   80
Live, and be happy long on your own Terms:
Only consent to yield, and you shall have
What Terms you can propose, for you, and yours.

Oro. Consent to yield! shall I betray my self?

Gov. Alas! we cannot fear, that your small Force,
The Force of two, with a weak Womans Arm,
Shou'd Conquer us. I speak in the regard
And Honour of your Worth, in my desire
And forwardness to serve so great a Man.
I wou'd not have it lie upon my Thoughts,   90
That I was the occasion of the fall
Of such a Prince, whose Courage carried on
In a more Noble Cause, wou'd well deserve
The Empire of the World.

Oro. You can speak fair.

Gov. Your Undertaking, tho' it wou'd have brought
So great a loss to us, we must all say
Was generous, and noble; and shall be
Regarded only as the Fire of Youth,
That will break out sometimes in Gallant Sort.   100
We'll think it but the Natural Impulse,
A rash impatience of Liberty:
No otherwise.

Oro. Think it what you will.
I was not born to render an Account
Of what I do, to any but my self.

[*Blanford comes forward.*

Blan. I'm glad you have proceeded by fair means.

[*To the Governour.*

I came to be a Mediator.

Gov. Try what you can work upon him.

Oro. Are you come against me too?   110

Blan. Is this to come against you?

[*Offering his Sword to* Oroon.

Unarm'd to put my self into your Hands?
I come, I hope, to serve you.

Oro. You have serv'd me;
I thank you for 't: And I am pleas'd to think
You were my Friend, while I had need of one:
But now 'tis past; this farewell; and be gone.

[*Embraces him.*

Blan. It is not past, and I must serve you still.
I wou'd make up these Breaches, which the Sword
Will widen more; and close us all in Love.   120

Oro. I know what I have done, and I shou'd be
A Child to think they ever can Forgive:
Forgive! Were there but that, I wou'd not live
To be Forgiven: Is there a Power on Earth,
That I can ever need forgiveness from?

Blan. You sha' not need it.

Oro. No, I wonnot need it.

Blan. You see he offers you your own Conditions,

For you, and yours.

   Oro. I must Capitulate?   130
Precariously Compound, on stinted Terms,
To save my Life?

   Blan. Sir, he Imposes none.
You make 'em for your own Security.
If your great Heart cannot descend to treat,
In adverse Fortune, with an Enemy:
Yet sure, your Honour 's safe, you may accept
Offers of Peace, and Safety from a Friend.

   Gov. He will rely on what you say to him:
                              [To Blanford.
Offer him what you can, I will confirm,   140
And make all good: Be you my Pledge of Trust.

   Blan. I'le answer with my Life for all he says.

   Gov. Ay, do, and pay the Forfeit if you please.
                                  [Aside.

   Blan. Consider, Sir, can you consent to throw
That Blessing from you, you so hardly found,
                            [Of Imoinda.
And so much valu'd once?

   Oro. Imoinda! Oh!
'Tis She that holds me on this Argument
Of tedious Life: I cou'd resolve it soon,
Were this curst Being only in Debate.   150
But my *Imoinda* struggles in my Soul:
She makes a Coward of me: I Confess
I am afraid to part with Her in Death:
And more afraid of Life to lose Her here.

   Blan. This way you must lose her, think upon
The weakness of her Sex, made yet more weak
With her Condition, requiring Rest,
And soft Indulging Ease, to nurse your Hopes,
And make you a glad Father.

   Oro. There I feel a Father's Fondness, and a
     Husband's Love.   160
They seize upon my Hart, strain all its strings,
To pull me to 'em, from my stern resolve.

Husband, and Father! All the melting Art
Of Eloquence lives in those softning Names.
Methinks I see the Babe, with Infant Hands,
Pleading for Life, and begging to be born:
Shall I forbid his Birth? Deny him Light?
The Heavenly Comforts of all-cheering Light?
And make the Womb the Dungeon of his Death?
His Bleeding Mother his sad Monument?   170
These are the Calls of Nature, that call loud,
They will be heard, and Conquer in their Cause:
He must not be a Man, who can resist 'em.
No, my *Imoinda*! I will venture all
To save thee, and that little Innocent:
The World may be a better Friend to him,
Than I have found it. Now I yield my self:
                              [*Gives up his Sword.*
The Conflict's past, and we are in your Hands.
          [*Several Men get about* Oroonoko, *and* Aboan,
                    and seize 'em.

  Gov. So you shall find you are: Dispose of them,
As I commanded you.   180
  Blan. Good Heaven forbid! You cannot mean——
  Gov. This is not your Concern.
                    [*To* Blanford *who goes to* Oroonoko.
I must take care of you.   [*To* Imoinda.
  Imo. I'm at the end
Of all my Care: Here I will die with him.
                              [*Holding* Oroonoko.
  Oro. You shall not force her from me.
                              [*he holds her.*
  Gov. Then I must   [*they force her from him.*
Try other means, and Conquer Force by Force:
Break, cut off his Hold, bring her away.
  Imo. I do not ask to Live, kill me but here.   190
  Oro. O Bloody Dogs! Inhumane Murderers.
          [Imoinda *forct out of one Door by the Governour,
            and others.* Oroonoko *and* Aboan *hurried
            out of another.*   [*Exeunt Omnes.*

ACT V SCENE I.

Enter Stanmore, Lucia, Charlott.

Stan. 'Tis strange we cannot hear of him: Can no body give an account of him?

Luc. Nay, I begin to despair: I give him for gone.

Stan. Not so I hope.

Luc. There are so many disturbances in this devilish Country! Wou'd we had never seen it.

Stan. This is but a cold welcome for you, Madam, after so troublesome a Voyage.

Char. A cold Welcome indeed, Sir, without my Cousin *Welldon.* He was the best Friend I had in the World.   11

Stan. He was a very good Friend of yours indeed, Madam.

Luc. They have made him away, Murder'd him for his Mony, I believe, he took a considerable Sum out with him, I know, that has been his Ruin.

Stan. That has done him no Injury, to my knowledge: For this Morning he put into my Custody what you speak of, I suppose a Thousand Pounds, for the use of this Lady.   20

Char. I was always oblig'd to him: and he has shown his Care of me, in placing my little Affairs in such Honourable Hands.

Stan. He gave me a particular charge of you, Madam, very particular, so particular, that you will be surpriz'd when I tell you.

Char. What, pray Sir.

Stan. I am engag'd to get you a Husband, I promis'd that before I saw you; and now I have seen you, you must give me leave to offer you my self.   30

Luc. Nay, Cozen, never be coy upon the matter, to my Knowledge my Brother always design'd you for this Gentleman.

Stan. You hear, Madam, he has given me his

Interest, and 'tis the Favour I wou'd have begg'd of him. Lord! you are so like him——

Char. That you are oblig'd to say you like me for his Sake.

Stan. I shou'd be glad to love you for your own. 39

Char. If I shou'd consent to the fine things you can say to me, how wou'd you look at last, to find 'em thrown away upon an old Acquaintance?

Stan. An old Acquaintance!

Char. Lord, how easily are you Men to be impos'd upon! I am no Cozen newly arriv'd from *England*, not I; but the very *Welldon* you wot of.

Stan. *Welldon*!

Char. Not murdered, nor made away, as my Sister wou'd have you believe, but am in very good Health, your old friend in Breeches that was, and now your humble Servant in Petticoats. 51

Stan. I'm glad we have you agen.
But what service can you do me in Petticoats, pray?

Char. Can't you tell what?

Stan. Not I, by my troth: I have found my Friend, and lost my Mistress, it seems, which I did not expect from your Petticoats.

Char. Come, come, you have had a Friend of your Mistress long enough, 'tis high time now to have a Mistress of your Friend. 60

Stan. What do you say?

Char. I am a Woman, Sir.

Stan. A Woman!

Char. As arrant a Woman as you wou'd have had me but now, I assure you.

Stan. And at my Service?

Char. If you have any for me in Petticoats.

Stan. Yes, yes, I shall find you employment.

Char. You wonder at my proceeding, I believe.

Stan. 'Tis a little extraordinary, indeed. 70

Char. I have taken some pains to come into your Favour.

Stan. You might have had it cheaper a great deal.

Char. I might have marry'd you in the Person of my English Cozen, but cou'd not consent to cheat you, ev'n in the thing I had a mind to.

Stan. 'Twas done as you do every thing.

Char. I need not tell you, I made that little Plot, and carry'd it on only for this Opportunity. I was resolv'd to see whether you lik't me as a Woman, or not: if I had found you indifferent, I wou'd have indeavour'd to have been so too: but you say you like me, and therefore I have ventur'd to discover the truth.　　　　　　　　　　　　　　　84

Stan. Like you! I like you so well, that I'm afraid you won't think Marriage a proof on 't: shall I give you any other?

Char. No, no, I'm inclin'd to believe you, and that shall convince me. At more leisure I'le satisfie you how I came to be in Mans Cloaths, for no ill I assure you, tho' I have happen'd to play the Rogue in 'em: They have assisted me in marrying my Sister, and have gone a great way in befriending your Cozen *Jack* with the Widow. Can you forgive me for pimping for your Family?　　　　　　　　95

Enter Jack Stanmore.

Stan. So, *Jack*, what News with you?

J. Stan. I am the forepart of the Widow, you know, She 's coming after with the body of the Family, the young Squire in her hand, my Son-in-Law that is to be, with the Help of Mr. *Welldon.*　　　　　100

Char. Say you so, Sir? [*Clapping* Jack *upon the back.*

Enter Widow Lackitt *with her Son* Daniel.

Wid. So, Mrs. *Lucy*, I have brought him about agen, I have Chastis'd him, I have made him as supple as a Glove for your wearing, to pull on, or throw off, at your pleasure. Will you ever Rebell again? Will you, Sirrah? But come, come, down on your Marrow

Bones, and ask her forgiveness. [Daniel *Kneels.* Say after me, pray forsooth Wife.

Dan. Pray forsooth Wife.   109

Luc. Well, well, this is a Day of good Nature, and so I take you into Favour: But first take the Oath of Allegiance.   [*He kisses her Hand, and rises.* If ever you do so agen——

Dan. Nay Marry if I do, I shall have the worst on 't.

Luc. Here 's a Stranger, forsooth, wou'd be glad to be known to you, a Sister of mine, pray salute her.
                                        [*starts at* Charlott.

Wid. Your Sister! Mrs. *Lucy*! what do you mean? This is your Brother, Mr. *Welldon*; do you think I do not know Mr. *Welldon*?

Luc. Have a care what you say: This Gentleman 's about Marrying her: You may spoil all.   121

Wid. Fiddle faddle, what! You wou'd put a trick upon me.

Char. No faith, Widow, the Trick is over, it has taken sufficiently, and now I will teach you the Trick, To prevent your being Cheated another time.

Wid. How! Cheated, Mr. *Welldon*!

Char. Why, ay, you will always take things by the wrong Handle, I see you will have me Mr. *Welldon*: I grant you, I was Mr. *Welldon* a little while to please you, or so: But Mr. *Stanmore* here has perswaded me into a Woman agen.   132

Wid. A Woman! Pray let me speak with you.
                                        [*drawing her aside.*
You are not in earnest, I hope? A Woman!

Char. Really a Woman.

Wid. Gad's my Life! I could not be cheated in every thing: I know a Man from a Woman at these Years, or the Devil 's in 't.
Pray, did not you marry me?

Char. You wou'd have it so.   140

Wid. And did not I give you a Thousand Pounds this Morning?

Char. Yes indeed, 'twas more than I deserv'd:
But you had your Penniworth for your Penny, I
suppose:
You seem'd to be pleas'd with your Bargain.

Wid. A rare Bargain I have made on 't, truly. I
have laid out my Money to fine purpose upon a
Woman.

Char. You wou'd have a Husband, and I provided
for you as well as I cou'd.　　　　　　　　　151

Wid. Yes, yes, you have provided for me.

Char. And you have paid me very well for 't, I
thank you.

Wid. 'Tis very well; I may be with Child too, for
ought I know, and may go look for the Father.

Char. Nay, if you think so, 'tis time to look about
you indeed. Ev'n make up the matter as well as
you can, I advise you as a Friend, and let us live
Neighbourly and Lovingly together.　　　　　160

Wid. I have nothing else for it, that I know now.

Char. For my part, Mrs. *Lackit*, your Thousand
Pounds will Engage me not to laugh at you. Then
my Sister is Married to your Son, he is to have half
your Estate, I know; and indeed they may live upon
it, very comfortably to themselves, and very creditably
to you.

Wid. Nay, I can blame no body but my self.

Char. You have enough for a Husband still,
And that you may bestow upon honest *Jack Stanmore.*

Wid. Is he the Man then?　　　　　　　　　171

Char. He is the Man you are oblig'd to.

J. Stan. Yes, Faith, Widow, I am the Man: I have
done fairly by you, you find, you know what you have
to trust to before hand.

Wid. Well, well, I see you will have me, ev'n Marry
me, and make an end of the business.

Stan. Why, that 's well said, now we are all agreed,
and all provided for. [*A Servant Enters to* Stanmore.

Serv. Sir, Mr. *Blandford* desires you to come to him,

and bring as many of your Friends as you can with
you.   182
   Stan. I come to him. You'll all go along with me.
Come, young Gentleman, Marriage is the fashion,
you see, you must like it now.
   Dan. If I don't, how shall I help my self?
   Luc. Nay, you may hang your self in the Noose,
if you please,
But you'll never get out on't with struggling.
   Dan. Come then, let's ev'n jogg on in the old Road.
Cuckold, or worse, I must be now contented: 191
I'm not the first has marry'd, and repented.

                                                      [*Exeunt.*

SCENE II.

Enter Governour *with* Blanford, *and Planters.*

   Blan. Have you no Reverence of future Fame?
No awe upon your actions, from the Tongues,
The censuring Tongues of Men, that will be free?
If you confess Humanity, believe
There is a God, or Devil, to reward
Our doings here, do not provoke your Fate.
The Hand of Heaven is arm'd against these Crimes,
With hotter Thunder-Bolts, prepar'd to shoot,
And Nail you to the Earth, a sad Example;
A Monument of Faithless Infamy.   10

Enter Stanmore, J. Stanmore, Charlott, Lucy, Widow, *and* Daniel.

So, *Stanmore,* you I know, the Women too
Will join with me: 'Tis *Oroonoko's* Cause,
A Lover's Cause, a wretched Woman's Cause
That will become your Intercession.

                                                [*To the Women.*
   1. *Plan.* Never mind 'em, Governour; he ought to
be made an Example for the good of the Plantation.

2. *Plan.* Ay, ay, 'twill frighten the Negroes from
Attempting the like agen.

1. *Plan.* What rise against their Lords and Masters!
At this rate no Man is safe from his own Slaves.   20

2. *Plan.* No, no more he is. Therefore, one and all,
Governour, we declare for Hanging.

Om. Plan. Ay, ay, hang him, hang him.

Wid. What! Hang him! O! forbid it, Governour.

Char. ⎱
Lucy. ⎰ We all Petition for him.

J. Stan. They are for a Holy-Day; Guilty or not,
Is not the Business, hanging is their Sport.

Blan. We are not sure so wretched, to have these,
The Rabble, judge for us; the changing Croud;
The Arbitrary Guard of Fortune's Power,   30
Who wait to catch the Sentence of her Frowns,
And hurry all to ruine she Condemns.

Stan. So far from farther Wrong, that 'tis a shame
He shou'd be where he is: Good Governour
Order his Liberty: He yielded up
Himself, his all, at your discretion.

Blan. Discretion! no, he yielded on your word;
And I am made the cautionary Pledge,
The Gage, and Hostage of your keeping it.
Remember, Sir, he yielded on your word;   40
Your Word! which honest Men will think should be
The last resort of Truth, and trust on Earth:
There's no Appeal beyond it, but to Heaven:
An Oath is a recognisance to Heaven,
Binding us over, in the Courts above,
To plead to the Indictment of our Crimes.
That those who 'scape this World should suffer
    there.
But in the common Intercourse of Men,
(Where the dread Majesty is not Invoak'd,
His Honour not immediately concern'd,   50
Not made a Party in our Interests,)
Our Word is all to be rely'd upon.

Wid. Come, come, You'l be as good as your Word, we know.

Stan. He 's out of all power of doing any harm now, If he were dispos'd to it.

Char. But he is not dispos'd to it.

Blan. To keep him, where he is, will make him soon Find out some desperate way to Liberty: He'll hang himself, or dash out his mad Brains.

Char. Pray try him by gentle Means: 60 We'll all be Sureties for him.

Om. All, all.

Luc. We will all answer for him now.

Gov. Well, you will have it so, do what you please, Just what you will with him, I give you leave. [*Exit.*

Blan. We thank you, Sir; this way, pray come with me. [*Exeunt.*

> *The Scene drawn shews* Oroonoko *upon his Back, his Legs and Arms stretcht out, and chain'd to the Ground.*

Enter Blanford, Stanmore, *&c.*

Blan. O miserable Sight! help every one, Assist me all to free him from his Chains.

[*They help him up, and bring him forward, looking down.*
Most injur'd Prince! how shall we clear our selves? We cannot hope you will vouchsafe to hear, 70 Or credit what we say in the Defence, And Cause of our suspected Innocence.

Stan. We are not guilty of your Injuries, No way consenting to 'em; but abhor, Abominate, and loath this Cruelty.

Blan. It is our Curse, but make it not our Crime. A heavy curse upon us, that we must Share any thing in common, ev'n the Light, The Elements, and Seasons, with such Men, Whose Principles, like the fam'd Dragons Teeth, 80 Scatter'd, and sown, wou'd shoot a Harvest up Of fighting Mischiefs, to confound themselves,

And ruin all about 'em.

 Stan. Profligates!
Whose bold *Titanian* Impiety
Wou'd once agen pollute their Mother Earth,
Force her to teem with her old monstrous Brood
Of Gyants, and forget the Race of Men.

 Blan. We are not so: believe us innocent.
We come prepar'd with all our Services,   90
To offer a Redress of your base Wrongs.
Which way shall we employ 'em?

 Stan. Tell us, Sir, if there is any thing that can
  attone;
But nothing can; that may be some amends——

 Oro. If you wou'd have me think you are not all
Confederates, all accessory to
The base Injustice of your Governour:
If you wou'd have me live, as you appear
Concern'd for me, if you wou'd have me live
To thank, and bless you, there is yet a Way 100
To tye me ever to your honest Love:
Bring my *Imoinda* to me; give me her,
To charm my Sorrows, and, if possible,
I'le sit down with my Wrongs; never to rise
Against my Fate, or think of Vengeance more.

 Blan. Be satisfi'd, you may depend upon us,
We'll bring her safe to you, and suddenly.

 Char. We wonnot leave you in so good a work.

 Wid. No, no, we'll go with you.

 Blan. In the mean time   110
Endeavour to forget, Sir, and forgive:
And hope a better Fortune.   [*Exeunt.*

Oroonoko alone.

 Oro. Forget! forgive! I must indeed forget,
When I forgive: but while I am a Man,
In Flesh, that bears the living mark of Shame,
The print of his dishonourable Chains,
My Memory still rousing up my Wrongs,

I never can forgive this Governour;
This Villain; the disgrace of Trust, and Place,
And just Contempt of delegated Power.   120
What shall I do? If I declare my self,
I know him, he will sneak behind his Guard
Of Followers, and brave me in his Fears.
Else, Lyon like, with my devouring Rage,
I wou'd rush on him, fasten on his Throat,
Tear wide a Passage to his treacherous Heart,
And that way lay him open to the World. [*Pausing.*
If I shou'd turn his Christian Arts on him,
Promise him, speak him fair, flatter, and creep,
With fawning Steps, to get within his Faith,   130
I cou'd betray him then, as he has me.
But am I sure by that to right my self?
Lying 's a certain Mark of Cowardise:
And when the Tongue forgets its Honesty,
The Heart and Hand may drop their functions
          too,
And nothing worthy be resolv'd, or done.
The Man must go together, bad, or good:
In one part frail, he soon grows weak in all.
Honour shou'd be concern'd in Honour's Cause,
That is not to be cur'd by Contraries,   140
As Bodies are, whose Health is often drawn
From rankest Poysons. Let me but find out
An honest Remedy, I have the Hand,
A ministring Hand, that will apply it Home. [*Exit.*

S C E N E *the Governour's House.*

Enter Governour.

Gov. I wou'd not have her tell me, she consents:
In Favour of the Sexes Modesty,
That still shou'd be presum'd, because there is
A greater Impudence in owning it,
Than in allowing all that we can do.
This Truth I know, and yet against my self,

(So unaccountable are Lovers ways)
I talk, and lose the Opportunities,
Which Love, and she expects I shou'd employ:
Ev'n she expects: for when a Man has said   10
All that is fit, to save the Decency,
The Women know the rest is to be done.
I wonnot disappoint her.   [*Going.*

 Enter to him Blanford, *the Stanmores, Daniel,*
  Mrs. Lackit, Charlot, *and* Lucy.

 Wid. O Governour! I'm glad we have lit upon you.
 Gov. Why! what's the Matter?
 Char. Nay, nothing extraordinary. But one good
Action
Draws on another. You have given the Prince his
  Freedom:
Now we come a begging for his Wife:
You won't refuse us.
 Gov. Refuse you. No, no, what have I to do to
refuse you?   21
 Wid. You won't refuse to send her to him, she
means.
 Gov. I send her to him!
 Wid. We have promis'd him to bring her.
 Gov. You do very well; 'tis Kindly done of you:
Ev'n carry her to him, with all my Heart.
 Luc. You must tell us where she is.
 Gov. I tell you! why, don't you know?
 Blan. Your Servants say she's in the House.   30
 Gov. No, no, I brought her home at first indeed;
but I thought it wou'd not look well to keep her here:
I remov'd her in the Hurry, only to take care of her.
What! she belongs to you: I have nothing to do with
her.
 Char. But where is she now, Sir?
 Gov. Why, Faith, I can't say certainly: you'll hear
of her at *Parham* House, I suppose: there, or there-
abouts: I think I sent her there.

Blan. I'le have an Eye on him.   [*Aside.* 40
                                [*Exeunt all but the Governour.*

Gov. I have ly'd my self into a little Time;
And must employ it: they'll be here agen;
But I must be before 'em.

                [*Going out, he meets* Imoinda, *and seizes her.*
Are you come!
I'le court no longer for a Happiness
That is in mine own keeping: you may still
Refuse to grant, so I have Power to take.
The Man that asks deserves to be deny'd.

                [*She disengages one hand, and draws his Sword
                from his side upon him, Governour starts and
                retires,* Blanford *enters behind him.*

Imo. He does indeed, that asks unworthily.
Blan. You hear her, Sir, that asks unworthily. 50
Gov. You are no Judge.
Blan. I am of my own Slave.
Gov. Begone, and leave us.
Blan. When you let her go.
Gov. To fasten upon you.
Blan. I must defend my self.
Imo. Help, Murder, help.

                [Imoinda *retreats towards the door, favour'd by*
                Blanford, *when they are clos'd, she throws
                down the Sword, and runs out. Governour
                takes up the Sword, they fight, close, and fall,*
                Blanford *upon him. Servants enter, and part
                'em.*

Gov. She shannot 'scape me so. I've gone too far,
Not to go farther. Curse on my delay:
But yet she is, and shall be in my Power.   60

Blan. Nay then it is the War of Honesty:
I know you, and will save you from your self.

Gov. All come along with me.   [*Exeunt.*

SCENE *the last.*

Oroonoko *Enters.*

Oro. To Honour bound! and yet a Slave to Love!
I am distracted by their rival Powers,
And both will be obey'd. O great Revenge!
Thou Raiser, and Restorer of faln Fame!
Let me not be unworthy of thy Aid,
For stopping in thy course: I still am thine:
But can't forget I am *Imoinda*'s too.
She calls me from my Wrongs to rescue her.
No man condemn me, who has never felt
A womans Power, or try'd the Force of Love: 10
All tempers yield, and soften in those fires:
Our Honours, Interests resolving down,
Run in the gentle Current of our Joys:
But not to sink, and drown our Memory:
We mount agen to Action, like the Sun,
That rises from the Bosom of the Sea,
To run his glorious Race of Light anew,
And carry on the World. Love, Love will be
My first Ambition, and my Fame the next.

Aboan *enters bloody.*

My Eyes are turn'd against me, and combine   20
With my sworn Enemies, to represent
This spectacle of Honour. *Aboan*!
My ever faithful Friend!
    Abo. I have no Name,
That can distinguish me from the vile Earth,
To which I'm going: a poor, abject worm,
That crawl'd awhile upon a bustling World,
And now am trampled to my Dust agen.
    Oro. I see thee gasht, and mangled.
    Abo. Spare my shame   30
To tell how they have us'd me: but believe
The Hangman's Hand wou'd have been merciful.
Do not you scorn me, Sir, to think I can

313   L

Intend to live under this Infamy.
I do not come for pity, to complain.
I've spent an honourable Life with you;
The earliest Servant of your rising Fame,
And wou'd attend it with my latest care:
My life was yours, and so shall be my death.
You must not live.   40
Bending and sinking, I have dragg'd my Steps
Thus far, to tell you that you cannot live:
To warn you of those Ignominious wrongs,
Whips, Rods, and all the Instruments of death,
Which I have felt, and are prepar'd for you.
This was the Duty that I had to pay.
'Tis done, and now I beg to be discharg'd.
    Oro. What shall I do for thee?
    Abo. My Body tires,
And wonnot bear me off to Liberty: 50
I shall agen be taken, made a Slave.
A Sword, a Dagger yet wou'd rescue me.
I have not Strength to go to find out Death:
You must direct him to me.
    Oro. Here he is,   [*Gives him a Dagger.*
The only present I can make thee now:
And next the honourable means of Life,
I wou'd bestow the honest means of Death.
    Abo. I cannot stay to thank you. If there is
A Being after this, I shall be yours   60
In the next World, your faithful Slave agen.
This is to try [*Stabs himself.*] I had a living Sense
Of all your royal Favours, but this last
Strikes through my Heart. I wonnot say farewell,
For you must follow me.   [*dyes.*
    Oro. In Life, and death,
The Guardian of my Honour! follow thee!
I shou'd have gone before thee: then perhaps
Thy Fate had been prevented. All his Care
Was to preserve me from the barbarous Rage   70
That wrong'd him, only for being mine.

Why, why, you Gods! Why am I so accurst,
That it must be a Reason of your Wrath,
A Guilt, a Crime sufficient to the Fate
Of any one, but to belong to me?
My Friend has found it, and my Wife will soon:
My Wife! the very Fear's too much for Life:
I can't support it. Where? *Imoinda*! Oh!
   [*Going out, she meets him, running into his Arms.*
Thou bosom Softness! Down of all my Cares!
I cou'd recline my thoughts upon this Breast 80
To a forgetfulness of all my Griefs,
And yet be happy: but it wonnot be.
Thou art disorder'd, pale, and out of Breath!
If Fate pursues thee, find a shelter here.
What is it thou woud'st tell me?
 Imo. 'Tis in vain to call him Villain.
 Oro. Call him Governour: is it not so?
 Imo. There's not another sure.
 Oro. Villain's the common name of Mankind here:
But his most properly. What! what of him? 90
I fear to be resolv'd, and must enquire.
He had thee in his Power.
 Imo. I blush to think it.
 Oro. Blush! to think what?
 Imo. That I was in his Power.
 Oro. He cou'd not use it?
 Imo. What can't such men do?
 Oro. But did he? durst he?
 Imo. What he cou'd, he dar'd.
 Oro. His own Gods damn him then: for ours have
  none, 100
No Punishment for such unheard-of Crimes.
 Imo. This Monster, cunning in his Flatteries,
When he had weary'd all his useless Arts,
Leapt out, fierce as a beast of prey, to seize me.
I trembled, fear'd.
 Oro. I fear, and tremble now.
What cou'd preserve thee? what deliver thee?

Imo. That worthy Man, you us'd to call your
    Friend——

Oro. Blanford.

Imo. Came in, and sav'd me from his Rage.   110

Oro. He was a Friend indeed to rescue thee!
And for his sake, I'le think it possible
A Christian may be yet an honest man.

Imo. O! did you know what I have strugl'd through,
To save me yours, sure you wou'd promise me
Never to see me forc't from you agen.

Oro. To promise thee! O! do I need to promise?
But there is now no farther use of Words.
Death is security for all our fears.

                  [Shews Aboan's *body on the floor.*
And yet I cannot trust him.   120

Imo. Aboan!

Oro. Mangled, and torn, resolv'd to give me time
To fit my self for what I must expect,
Groan'd out a warning to me, and expir'd.

Imo. For what you must expect?

Oro. Wou'd that were all.

Imo. What! to be butcher'd thus——

Oro. Just as thou see'st.

Imo. By barbarous Hands, to fall at last their Prey!

Oro. I have run the Race with Honour, shall I now
Lag, and be overtaken at the Goal?   131

Imo. No.

Oro. I must look back to thee.   *[Tenderly.*

Imo. You shannot need.
I'm always present to your purpose, say,
Which way wou'd you dispose me?

Oro. Have a care,
Thou'rt on a Precipice, and dost not see
Whither that question leads thee. O! too soon
Thou dost enquire what the assembled Gods   140
Have not determin'd, and will latest doom.
Yet this I know of Fate, this is most certain,
I cannot, as I wou'd, dispose of thee:

And, as I ought, I dare not. Oh *Imoinda*!

Imo. Alas! that sigh! why do you tremble so?
Nay then 'tis bad indeed, if you can weep.

Oro. My Heart runs over, if my gushing Eyes
Betray a weakness which they never knew,
Believe, thou, only thou cou'dst cause these tears.
The Gods themselves conspire with faithless Men
To our destruction.   151

Imo. Heaven and Earth our Foes!

Oro. It is not always granted to the great,
To be most happy: If the angry Pow'rs
Repent their Favours, let 'em take 'em back:
The hopes of Empire, which they gave my youth,
By making me a Prince, I here resign.
Let 'em quench in me all those glorious Fires,
Which kindled at their beams: that lust of Fame,
The Fevor of Ambition, restless still,   160
And burning with the sacred Thirst of Sway,
Which they inspir'd, to qualifie my Fate,
And make me fit to govern under them,
Let 'em extinguish. I submit my self
To their high pleasure, and devoted Bow
Yet lower, to continue still a Slave;
Hopeless of liberty: and if I cou'd
Live after it, wou'd give up Honour too,
To satisfie their Vengeance, to avert
This only Curse, the curse of losing thee.   170

Imo. If Heav'n cou'd be appeas'd, these cruel
      Men
Are not to be entreated, or believ'd:
O! think on that, and be no more deceiv'd.

Oro. What can we do?

Imo. Can I do any thing?

Oro. But we were born to suffer.

Imo. Suffer both,
Both die, and so prevent 'em.

Oro. By thy Death!
O! let me hunt my travel'd Thoughts again;   180

Range the wide waste of desolate despair;
Start any hope. Alas! I lose my self,
'Tis Pathless, Dark, and Barren all to me.
Thou art my only guide, my light of Life,
And thou art leaving me: Send out thy Beams
Upon the Wing; let 'em fly all around,
Discover every way: Is there a dawn,
A glimmering of comfort? the great God,
That rises on the World, must shine on us.

 Imo. And see us set before him.   190

 Oro. Thou bespeak'st, and goes before me.

 Imo. So I wou'd, in Love:
In the dear unsuspected part of Life,
In Death for Love. Alas! what hopes for me?
I was preserv'd but to acquit my self,
To beg to die with you.

 Oro. And can'st thou ask it?
I never durst enquire into my self
About thy fate, and thou resolv'st it all.

 Imo. Alas! my Lord! my Fate's resolv'd in yours.

 Oro. O! keep thee there: Let not thy Virtue
  shrink   201
From my support, and I will gather strength,
Fast as I can to tell thee——

 Imo. I must die.
I know 'tis fit, and I can die with you.

 Oro. O! thou hast banisht hence a thousand
  fears,
Which sicken'd at my Heart, and quite unman'd me.

 Imo. Your fear's for me, I know you fear'd my
  strength,
And cou'd not overcome your tenderness,
To pass this Sentence on me: and indeed 210
There you were kind, as I have always found you,
As you have ever been: for tho' I am
Resign'd, and ready to obey my doom,
Methinks it shou'd not be pronounc'd by you.

 Oro. O! that was all the labour of my grief.

My heart, and tongue forsook me in the strife:
I never cou'd pronounce it.
 Imo. I have for you, for both of us.
 Oro. Alas! for me! my death
I cou'd regard as the last Scene of life,   220
And act it thro' with joy, to have it done.
But then to part with thee——
 Imo. 'Tis hard to part.
But parting thus, as the most happy must,
Parting in death, makes it the easier.
You might have thrown me off, forsaken me,
And my misfortunes: that had been a death
Indeed of terror, to have trembled at.
 Oro. Forsaken! thrown thee off!
 Imo. But 'tis a pleasure more than life can give, 230
That with unconquer'd Passion to the last,
You struggle still, and fain wou'd hold me to you.
 Oro. Ever, ever, and let those stars, which are my
   Enemies,
Witness against me in the other World,
If I wou'd leave this Mansion of my Bliss,
To be the brightest Ruler of their Skies.
O! that we cou'd incorporate, be one,
          [Embracing her.
One Body, as we have been long one Mind:
That blended so, we might together mix,
And losing thus our Beings to the World, 240
Be only found to one another Joys.
 Imo. Is this the way to part?
 Oro. Which is the way?
 Imo. The God of Love is blind, and cannot find it.
But quick, make haste, our Enemies have Eyes
To find us out, and shew us the worst way
Of parting; think on them.
 Oro. Why dost thou wake me?
 Imo. O! no more of Love.
For if I listen to you, I shall quite   250
Forget my Dangers, and desire to live.

I can't live yours.   *[Takes up the Dagger.*

   Oro. There all the Stings of Death
Are shot into my Heart—what shall I do?

   Imo. This Dagger will instruct you.   *[Gives it him.*

   Oro. Ha! this Dagger!
Like Fate, it points me to the horrid Deed.

   Imo. Strike, strike it home, and bravely save us
    both.
There is no other Safety.

   Oro. It must be——   260
But first a dying Kiss——   *[Kisses her.*
This last Embrace——   *[Embracing her.*
And now——

   Imo. I'm ready.

   Oro. O! where shall I strike?
Is there a smallest grain of that lov'd Body
That is not dearer to me than my Eyes,
My bosom'd Heart, and all the live Blood there?
Bid me cut off these Limbs, hew off these Hands,
Dig out these Eyes, tho' I wou'd keep them last   270
To gaze upon thee: but to murder thee!
The Joy, and Charm of every ravisht Sense,
My Wife! forbid it Nature.

   Imo. 'Tis your Wife,
Who on her knees conjures you. O! in time
Prevent those Mischeifs that are falling on us.
You may be hurry'd to a shameful Death,
And I too drag'd to the vile Governour:
Then I may cry aloud: when you are gone,
Where shall I find a Friend agen to save me?   280

   Oro. It will be so. Thou unexampled Virtue!
Thy Resolution has recover'd mine:
And now prepare thee.

   Imo. Thus with open Arms,
I welcome you, and Death.
       *[He drops his Dagger as he looks on her, and
        throws himself on the Ground.*

   Oro. I cannot bear it.

O let me dash against this Rock of Fate.
Dig up this Earth, tear, tear her Bowels out,
To make a Grave, deep as the Center down,
To swallow wide, and bury us together.   290
It wonnot be. O! then some pitying God
(If there be one a Friend to Innocence)
Find yet a way to lay her Beauties down
Gently in Death, and save me from her Blood.

Imo. O rise, 'tis more than Death to see you
    thus.
I'le ease your Love, and do the Deed my self——
       [She takes up the Dagger, he rises in haste to take
         it from her.

Oro. O! hold, I charge thee, hold.

Imo. Tho' I must own
It wou'd be nobler for us both from you.

Oro. O! for a Whirlwind's Wing to hurry us   300
To yonder Clif, which frowns upon the Flood:
That in Embraces lockt we might plunge in,
And perish thus in one anothers Arms.

Imo. Alas! what shout is that?

Oro. I see 'em coming.
They shannot overtake us. This last Kiss.
And now farewell.

Imo. Farewel, farewel for ever.

Oro. I'le turn my Face away, and do it so.
Now, are you ready?   310

Imo. Now. But do not grudge me
The Pleasure in my Death of a last look,
Pray look upon me——Now I'm satisfied.

Oro. So Fate must be by this.
       [Going to stab her, he stops short, she lays her
         hands on his, in order to give the blow.

Imo. Nay then I must assist you.
And since it is the common Cause of both,
'Tis just that both shou'd be employ'd in it.
Thus, thus 'tis finisht, and I bless my Fate,
       [Stabs her self.

That where I liv'd, I die, in these lov'd Arms,   [*Dyes.*
    Oro. She's gone. And now all's at an End with me.
Soft, lay her down. O we will part no more.   321
                                    [*Throws himself by her.*
But let me pay the tribute of my Grief,
A few sad Tears to thy lov'd Memory,
And then I follow——   [*Weeps over her.*
But I stay too long.   [*A noise agen.*
The Noise comes nearer. Hold, before I go,
There's something wou'd be done. It shall be so.
And then, *Imoinda*, I'le come all to thee.   [*Rises.*

    [*Blanford, and his party, enters before the* Governour
        and his party, Swords drawn on both sides.

    Gov. You strive in vain to save him, he shall die.
    Blan. Not while we can defend him with our
        lives.   330
    Gov. Where is he?
    Oro. Here's the Wretch whom you wou'd have.
Put up your Swords, and let not civil broils
Engage you in the cursed cause of one,
Who cannot live, and now entreats to die.
This object will convince you.
    Blan. 'Tis his Wife!   [*They gather about the Body.*
Alas! there was no other Remedy.
    Gov. Who did the bloody Deed?
    Oro. The Deed was mine: 340
Bloody I know it is, and I expect
Your Laws shou'd tell me so. Thus self-condemn'd,
I do resign my self into your Hands,
The Hands of Justice——But I hold the Sword
For you—and for my self.
            [*Stabs the Governour, and himself, then throws
                himself by* Imoinda's *Body.*
    Stan. He has kill'd the Governour, and stab'd
        himself.
    Oro. 'Tis as it shou'd be now. I have sent his Ghost
To be a Witness of that Happiness

In the next World, which he deny'd us here.　[*Dyes.*

　Blan. I hope there is a place of Happiness　　350
In the next World for such exalted Virtue.
Pagan, or Unbeliever, yet he liv'd
To all he knew: And if he went astray,
There's Mercy still above to set him right.
But Christians guided by the Heavenly Ray
Have no excuse if we mistake our Way.

FINIS.

EPILOGUE,

Written by Mr. *Congreve*, and Spoken by Mrs. *Verbruggen*.

You see, we try all Shapes, and Shifts, and Arts,
To tempt your Favours, and regain your Hearts.
We weep, and laugh, joyn mirth and grief together,
Like Rain and Sunshine mixt, in April weather.
Your different tasts divide our Poet's Cares:
One foot the Sock, t'other the Buskin wears:
Thus, while he strives to please, he's forc'd to do't,
Like Volscius, *hip-hop, in a single Boot.*
Criticks, he knows, for this may damn his Books:
But he makes Feasts for Friends, and not for Cooks.   10
Tho' Errant-Knights of late no favour find,
Sure you will be to Ladies-Errant kind.
To follow Fame, Knights-Errant make profession: ⎫
We Damsels flye, to save our Reputation: ⎬
So they, their Valour show, we, our Discretion.   ⎭
To Lands of Monsters, and fierce Beasts they go: ⎫
We, to those Islands, where Rich Husbands grow: ⎬
Tho' they're no Monsters, we may make 'em so.   ⎭
If they're of English *growth, they'll bear't with patience:*
But save us from a Spouse of Oroonoko's *Nations!*   20
Then bless your Stars, you happy London *Wives,*
Who love at large, each day, yet keep your lives:
Nor envy poor Imoinda's *doating blindness,*
Who thought her Husband kill'd her out of kindness.
Death with a Husband ne'er had shewn such Charms,
Had she once dy'd within a Lover's Arms.

8 *Volscius*] In *The Rehearsal*, by the Duke of Buckingham, 1671. In Act III, Scene II, Prince Volscius starts putting on his boots to sally forth, but meanwhile falls in love, and goes off the stage while ' one hasty Boot is on, the other off '. As Mr. Bayes remarks, ' To go off hip hop, hip hop, upon this occasion, is a thousand times better than **any** conclusion in the world, I gad.'

Her error was from ignorance proceeding:
Poor Soul! she wanted some of our Town Breeding.
Forgive this Indians fondness of her Spouse;
Their Law no Christian Liberty allows: 30
Alas! they make a Conscience of their Vows!
If Virtue in a Heathen be a fault;
Then Damn the Heathen School, where she was taught.
She might have learn'd to Cuckold, Jilt, and Sham,
Had Covent-Garden been in Surinam.

FINIS.

THE
FAIR PENITENT.
A
TRAGEDY.

As it is Acted at the

NEW THEATRE
IN
Little Lincolns-Inn-Fields.

By Her MAJESTY's SERVANTS.

Written by *N. ROWE*, Esq;

Quin morere, ut merita es, ferroque averte dolorem.
Virg. Æn. Lib. 4.

LONDON,
Printed for *Jacob Tonson*, within *Grays-Inn Gate* next
Grays-Inn Lane. 1703.

TO HER

G R A C E

THE

DUTCHESS

OF

O R M O N D.

MADAM,

The Privilege of Poetry (or it may be the Vanity of
the Pretenders to it) has given 'em a kind of Right
to pretend, at the same time, to the Favour of those,
whom their high Birth and excellent Qualities have
plac'd in a very distinguishing manner above the rest
of the World. If this be not a receiv'd Maxim, yet
I am sure I am to wish it were, that I may have at
least some kind of Excuse for laying this Tragedy at
Your Grace's Feet. I have too much reason to fear
that it may prove but an indifferent Entertainment
to Your Grace, since if I have any way succeeded
in it, it has been in describing those violent Passions
which have been always Strangers to so happy a
Temper, and so noble and so exalted a Virtue as Your
Grace is Mistress of. Yet for all this, I cannot but
confess the Vanity which I have, to hope that there
may be something so moving in the Misfortunes and
Distress of the Play, as may be not altogether unworthy of Your Grace's Pity. This is one of the main
Designs of Tragedy, and to excite this generous Pity

Dutchess of Ormond] The second wife of the Duke of
Ormonde, Mary, the eldest surviving daughter of the first
Duke of Beaufort. She died in 1733, when her husband
was in exile, after having taken part in the rebellion of
1715. In 1733 the Duke was residing at Avignon.

in the greatest Minds, may pass for some kind of Success in this way of Writing. I am sensible of the Presumption I am guilty of by this Hope, and how much it is that I pretend to in Your Grace's Approbation; if it be my good Fortune to meet with any little Share of it, I shall always look upon it as much more to me than the general Applause of the Theatre, or even the Praise of a good Critick. Your Grace's Name is the best Protection this Play can hope for, since the World, ill natur'd as it is, agrees in an universal Respect and Deference for Your Grace's Person and Character. In so censorious an Age as this is, where Malice furnishes out all the Publick Conversations, where every Body pulls and is pull'd to pieces of course, and where there is hardly such a thing as being merry, but at another's Expence; yet by a publick and uncommon Justice to the Dutchess of *Ormond*, Her Name has never been mention'd, but as it ought, tho' She has Beauty enough to provoke Detraction from the Fairest of Her own Sex, and Virtue enough to make the Loose and Dissolute of the other (a very formidable Party) Her Enemies. Instead of this they agree to say nothing of Her but what She deserves, That Her Spirit is worthy of Her Birth; Her Sweetness, of the Love and Respect of all the World; Her Piety, of Her Religion; Her Service, of Her Royal Mistress; and Her Beauty and Truth, of Her Lord; that in short every part of Her Character is Just, and that She is the best Reward for one of the greatest Hero's this Age has produc'd. This, Madam, is what You must allow People every where to say; those whom You shall leave behind You in *England* will have something further to add, the Loss we shall suffer by your Grace's Journey to *Ireland*; the Queen's Pleasure, and the Impatient

35 *Journey to Ireland*] In this year the Duke of Ormonde was made Viceroy of Ireland, succeeding the Earl of Rochester, the father of Anne Hyde, his first wife.

Wishes of that Nation are about to deprive us of Two of our Publick Ornaments. But there is no arguing against Reasons so prevalent as these. Those who shall lament your Grace's Absence will yet acquiesce in the Wisdom and Justice of Her Majesty's Choice: Among all whose Royal Favours none cou'd be so agreeable, upon a thousand Accounts, to that People, as the Duke of *Ormond.* With what Joy, what Acclamations shall they meet a Governor, who beside their former Obligations to His Family, has so lately ventur'd His Life and Fortune for their Preservation? What Duty, what Submission shall they not pay to that Authority which the Queen has delegated to a Person so dear to 'em? And with what Honour, what Respect shall they receive Your Grace, when they look upon You as the Noblest and Best Pattern Her Majesty cou'd send 'em, of her own Royal Goodness, and Personal Virtues? They shall behold Your Grace with the same Pleasure the *English* shall take when ever it shall be their good Fortune to see You return again to Your Native Country. In *England* Your Grace is become a Publick Concern, and as Your going away will be attended with a general Sorrow, so Your Return shall give as general a Joy; and to none of those many, more than to,

> *Madam,*
>
> > *Your Grace's*
> >
> > > *most Obedient, and*
> > >
> > > > *most Humble Servant,*
> > > >
> > > > > N. ROWE.

PROLOGUE,

Spoken by Mr. *Betterton*.

Long has the Fate of Kings and Empires been
The common Bus'ness of the Tragick Scene,
As if Misfortune made the Throne her Seat,
And none cou'd be unhappy but the Great.
Dearly, 'tis true, each buys the Crown he wears,
And many are the mighty Monarch's Cares:
By foreign Foes and home-bred Factions prest,
Few are the Joys he knows, and short his Hours of Rest.
Stories like these with Wonder we may hear,
But far remote, and in a higher Sphere,   10
We ne'er can pity what we ne'er can share.
Like distant Battles of the Pole and Swede,
Which frugal Citizens o'er Coffee read;
Careless for who shall fail or who succeed.
Therefore an humbler Theme our Author chose,
A melancholy Tale of private Woes:
No Princes here lost Royalty bemoan,
But you shall meet with Sorrows like your own;
Here see imperious Love his Vassals treat,
As hardly as Ambition does the Great;   20
See how succeeding Passions rage by turns,
How fierce the Youth with Joy and Rapture burns,
And how to Death, for Beauty lost, he mourns.

Let no nice Taste the Poet's Art arraign,
If some frail vicious Characters he feign:
Who Writes shou'd still let Nature be his Care,
Mix Shades with Lights, and not paint all things fair,
But shew you Men and Women as they are.

12 Swede] A reference to the ruinous wars of Charles XII against Augustus of Poland.

With Deference to the Fair he bad me say,
Few to Perfection ever found the Way; 30
Many in many Parts are known t' excel,
But 'twere too hard for One to act all well;
Whom justly Life should through each Scene commend,
The Maid, the Wife, the Mistress, and the Friend:
This Age, 'tis true, has one great Instance seen,
And Heav'n in Justice made that One a Queen.

Dramatis Personæ.

MEN.

Sciolto, a Nobleman of *Genoa*, Father to *Calista*. } Mr. *Bowman*.

Altamont, a young Lord, in Love with *Calista*, and design'd her Husband by *Sciolto*. } Mr. *Verbruggen*.

Horatio, his Friend.   Mr. *Betterton*.

Lothario, a young Lord, Enemy to *Altamont*. } Mr. *Powell*.

Rossano, his Friend.   Mr. *Baily*.

WOMEN.

Calista, Daughter to *Sciolto*.   Mrs. *Barry*.

Lavinia, Sister to *Altamont*, and Wife to *Horatio*. } Mrs. *Bracegirdle*.

Lucilla, Confident to *Calista*.   Mrs. *Prince*.

Servants to *Sciolto*.

SCENE, *Sciolto*'s Palace and Garden, with some part of the Street near it, in GENOA.

THE

FAIR PENITENT.

ACT I. SCENE I.

SCENE, *a Garden belonging to* Sciolto's *Palace.*

Enter Altamont *and* Horatio.

Alta. Let this auspicious Day be ever sacred,
No Mourning, no Misfortunes happen on it;
Let it be markt for Triumphs and Rejoycings;
Let happy Lovers ever make it holy,
Chuse it to bless their Hopes, and crown their
　Wishes,
This happy Day that gives me my *Calista.*

　Hor. Yes, *Altamont*; to Day thy better Stars
Are join'd, to shed their kindest Influence on thee:
Sciolto's noble Hand, that rais'd thee first,　　9
Half dead and drooping o'er thy Father's Grave,
Compleats its Bounty, and restores thy Name
To that high Rank and Lustre which it boasted,
Before ungrateful *Genoa* had forgot
The Merit of thy Godlike Father's Arms;
Before that Country which he long had serv'd,
In watchful Councils, and in Winter Camps,
Had cast off his white Age to Want and Wretchedness,
And made their Court to faction by his Ruin.

　Alt. Oh great *Sciolto*! oh my more than Father!
Let me not live, but at thy very Name　　20
My eager Heart springs up, and leaps with Joy.
When I forget the vast vast Debt I owe thee,
Forget! (but 'tis impossible) then let me
Forget the Use and Privilege of Reason.

Be driven from the Commerce of Mankind,
To wander in the Desart among Brutes,
To bear the various Fury of the Seasons,
The Night's unwholsom Dew and Noon-day's Heat,
To be the Scorn of Earth and Curse of Heav'n.

   Hor. So open, so unbounded was his Goodness, 30
It reach'd ev'n me, because I was thy Friend.
When that Great Man I lov'd, thy Noble Father,
Bequeath'd thy gentle Sister to my Arms,
His last dear Pledge and Legacy of Friendship,
That happy Tye made me *Sciolto*'s Son;
He call'd us his, and with a Parent's Fondness
Indulg'd us in his Wealth, blest us with Plenty,
Heal'd all our Cares, and sweeten'd Love it self.

   Alt. By Heav'n, he found my Fortunes so aban-
don'd,
That nothing but a Miracle could raise 'em; 40
My Father's Bounty, and the State's Ingratitude,
Had strip'd him bare, nor left him ev'n a Grave;
Undone my self, and sinking with his Ruin,
I had no Wealth to bring, nothing to succour him,
But fruitless Tears.

   Hor. Yet what thou cou'dst thou didst,
And didst it like a Son; when his hard Creditors,
Urg'd and assisted by *Lothario*'s Father,
(Foe to thy House, and Rival of their Greatness)
By Sentence of the cruel Law, forbid 50
His venerable Corps to rest in Earth,
Thou gav'st thy self a Ransom for his Bones;
With Piety uncommon, didst give up
Thy hopeful Youth to Slaves who ne'er knew Mercy,
Sour, unrelenting, Mony-loving Villains,
Who laugh at Human Nature and Forgiveness,
And are like Fiends the Factors for Destruction.
Heav'n, who beheld the pious Act, approv'd it,
And bad *Sciolto*'s Bounty be its Proxy,
To bless thy filial Virtue with Abundance. 60

   Alt. But see he comes, the Author of my Happiness,

The Man who sav'd my Life from deadly Sorrow,
Who bids my Days be blest with Peace and Plenty,
And satisfies my Soul with Love and Beauty.

Enter Sciolto, *he runs to* Altamont *and embraces him.*

Sci. Joy to thee, *Altamont*! Joy to my self!
Joy to this happy Morn, that makes thee mine,
That kindly grants what Nature had deny'd me,
And makes me Father of a Son like thee.

Alt. My Father! oh let me unlade my Breast,
Pour out the fullness of my Soul before you,   70
Show ev'ry tender, ev'ry grateful Thought,
This wond'rous Goodness stirs. But 'tis impossible,
And Utterance all is vile; since I can only
Swear you reign here, but never tell how much.

Sci. It is enough; I know thee thou art honest;
Goodness innate, and Worth hereditary
Are in thy Mind; thy noble Father's Virtues
Spring freshly forth, and blossom in thy Youth.

Alt. Thus Heav'n from nothing rais'd his fair
          Creation,
And then with wond'rous Joy beheld its Beauty,   80
Well pleas'd to see the Excellence he gave.

Sci. Oh noble Youth! I swear since first I knew thee,
Ev'n from that day of Sorrows when I saw thee,
Adorn'd and lovely in thy filial Tears,
The Mourner and Redeemer of thy Father,
I set thee down and seal'd thee for my own:
Thou art my Son, ev'n near me as *Calista.*
Horatio and *Lavinia* too are mine; [*Embraces* Horatio.
All are my Children, and shall share my Heart.
But wherefore waste we thus this happy Day?   90
The laughing Minutes summon thee to Joy,
And with new Pleasures court thee as they pass;
Thy waiting Bride ev'n chides thee for delaying,
And swears thou com'st not with a Bridegroom's Haste.

Alt. Oh! could I hope there was one Thought of
          Altamont,

One kind Remembrance in *Calista's* Breast,
The Winds, with all their Wings, would be too slow
To bear me to her Feet. For oh! my Father,
Amidst this Stream of Joy that bears me on,
Blest as I am, and honour'd in your Friendship,   100
There is one Pain that hangs upon my Heart.

   Sci. What means my Son?

   Alt. When, at your Intercession,
Last Night *Calista* yielded to my Happiness,
Just e'er we parted, as I seal'd my Vows
With Rapture on her Lips, I found her Cold,
As a dead Lover's Statue on his Tomb;
A rising storm of Passion shook her Breast,
Her Eyes a piteous show'r of Tears let fall,   109
And then she sigh'd as if her Heart were breaking.
With all the tend'rest Eloquence of Love
I beg'd to be a Sharer in her Grief;
But she, with Looks averse, and Eyes that froze me,
Sadly reply'd, her Sorrows were her own,
Nor in a Father's Pow'r to dispose of.

   Sci. Away! it is the Cosenage of their Sex,
One of the common Arts they practise on us,
To sigh and weep, then when their Hearts beat high,
With expectation of the coming Joy: 119
Thou hast in Camps, and fighting Fields been bred,
Unknowing in the Subtleties of Women;
The Virgin Bride, who swoons with deadly Fear,
To see the end of all her Wishes near,
When blushing from the Light and publick Eyes,
To the kind Covert of the Night she flies,
With equal Fires to meet the Bridegroom moves,
Melts in his Arms, and with a loose she loves.

                             [*Exeunt.*

       Enter Lothario *and* Rossano.

   Loth. The Father and the Husband!

   Ross. Let them pass,
They saw us not.   130

   Loth. I care not if they did,

E're long I mean to meet 'em Face to Face,
And gaul 'em with my Triumph o'er *Calista*.
   Ross. You lov'd her once.
   Loth. I lik'd her, wou'd have marry'd her,
But that it pleas'd her Father to refuse me,
To make this Honourable Fool her Husband.
For which, if I forget him, may the Shame
I mean to brand his Name with, stick on mine.   139
   Ross. She, gentle Soul, was kinder than her Father.
   Loth. She was, and oft in private gave me hearing,
'Till by long list'ning to the soothing Tale,
At length her easie Heart was wholly mine.
   Ross. I have heard you oft describe her, Haughty,
     Insolent,
And fierce with high Disdain; it moves my wonder,
That Virtue thus defended, should be yielded
A prey to loose Desires.
   Loth. Hear, then I'll tell thee.
Once in a lone, and secret Hour of Night,
When ev'ry Eye was clos'd, and the pale Moon   150
And Stars alone, shone conscious of the Theft,
Hot with the *Tuscan* Grape, and high in Blood,
Hap'ly I stole unheeded to her Chamber.
   Ross. That Minute sure was lucky.
   Loth. Oh 'twas great.
I found the Fond, Believing, Love-sick Maid,
Loose, unattir'd, warm, tender, full of Wishes;
Fierceness and Pride, the Guardians of her Honour,
Were charm'd to Rest, and Love alone was waking.
Within her rising Bosom all was calm,   160
As peaceful Seas that know no Storms, and only
Are gently lifted up and down by Tides.
I snatch'd the glorious, golden Opportunity,
And with prevailing, youthful Ardour prest her,
'Till with short Sighs, and murmuring Reluctance,
The yielding Fair one gave me perfect Happiness.
Ev'n all the live-long Night we past in Bliss,
In Extacies too fierce to last for ever;

At length the Morn and cold Indifference came;
When fully sated with the luscious Banquet, 170
I hastily took leave, and left the Nymph
To think on what was past, and sigh alone.

   Ross. You saw her soon again.

   Loth. Too soon I saw her;
For oh! that Meeting was not like the former;
I found my Heart no more beat high with Transport,
No more I sigh'd, and languish'd for Enjoyment,
'Twas past, and Reason took her turn to reign,
While ev'ry Weakness fell before her Throne.

   Ross. What of the Lady? 180

   Loth. With uneasie Fondness
She hung upon me, wept, and sigh'd, and swore
She was undone; talk'd of a Priest and Marriage,
Of flying with me from her Father's Pow'r;
Call'd ev'ry Saint and blessed Angel down,
To witness for her that she was my Wife.
I started at that Name.

   Ross. What Answer made you?

   Loth. None; but pretending sudden Pain and Illness
Escap'd the Persecution; two Nights since, 190
By Message urg'd, and frequent Importunity,
Again I saw her. Strait with Tears and Sighs,
With swelling Breasts, with Swooning, with Distraction,
With all the Subtleties, and pow'rful Arts
Of wilful Woman lab'ring for her purpose,
Again she told the same dull nauseous Tale.
Unmov'd, I beg'd her spare th' ungrateful Subject,
Since I resolv'd, that Love and Peace of Mind
Might flourish long inviolate betwixt us,
Never to load it with the Marriage Chain; 200
That I would still retain her in my Heart,
My ever gentle Mistress, and my Friend;
But for those other Names of Wife and Husband,
They only meant Ill-nature, Cares, and Quarrels.

Ross. How bore she this Reply?
  Loth. Ev'n as the Earth,
When, (Winds pent up, or eating Fires beneath
Shaking the Mass) she labours with Destruction.
At first her Rage was dumb, and wanted Words, 209
But when the Storm found way, 'twas wild and
    loud.
Mad as the Priestess of the *Delphick* God,
Enthusiastick Passion swell'd her Breast,
Enlarg'd her Voice, and ruffled all her Form;
Proud, and disdainful of the Love I profferr'd,
She call'd me Villain! Monster! Base! Betrayer!
At last, in very bitterness of Soul,
With deadly Imprecations on her self,
She vow'd severely ne'er to see me more;
Then bid me fly that minute; I obey'd,
And bowing left her to grow cool at leisure.   220
  Ross. She has relented since, else why this Message,
To meet the Keeper of her Secrets here
This Morning?
  Loth. See the Person whom you nam'd.

Enter Lucilla.

Well, my Embassadress, what must we treat of?
Come you to menace War and proud Defiance,
Or does the peaceful Olive grace your Message?
Is your Fair Mistress calmer? does she soften?
And must we love again? Perhaps she means
To treat in Juncture with her new Ally,   230
And make her Husband Party to th' Agreement.
  Lucill. Is this well done, my Lord? Have you put
    off
All Sense of Human Nature? keep a little,
A little Pity to distinguish Manhood,
Lest other Men, tho' cruel, should disclaim you,
And judge you to be number'd with the Brutes.
  Loth. I see thou'st learnt to rail.
  Lucill. I've learnt to weep;

That Lesson my sad Mistress often gives me;
By Day she seeks some melancholy Shade,   240
To hide her Sorrows from the prying World;
At Night she watches all the long long Hours,
And listens to the Winds and beating Rain,
With Sighs as loud, and Tears that fall as fast.
Then ever and anon she wrings her Hands,
And crys, false! false *Lothario*.

 Loth. Oh no more!
I swear thou'lt spoil thy pretty Face with Crying,
And thou hast Beauty that may make thy Fortune;
Some keeping Cardinal shall doat upon thee,   250
And barter his Church Treasure for thy Freshness.

 Lucill. What! shall I sell my Innocence and Youth,
For Wealth or Titles, to perfidious Man!
To Man! who makes his Mirth of our Undoing!
The base, profest Betrayer of our Sex;
Let me grow old in all Misfortunes else,
Rather than know the Sorrows of *Calista*.

 Loth. Does she send thee to chide in her behalf?
I swear thou dost it with so good a Grace,
That I cou'd almost love thee for thy frowning.   260

 Lucill. Read there, my Lord, there, in her own sad
  Lines,   [*Giving a Letter.*
Which best can tell the Story of her Woes,
That Grief of Heart which your Unkindness gives her.
  Lothario *reads.*]
 *Your Cruelty...Obedience to my Father...give my Hand
 to* Altamont.
By Heav'n! 'tis well; such ever be the Gifts,
With which I greet the Man whom my Soul hates.
            [*Aside.*

But to go on!
 *...Wish...Heart...Honour...too faithless...Weakness...to
 morrow...last Trouble...lost* Calista.   270
Women I see can change as well as Men;
She writes me here, forsaken as I am,
That I should bind my Brows with mournful Willow,

For she has given her Hand to *Altamont*:
Yet tell the Fair Inconstant——
   Lucill. How, my Lord?
   Loth. Nay, no more angry Words, say to *Calista*,
The humblest of her Slaves shall wait her Pleasure;
If she can leave her happy Husband's Arms,
To think upon so lost a thing as I am.   280
   Lucill. Alas! for pity come with gentler Looks;
Wound not her Heart with this unmanly Triumph;
And tho' you love her not, yet swear you do,
So shall Dissembling once be virtuous in you.
   Loth. Ha! who comes here?
   Lucill. The Bridegroom's Friend, *Horatio*.
He must not see us here; to morrow early
Be at the Garden Gate.
   Loth. Bear to my Love   289
My kindest Thoughts, and swear I will not fail her.

        Lothario *putting up the Letter hastily, drops it
           as he goes out.*
        Exeunt Lothario *and* Rossano *one way,* Lucilla
           another.

          Enter Horatio.

   Hor. Sure 'tis the very Error of my Eyes:
Waking I dream, or I beheld *Lothario*;
He seem'd conferring with *Calista*'s Woman:
At my approach they started, and retir'd.
What Business cou'd he have here, and with her?
I know he bears the noble *Altamont*
Profest and deadly Hate——What Paper's this?
               [*Taking up the Letter.*
Ha! to *Lothario* —'s Death! *Calista*'s Name!   298
               [*opening it.*
Confusion and Misfortune!   [*Reads.*

   *Your Cruelty has at length determin'd me, and I have
resolv'd this Morning to yield a perfect Obedience to my
Father, and to give my Hand to* Altamont, *in spight of
my Weakness for the false* Lothario. *I could almost wish*

*I had that Heart, and that Honour to bestow with it, which
you have robb'd me of:*

Damnation! to the rest——   *[Reads again.*

*But oh! I fear, could I retrieve 'em I should again be undone
by the too faithless, yet too lovely* Lothario; *this is the
last weakness of my Pen, and to morrow shall be the last
in which I will indulge my Eyes.* Lucilla *shall conduct
you if you are kind enough to let me see you; it shall be the
last Trouble you shall meet with from*   312
                              The lost *Calista.*

The lost indeed! for thou art gone as far
As there can be Perdition. Fire and Sulphur,
Hell is the sole Avenger of such Crimes.
Oh that the Ruin were but all thy own!
Thou wilt ev'n make thy Father curse his Age,
At sight of this black Scrowl, the gentle *Altamont,*
(For oh! I know his Heart is set upon thee)   320
Shall droop and hang his discontented Head,
Like Merit scorn'd by insolent Authority,
And never grace the Publick with his Virtues.——
Perhaps ev'n now he gazes fondly on her,
And thinking Soul and Body both alike,
Blesses the perfect Workmanship of Heav'n;
Then sighing to his ev'ry Care, speaks Peace,
And bids his Heart be satisfy'd with Happiness.
Oh wretched Husband! while she hangs about thee
With idle Blandishments, and plays the fond one,
Ev'n then her hot Imagination wanders,   331
Contriving Riot, and loose scapes of Love;
And while she clasps thee close makes thee a
     Monster.
What if I give this Paper to her Father?
It follows that his Justice dooms her dead,
And breaks his Heart with Sorrow; hard Return,
For all the Good his Hand has heap'd on us:
Hold, let me take a Moment's Thought.

Enter Lavinia.

Lav. My Lord!
Trust me it joys my Heart that I have found you. 340
Enquiring wherefore you had left the Company,
Before my Brother's Nuptial Rites were ended,
They told me you had felt some sudden Illness;
Where are you sick? Is it your Head? your Heart?
Tell me my Love, and ease my anxious Thoughts,
That I may take you gently in my Arms,
Sooth you to Rest, and soften all your Pains.

Hor. It were unjust, no let me spare my Friend,
Lock up the fatal Secret in my Breast,
Nor tell him that which will undo his Quiet.   350

Lav. What means my Lord?

Hor. Ha! saidst thou my *Lavinia*?

Lav. Alas you know not what you make me suffer;
Why are you pale? Why did you start and tremble?
Whence is that Sigh? And wherefore are your Eyes
Severely rais'd to Heav'n? The sick Man thus,
Acknowledging the Summons of his Fate,
Lifts up his feeble Hands and Eyes for Mercy,
And with Confusion thinks upon his Audit.   359

Hor. Oh no! thou hast mistook my Sickness quite,
These Pangs are of the Soul. Wou'd I had met
Sharpest Convulsions, spotted Pestilences,
Or any other deadly Foe to Life,
Rather than heave beneath this load of Thought.

Lav. Alas, what is it? Wherefore turn you from me?
Why did you falsly call me your *Lavinia*,
And swear I was *Horatio*'s better half,
Since now you mourn unkindly by your self,
And rob me of my Partnership of Sadness?
Witness you Holy Pow'rs, who know my Truth,   370
There cannot be a Chance in Life so miserable,
Nothing so very hard but I cou'd bear it,
Much rather than my Love shou'd treat me coldly,
And use me like a Stranger to his Heart.

Hor. Seek not to know what I wou'd hide from all,

But most from thee. I never knew a Pleasure,
Ought that was joyful, fortunate, or good,
But strait I ran to bless thee with the Tidings,
And laid up all my Happiness with thee: 379
But wherefore, wherefore should I give thee Pain?
Then spare me, I conjure thee, ask no further;
Allow my melancholy Thoughts this privilege,
And let 'em brood in secret o'er their Sorrows.

　　Lav. It is enough, chide not, and all is well;
Forgive me if I saw you sad, *Horatio*,
And ask'd to weep out part of your Misfortunes;
I wo' not press to know what you forbid me.
Yet, my lov'd Lord, yet you must grant me this,
Forget your Cares for this one happy Day,
Devote this Day to Mirth, and to your *Altamont*; 390
For his dear sake let Peace be in your Looks.
Ev'n now the jocund Bridegroom wants your Wishes,
He thinks the Priest has but half blest his Marriage,
'Till his Friend Hails him with the sound of Joy.

　　Hor. Oh never! never! never! Thou art innocent,
Simplicity from Ill, pure native Truth,
And Candour of the Mind adorn thee ever;
But there are such, such false ones in the World,
'Twou'd fill thy gentle Soul with wild Amazement
To hear their Story told. 400

　　Lav. False ones, my Lord?

　　Hor. Fatally Fair they are, and in their Smiles,
The Graces, little Loves, and young Desires inhabit;
But all that gaze upon 'em are undone,
For they are false; luxurious in their Appetites,
And all the Heav'n they hope for is Variety:
One Lover to another still succeeds,
Another, and another after that,
And the last Fool is welcome as the former;
'Till having lov'd his Hour out, he gives place, 410
And mingles with the Herd that went before him.

　　Lav. Can there be such? And have they peace of
　　Mind?

Have they in all the Series of their changing
One happy Hour? If Women are such things,
How was I form'd so different from my Sex?
My little Heart is satisfy'd with you,
You take up all her room; as in a Cottage
Which harbours some Benighted Princely Stranger,
Where the good Man, proud of his Hospitality,
Yields all his homely Dwelling to his Guest,   420
And hardly keeps a Corner for himself.

 Hor. Oh were they all like thee Men would adore
  'em,
And all the Bus'ness of their Lives be loving;
The Nuptial Band shou'd be the Pledge of Peace,
And all Domestick Cares and Quarrels cease;
The World shou'd learn to love by Virtuous Rules,
And Marriage be no more the Jest of Fools.

          [*Exeunt.*

End of the First Act.

ACT II. SCENE I.

S C E N E, *a Hall.*

Enter Calista *and* Lucilla.

 Cal. Be dumb for ever, silent as the Grave,
Nor let thy fond officious Love disturb
My solemn Sadness, with the sound of Joy.
If thou wilt sooth me, tell some dismal Tale
Of pining Discontent, and black Despair;
For oh! I've gone around thro' all my Thoughts,
But all are Indignation, Love, or Shame,
And my dear Peace of Mind is lost for ever.

 Luc. Why do you follow still that wand'ring Fire
That has miss-led your weary Steps, and leaves you
Benighted in a Wilderness of Woe?   11
That false *Lothario*! Turn from the Deceiver;
Turn, and behold where gentle *Altamont*,

Kind as the softest Virgin of our Sex,
And faithful as the simple Village Swain,
That never knew the Courtly Vice of Changing,
Sighs at your Feet, and wooes you to be happy.

Cal. Away, I think not of him. My sad Soul
Has form'd a dismal melancholy Scene,
Such a Retreat as I wou'd wish to find;   20
An unfrequented Vale, o'er-grown with Trees
Mossie and old, within whose lonesom Shade,
Ravens, and Birds ill-omen'd, only dwell;
No Sound to break the Silence, but a Brook
That bubling winds among the Weeds; no Mark
Of any Human Shape that had been there,
Unless a Skeleton of some poor Wretch,
Who had long since, like me, by Love undone,
Sought that sad Place out to despair and die in.

Luc. Alas for Pity!   30

Cal. There I fain wou'd hide me,
From the base World, from Malice, and from Shame;
For 'tis the solemn Counsel of my Soul,
Never to live with publick Loss of Honour:
'Tix fix'd to die, rather than bear the Insolence
Of each affected She that tells my Story,
And blesses her good Stars that she is virtuous.
To be a Tale for Fools! Scorn'd by the Women,
And pity'd by the Men! oh insupportable!   39

Luc. Can you perceive the manifest Destruction,
The gaping Gulf that opens just before you,
And yet rush on, tho' conscious of the Danger?
Oh hear me, hear your ever faithful Creature;
By all the Good I wish, by all the Ill
My trembling Heart forebodes, let me intreat you,
Never to see this faithless Man again:
Let me forbid his coming.

Cal. On thy Life
I charge thee no: my Genius drives me on;
I must, I will behold him once again: 50
Perhaps it is the Crisis of my Fate,

And this one Enterview shall end my Cares.
My lab'ring Heart, that swells with Indignation,
Heaves to discharge the Burthen; that once done,
The busie thing shall rest within its Cell,
And never beat again.

   Luc. Trust not to that;
Rage is the shortest Passion of our Souls,
Like narrow Brooks that rise with sudden Show'rs,
It swells in haste, and falls again as soon;   60
Still as it ebbs the softer Thoughts flow in,
And the Deceiver Love supplies its place.

   Cal. I have been wrong'd enough, to arm my Temper
Against the smooth Delusion; but alas!
(Chide not my Weakness, gentle Maid, but pity me)
A Woman's Softness hangs about me still:
Then let me blush, and tell thee all my Folly.
I swear I could not see the dear Betrayer
Kneel at my Feet, and sigh to be forgiven,
But my relenting Heart would pardon all,   70
And quite forget 'twas he that had undone me.

   Luc. Ye sacred Powers, whose gracious Providence
Is watchful for our Good, guard me from Men,
From their deceitful Tongues, their Vows and Flatteries;
Still let me pass neglected by their Eyes,
Let my Bloom wither, and my Form decay,
That none may think it worth his while to ruin me,
And fatal Love may never be my Bane.

   Cal. Ha! *Altamont? Calista* now be wary,
And guard thy Soul's Accesses with Dissembling;   80
Nor let this Hostile Husband's Eyes explore
The warring Passions, and tumultuous Thoughts,
That rage within thee, and deform thy Reason.

         Enter Altamont.

   Alt. Be gone my Cares, I give you to the Winds,
Far to be born, far from the happy *Altamont*;

For from this sacred *Æra* of my Love,
A better Order of succeeding Days
Come smiling forward, white and lucky all.
Calista is the Mistress of the Year,
She crowns the Seasons with auspicious Beauty,   90
And bids ev'n all my Hours be good and joyful.

Cal. If I was ever Mistress of such Happiness,
Oh! wherefore did I play th' unthrifty Fool,
And wasting all on others, leave my self
Without one Thought of Joy to give me Comfort?

Alt. Oh mighty Love! Shall that fair Face profane
This thy great Festival with Frowns and Sadness!
I swear it sha' not be, for I will wooe thee
With Sighs so moving, with so warm a Transport,
That thou shalt catch the gentle Flame from me,   100
And kindle into Joy.

Cal. I tell thee, *Altamont*,
Such Hearts as ours were never pair'd above,
Ill suited to each other; join'd, not match'd;
Some sullen Influence, a Foe to both,
Has wrought this fatal Marriage to undo us.
Mark but the Frame and Temper of our Minds,
How very much we differ. Ev'n this Day,
That fills thee with such Extasie and Transport,   109
To me brings nothing that should make me bless it.
Or think it better than the Day before,
Or any other in the Course of Time,
That dully took its turn, and was forgotten.

Alt. If to behold thee as my Pledge of Happiness,
To know none fair, none excellent beside thee;
If still to love thee with unweary'd Constancy,
Through ev'ry Season, ev'ry Change of Life,
Through wrinkled Age, through Sickness and Mis-
        fortune,
Be worth the least Return of grateful Love,
Oh then let my *Calista* bless this Day,   120
And set it down for happy.

Cal. 'Tis the Day

In which my Father gave my Hand to *Altamont*;
As such I will remember it for ever.

   Enter Sciolto, Horatio, *and* Lavinia.

 Sci. Let Mirth go on, let Pleasure know no pause,
But fill up ev'ry Minute of this Day.
'Tis yours, my Children, sacred to your Loves;
The glorious Sun himself for you looks gay,
He shines for *Altamont* and for *Calista.*
Let there be Musick, let the Master touch 130
The sprightly String, and softly-breathing Flute,
'Till Harmony rouse ev'ry gentle Passion,
Teach the cold Maid to lose her Fears in Love,
And the fierce Youth to languish at her Feet.
Begin, ev'n Age it self is chear'd with Musick,
It wakes a glad Remembrance of our Youth,
Calls back past Joys, and warms us into Transport.
   [*Here an Entertainment of Musick and Dancing.*

SONG.

By Mr. *CONGREVE.*

I.

Ah stay! ah turn! ah whither would you fly
 Too charming, too relentless Maid?
I follow not to Conquer but to Die, 140
 You of the fearful are afraid.

II.

In vain I call; for she like fleeting Air,
 When prest by some tempestuous Wind,
Flies swifter from the Voice of my Despair,
 Nor casts one pitying Look behind.

 Sci. Take care my Gates be open, bid all welcome;
All who rejoice with me to Day are Friends:
Let each indulge his Genius, each be glad,

Jocund and free, and swell the Feast with Mirth.
The sprightly Bowl shall chearfully go round,   150
None shall be grave, nor too severely wise;
Losses and Disappointments, Cares and Poverty,
The rich Man's Insolence, and great Man's Scorn,
In Wine shall be forgotten all. To Morrow
Will be too soon to think, and to be wretched.
Oh! grant, ye Powers, that I may see these happy,
                    [*Pointing to* Alt. *and* Calista.
Compleatly blest, and I have Life enough;
And leave the rest indifferently to Fate.   [*Exeunt.*

                Manet Horatio.

Hor. What if, while all are here intent on Revelling,
I privately went forth, and sought *Lothario?*   160
This Letter may be forg'd; perhaps the Wantonness
Of his vain Youth, to stain a Lady's Fame;
Perhaps his Malice, to disturb my Friend.
Oh no! my Heart forebodes it must be true.
Methought ev'n now I mark'd the starts of Guilt,
That shook her Soul; tho' damn'd Dissimulation
Skreen'd her dark Thoughts, and set to publick View
A specious Face of Innocence and Beauty.
Oh false Appearance! What is all our Soveraignty,
Our boasted Pow'r? when they oppose their Arts,
Still they prevail, and we are found their Fools.   171
With such smooth Looks, and many a gentle Word,
The first fair She beguil'd her easie Lord;
Too blind with Love and Beauty to beware,
He fell unthinking in the fatal Snare;
Nor cou'd believe, that such a Heav'nly Face
Had bargain'd with the Devil, to damn her wretched
            Race.   [*Exit.*

SCENE II.

S C E N E, *the Street near* Sciolto's *Palace.*

Enter Lothario *and* Rossano.

Loth. To tell thee then the Purport of my Thoughts;
The Loss of this fond Paper would not give me
A moment of Disquiet, were it not
My Instrument of Vengeance on this *Altamont*:
Therefore I mean to wait some Opportunity
Of speaking with the Maid we saw this Morning.

Ross. I wish you, Sir, to think upon the Danger
Of being seen; to Day their Friends are round 'em,
And any Eye, that lights by chance on you,
Shall put your Life and Safety to the Hazard.   10
                              [*They confer aside.*

Enter Horatio.

Hor. Still I must doubt some Mystery of Mischief,
Some Artifice beneath; *Lothario*'s Father
I knew him well, he was sagacious, cunning,
Fluent in Words, and bold in peaceful Councils,
But of a cold, unactive hand in War.
Yet with these Coward's Virtues he undid
My unsuspecting, valiant, honest Friend.
This Son, if Fame mistakes not, is more hot,
More open, and unartful.—Ha! he's here!   19
                              [*Seeing him.*

Loth. Damnation! He again!——This second time
To Day he has crost me like my evil Genius.

Hor. I sought you, Sir.

Loth. 'Tis well then I am found.

Hor. 'Tis well you are: The Man who wrongs my
    Friend
To the Earth's utmost Verge I wou'd pursue;
No Place, tho' e'er so holy, shou'd protect him;
No Shape that artful Fear e'er form'd shou'd hide him,
'Till he fair Answer made, and did me Justice.

Loth. Ha! dost thou know me? that I am *Lothario*?
As great a Name as this proud City boasts of.   30
Who is this mighty Man then, this *Horatio*,
That I should basely hide me from his Anger,
Lest he should chide me for his Friend's Displeasure?

Hor. The Brave, 'tis true, do never shun the Light,
Just are their Thoughts, and open are their Tempers,
Freely without Disguise they love and hate,
Still are they found in the fair face of Day,
And Heav'n and Men are Judges of their Actions.

Loth. Such let 'em be of mine; there's not a Purpose,
Which my Soul ever fram'd, or my Hand acted,   40
But I could well have bid the World look on,
And what I once durst do, have dar'd to justifie.

Hor. Where was this open Boldness, this free Spirit?
When but this very Morning I surpriz'd thee,
In base, dishonest Privacy, consulting
And bribing a poor mercenary Wretch,
To sell her Lady's Secrets, stain her Honour,
And with a forg'd Contrivance blast her Virtue:
At Sight of me thou fledst!

Loth. Ha! Fled from thee?   50

Hor. Thou fled'st, and Guilt was on thee; like a Thief,
A Pilferer descry'd in some dark Corner,
Who there had lodg'd, with mischievous Intent
To rob and ravage at the Hour of Rest,
And do a Midnight Murder on the Sleepers.

Loth. Slave! Villain!——

[*Offers to draw,* Rossano *holds him.*
Ross. Hold, my Lord! think where you are,
Think how unsafe, and hurtful to your Honour,
It were to urge a Quarrel in this Place,
And shock the peaceful City with a Broil.   60

Loth. Then since thou dost provoke my Vengeance, know
I wou'd not for this City's Wealth, for all

Which the Sea wafts to our *Ligurian* Shoar,
But that the Joys I reap'd with that fond Wanton,
The Wife of *Altamont*, shou'd be as publick
As is the Noon-day Sun, Air, Earth, or Water,
Or any common Benefit of Nature:
Think'st thou I meant the Shame shou'd be conceal'd?
Oh no! by Hell and Vengeance, all I wanted
Was some fit Messenger to bear the News   70
To the dull doating Husband; now I have found him,
And thou art he.

   Hor. I hold thee base enough,
To break through Law, and spurn at Sacred Order,
And do a brutal Injury like this;
Yet mark me well, young Lord, I think *Calista*
Too Nice, too Noble, and too Great of Soul,
To be the Prey of such a Thing as thou art.
'Twas base and poor, unworthy of a Man,
To forge a Scrowl so villanous and loose,   80
And Mark it with a noble Lady's Name;
These are the mean, dishonest Arts of Cowards,
Strangers to Manhood, and to glorious Dangers;
Who bred at Home in Idleness and Riot,
Ransack for Mistresses th' unwholsome Stews,
And never know the worth of virtuous Love.

   Loth. Think'st thou I forg'd the Letter? Think so
     still,
'Till the broad Shame comes staring in thy Face,
And Boys shall hoot the Cuckold as he passes.

   Hor. Away, no Woman cou'd descend so low: 90
A skipping, dancing, worthless Tribe you are,
Fit only for your selves, your Herd together;
And when the circling Glass warms your vain Hearts,
You talk of Beauties that you never saw,
And fancy Raptures that you never knew.
Legends of Saints, who never yet had Being,
Or being, ne'er were Saints, are not so false
As the fond Tales which you recount of Love.

   Loth. But that I do not hold it worth my Leisure,

I cou'd produce such damning Proof—— 100
　　Hor. 'Tis false,
You blast the Fair with Lies because they scorn you,
Hate you like Age, like Ugliness and Impotence:
Rather than make you blest they wou'd die Virgins,
And stop the Propagation of Mankind.
　　Loth. It is the Curse of Fools to be secure,
And that be thine and *Altamont*'s: Dream on,
Nor think upon my Vengeance 'till thou feel'st it.
　　Hor. Hold, Sir, another Word, and then farewell;
Tho' I think greatly of *Calista*'s Virtue, 110
And hold it far beyond thy Pow'r to hurt;
Yet as she shares the Honour of my *Altamont*,
That Treasure of a Soldier, bought with Blood,
And kept at Life's Expence, I must not have
(Mark me, young Sir) her very Name prophan'd.
Learn to restrain the Licence of your Speech;
'Tis held you are too lavish; when you are met
Among your Set of Fools, talk of your Dress,
Of Dice, of Whores, of Horses, and your Selves;
'Tis safer, and becomes your Understandings. 120
　　Loth. What if we pass beyond this solemn Order?
And, in Defiance of the stern *Horatio*,
Indulge our gayer Thoughts, let Laughter loose,
And use his sacred Friendship for our Mirth.
　　Hor. 'Tis well! Sir, you are pleasant——
　　Loth. By the Joys,
Which yet my Soul has uncontroll'd pursu'd,
I wou'd not turn aside from my least Pleasure,
Tho' all thy Force were arm'd to bar my Way; 129
But like the Birds, great Nature's happy Commoners,
That haunt in Woods, in Meads, and flow'ry Gardens,
Rifle the Sweets, and taste the choicest Fruits,
Yet scorn to ask the Lordly Owners leave.
　　Hor. What Liberty has vain presumptuous Youth,
That thou shou'dst dare provoke me unchastis'd?
But henceforth, Boy, I warn thee shun my Walks;
If in the Bounds of yon forbidden Place

Again thou'rt found, expect a Punishment,
Such as great Souls, impatient of an Injury,   139
Exact from those who wrong 'em much, ev'n Death;
Or something worse; an injur'd Husband's Vengeance
Shall print a thousand Wounds, tear thy fine Form,
And scatter thee to all the Winds of Heav'n.

Loth. Is then my Way in *Genoa* prescrib'd,
By a Dependant on the wretched *Altamont,*
A talking Sir, that brawls for him in Taverns,
And vouches for his Valour's Reputation?——

Hor. Away, thy Speech is fouler than thy Manners.

Loth. Or if there be a Name more vile, his Parasite,
A Beggar's Parasite!——   150

Hor. Now learn Humanity,
                    [*Offers to strike him,* Rossano *interposes.*
Since Brutes and Boys are only taught with Blows,

Loth. Damnation!   [*They Draw.*

Ross. Hold, this goes no further here,
Horatio, 'tis too much; already see,
The Crowd are gath'ring to us.

Loth. Oh *Rossano!*
Or give me way, or thou'rt no more my Friend.

Ross. Sciolto's Servants too have ta'ne the Alarm;
You'll be opprest by Numbers, be advis'd,   160
Or I must force you hence; take 't on my Word,
You shall have Justice done you on *Horatio.*
Put up, my Lord.

Loth. This wo' not brook Delay;
West of the Town a Mile, among the Rocks,
Two Hours e'er Noon to morrow I expect thee,
Thy single Hand to mine.

Hor. I'll meet thee there.

Loth. To morrow, oh my better Stars! to morrow,
Exert your Influence, shine strongly for me;   170
'Tis not a common Conquest I wou'd gain,
Since Love, as well as Arms, must grace my Triumph.
                    [*Exeunt* Lothario *and* Rossano.

Hor. Two Hours e'er Noon to morrow! ha! e'er that

He sees *Calista*! oh unthinking Fool——
What if I urg'd her with the Crime and Danger?
If any Spark from Heav'n remain unquench'd
Within her Breast, my Breath perhaps may wake it;
Cou'd I but prosper there, I wou'd not doubt
My Combat with that loud vain-glorious Boaster,
Were you, ye Fair, but cautious whom ye trust,   180
Did you but think how seldom Fools are just,
So many of your Sex wou'd not in vain,
Of broken Vows and faithless Men complain.
Of all the various Wretches Love has made,
How few have been by Men of Sense betray'd?
Convinc'd by Reason, they your Pow'r confess,
Pleas'd to be happy, as you're pleas'd to bless,
And conscious of your Worth, can never love you less.
                                                    [*Exit.*

End of the Second Act.

ACT III. SCENE I.

SCENE, *an Apartment in* Sciolto's *Palace.*

Enter Sciolto *and* Calista.

Sci. Now by my Life, my Honour, 'tis too much;
Have I not mark'd thee wayward as thou art,
Perverse and sullen all this Day of Joy?
When ev'ry Heart was chear'd, and Mirth went round,
Sorrow, Displeasure, and repining Anguish
Sate on thy Brow; like some malignant Planet,
Foe to the Harvest, and the healthy Year,
Who scouls adverse, and lours upon the World;
When all the other Stars, with gentle Aspect,
Propitious shine, and meaning Good to Man.   10
    Cal. Is then the Task of Duty half perform'd?
Has not your Daughter giv'n her self to *Altamont*,
Yielded the native Freedom of her Will,
To an Imperious Husband's lordly Rule,

To gratifie a Father's stern Command?

  Sci. Dost thou complain?

  Cal. For pity do not frown then,
If in despight of all my vow'd Obedience,
A Sigh breaks out, or a Tear falls by chance;   19
For oh! that Sorrow which has drawn your Anger,
Is the sad Native of *Calista*'s Breast,
And once possest will never quit its Dwelling,
'Till Life, the Prop all, shall leave the Building,
To tumble down, and moulder into Ruin.

  Sci. Now by the sacred Dust of that dear Saint
That was thy Mother, by her wond'rous Goodness,
Her soft, her tender, most complying Sweetness,
I swear some sullen Thought that shuns the Light,
Lurks underneath that Sadness in thy Visage.   29
But mark me well, tho' by yon Heaven I love thee,
As much, I think, as a fond Parent can;
Yet shou'dst thou (which the Pow'rs above forbid)
E'er stain the Honour of thy Name with Infamy,
I cast thee off, as one whose Impious Hands
Had rent asunder Nature's nearest Ties,
Which once divided never join again.
To Day, I have made a noble Youth thy Husband,
Consider well his Worth, reward his Love,
Be willing to be happy, and thou art so.

                              [*Exit* Sciolto.

  Cal. How hard is the Condition of our Sex,   40
Thro' ev'ry State of Life the Slaves of Man?
In all the dear delightful Days of Youth,
A rigid Father dictates to our Wills,
And deals out Pleasure with a scanty Hand;
To his, the Tyrant Husband's Reign succeeds
Proud with Opinion of superior Reason,
He holds Domestick Bus'ness and Devotion
All we are capable to know, and shuts us,
Like Cloyster'd Ideots, from the World's Acquaintance,

  23 the Prop all] Suggested emendation, the Prop of all.

And all the Joys of Freedom; wherefore are we   50
Born with high Souls, but to assert our selves,
Shake off this vile Obedience they exact,
And claim an equal Empire o'er the World?

Enter Horatio.

Hor. She's here! yet oh! my Tongue is at a loss,
Teach me, some Pow'r, that happy Art of Speech,
To dress my Purpose up in gracious Words;
Such as may softly steal upon her Soul,
And never waken the Tempestuous Passions.
By Heaven she weeps!——Forgive me, Fair *Calista*,
If I presume, on Privilege of Friendship,   60
To join my Grief to yours, and mourn the Evils
That hurt your Peace, and quench those Eyes in Tears.

Cal. To steal unlook'd for on my private Sorrow,
Speaks not the Man of Honour, nor the Friend,
But rather means the Spy.

Hor. Unkindly said!
For oh! as sure as you accuse me falsly,
I come to prove my self *Calista*'s Friend.

Cal. You are my Husband's Friend, the Friend of
  Altamont.

Hor. Are you not one? Are you not join'd by
  Heav'n,   70
Each interwoven with the other's Fate?
Are you not mix'd like Streams of meeting Rivers,
Whose blended Waters are no more distinguish'd,
But roul into the Sea, one common Flood?
Then, who can give his Friendship, but to one?
Who can be *Altamont*'s, and not *Calista*'s?

Cal. Force, and the Wills of our Imperious Rulers,
May bind two Bodies in one wretched Chain;
But Minds will still look back to their own Choice.
So the poor Captive in a Foreign Realm,   80
Stands on the Shoar, and sends his Wishes back
To the dear Native Land from whence he came.

Hor. When Souls that shou'd agree to Will the same,

To have one common Object for their Wishes,
Look different ways, regardless of each other,
Think what a Train of Wretchedness ensues:
Love shall be banish'd from the Genial Bed,
The Nights shall all be lonely and unquiet,
And ev'ry Day shall be a Day of Cares.   89

Cal. Then all the boasted Office of thy Friendship,
Was but to tell *Calista* what a Wretch she is;
Alas! what needed that?

Hor. Oh! rather say,
I came to tell her how she might be happy;
To sooth the secret Anguish of her Soul,
To comfort that Fair Mourner, that forlorn one,
And teach her Steps to know the Paths of Peace.

Cal. Say thou to whom this Paradise is known,
Where lyes the blissful Region? Mark my way to it,
For oh! 'tis sure, I long to be at Rest.   100

Hor. Then——to be Good is to be Happy;——
        Angels
Are happier than Mankind, because they are better.
Guilt is the source of Sorrow; 'tis the Fiend,
The avenging Fiend, that follows us behind
With Whips and Stings; the blest know none of this,
But rest in everlasting Peace of Mind,
And find the height of all their Heav'n is Goodness.

Cal. And what bold Parasite's officious Tongue
Shall dare to tax *Calista*'s Name with Guilt?   109

Hor. None shou'd; but 'tis a busie, talking World,
That with licentious Breath blows like the Wind,
As freely on the Palace, as the Cottage.

Cal. What mystick Riddle lurks beneath thy Words,
Which thou wou'dst seem unwilling to express,
As if it meant Dishonour to my Virtue?
Away with this ambiguous shuffling Phrase,
And let thy Oracle be understood.

Hor. *Lothario!*

Cal. Ha! what wou'dst thou mean by him?

Hor. *Lothario* and *Calista!*——Thus they join   120

Two Names, which Heav'n decreed shou'd never
   meet;
Hence have the Talkers of this populous City,
A shameful Tale to tell for publick Sport,
Of an unhappy Beauty, a false Fair one,
Who plighted to a noble Youth her Faith,
When she had giv'n her Honour to a Wretch.

   Cal. Death! and Confusion! Have I liv'd to this?
Thus to be treated with unmanly Insolence!
To be the Sport of a loose Ruffian's Tongue!
Thus to be us'd! thus! like the vilest Creature,   130
That ever was a Slave to Vice and Infamy.

   Hor. By Honour and fair Truth, you wrong me
   much,
For on my Soul nothing but strong Necessity,
Cou'd urge my Tongue to this ungrateful Office:
I came with strong Reluctance, as if Death
Had stood a-cross my Way, to save your Honour,
Yours and *Sciolto*'s, yours and *Altamont*'s;
Like one who ventures thro' a burning Pile,
To save his tender Wife, with all her Brood
Of little Fondlings, from the dreadful Ruin.   140

   Cal. Is this! Is this the famous Friend of *Altamont*,
For noble Worth, and Deeds of Arms renown'd?
Is this! this Tale bearing, officious Fellow,
That watches for Intelligence from Eyes;
This wretched *Argus* of a jealous Husband,
That fills his easie Ears with monstrous Tales,
And makes him toss, and rave, and wreak at length
Bloody Revenge on his defenceless Wife;
Who guiltless dies, because her Fool ran mad.

   Hor. Alas! this Rage is vain, for if your Fame,   150
Or Peace be worth your Care, you must be calm,
And listen to the Means are left to save 'em.
'Tis now the lucky Minute of your Fate,
By me your Genius speaks, by me it warns you,
Never to see that curst *Lothario* more;
Unless you mean to be despis'd, be shunn'd,

By all your virtuous Maids and noble Matrons;
Unless you have devoted this rare Beauty
To Infamy, Diseases, Prostitution——   159
   Cal. Dishonour blast thee, base, unmanner'd Slave!
That dar'st forget my Birth, and sacred Sex,
And shock me with the rude unhallow'd Sound.
   Hor. Here kneel, and in the awful Face of Heav'n,
Breath out a solemn Vow, never to see,
Nor think, if possible, on him that ruin'd thee;
Or by my *Altamont*'s dear Life I swear,
This Paper!—Nay you must not fly!—This Paper,
                              [*Holding her.*
This guilty Paper shall divulge your Shame.——
   Cal. What meanst thou by that Paper? What
      Contrivance
Hast thou been forging to deceive my Father,   170
To turn his Heart against his wretched Daughter,
That *Altamont* and thou may share his Wealth?
A Wrong like this will make me ev'n forget
The Weakness of my Sex.—Oh for a Sword,
To urge my Vengeance on the villanous Hand
That forg'd the Scrowl.
   Hor. Behold, can this be forg'd?
See where *Calista*'s Name——
                [*Shewing the Letter near.*
   Cal. To Atoms thus,   [*Tearing it.*
Thus let me tear the vile, detested Falshood,   180
The wicked, lying Evidence of Shame.
   Hor. Confusion!
   Cal. Henceforth, thou officious Fool,
Meddle no more, nor dare ev'n on thy Life
To breath an Accent that may touch my Virtue:
I am my self the Guardian of my Honour,
And wo' not bear so insolent a Monitor.

Enter Altamont.

   Alt. Where is my Life, my Love, my charming Bride,
Joy of my Heart, and Pleasure of my Eyes,

The Wish, the Care, and Bus'ness of my Youth?   190
Oh! let me find her, snatch her to my Breast,
And tell her she delays my Bliss too long,
'Till my soft Soul ev'n sickens with Desire.
Disorder'd!—and in Tears! *Horatio* too!
My Friend is in Amaze!—What can it mean?
Tell me, *Calista*, who has done thee wrong,
That my swift Sword may find out the Offender,
And do thee ample Justice.

   Cal. Turn to him!

   Alt. Horatio!   200

   Cal. To that Insolent.

   Alt. My Friend!
Cou'd he do this? He, who was half my self!
One Faith has ever bound us, and one Reason
Guided our Wills: Have I not found him just,
Honest as Truth it self? And cou'd he break
The Sanctity of Friendship? Cou'd he wound
The Heart of *Altamont* in his *Calista*?

   Cal. I thought what Justice I should find from
     thee!
Go fawn upon him, listen to his Tale,   210
Applaud his Malice, that wou'd blast my Fame,
And treat me like a common Prostitute.
Thou art perhaps Confederate in his Mischief,
And wilt believe the Legend, if he tells it.

   Alt. Oh Impious! What presumptuous Wretch
     shall dare
To offer at an Injury like that?
Priesthood, nor Age, nor Cowardise it self,
Shall save him from the Fury of my Vengeance.

   Cal. The Man who dar'd to do it was *Horatio*!
Thy darling Friend! 'Twas *Altamont*'s *Horatio*!   220
But mark me well! While thy divided Heart
Doats on a Villain that has wrong'd me thus,
No Force shall drag me to thy hated Bed;
Nor can my cruel Father's Pow'r do more
Than shut me in a Cloyster; there, well pleas'd,

Religious Hardships will I learn to bear,
To fast, and freeze at Midnight Hours of Pray'r;
Nor think it hard, within a lonely Cell,
With melancholy, speechless Saints to dwell;
But bless the Day I to that Refuge ran,   230
Free from the Marriage Chain, and from that Tyrant,
    Man.   [*Exit* Calista.

   Alt. She's gone; and as she went, Ten thousand
    Fires
Shot from her angry Eyes, as if she meant
Too well to keep the cruel Vow she made.
Now as thou art a Man, *Horatio*, tell me,
What means this wild Confusion in thy Looks?
As if thou wert at variance with thy self,
Madness and Reason combating within thee,
And thou wert doubtful which shou'd get the better.

   Hor. I wou'd be dumb for ever, but thy Fate 240
Has otherwise decreed it; thou hast seen
That Idol of thy Soul, that fair *Calista*,
Thou hast beheld her Tears.

   Alt. I have seen her weep,
I have seen that lovely one, that dear *Calista*,
Complaining in the Bitterness of Sorrow,
That thou! my Friend! *Horatio*! thou hadst wrong'd
    her.

   Hor. That I have wrong'd her! Had her Eyes
    been fed
From that rich Stream which warms her Heart, and
    number'd
For ev'ry falling Tear a Drop of Blood,   250
It had not been too much; for she has ruin'd thee,
Ev'n thee, my *Altamont*! She has undone thee.

   Alt. Dost thou join Ruin with *Calista*'s Name?
What is so fair, so exquisitely good?
Is she not more than Painting can express,
Or youthful Poets fancy, when they love?
Does she not come, like Wisdom, or good Fortune,
Repleat with Blessings, giving Wealth and Honour?

The Dowry which she brings is Peace and Pleasure,
And everlasting Joys are in her Arms.   260

    Hor. It had been better thou hadst liv'd a Beggar,
And fed on Scraps at great Mens surly Doors,
Than to have match'd with one so false, so fatal.——

    Alt. It is too much for Friendship to allow
    thee;
Because I tamely bore the Wrong thou didst her,
Thou dost avow the barb'rous, brutal Part,
And urge the Injury ev'n to my Face.

    Hor. I see she has got Possession of thy Heart,
She has charm'd thee, like a Siren, to her Bed,   269
With Looks of Love, and with enchanting Sounds:
Too late the Rocks and Quick-sands will appear.
When thou art wreckt upon the faithless Shoar,
Then vainly wish thou hadst not left thy Friend,
To follow her Delusion.

    Alt. If thy Friendship
Do churlishly deny my Love a Room,
It is not worth my keeping, I disclaim it.

    Hor. Canst thou so soon forget what I've been to
    thee?
I shar'd the Task of Nature with thy Father,
And form'd with Care thy unexperienc'd Youth   280
To Virtue and to Arms.
Thy noble Father, oh thou light young Man!
Wou'd he have us'd me thus? One Fortune fed us,
For his was ever mine, mine his, and both
Together flourish'd, and together fell.
He call'd me Friend, like thee; wou'd he have left
    me
Thus? for a Woman? nay, a vile one too?

    Alt. Thou canst not, dar'st not mean it; speak
    again,
Say, who is vile? but dare not name *Calista.*

    Hor. I had not spoke at first, unless compell'd,   290
And forc'd to clear my self; but since thus urg'd,
I must avow I do not know a viler.

Alt. Thou wert my Father's Friend, he lov'd thee
well;
A kind of venerable Mark of him
Hangs round thee, and protects thee from my
Vengeance:
I cannot, dare not lift my Sword against thee,
But henceforth never let me see thee more.
                                    [*Going out.*
Hor. I love thee still, ungrateful as thou art,
And must, and will preserve thee from Dishonour,
Ev'n in despight of thee.   [*Holds him.*
Alt. Let go my Arm.   301
Hor. If Honour be thy Care, if thou wou'dst live,
Without the Name of credulous, wittal Husband,
Avoid thy Bride, shun her detested Bed,
The Joys it yields are dash'd with Poyson.——
Alt. Off!
To urge me but a Minute more is fatal.
Hor. She is polluted! stain'd!
Alt. Madness and Raving!
But hence!   310
Hor. Dishonour'd by the Man you hate.——
Alt. I prithee loose me yet, for thy own sake,
If Life be worth the keeping.——
Hor. By *Lothario.*
Alt. Perdition take thee, Villain, for the Falshood.
                                    [*Strikes him.*
Now nothing but thy Life can make Atonement.
Hor. A Blow! Thou hast us'd well.——   [*Draws.*
Alt. This to thy Heart.——
Hor. Yet hold!——By Heav'n his Father's in his
Face.
Spight of my Wrongs my Heart runs o'er with
Tenderness,   320
And I cou'd rather die my self, than hurt him.
Alt. Defend thy self, for by my much wrong'd
Love,
I swear the poor Evasion shall not save thee.

Hor. Yet hold! thou know'st I dare!——Think how
    we've liv'd——

        [*They fight*; Altamont *presses on* Horatio, *who
        retires.*

Nay! then 'tis brutal Violence! And thus,
Thus Nature bids me guard the Life she gave.

        [*They fight.*

    Lavinia *Enters, and runs between their Swords.*

    Lav. My Brother! my *Horatio*! is it possible?
Oh! turn your cruel Swords upon *Lavinia*.
If you must quench your impious Rage in Blood,
Behold, my Heart shall give you all her Store,   330
To save those dearer Streams that flow from yours.

    Alt. 'Tis well thou hast found a Safeguard; none
    but this,
No Pow'r on Earth cou'd save thee from my Fury.

    Lav. Oh fatal, deadly Sound!

    Hor. Safety from thee!
Away, vain Boy! Hast thou forgot the Reverence
Due to my Arm, thy first, thy great Example,
Which pointed out thy way to noble Daring,
And shew'd thee what it was to be a Man.

    Lav. What busie, medling Fiend, what Foe to
    Goodness,   340
Could kindle such a Discord? Oh! lay by
Those most ungentle Looks, and angry Weapons,
Unless you mean my Griefs, and killing Fears,
Should stretch me out at your relentless Feet,
A wretched Coarse, the Victim of your Fury.

    Hor. Ask'st thou what made us Foes? 'twas base
    Ingratitude;
'Twas such a Sin to Friendship, as Heaven's Mercy,
That strives with Man's untoward, monstrous
    Wickedness,
Unweary'd with Forgiving, scarce cou'd pardon.
He who was all to me, Child! Brother! Friend!   350
With barb'rous, bloody Malice, sought my Life.

Alt. Thou art my Sister, and I would not make thee
The lonely Mourner of a widdow'd Bed,
Therefore thy Husband's Life is safe; but warn him,
No more to know this Hospitable Roof.
He has but ill repaid *Sciolto*'s Bounty;
We must not meet; 'tis dangerous; farewel.
                              [*He is going,* Lavinia *holds him.*

Lav. Stay *Altamont*, my Brother stay, if ever
Nature, or what is nearer much than Nature,
The kind Consent of our agreeing Minds,   360
Have made us dear to one another, stay,
And speak one gentle Word to your *Horatio*.
Behold, his Anger melts, he longs to love you,
To call you Friend, then press you hard, with all
The tender, speechless Joy of Reconcilement.
    Alt. It cannot, sha' not be!—you must not hold me.
    Lav. Look kindly then!
    Alt. Each Minute that I stay,
Is a new Injury to fair *Calista*.
From thy false Friendship, to her Arms I'll fly;   370
There, if in any pause of Love I rest,
Breathless with Bliss, upon her panting Breast,
In broken, melting Accents I will swear,
Henceforth to trust my Heart with none but her;
Then own the Joys, which on her Charms attend,
Have more than paid me for my faithless Friend.
                        [Altamont *breaks from* Lavinia, *and Exit.*

Hor. Oh raise thee, my *Lavinia*, from the Earth;
It is too much, this Tide of flowing Grief,
This wond'rous waste of Tears, too much to give,
To an ungrateful Friend, and cruel Brother.   380
    Lav. Is there not cause for Weeping? Oh *Horatio*!
A Brother and a Husband were my Treasure,
'Twas all the little Wealth, that poor *Lavinia*

Sav'd from the Shipwreck of her Father's Fortunes.
One half is lost already; if thou leav'st me,
If thou shou'dst prove unkind to me, as *Altamont*,
Whom shall I find to pity my Distress,
To have Compassion on a helpless Wanderer,
And give her where to lay her wretched Head?

    Hor. Why dost thou wound me with thy soft
      Complainings?   390
Tho' *Altamont* be false, and use me hardly,
Yet think not I impute his Crimes to thee.
Talk not of being forsaken, for I'll keep thee,
Next to my Heart, my certain Pledge of Happiness.
Heav'n form'd thee gentle, fair, and full of Goodness,
And made thee all my Portion here on Earth;
It gave thee to me, as a large amends,
For Fortune, Friends, and all the World beside.

    Lav. Then you will love me still, cherish me ever,
And hide me from Misfortune in your Bosom: 400
Here end my Cares, nor will I lose one Thought,
How we shall live, or purchase Food and Raiment.
The holy Pow'r, who clothes the senseless Earth,
With Woods, with Fruits, with Flow'rs, and verdant
    Grass,
Whose bounteous Hand feeds the whole Brute
    Creation,
Knows all our Wants, and has enough to give us.

    Hor. From *Genoa*, from Falshood and Inconstancy,
To some more honest distant Clime we'll go;
Nor will I be beholding to my Country,
For ought but thee, the Partner of my Flight.   410

    Lav. Yes, I will follow thee; forsake, for thee,
My Country, Brother, Friends, ev'n all I have;
Tho' mine's a little all; yet were it more,
And better far, it shou'd be left for thee,
And all that I wou'd keep shou'd be *Horatio*.
So when the Merchant sees his Vessel lost,
Tho' richly Freighted from a Foreign Coast,
Gladly, for Life, the Treasure he wou'd give;

And only wishes to escape, and live.
Gold and his Gains no more employ his Mind, 420
But driving o'er the Billows with the Wind,
Cleaves to one faithful Plank, and leaves the rest
　　behind.

[Exeunt.

End of the Third Act.

ACT IV. SCENE I.

SCENE, *a Garden.*

Enter Altamont.

Alt. With what unequal Tempers are we form'd?
One Day the Soul, supine with Ease and Fulness,
Revels secure, and fondly tells her self,
The Hour of Evil can return no more;
The next, the Spirit's pall'd, and sick of Riot,
Turn all to Discord, and we hate our Beings,
Curse the past Joy, and think it Folly all,
And Bitterness, and Anguish. Oh! last Night!
What has ungrateful Beauty paid me back, 9
For all that Mass of Friendship which I squander'd?
Coldness, Aversion, Tears, and sullen Sorrow,
Dash'd all my Bliss, and damp'd my Bridal Bed.
Soon as the Morning dawn'd, she vanish'd from me,
Relentless to the gentle Call of Love.
I have lost a Friend, and I have gain'd——a Wife!
Turn not to Thought my Brain; but let me find
Some unfrequented Shade; there lay me down,
And let forgetful Dulness steal upon me,
To soften and asswage this Pain of Thinking. *[Exit.*

Enter Lothario *and* Calista.

Loth. Weep not my Fair, but let the God of Love
Laugh in thy Eyes, and Revel in thy Heart, 21
Kindle again his Torch, and hold it high,
To light us to new Joys; nor let a Thought

Of Discord, or Disquiet past, molest thee;
But to a long Oblivion give thy Cares,
And let us melt the present Hour in Bliss.

   Cal. Seek not to sooth me with thy false Endear-
     ments,
To Charm me with thy Softness; 'tis in vain;
Thou can'st no more betray, nor I be ruin'd.
The Hours of Folly, and of fond Delight,   30
Are wasted all and fled; those that remain
Are doom'd to Weeping, Anguish, and Repentance.
I come to charge thee with a long Account,
Of all the Sorrows I have known already,
And all I have to come; thou hast undone me.

   Loth. Unjust *Calista*! Dost thou call it Ruin,
To Love as we have done; to melt, to languish,
To wish for somewhat exquisitely Happy,
And then be blest ev'n to that Wish's height?
To die with Joy, and streight to live again,   40
Speechless to gaze, and with tumultuous Transport—

   Cal. Oh! let me hear no more, I cannot bear it,
'Tis deadly to Remembrance; let that Night,
That guilty Night, be blotted from the Year,
Let not the Voice of Mirth, or Musick know it,
Let it be dark and desolate, no Stars
To glitter o'er it; let it wish for Light,
Yet want it still, and vainly wait the Dawn;
For 'twas the Night that gave me up to Shame,
To Sorrow, to perfidious, false *Lothario*.   50

   Loth. Hear this, ye Pow'rs, mark how the Fair
     Deceiver
Sadly complains of violated Truth;
She calls me false, ev'n She, the faithless She,
Whom Day and Night, whom Heav'n and Earth
     have heard
Sighing to vow, and tenderly protest,
Ten Thousand times, she wou'd be only mine;
And yet, behold, she has giv'n her self away,
Fled from my Arms, and wedded to another,

Ev'n to the Man whom most I hate on Earth.——

   Cal. Art thou so base, to upbraid me with a Crime,
Which nothing but thy Cruelty cou'd cause?   61
If Indignation, raging in my Soul,
For thy unmanly Insolence and Scorn,
Urg'd me to do a Deed of Desperation,
And wound my self to be reveng'd on thee,
Think whom I shou'd devote to Death and Hell,
Whom Curse, as my Undoer; but *Lothario*;
Hadst thou been Just, not all *Sciolto*'s Pow'r,
Not all the Vows and Pray'rs of sighing *Altamont*,
Cou'd have prevail'd, or won me to forsake thee. 70

   Loth. How have I fail'd in Justice or in Love?
Burns not my Flame as brightly as at first?
Ev'n now my Heart beats high, I languish for thee,
My Transports are as fierce, as strong my Wishes,
As if thou hadst never blest me with thy Beauty.

   Cal. How didst thou dare to think that I wou'd live
A Slave to base Desires, and brutal Pleasures,
To be a wretched Wanton for thy Leisure,
To toy, and waste an Hour of idle Time with?
My Soul disdains thee for so mean a Thought. 80

   Loth. The driving Storm of Passion will have way,
And I must yield before it; wer't thou calm,
Love, the poor Criminal, whom thou hast doom'd,
Has yet a thousand tender things to plead,
To charm thy Rage, and mitigate his Fate.

Enter behind them Altamont.

   Alt. I have lost my Peace——Ha! do I live, and
   wake!——

   Cal. Hadst thou been true, how happy had I been?
Nor *Altamont*, but thou hadst been my Lord.
But wherefore nam'd I Happiness with thee?
It is for thee, for thee, that I am curst;   90
For thee, my secret Soul each Hour arraigns me,
Calls me to answer for my Virtue stain'd,
My Honour lost to thee; for thee it haunts me,

With stern *Sciolto* vowing Vengeance on me;
With *Altamont* complaining for his Wrongs——

 Alt. Behold him here—— [*Coming forward.*
 Cal. Ah!——   [*Starting.*

 Alt. The Wretch! whom thou hast made,
Curses and Sorrows hast thou heap'd upon him, 99
And Vengeance is the only Good is left. [*Drawing.*

 Loth. Thou hast ta'ne me somewhat unawares,
  'tis true,
But Love and War take turns like Day and Night,
And little Preparation serves my turn,
Equal to both, and arm'd for either Field.
We've long been Foes, this Moment ends our Quarrel;
Earth, Heav'n and Fair *Calista* judge the Combat.

 Cal. Distraction! Fury! Sorrow! Shame! and
  Death!

 Alt. Thou hast talk'd too much, thy Breath is
  Poison to me,
It taints the ambient Air; this for my Father,
This for *Sciolto*, and this last for *Altamont*. 110

   [*They Fight*; Lothario *is wounded once or twice,
   and then falls.*

 Loth. Oh *Altamont*! thy Genius is the stronger,
Thou hast prevail'd!——My fierce, ambitious Soul
Declining droops, and all her Fires grow pale;
Yet let not this Advantage swell thy Pride,
I Conquer'd in my turn, in Love I Triumph'd:
Those Joys are lodg'd beyond the reach of Fate;
That sweet Revenge comes smiling to my Thoughts,
Adorns my Fall, and chears my Heart in Dying.
            [*Dies.*

 Cal. And what remains for me? Beset with Shame,
Encompas'd round with Wretchedness, there is 120
But this one way, to break the Toil and 'scape.

   [*She catches up* Lothario's *Sword, and offers to
   kill her self*; Altamont *runs to her, and
   wrests it from her.*

 Alt. What means thy frantick Rage?

 Cal. Off! let me go.

 Alt. Oh! thou hast more than murder'd me, yet still,
Still art thou here! and my Soul starts with Horror,
At thought of any Danger that may reach thee.

 Cal. Think'st thou I mean to live? to be forgiven?
Oh! thou hast known but little of *Calista*;
If thou hadst never heard my Shame, if only
The midnight Moon, and silent Stars had seen it, 130
I wou'd not bear to be reproach'd by them,
But dig down deep to find a Grave beneath,
And hide me from their Beams.

 Sciolto within.] What ho! my Son!

 Alt. It is *Sciolto* calls; come near, and find me,
The wretched'st Thing of all my Kind on Earth.

 Cal. Is it the Voice of Thunder, or my Father?
Madness! Confusion! let the Storm come on,
Let the tumultuous Roar drive all upon me,
Dash my devoted Bark; ye Surges, break it; 140
'Tis for my Ruin that the Tempest rises.
When I am lost, sunk to the bottom low,
Peace shall return, and all be calm again.

Enter Sciolto.

 Sci. Ev'n now *Rossano* leap'd the Garden Walls——
Ha! Death has been among you——Oh my Fears!
Last Night thou hadst a diff'rence with thy Friend,
The Cause thou gav'st me for it was a damn'd one;
Didst thou not wrong the Man who told thee Truth?
Answer me quick——

 Alt. Oh! press me not to speak, 150
Ev'n now my Heart is breaking, and the mention
Will lay me dead before you; see that Body,
And guess my Shame! my Ruin! oh *Calista*!

 Sci. It is enough! but I am slow to Execute,
And Justice lingers in my lazy Hand;
Thus let me wipe Dishonour from my Name,

And cut thee from the Earth, thou Stain to Goodness.——

        [*Offers to kill* Calista, Altamont *holds him.*

    Alt. Stay thee, *Sciolto*, thou rash Father stay,
Or turn the Point on me, and thro' my Breast,
Cut out the bloody Passage to *Calista*;   160
So shall my Love be perfect, while for her
I die, for whom alone I wish'd to live.

    Cal. No, *Altamont*! my Heart, that scorn'd thy Love,
Shall never be indebted to thy Pity;
Thus torn, defac'd, and wretched as I seem,
Still I have something of *Sciolto*'s Virtue.
Yes! yes, my Father, I applaud thy Justice,
Strike home, and I will bless thee for the Blow;
Be merciful, and free me from my Pain,
'Tis sharp, 'tis terrible, and I cou'd curse   170
The chearful Day, Men, Earth, and Heav'n, and Thee,
Ev'n thee, thou venerable good Old Man,
For being Author of a Wretch like me.

    Alt. Listen not to the Wildness of her Raving,
Remember Nature! Shou'd thy Daughter's Murder
Defile that Hand, so just, so great in Arms,
Her Blood wou'd rest upon thee to Posterity,
Pollute thy Name, and fully all thy Wars.

    Cal. Have I not wrong'd his gentle Nature much?
And yet behold him pleading for my Life.   180
Lost as thou art, to Virtue, oh *Calista*!
I think thou canst not bear to be outdone;
Then haste to die, and be oblig'd no more.

    Sci. Thy pious Care has giv'n me time to think,
And sav'd me from a Crime; then rest my Sword;
To Honour have I kept thee ever sacred,
Nor will I stain thee with a rash Revenge;
But, mark me well, I will have Justice done;
Hope not to bear away thy Crimes unpunish'd,
I will see Justice executed on thee,   190
Ev'n to a *Roman* strictness; and thou, Nature,
Or whatsoe'er thou art that plead'st within me,

Be still, thy tender Strugglings are in vain.
   Cal. Then am I doom'd to live, and bear your
     Triumph?
To groan beneath your Scorn and fierce Upbraidings,
Daily to be reproach'd, and have my Misery
At Morn, at Noon and Night told over to me,
Lest my Remembrance might grow pitiful,
And grant a Moment's Interval of Peace;
Is this, is this the Mercy of a Father?   200
I only beg to die, and he denies me.
   Sci. Hence from my sight, thy Father cannot bear
     thee;
Fly with thy Infamy to some dark Cell,
Where on the Confines of Eternal Night,
Mourning, Misfortune, Cares, and Anguish dwell;
Where ugly Shame hides her opprobrious Head,
And Death and Hell detested Rule maintain;
There howl out the remainder of thy Life,
And wish thy Name may be no more remember'd.
   Cal. Yes, I will fly to some such dismal Place,   210
And be more curst than you can wish I were;
This fatal Form that drew on my Undoing,
Fasting, and Tears, and Hardship shall destroy,
Nor Light, nor Food, nor Comfort will I know,
Nor ought that may continue hated Life.
Then when you see me meagre, wan, and chang'd,
Stretch'd at my Length, and dying in my Cave,
On that cold Earth I mean shall be my Grave,
Perhaps you may relent, and sighing say,   219
At length her Tears have wash'd her Stains away,
At length 'tis time her Punishment shou'd cease;
Die thou, poor suff'ring Wretch, and be at peace.
                      [Exit Calista.
   Sci. Who of my Servants wait there?

     Enter two or three Servants.

On your Lives
Take care my Doors be guarded well, that none

Pass out, or enter, but by my Appointment.

[*Exeunt Servants.*

Alt. There is a fatal Fury in your Visage,
It blazes fierce, and menaces Destruction:
My Father, I am sick of many Sorrows,
Ev'n now my easie Heart is breaking with 'em,   230
Yet, above all, one Fear distracts me most,
I tremble at the Vengeance which you meditate,
On the poor, faithless, lovely, dear *Calista*.

Sci. Hast thou not read what brave *Virginius* did?
With his own Hand he slew his only Daughter,
To save her from the fierce *Decemvir*'s Lust.
He slew her yet unspotted, to prevent
The Shame which she might know. Then what
          shou'd I do?——
But thou hast ty'd my Hand.——I wo' not kill her;
Yet by the Ruin she has brought upon us,   240
The common Infamy that brands us both,
She sha' not 'scape.

Alt. You mean that she shall dye then.

Sci. Ask me not what, nor how I have resolv'd,
For all within is Anarchy and Uproar.
Oh *Altamont*! what a vast Scheme of Joy
Has this one Day destroy'd! Well did I hope
This Daughter wou'd have blest my latter Days,
That I shou'd live to see you the World's Wonder;
So happy, great, and good, that none were like you.
While I, from busie Life and Care set free,   251
Had spent the Ev'ning of my Age at home,
Among a little prattling Race of yours:
There, like an old Man talk'd awhile, and then
Lain down and slept in Peace. Instead of this,
Sorrow and Shame must bring me to my Grave;
Oh damn her! damn her!

Enter a Servant.

Ser. Arm your self, my Lord,
Rossano, who but now escap'd the Garden,

Has gather'd in the Street a Band of Rioters,   260
Who threaten you, and all your Friends, with Ruin,
Unless *Lothario* be return'd in safety.

Sci. By Heav'n, their Fury rises to my Wish,
Nor shall Misfortune know my House alone,
But thou, *Lothario,* and thy Race, shall pay me,
For all the Sorrows which my Age is curst with.
I think my Name as great, my Friends as potent,
As any in the State; all shall be summon'd,
I know that all will joyn their Hands to ours,
And vindicate thy Vengeance. Raise the Body,   270
And bear it in; his Friends shall buy him dearly,
I will have Blood for Ransom: When our Force
Is full, and arm'd, we shall expect thy Sword,
To join with us, and sacrifice to Justice.——

[Exit Sciolto.
[The Body of Lothario *is carried off by Servants.*
Manet Altamont.

Alt. There is a stupid Weight upon my Senses,
A dismal sullen Stillness, that succeeds
The Storm of Rage and Grief, like silent Death,
After the Tumult and the Noise of Life.
Wou'd it were Death, as sure 'tis wond'rous like it,
For I am sick of Living, my Soul 's pall'd,   280
She kindles not with Anger or Revenge;
Love was th' informing, active Fire within,
Now that is quench'd, the Mass forgets to move,
And longs to mingle with its kindred Earth.

*A tumultuous Noise, with clashing of Swords, as at a little
distance.*
Enter Lavinia, *with two Servants, their Swords drawn.*

Lav. Fly, swiftly fly, to my *Horatio's* Aid,
Nor lose you vain, officious Cares on me;
Bring me my Lord, my Husband to my Arms,
He is *Lavinia's* Life, bring him me safe,
And I shall be at ease, be well and happy.   289

[Exeunt Servants.

Alt. Art thou *Lavinia*? Oh! what barb'rous Hand
Could wrong thy poor, defenceless Innocence,
And leave such Marks of more than savage Fury?

Lav. My Brother! Oh my Heart is full of Fears;
Perhaps ev'n now my dear *Horatio* bleeds.——
Not far from hence, as passing to the Port,
By a mad Multitude we were surrounded,
Who ran upon us with uplifted Swords,
And cry'd aloud for Vengeance, and *Lothario*.
My Lord, with ready Boldness stood the Shock,
To shelter me from Danger, but in vain,   300
Had not a Party, from *Sciolto*'s Palace,
Rush'd out, and snatch'd me from amidst the Fray.

Alt. What of my Friend?

Lav. Ha! by my Joys 'tis he,   [*Looking out.*
He lives, he comes to bless me, he is safe!——

Enter Horatio, *with two or three Servants, their Swords drawn.*

1 *Serv.* 'Twere at the utmost hazard of your Life
To venture forth again, 'till we are stronger;
Their Number trebles ours.

Hor. No matter, let it;
Death is not half so shocking as that Traitor.   310
My honest Soul is mad with Indignation,
To think her Plainness could be so abus'd,
As to mistake that Wretch, and call him Friend;
I cannot bear the Sight.

Alt. Open thou Earth,
Gape wide, and take me down to thy dark Bosom,
To hide me from *Horatio*.

Hor. Oh *Lavinia*,
Believe not but I joy to see thee safe:
Wou'd our ill Fortune had not drove us hither;   320
I cou'd ev'n wish, we rather had been wreckt
On any other Shoar, than sav'd on this.

Lav. Oh let us bless the Mercy that preserv'd us,
That gracious Pow'r that sav'd us for each other:

And to adorn the Sacrifice of Praise,
Offer Forgiveness too; be thou like Heav'n,
And put away th' Offences of thy Friend,
Far, far from thy Remembrance.

 Alt. I have mark'd him,
To see if one forgiving Glance stole hither, 330
If any Spark of Friendship were alive,
That wou'd, by Sympathy, at meeting glow,
And strive to kindle up the Flame anew;
'Tis lost, 'tis gone, his Soul is quite estrang'd,
And knows me for its Counter-part no more.

 Hor. Thou know'st thy Rule, thy Empire in
  Horatio,
Nor canst thou ask in vain, command in vain,
Where Nature, Reason, nay where Love is Judge;
But when you urge my Temper, to comply
With what it most abhors, I cannot do it. 340

 Lav. Where didst thou get this sullen, gloomy
  Hate?
It was not in thy Nature to be thus;
Come put it off, and let thy Heart be chearful,
Be gay again, and know the Joys of Friendship,
The Trust, Security, and mutual Tenderness,
The double Joys, where each is glad for both;
Friendship, the Wealth, the last Retreat and Strength,
Secure against ill Fortune, and the World.

 Hor. I am not apt to take a light Offence,
But patient of the Failings of my Friends, 350
And willing to forgive; but when an Injury
Stabs to the Heart, and rouses my Resentment,
(Perhaps it is the Fault of my rude Nature)
I own I cannot easily forget it.

 Alt. Thou hast forgot me.

 Hor. No.

 Alt. Why are thy Eyes
Impatient of me then, scornful and fierce?

 Hor. Because they speak the meaning of my Heart,
Because they are honest, and disdain a Villain. 360

Alt. I have wrong'd thee much, *Horatio*.

Hor. True thou hast:
When I forget it, may I be a Wretch,
Vile as thy self, a false perfidious Fellow,
An infamous, believing, *British* Husband.

Alt. I've wrong'd thee much, and Heav'n has well
aveng'd it.
I have not, since we parted, been at Peace,
Nor known one Joy sincere; our broken Friendship
Pursu'd me to the last Retreat of Love,
Stood glaring like a Ghost, and made me cold with
Horror.   370
Misfortunes on Misfortunes press upon me,
Swell o'er my Head, like Waves, and dash me down.
Sorrow, Remorse, and Shame, have torn my Soul,
They hang like Winter on my Youthful Hopes,
And blast the Spring and Promise of my Year.

Lav. So Flow'rs are gather'd to adorn a Grave,
To lose their Freshness amongst Bones and Rotten-
ness,
And have their Odours stifled in the Dust.
Canst thou hear this, thou cruel, hard *Horatio*?
Canst thou behold thy *Altamont* undone?   380
That gentle, that dear Youth! canst thou behold him,
His poor Heart broken, Death in his pale Visage,
And groaning out his Woes, yet stand unmov'd?

Hor. The Brave and Wise I pity in Misfortune,
But when Ingratitude and Folly suffers,
'Tis Weakness to be touch'd.

Alt. I wo' not ask thee
To pity or forgive me, but confess,
This Scorn, this Insolence of Hate is just;
'Tis Constancy of Mind, and manly in thee.   390
But oh! had I been wrong'd by thee, *Horatio*,
There is a yielding Softness in my Heart
Cou'd ne'er have stood it out, but I had ran,
With streaming Eyes, and open Arms, upon thee,
And prest thee close, close!

Hor. I must hear no more,
The Weakness is contagious, I shall catch it,
And be a tame fond Wretch.
    Lav. Where wou'dst thou go?   399
Wou'dst thou part thus? You sha' not, 'tis impossible;
For I will bar thy Passage, kneeling thus;
Perhaps thy cruel Hand may spurn me off,
But I will throw my Body in thy way,
And thou shalt trample o'er my faithful Bosom,
Tread on me, wound me, kill me e'er thou pass.
    Alt. Urge not in vain thy pious Suit, *Lavinia*,
I have enough to rid me of my Pain.
Calista, thou hadst reach'd my Heart before;
To make all sure, my Friend repeats the Blow:
But in the Grave our Cares shall be forgotten,   410
There Love and Friendship cease.   [*Falls.*
    [*Lavinia runs to him, and endeavours to raise him.*
    Lav. Speak to me, *Altamont.*
He faints! he dies! Now turn and see thy Triumph;
My Brother! But our Cares shall end together;
Here will I lay me down by thy dear Side,
Bemoan thy too hard Fate, then share it with thee,
And never see my cruel Lord again.
    [*Horatio runs to* Altamont, *and raises him in
       his Arms.*
    Hor. It is too much to bear! Look up, my *Altamont*!
My stubborn, unrelenting Heart has kill'd him.
Look up and bless me, tell me that thou liv'st.   420
Oh! I have urg'd thy Gentleness too far;
                        [*He revives.*
Do thou and my *Lavinia* both forgive me;
A Flood of Tenderness comes o'er my Soul;
I cannot speak!——I love! forgive! and pity thee.——
    Alt. I thought that nothing cou'd have stay'd my
      Soul,
That long e'er this her Flight had reach'd the Stars;
But thy known Voice has lur'd her back again.
Methinks I fain wou'd set all right with thee,

Make up this most unlucky Breach, and then,   429
With thine, and Heav'n's Forgiveness on my Soul,
Shrink to my Grave, and be at ease for ever.

    Hor. By Heav'n my Heart bleeds for thee; ev'n this
      moment
I feel thy Pangs of disappointed Love.
Is it not pity that this Youth shou'd fail,
That all this wond'rous Goodness shou'd be lost,
And the World never know it? oh my *Altamont*!
Give me thy Sorrows, let me bear 'em for thee,
And shelter thee from Ruin.

    Lav. Oh my Brother!
Think not but we will share in all thy Woes,   440
We'll sit all day, and tell sad Tales of Love,
And when we light upon some faithless Woman,
Some Beauty, like *Calista*, false and fair,
We'll fix our Grief, and our Complaining, there;
We'll curse the Nymph that drew the Ruin on,
And mourn the Youth that was like thee undone.

                           [*Exeunt.*

End of the Fourth Act.

ACT V. SCENE I.

SCENE *is a Room hung with Black; on one side,
Lothario's Body on a Bier; on the other, a Table with
a Skull and other Bones, a Book, and a Lamp on it.*

Calista *is discover'd on a Couch in Black, her Hair hanging
loose and disordered: After Musick and a Song, she rises
and comes forward.*

SONG.

I.

    Hear, you Midnight Phantoms, hear,   ⎫
    You who pale and wan appear,   ⎬
    And fill the Wretch, who wakes, with Fear. ⎭
    You who wander, scream, and groan,
    Round the Mansions once your own,

You, whom still your Crimes upbraid,
You, who rest not with the dead;
From the Coverts where you stray,
Where you lurk, and shun the Day,
From the Charnel, and the Tomb,   10
Hither haste ye, hither come.

II.

Chide Calista *for Delay,*   ⎤
Tell her, 'tis for her you stay; ⎥
Bid her die, and come away.   ⎦
See the Sexton with his Spade,
See the Grave already made;
Listen, Fair one, to thy Knell,
This Musick is thy passing Bell.

Cal. 'Tis well! these Solemn Sounds, this Pomp of
        Horror,
Are fit to feed the Frenzy in my Soul,   20
Here's room for Meditation, ev'n to Madness,
'Till the Mind burst with Thinking; this dull Flame
Sleeps in the Socket; sure the Book was left
To tell me something;——for Instruction then——
He teaches holy Sorrow, and Contrition,
And Penitence;——Is it become an Art then?
A Trick that lazy, dull, luxurious Gown-men
Can teach us to do over; I'll no more on't;
                        [*Throwing away the Book.*
I have more real Anguish in my Heart,
Than all their Pedant Discipline e'er knew.   30
What Charnel has been rifl'd for these Bones?
Fye! this is Pageantry;——they look uncouthly,
But what of that? If he or she that own'd 'em,
Safe from Disquiet, sit, and smile to see
The Farce, their miserable Relicks play.
But here's a Sight is terrible indeed;
Is this that Haughty, Gallant, Gay *Lothario,*
That dear perfidious——Ah!——how Pale he looks!
How Grim with clotted Blood, and those dead Eyes!

Ascend ye Ghosts, fantastick Forms of Night,   40
In all your diff'rent, dreadful Shapes ascend,
And match the present Horror if you can.

Enter Sciolto.

  Sci. This Dead of Night, this silent Hour of Dark-
     ness,
Nature for Rest ordain'd, and soft Repose,
And yet Distraction, and tumultuous Jars,
Keep all our frighted Citizens awake;
The Senate, weak, divided, and irresolute,
Want Pow'r to succour the afflicted State.
Vainly in Words and long Debates they're Wise,   49
While the fierce Factions scorn their peaceful Orders,
And drown the Voice of Law in Noise and Anarchy.
Amidst the general Wreck, see where she stands,
                   [*Pointing to* Calista.
Like *Hellen*, in the Night when *Troy* was sack'd,
Spectatress of the Mischief which she made.

  Cal. It is *Sciolto*! be thy self, my Soul;
Be strong to bear this fatal Indignation,
That he may see thou art not lost so far,
But somewhat still of his great Spirit lives
In the forlorn *Calista*.

  Sci. Thou wert once   60
My Daughter.

  Cal. Happy were it I had dy'd,
And never lost that Name.

  Sci. That 's something yet;
Thou wer't the very Darling of my Age;
I thought the Day too short to gaze upon thee,
That all the Blessings I cou'd gather for thee,
By Cares on Earth, and by my Pray'rs to Heav'n,
Were little for my Fondness to bestow;   69
Why didst thou turn to Folly then, and curse me?

  Cal. Because my Soul was rudely drawn from yours;
A poor imperfect Copy of my Father,
Where Goodness. and the strength of manly Virtue,

Was thinly planted, and the idle Void
Fill'd up with light Belief, and easie Fondness;
It was, because I lov'd, and was a Woman.
   Sci. Hadst thou been honest, thou hadst been a
     Cherubin;
But of that Joy, as of a Gem long lost,
Beyond Redemption gone, think we no more.
Hast thou e'er dar'd to meditate on Death?   80
   Cal. I have, as on the end of Shame and Sorrow.
   Sci. Ha! answer me! say, hast thou coolly thought?
'Tis not the Stoick's Lessons got by Rote,
The Pomp of Words, and Pedant Dissertations,
That can sustain thee in that Hour of Terror:
Books have taught Cowards to talk nobly of it,
But when the Trial comes, they start, and stand
     aghast;
Hast thou consider'd what may happen after it?   88
How thy Account may stand, and what to answer?
   Cal. I have turn'd my Eyes inward upon my self,
Where foul Offence, and Shame have laid all waste;
Therefore my Soul abhors the wretched Dwelling,
And longs to find some better place of Rest.
   Sci. 'Tis justly thought, and worthy of that Spirit
That dwelt in ancient *Latian* Breasts, when *Rome*
Was Mistress of the World. I wou'd go on,
And tell thee all my Purpose, but it sticks,
Here at my Heart, and cannot find a way.
   Cal. Then spare the Telling, if it be a Pain,   99
And write the Meaning with your Ponyard here.
   Sci. Oh! truly guess'd—seest thou this trembling
     Hand——   [*Holding up a Dagger.*
Thrice Justice urg'd——and thrice the slack'ning
     Sinews
Forgot their Office, and confest the Father;
At length the stubborn Virtue has prevail'd,
It must, it must be so——Oh! take it then,
                [*Giving the Dagger.*
And know the rest untaught.

Cal. I understand you,
It is but thus, and both are satisfy'd.

> [*She offers to kill her self,* Sciolto *catches hold
> of her Arm.*

Sci. A Moment, give me yet a Moment's space;
The stern, the rigid Judge has been obey'd;   110
Now Nature, and the Father claim their turns;
I have held the Ballance with an Iron Hand,
And put off ev'ry tender, human Thought,
To doom my Child to Death; but spare my Eyes
The most unnatural Sight, lest their Strings crack,
And my old Brain split, and grow Mad with Horror.

Cal. Ha! Is it possible? And is there yet
Some little, dear Remain of Love and Tenderness,
For poor, undone *Calista*, in your Heart?

Sci. Oh! when I think what Pleasure I took in
thee,   120
What Joys thou gav'st me in thy prattling Infancy,
Thy sprightly Wit, and early blooming Beauty,
How I have stood, and fed my Eyes upon thee,
Then lifted up my Hands, and wond'ring, blest thee;
By my strong Grief, my Heart ev'n melts within me,
I cou'd curse Nature, and that Tyrant, Honour,
For making me thy Father, and thy Judge;
Thou art my Daughter still.

Cal. For that kind Word,
Thus let me fall, thus humbly to the Earth;   130
Weep on your Feet, and bless you for this Goodness;
Oh! 'tis too much for this offending Wretch,
This Parricide, that murders with her Crimes,
Shortens her Father's Age, and cuts him off,
E'er little more than half his Years be number'd.

Sci. Wou'd it were otherwise!—but thou must
die.——

Cal. That I must die! it is my only Comfort;
Death is the Privilege of human Nature,
And Life without it were not worth our taking;   139
Thither the Poor, the Pris'ner, and the Mourner,

Fly for Relief, and lay their Burthens down.
Come then, and take me now to thy cold Arms,
Thou meagre Shade; here let me breathe my last,
Charm'd with my Father's Pity and Forgiveness,
More than if Angels tun'd their Golden Viols,
And sung a *Requiem* to my parting Soul.

 Sci. I am summon'd hence, e'er this my Friends
  expect me,
There is I know not what of sad Presage,
That tells me, I shall never see thee more;
If it be so, this is our last Farewel,   150
And these the parting Pangs which Nature feels,
When Anguish rends the Heart-strings—Oh! my
  Daughter.   [*Exit* Sciolto.

 Cal. Now think thou, curst *Calista*, now behold
The Desolation, Horror, Blood, and Ruin,
Thy Crimes, and fatal Folly spread around,
That loudly cry for Vengeance on thy Head;
Yet Heav'n, who knows our weak, imperfect Natures,
How blind with Passions, and how prone to Evil,
Makes not too strict Enquiry for Offences,
But is aton'd by Penitence and Pray'r: 160
Cheap Recompence! here 'twould not be receiv'd,
Nothing but Blood can make the Expiation
And cleanse the Soul from inbred, deep Pollution.
And see, another injur'd Wretch is come,
To call for Justice from my tardy Hand.

    Enter Altamont.

 Alt. Hail to you Horrors! hail thou House of
  Death!
And thou the lovely Mistress of these Shades,
Whose Beauty gilds the more than midnight Darkness,
And makes it grateful as the Dawn of Day.
Oh! take me in a Fellow-Mourner with thee,   170
I'll number Groan for Groan, and Tear for Tear;
And when the Fountain of thy Eyes are dry,
Mine shall supply the Stream, and weep for both.

Cal. I know thee well, thou art the injur'd *Altamont*,
Thou com'st to urge me with the Wrongs I ha' done
    thee;
But know I stand upon the Brink of Life,
And in a Moment mean to set me free
From Shame, and thy Upbraiding.

    Alt. Falsly, falsly
Dost thou accuse me; when did I complain,   180
Or murmur at my Fate? For thee I have
Forgot the Temper of *Italian* Husbands,
And Fondness has prevail'd upon Revenge;
I bore my load of Infamy with Patience,
As Holy Men do Punishments from Heav'n,
Nor thought it hard, because it came from thee;
Oh! then forbid me not to mourn thy Loss,
To wish some better Fate had rul'd our Loves,
And that *Calista* had been mine, and true.   189

    Cal. Oh! *Altamont*, 'tis hard for Souls like mine,
Haughty and fierce, to yield they have done amiss;
But oh! behold my proud, disdainful Heart,
Bends to thy gentler Virtue; yes, I own,
Such is thy Truth, thy Tenderness and Love,
Such are the Graces that adorn thy Youth,
That were I not abandon'd to Destruction,
With thee I might have liv'd, for Ages blest,
And dy'd in Peace within thy faithful Arms.

    Alt. Then Happiness is still within our reach;   199
Here let Remembrance lose our past Misfortunes,
Tear all Records that hold the fatal Story;
Here let our Joys begin, from hence go on
In long successive Order.

    Cal. What! in Death?

    Alt. Then art thou fix'd to die?——But be it so,
We'll go together, my advent'rous Love
Shall follow thee to those uncertain Beings;
Whether our lifeless Shades are doom'd to wander,
In gloomy Groves, with discontented Ghosts,

Or whether thro' the upper Air we fleet, 210
And tread the Fields of Light, still I'll pursue thee,
'Till Fate ordains that we shall part no more.

Cal. Oh no! Heav'n has some better Lot in store
To Crown thee with; live, be happy long;
Live for some Maid that shall deserve thy Goodness,
Some kind, unpractis'd Heart, that never yet
Has listen'd to the false ones of thy Sex,
Nor known the Arts of ours; she shall reward thee,
Meet thee with Virtues equal to thy own, 219
Charm thee with Sweetness, Beauty, and with Truth,
Be blest in thee alone, and thou in her.

Enter Horatio.

Hor. Now mourn indeed, ye miserable Pair,
For now the Measure of your Woes is full.

Alt. What dost thou mean, *Horatio*?

Hor. Oh! 'tis dreadful;
The great, the good *Sciolto* dies this Moment.

Cal. My Father!

Alt. That's a deadly Stroak indeed.

Hor. Not long ago he privately went forth,
Attended but by few, and those unbidden; 230
I heard which way he took, and strait pursu'd him,
But found him compass'd by *Lothario's* Faction,
Almost alone, amidst a Crowd of Foes;
Too late we brought him Aid, and drove them back;
E'er that his frantick Valour had provok'd,
The Death he seem'd to wish for from their Swords.

Cal. And dost thou bear me yet, thou patient
Earth?
Dost thou not labour with my murd'rous Weight?
And you ye glitt'ring, heav'nly Host of Stars, 239
Hide your Fair Heads in Clouds, or I shall blast you
For I am all Contagion, Death, and Ruin,
And Nature sickens at me; rest thou World,
This Parricide shall be thy Plague no more;
Thus, thus I set thee free.   [*Stabs her self.*

Hor. Oh! fatal Rashness.

Alt. Thou dost instruct me well; to lengthen Life,
Is but to trifle now.

> [Altamont *offers to kill himself*; Horatio *prevents him, and wrests his Sword from him.*

Hor. Ha! what means
The frantick *Altamont?* Some Foe to Man
Has breath'd on ev'ry Breast Contagious Fury,   250
And Epidemick Madness.

Enter Sciolto, *pale and bloody, supported by Servants.*

Cal. Oh my Heart!
Well may'st thou fail, for see the Spring that fed
Thy Vital Stream is wasted, and runs low.
My Father! will you now at last forgive me,
If after all my Crimes, and all your Suff'rings,
I call you once again by that dear Name?
Will you forget my Shame, and those wide Wounds,
Lift up your Hand, and bless me e'er I go
Down to my dark Abode.   260

Sci. Alas! my Daughter!
Thou hast rashly ventur'd in a stormy Sea,
Where Life, Fame, Virtue, all were wreck'd and lost;
But sure thou hast born thy part in all the Anguish,
And smarted with the Pain, then rest in Peace,
Let Silence and Oblivion hide thy Name,
And save thee from the Malice of Posterity;
And may'st thou find with Heav'n the same Forgiveness,
As with thy Father here.——Die, and be happy.   269

Cal. Celestial Sounds! Peace dawns upon my Soul,
And ev'ry Pain grows less.——Oh! gentle *Altamont,*
Think not too hardly of me when I'm gone,
But pity me.——Had I but early known
Thy wond'rous Worth, thou excellent young Man,
We had been happier both:——Now 'tis too late,
And yet my Eyes take Pleasure to behold thee,

Thou art their last dear Object.——Mercy, Heav'n!
                                              [*She dies.*

  Alt. Cold! dead and cold! and yet thou art not
     chang'd,
But lovely still! Hadst thou a thousand Faults,
What Heart so hard, what Virtue so severe,   280
But at that Beauty must of force relented,
Melted to Pity, Love, and to Forgiveness?
  Sci. Oh! turn thee from the fatal Object; *Altamont*,
Come near, and let me bless thee e'er I die.
To thee, and brave *Horatio*, I bequeath
My Fortunes.——Lay me by thy Noble Father,
And love my Memory as thou hast done his,
For thou hast been my Son.——Oh! gracious
     Heav'n!
Thou that hast endless Blessings still in store,
For Virtue, and for filial Piety,   290
Let Grief, Disgrace, and Want be far away,
But multiply thy Mercies on his Head;
Let Honour, Greatness, Goodness, still be with him,
And Peace in all his Ways.——   [*He dies.*
  Alt. Take, take it all;
To thee, *Horatio*, I resign the Gift,
While I pursue my Father and my Love,
And find my only Portion in the Grave.
  Hor. The Storm of Grief bears hard upon his Youth,
And bends him like a drooping Flower to Earth.   300
Raise him, and bear him in.
                         [*Altamont is carried off.*
By such Examples are we taught to prove,
The Sorrows that attend unlawful Love;
Death, or some worse Misfortunes, soon divide
The injur'd Bridegroom from his guilty Bride:
If you wou'd have the Nuptial Union last,
Let Virtue be the Bond that ties it fast.
                                [*Exeunt omnes.*

The End of the Fifth Act.

EPILOGUE,

Spoken by Mrs. *Bracegirdle*, who play'd *Lavinia*.

You see the tripping Dame cou'd find no Favour, }
Dearly she paid for Breach of good Behaviour, }
Nor cou'd her loving Husband's Fondness save her. }
Italian Ladies lead but scurvy Lives,
There's dreadful dealing with Eloping Wives;
Thus 'tis, because these Husbands are obey'd
By force of Laws, which for themselves they made.
With Tales of old Prescriptions they confine, }
The Right of Marriage-rule to their Male Line, }
And Huff, and Domineer by Right Divine. }   10
Had we the Pow'r we'd make the Tyrants know,
What 'tis to fail in Duties which they owe;
We'd teach the saunt'ring Squire, who loves to roam,
Forgetful of his own dear Spouse and Home;
Who Snores at Night supinely by her side,
'Twas not for this the Nuptial Knot was ty'd.
The plodding Petty-fogger, and the Cit,
Have learn'd at least this Modern way of Wit:
Each ill-bred, senseless Rogue, tho' ne'er so dull,
Has th' Impudence to think his Wife a Fool;   20
He spends the Night, where merry Wags resort,
With joking Clubs, and Eighteen-penny Port,
While she poor Soul's contented to regale,
By a sad Sea-cole Fire, with Wigs and Ale.
Well may the Cuckold-making Tribe find Grace,
And fill an absent Husband's empty place:
If you wou'd e'er bring Constancy in Fashion,
You Men must first begin the Reformation.
Then shall the Golden Age of Love return,
No Turtle for her wand'ring Mate shall mourn,   30
No Foreign Charms shall cause Domestick Strife,
But ev'ry marry'd Man shall toast his Wife;
Phillis shall not be to the Country sent,
For Carnivals in Town to keep a tedious Lent:
Lampoons shall cease, and envious Scandal die,
And all shall live in Peace like my good Man and I.

C A T O.

A

T R A G E D Y.

As it is Acted at the

THEATRE-ROYAL in *Drury-Lane,*

B Y

HIS MAJESTY'S SERVANTS.

Ecce Spectaculum dignum, ad quod respiciat, intentus operi suo, Deus!
Ecce par Deo dignum, vir fortis cum malâ fortunâ compositus! Non
video, inquam, quid habeat in terris Jupiter pulchrius, si convertere
animum velit, quàm ut spectet Catonem, jam partibus non semel
fractis, nihilominùs inter ruinas publicas erectum.

Sen. de Divin. Prov.

V E R S E S
TO THE
A U T H O R
OF THE
TRAGEDY of *CATO*.

While you the fierce divided Britons *awe,*
And Cato *with an equal virtue, draw,*
While Envy *is it self in Wonder lost,*
And Factions strive who shall applaud you most;
Forgive the fond ambition of a friend,
Who hopes himself, not you, to recommend,
And join th' applause which all the Learn'd bestow
On one, to whom a perfect work they owe.
To my * *light Scenes I once inscrib'd your name,*
And impotently strove to borrow fame: 10
Soon will that die, which adds thy name to mine;
Let me, then, live, join'd to a work of thine.

RICHARD STEELE.

Tho' Cato *shines in* Virgil's *epick song,*
Prescribing laws among th' Elysian *throng;*
Tho' Lucan's *verse, exalted by his name,*
O'er Gods themselves has rais'd the Heroe's fame;
The Roman *stage did ne'er his image see,*
Drawn at full length; a task reserv'd for thee.
By thee we view the finish'd figure rise,
And awful march before our ravish'd eyes;
We hear his voice, asserting virtue's cause;
His fate renew'd our deep attention draws,   10
Excites by turns our various hopes and fears,
And all the patriot in thy scene appears.

On Tyber's *banks thy thought was first inspir'd;*
'Twas there, to some indulgent grove retir'd,

* Tender Husband, *Dedicated to Mr.* Addison.

Rome's *ancient fortunes rolling in thy mind,*
Thy happy Muse *this manly work design'd:*
Or in a dream thou saw'st Rome's Genius *stand,*
And, leading Cato *in his sacred hand,*
Point out th' immortal subject of thy lays,
And ask this labour to record his praise.   20

'Tis done—the Heroe *lives, and charms our age!*
While nobler morals grace the British *stage.*
Great Shakespear's *ghost, the solemn strain to hear,*
(Methinks I see the laurel'd Shade *appear!)*
Will hover o'er the Scene, *and wond'ring view*
His fav'rite Brutus *rival'd thus by you.*
Such Roman *greatness in each action shines,*
Such Roman *eloquence adorns your lines,*
That sure the Sybills *books this year foretold,*
And in some mystick leaf was seen inroll'd,   30
    '*Rome, turn thy mournful eyes from* Africk's *shore,*
    '*Nor in her sands thy* Cato's *tomb explore!*
    '*When thrice six hundred times the circling Sun*
    '*His annual race shall thro' the* Zodiack *run,*
    '*An Isle remote his monument shall rear,*
    '*And every generous* Briton *pay a tear.*'

J. HUGHES.

What do we see! is Cato *then become*
A greater name in Britain *than in* Rome?
Does mankind now admire his virtues more,
Tho' Lucan, Horace, Virgil *wrote before?*
How will Posterity this truth explain?
"Cato *begins to live in* Anna's *reign:*"
The world's great chiefs, in council or in arms,
Rise in your lines with more exalted charms;
Illustrious deeds in distant nations wrought,
And virtues by departed Heroes *taught,*   10
Raise in your soul a pure immortal flame,
Adorn your life, and consecrate your fame;

To your renown all ages you subdue,
And Cæsar fought, and Cato bled for you.

All Souls College,
    Oxon.   EDWARD YOUNG.

  'Tis nobly done thus to enrich the stage,
And raise the thoughts of a degenerate age,
To show, how endless joys from freedom spring:
How life in bondage is a worthless thing.
The inborn greatness of your soul we view,
You tread the paths frequented by the few.
With so much strength you write, and so much ease,
Virtue, and sense! how durst you hope to please?
Yet crowds the sentiments of every line
Impartial clap'd, and own'd the work divine.   10
Even the sour Criticks, who malicious came,
Eager to censure, and resolv'd to blame,
Finding the Heroe regularly rise,
Great, while he lives, but greater, when he dies,
Sullen approv'd, too obstinate to melt,
And sicken'd with the pleasures, which they felt.
Not so the Fair their passions secret kept,
Silent they heard, but as they heard, they wept,
When gloriously the blooming Marcus dy'd,
And Cato told the Gods, I'm satisfy'd.   20

  See! how your lays the British youth inflame!
They long to shoot, and ripen into fame;
Applauding theatres disturb their rest,
And unborn Cato's heave in every breast;
Their nightly dreams their daily thoughts repeat,
And pulses high with fancy'd glories beat.
So, griev'd to view the Marathonian spoils,
The young Themistocles vow'd equal toils;
Did then his schemes of future honours draw
From the long triumphs which with tears he saw.   30

  How shall I your unrival'd worth proclaim,
Lost in the spreading circle of your fame!

We saw you the great William's praise rehearse,
And paint Britannia's joys in Roman verse.
We heard at distance soft, enchanting strains,
From blooming mountains, and Italian Plains.
Virgil began in English dress to shine,
His voice, his looks, his grandeur still divine.
From him too soon unfriendly you withdrew,
But brought the tuneful Ovid to our view.   40
Then, the delightful theme of every tongue,
Th' immortal Marlb'rough was your daring song;
From clime to clime the mighty victor flew,
From clime to clime as swiftly you pursue;
Still with the Heroe's glow'd the Poet's flame,
Still with his conquests you enlarg'd your fame.
With boundless raptures here the Muse could swell,
And on your Rosamond for ever dwell:
There opening sweets, and every fragrant flower
Luxuriant smile, a never-fading bower.   50
Next, human follies kindly to expose,
You change from numbers, but not sink in prose:
Whether in visionary scenes you play,
Refine our tastes, or laugh our crimes away.
Now, by the buskin'd Muse you shine confest,
The Patriot kindles in the Poet's breast.
Such energy of sense might pleasure raise,
Tho' unembellish'd with the charms of phrase:
Such charms of phrase would with success be crown'd,
Tho' nonsense flow'd in the melodious sound.   60
The chastest Virgin needs no blushes fear,
The Learn'd themselves, not uninstructed, hear.
The Libertine, in pleasures us'd to roul,
And idly sport with an immortal soul,
Here comes, and by the virtuous Heathen taught,
Turns pale, and trembles at the dreadful thought.

When e'er you traverse vast Numidia's plains,
What sluggish Briton in his Isle remains?
When Juba seeks the Tiger with delight,
We beat the thicket, and provoke the fight.   70

By the description warm'd, we fondly sweat,
And in the chilling East-wind pant with heat.
What eyes behold not, how the stream refines,
'Till by degrees the floating mirrour shines?
While hurricanes in circling eddies play,
Tear up the sands, and sweep whole plains away,
We shrink with horror, and confess our fear,
And all the sudden sounding ruine hear.
When purple robes, distain'd with blood, deceive,
And make poor Marcia *beautifully grieve,*   80
When she her secret thoughts no more conceals,
Forgets the woman, and her flame reveals,
Well may the Prince exult with noble pride,
Not for his Libyan *crown, but* Roman *bride.*

But I in vain on single features dwell,
While all the parts of the fair piece excell,
So rich the store, so dubious is the feast,
We know not, which to pass, or which to taste.
The shining incidents so justly fall,
We may the whole new scenes of transport call.   90
Thus jewellers confound our wandering eyes,
And with variety of gemms surprise.
Here Saphires, *here the* Sardian Stone *is seen,*
The Topaz *yellow, and the* Jasper *green.*
The costly Brilliant there, confus'dly bright,
From numerous surfaces darts trembling light.
The different colours mingling in a blaze,   ⎫
Silent we stand, unable where to praise,   ⎬
In pleasure sweetly lost ten thousand ways.   ⎭

Trinity College,
  Cambridge.   L. EUSDEN.

Too long hath Love engross'd Britannia's *stage,*
And sunk to softness all our tragic rage;
By that alone did empires fall or rise,
And fate depended on a fair one's eyes:
The sweet infection, mixt with dangerous art,
Debas'd our manhood, while it sooth'd the heart.

You scorn to raise a grief thy self must blame,
Nor from our weakness steal a vulgar fame:
A Patriot's fall may justly melt the mind,
And tears flow nobly, shed for all mankind.　　　10

How do our souls with gen'rous pleasure glow!
Our hearts exulting, while our eyes o'erflow,
When thy firm Hero stands beneath the weight
Of all his sufferings venerably great;
Rome's poor remains still shelt'ring by his side,
With conscious virtue, and becoming pride.

The aged Oak thus rears his head in air,
His sap exhausted, and his branches bare;
'Midst storms and earthquakes he maintains his state,
Fixt deep in earth, and fasten'd by his weight:　　　20
His naked boughs still lend the shepherds aid,
And his old trunk projects an awful shade.

Amidst the joys triumphant peace bestows,
Our Patriots sadden at his glorious woes,
Awhile they let the world's great bus'ness wait,
Anxious for Rome, and sigh for Cato's fate.
Here taught how ancient Heroes rose to fame,
Our Britons crowd, and catch the Roman flame,
Where states and senates well might lend an ear,
And Kings and Priests without a blush appear.　　　30

France boasts no more, but, fearful to engage,
Now first pays homage to her rival's stage,
Hastes to learn thee, and learning shall submit
Alike to British arms, and British wit:
No more she'll wonder, (forc'd to do us right)
Who think like Romans, could like Romans fight.

Thy Oxford smiles this glorious work to see,
And fondly triumphs in a son like thee.
The senates, consuls, and the gods of Rome,
Like old acquaintance at their native home,　　　40
In thee we find: each deed, each word exprest,
And every thought that swell'd a Roman breast.

We trace each hint that could thy soul inspire
With Virgil's *judgment, and with* Lucan's *fire;*
We know thy worth, and, give us leave to boast,
We most admire, because we know thee most.

Queen's-College,
   Oxon.   THO. TICKELL.

SIR,

When your generous labour first I view'd,
And Cato's *hands in his own blood imbru'd;*
That scene of death so terrible appears,
My soul could only thank you with her tears.
Yet with such wond'rous art your skilful hand
Does all the passions of the soul command,
That even my grief to praise and wonder turn'd,
And envy'd the great death which first I mourn'd.

What pen but yours could draw the doubtful strife,
Of honour struggling with the love of life?   10
Describe the Patriot, obstinately good,
As hovering o'er eternity he stood:
The wide, th' unbounded ocean lay before
His piercing sight, and Heaven the distant shore.
Secure of endless bliss, with fearless eyes, }
He grasps the dagger, and its point defies, }
And rushes out of Life, to snatch the glorious prize. }

How would old Rome *rejoice, to hear you tell*
How just her Patriot liv'd, how great he fell!
Recount his wond'rous probity and truth,   20
And form new Juba's *in the* British *youth.*
Their generous souls, when he resigns his breath,
Are pleas'd with ruine, and in love with death.
And when her conquering sword Britannia *draws,*
Resolve to perish, or defend her cause.
Now first on Albion's *theatre we see,*
A perfect image of what man should be;
The glorious character is now exprest,
Of virtue dwelling in a human breast.

Drawn at full length by your immortal lines,　　30
In Cato's soul, as in her Heaven she shines.

All-Souls College,
　　Oxon.　　　　　　　　　　　DIGBY COTES.

Left with the Printer by an unknown hand.

Now we may speak, since Cato speaks no more;
'Tis praise at length, 'twas rapture all before;
When crowded theatres with Iös rung
Sent to the skies, from whence thy genius sprung:
Even civil rage awhile in thine was lost;
And factions strove but to applaud thee most:
Nor could enjoyment pall our longing taste;
But every night was dearer than the last.

As when old Rome in a malignant hour
Depriv'd of some returning conqueror,　　10
Her debt of triumph to the dead discharg'd,
For fame, for treasure, and her bounds enlarg'd:
And, while his godlike figure mov'd along,　　⎫
Alternate passions fir'd th' adoring throng;　　⎬
Tears flow'd from every eye, and shouts from every tongue.　⎭
So in thy pompous lines has Cato far'd,
Grac'd with an ample, tho' a late reward:
A greater victor we in him revere;
A nobler triumph crowns his image here.

With wonder, as with pleasure, we survey　　20
A theme so scanty wrought into a play;
So vast a pile on such foundations plac'd;
Like Ammon's temple rear'd on Libya's waste:
Behold its glowing paint! its easie weight!
Its nice proportions! and stupendous height!
How chaste the conduct, how divine the rage!
A Roman Worthy on a Grecian stage!

But where shall Cato's praise begin or end;　　⎫
Inclin'd to melt, and yet untaught to bend,　　⎬
The firmest Patriot, and the gentlest Friend?　⎭
How great his genius, when the traytor croud　　31

Ready to strike the blow their fury vow'd;
Quell'd by his look, and listning to his lore,
Learn, like his passions, to rebel no more!
When, lavish of his boiling blood, to prove
The cure of slavish life, and slighted love,
Brave Marcus new in early death appears,
While Cato counts his wounds, and not his years;
Who, checking private grief, the publick mourns,
Commands the pity he so greatly scorns. 40
But when he strikes, (to crown his generous part)
That honest, staunch, impracticable heart;
No tears, no sobs pursue his parting breath;
The dying Roman shames the pomp of death.

O sacred Freedom, which the powers bestow
To season blessings, and to soften woe;
Plant of our growth, and aim of all our cares,
The toil of ages, and the crown of wars:
If, taught by thee, the Poet's wit has flow'd
In strains as precious as his Heroe's blood; 50
Preserve those strains, an everlasting charm
To keep that blood, and thy remembrance warm:
Be this thy guardian image still secure;
In vain shall force invade, or fraud allure;
Our great Palladium shall perform its part,
Fix'd and enshrin'd in every British heart.

The mind to virtue is by verse subdu'd;
And the true Poet is a public good.
This Britain feels, while, by your lines inspir'd,
Her free-born sons to glorious thoughts are fir'd. 60
In Rome had you espous'd the vanquish'd cause,
Enflam'd her senate, and upheld her laws;
Your manly scenes had liberty restor'd,
And given the just success to Cato's sword:
O'er Cæsar's arms your genius had prevail'd;
And the Muse triumph'd, where the Patriot fail'd.

AMBR. PHILIPS.

PROLOGUE,

By Mr. *POPE*.

Spoken by Mr. *WILKS*.

To wake the soul by tender strokes of art,
To raise the genius, and to mend the heart,
To make mankind in conscious virtue bold,
Live o'er each scene, and be what they behold:
For this the Tragic-Muse first trod the stage,
Commanding tears to stream thro' every age;
Tyrants no more their savage nature kept,
And foes to virtue wonder'd how they wept.
Our author shuns by vulgar springs to move
The Heroe's glory, or the Virgin's love; 10
In pitying Love we but our weakness show,
And wild Ambition well deserves its woe.
Here tears shall flow from a more generous cause,
Such tears as Patriots shed for dying laws:
He bids your breasts with ancient ardor rise,
And calls forth Roman drops from British eyes.
Virtue confest in human shape he draws,
What Plato thought, and God-like Cato was:
No common object to your sight displays,
But what with pleasure Heaven it self surveys; 20
A brave man struggling in the storms of fate,
And greatly falling with a falling state!
While Cato gives his little Senate laws,
What bosom beats not in his country's cause?
Who sees him act, but envies every deed?
Who hears him groan, and does not wish to bleed?
Even when proud Cæsar 'midst triumphal cars,
The spoils of nations, and the pomp of wars,
Ignobly vain, and impotently great,
Show'd Rome her Cato's figure drawn in state, 30
As her dead father's reverend image past,
The pomp was darken'd, and the day o'ercast,

The triumph ceas'd—tears gush'd from every eye,
The world's great victor pass'd unheeded by;
Her last good man dejected Rome *ador'd,*
And honour'd Cæsar's *less than* Cato's *sword.*

   Britons *attend: be worth like this approv'd,*
And show you have the virtue to be mov'd.
With honest scorn the first fam'd Cato *view'd*
Rome *learning arts from* Greece, *whom she subdu'd.*   40
Our scene precariously subsists too long
On French *translation, and* Italian *song:*
Dare to have sense your selves; assert the stage,
Be justly warm'd with your own native rage.
Such plays alone should please a British *ear,*
As Cato's *self had not disdain'd to hear.*

Dramatis Personæ.

MEN.

C A T O.	Mr. *Booth.*
Lucius, *a Senator.*	Mr. *Keen.*
Sempronius, *a Senator.*	Mr. *Mills.*
Juba, *Prince of* Numidia.	Mr. *Wilks.*
Syphax, *General of the* Numidians.	Mr. *Cibber.*
Portius, } *Sons of* Cato. Marcus, }	Mr. *Powell.* Mr. *Ryan.*
Decius, *Ambassador from* Cæsar.	Mr. *Bowman.*

Mutineers, Guards, &c.

WOMEN.

Marcia, *Daughter to* Cato.	Mrs. *Oldfield.*
Lucia, *Daughter to* Lucius.	Mrs. *Porter.*

S C E N E *a large Hall in the Governor's Palace
of* Utica.

Scene] Utica, to which Cato had led a small remnant of the republican party, marching across the Lybian desert, after the defeat of Pompey (47 B.C.) by Cæsar, who had always been Cato's bitter enemy.

C A T O.

ACT I. SCENE I.

PORTIUS, MARCUS.

Portius. The dawn is over-cast, the morning lours,
And heavily in clouds brings on the day,
The great, th' important day, big with the fate
Of *Cato* and of *Rome*——Our Father's Death
Would fill up all the guilt of Civil war,
And close the scene of blood.   Already *Cæsar*
Has ravaged more than half the globe, and sees
Mankind grown thin by his destructive sword:
Should he go further, numbers would be wanting
To form new battels, and support his crimes.   10
Ye Gods, what havock does Ambition make
Among your works!

Marcus. Thy steddy temper, *Portius*,
Can look on guilt, rebellion, fraud, and *Cæsar*,
In the calm lights of mild Philosophy;
I'm tortured, even to madness, when I think
On the proud victor: every time he's named
Pharsalia rises to my view!—I see
Th' insulting tyrant, prancing o'er the field
Strow'd with *Rome*'s citizens, and drench'd in slaughter,   20
His Horse's hoofs wet with Patrician blood!
Oh *Portius*, is there not some chosen curse,
Some hidden thunder in the stores of Heaven,
Red with uncommon wrath, to blast the man,
Who owes his greatness to his country's ruin?

Portius. Believe me, *Marcus*, 'tis an impious greatness,
And mixt with too much horrour to be envy'd:
How does the lustre of our father's actions,

Through the dark cloud of Ills that cover him,
Break out, and burn with more triumphant bright-
  ness!   30
His sufferings shine, and spread a glory round him;
Greatly unfortunate, he fights the cause
Of honour, virtue, liberty, and *Rome*.
His sword ne'er fell but on the guilty head;
Oppression, tyranny, and power usurp'd,
Draw all the vengeance of his arm upon 'em.
 Marcus. Who knows not this? but what can *Cato* do
Against a world, a base degenerate world,
That courts the yoke, and bows the neck to *Cæsar*?
Pent up in *Utica* he vainly forms   40
A poor epitome of *Roman* greatness,
And, cover'd with *Numidian* guards, directs
A feeble army, and an empty senate,
Remnants of mighty battels fought in vain.
By Heavens, such virtues, join'd with such success,
Distract my very soul: Our father's fortune
Would almost tempt us to renounce his precepts.
 Portius. Remember what our father oft has told us:
The ways of Heaven are dark and intricate,
Puzzled in mazes, and perplex'd with errors: 50
Our understanding traces 'em in vain,
Lost and bewilder'd in the fruitless search;
Nor sees with how much art the windings run,
Nor where the regular confusion ends.
 Marcus. These are suggestions of a mind at ease:
Oh *Portius*, didst thou taste but half the griefs
That wring my soul, thou couldst not talk thus coldly.
Passion unpity'd, and successless love,
Plant daggers in my heart, and aggravate
My other griefs. Were but my *Lucia* kind!— 60
 Portius. Thou see'st not that thy Brother is thy
  Rival:
But I must hide it, for I know thy temper. [*Aside.*
 Now, *Marcus*, now, thy virtue's on the proof:
Put forth thy utmost strength, work every nerve,

And call up all thy father in thy soul:
To quell the tyrant Love, and guard thy heart
On this weak side, where most our nature fails,
Would be a conquest worthy *Cato*'s son.
 Marcus. *Portius*, the counsel which I cannot take, 70
Instead of healing, but upbraids my weakness.
Bid me for honour plunge into a war
Of thickest foes, and rush on certain death,
Then shalt thou see that *Marcus* is not slow
To follow glory, and confess his father.
Love is not to be reason'd down, or lost
In high ambition, and a thirst of greatness;
'Tis second life, it grows into the soul,
Warms every vein, and beats in every pulse,
I feel it here: my resolution melts—
 Portius. Behold young *Juba*, the *Numidian* Prince!
With how much care he forms himself to glory, 81
And breaks the fierceness of his native temper
To copy out our Father's bright example.
He loves our sister *Marcia*, greatly loves her,
His eyes, his looks, his actions all betray it:
But still the smother'd fondness burns within him.
When most it swells, and labours for a vent,
The sense of honour and desire of fame
Drive the big passion back into his heart.
What! shall an *African*, shall *Juba*'s heir 90
Reproach great *Cato*'s son, and show the world
A virtue wanting in a *Roman* soul?
 Marcus. *Portius*, no more! your words leave stings
  behind 'em.
When-e'er did *Juba*, or did *Portius*, show
A virtue that has cast me at a distance,
And thrown me out in the pursuits of honour?
 Portius. *Marcus*, I know thy gen'rous temper well;
Fling but th' appearance of dishonour on it,
It strait takes fire, and mounts into a blaze.
 Marcus. A Brother's sufferings claim a Brother's
  pity.

Portius. Heaven knows I pity thee: behold my eyes
Even whilst I speak——Do they not swim in tears?
Were but my heart as naked to thy view,
Marcus would see it bleed in his behalf.

Marcus. Why then dost treat me with rebukes, instead
Of kind condoling cares, and friendly sorrow?

Portius. O *Marcus*, did I know the way to ease
Thy troubled heart, and mitigate thy pains,
Marcus, believe me, I could die to do it.

Marcus. Thou best of brothers, and thou best of
friends!   110
Pardon a weak distemper'd soul that swells
With sudden gusts, and sinks as soon in calms,
The sport of passions:——but *Sempronius* comes:
He must not find this softness hanging on me.   [*Exit.*

SCENE II.

SEMPRONIUS, PORTIUS.

Sempronius. Conspiracies no sooner should be
form'd
Than executed. What means *Portius* here?
I like not that cold youth. I must dissemble,
And speak a language foreign to my heart.   [*Aside.*
Good morrow *Portius*! let us once embrace,
Once more embrace; whilst yet we both are free.
To-morrow should we thus express our friendship,
Each might receive a slave into his arms:
This Sun perhaps, this morning Sun 's the last,
That e'er shall rise on *Roman* liberty.   10

Portius. My father has this morning call'd together
To this poor hall his little *Roman* Senate,
(The leavings of *Pharsalia*) to consult
If yet he can oppose the mighty torrent
That bears down *Rome*, and all her gods, before it,
Or must at length give up the world to *Cæsar*.

Sempronius. Not all the pomp and majesty of *Rome*
Can raise her Senate more than *Cato*'s presence.
His virtues render our assembly awful,
They strike with something like religious fear,   20
And make even *Cæsar* tremble at the head
Of armies flush'd with conquest: O my *Portius*,
Could I but call that wondrous Man my Father,
Would but thy sister *Marcia* be propitious
To thy friend's vows: I might be bless'd indeed!

Portius. Alas! *Sempronius*, would'st thou talk of love
To *Marcia*, whilst her father's life's in danger?
Thou might'st as well court the pale trembling Vestal,
When she beholds the holy flame expiring.

Sempronius. The more I see the wonders of thy race,
The more I'm charm'd. Thou must take heed, my
     Portius!   31
The world has all its eyes on *Cato*'s son.
Thy father's merit sets thee up to view,
And shows thee in the fairest point of light,
To make thy virtues, or thy faults, conspicuous.

Portius. Well dost thou seem to check my lingring
     here
On this important hour——I'll strait away,
And while the Fathers of the Senate meet
In close debate to weigh th' events of war,
I'll animate the soldiers' drooping courage,   40
With love of freedom, and contempt of life:
I'll thunder in their ears their country's cause,
And try to rouse up all that's *Roman* in 'em.
'Tis not in mortals to Command success,
But we'll do more, *Sempronius*; we'll Deserve it.
                                        [*Exit.*

Sempronius solus. Curse on the Stripling! how he
     apes his Sire!
Ambitiously sententious!——but I wonder
Old *Syphax* comes not; his *Numidian* genius
Is well disposed to mischief, were he prompt
And eager on it; but he must be spurr'd,   50

And every moment quickned to the course.
——*Cato* has us'd me ill: he has refused
His daughter *Marcia* to my ardent vows.
Besides, his baffled arms, and ruined cause,
Are bars to my ambition. *Cæsar*'s favour,
That show'rs down greatness on his friends, will raise me
To *Rome*'s first honours. If I give up *Cato*,
I claim in my reward his captive daughter.
But *Syphax* comes!——

SCENE III.

SYPHAX, SEMPRONIUS.

Syphax.——*Sempronius*, all is ready,
I've sounded my *Numidians*, man by man,
And find 'em ripe for a revolt: they all
Complain aloud of *Cato*'s discipline,
And wait but the command to change their master.
 Sempronius. Believe me, *Syphax*, there 's no time to waste;
Even whilst we speak, our Conqueror comes on,
And gathers ground upon us every moment.
Alas! thou know'st not *Cæsar*'s active soul,
With what a dreadful course he rushes on   10
From war to war: in vain has Nature form'd
Mountains and oceans to oppose his passage;
He bounds o'er all, victorious in his march;
The *Alpes* and *Pyreneans* sink before him,
Through winds and waves and storms he works his way,
Impatient for the battel: one day more
Will set the Victor thundering at our gates.
But tell me, hast thou yet drawn o'er young *Juba*?
That still would recommend thee more to *Cæsar*,
And challenge better terms.
 Syphax.   Alas! he 's lost,   20

He 's lost, *Sempronius*; all his thoughts are full
Of *Cato*'s virtues:——but I'll try once more
(For every instant I expect him here)
If yet I can subdue those stubborn principles
Of faith, of honour, and I know not what,
That have corrupted his *Numidian* temper,
And struck th' infection into all his soul.

   Sempronius. Be sure to press upon him every motive.
Juba's surrender, since his father's death,
Would give up *Africk* into *Cæsar*'s hands,   30
And make him Lord of half the burning Zone.

   Syphax. But is it true, *Sempronius*, that your Senate
Is call'd together? Gods! thou must be cautious!
Cato has piercing eyes, and will discern
Our frauds, unless they're cover'd thick with art.

   Sempronius. Let me alone, good *Syphax*, I'll conceal
My thoughts in passion ('tis the surest way;)
I'll bellow out for *Rome* and for my country,
And mouth at *Cæsar* 'till I shake the Senate.
Your cold hypocrisie 's a stale device,   40
A worn-out trick: would'st thou be thought in
     earnest?
Cloath thy feign'd zeal in rage, in fire, in fury!

   Syphax. In troth, thou'rt able to instruct grey-hairs,
And teach the wily *African* deceit!

   Sempronius. Once more, be sure to try thy skill on
     Juba.
Mean while I'll hasten to my *Roman* soldiers,
Inflame the mutiny, and underhand
Blow up their discontents, 'till they break out
Unlook'd-for, and discharge themselves on *Cato*.
Remember, *Syphax*, we must work in haste: 50
O think what anxious moments pass between
The birth of plots, and their last fatal periods.
Oh! 'tis a dreadful interval of time,
Fill'd up with horror all, and big with death!
Destruction hangs on every word we speak,
On every thought, 'till the concluding stroke

Determines all, and closes our design.   [*Exit.*

  Syphax solus. I'll try if yet I can reduce to reason
This head-strong youth, and make him spurn at *Cato*.
The time is short, *Cæsar* comes rushing on us——
But hold! young *Juba* sees me, and approaches.   61

SCENE IV.

JUBA, SYPHAX.

  Juba. SYPHAX, I joy to meet thee thus alone,
I have observed of late thy looks are fallen,
O'ercast with gloomy cares, and discontent;
Then tell me, *Syphax*, I conjure thee, tell me,
What are the thoughts that knit thy brow in frowns,
And turn thine eye thus coldly on thy Prince?

  Syphax. 'Tis not my talent to conceal my thoughts,
Or carry smiles and sun-shine in my face,
When discontent sits heavy at my heart.
I have not yet so much the *Roman* in me.   10

  Juba. Why do'st thou cast out such ungenerous terms
Against the Lords and Sov'reigns of the world?
Dost thou not see mankind fall down before them,
And own the force of their superior virtue?
Is there a nation in the wilds of *Africk*,
Amidst our barren rocks, and burning sands,
That does not tremble at the *Roman* name?

  Syphax. Gods! where 's the worth that sets this people up
Above your own *Numidia*'s tawny sons!
Do they with tougher sinews bend the bow?   20
Or flies the javelin swifter to its mark,
Launch'd from the vigour of a *Roman* arm?
Who like our active *African* instructs
The fiery steed, and trains him to his hand?
Or guides in troops th' embattled Elephant,
Loaden with war? these, these are arts, my Prince,

In which your *Zama* does not stoop to *Rome*.

  Juba. These all are virtues of a meaner rank,
Perfections that are placed in bones and nerves.
A *Roman* soul is bent on higher views: 30
To civilize the rude unpolish'd world,
And lay it under the restraint of laws;
To make Man mild, and sociable to Man;
To cultivate the wild licentious Savage
With wisdom, discipline, and liberal arts;
Th' embellishments of life: Virtues like these,
Make human nature shine, reform the soul,
And break our fierce barbarians into men.

  Syphax. Patience kind Heavens!——excuse an old
    man's warmth.
What are these wond'rous civilizing arts,   40
This *Roman* polish, and this smooth behaviour,
That render man thus tractable and tame?
Are they not only to disguise our passions,
To set our looks at variance with our thoughts,
To check the starts and sallies of the soul,
And break off all its commerce with the tongue;
In short, to change us into other creatures,
Than what our nature and the Gods design'd us?

  Juba. To strike thee dumb: turn up thy eyes to
    Cato!
There may'st thou see to what a godlike height 50
The *Roman* virtues lift up mortal man,
While good, and just, and anxious for his friends,
He 's still severely bent against himself;
Renouncing sleep, and rest, and food, and ease,
He strives with thirst and hunger, toil and heat;
And when his fortune sets before him all
The pomps and pleasures that his soul can wish,
His rigid virtue will accept of none.

  Syphax. Believe me, Prince, there 's not an *African*
That traverses our vast *Numidian* desarts   60
In quest of prey, and lives upon his bow,
But better practises these boasted virtues.

Coarse are his meals, the fortune of the chase,
Amidst the running stream he slakes his thirst,
Toils all the day, and at th' approach of night
On the first friendly bank he throws him down,
Or rests his head upon a rock 'till morn:
Then rises fresh, pursues his wonted game,
And if the following day he chance to find
A new repast, or an untasted spring,   70
Blesses his stars, and thinks it luxury.

 Juba. Thy prejudices, *Syphax*, won't discern
What virtues grow from ignorance and choice,
Nor how the Hero differs from the Brute.
But grant that others could with equal glory
Look down on pleasures, and the baits of sense;
Where shall we find the man that bears affliction,
Great and majestick in his griefs, like *Cato*?
Heavens! with what strength, what steadiness of mind,
He triumphs in the midst of all his sufferings!   80
How does he rise against a load of woes,
And thank the Gods that throw the weight upon him!

 Syphax. 'Tis pride, rank pride, and haughtiness of
  soul:
I think the *Romans* call it *Stoicism*.
Had not your royal father thought so highly
Of *Roman* virtue, and of *Cato*'s cause,
He had not fallen by a slave's hand, inglorious:
Nor would his slaughter'd army now have lain
On *Africk*'s sands, disfigur'd with their wounds,
To gorge the Wolves and Vultures of *Numidia*.   90

 Juba. Why do'st thou call my sorrows up afresh?
My Father's name brings tears into my eyes.

 Syphax. Oh! that you'd profit by your Father's
  ills!

 Juba. What would'st thou have me do?

 Syphax. Abandon *Cato*.

 Juba. Syphax, I should be more than twice an
  Orphan
By such a loss.

Syphax. Ay, there's the tie that binds you!
You long to call him Father.   *Marcia*'s charms
Work in your heart unseen, and plead for *Cato*.   100
No wonder you are deaf to all I say.

   Juba. *Syphax*, your zeal becomes importunate;
I've hitherto permitted it to rave,
And talk at large; but learn to keep it in,
Lest it should take more freedom than I'll give it.

   Syphax. Sir, your great father never used me thus.
Alas, he's dead! but can you e'er forget
The tender sorrows, and the pangs of nature,
The fond embraces, and repeated blessings,
Which you drew from him in your last farewel?   110
Still must I cherish the dear, sad, remembrance,
At once to torture, and to please my soul.
The good old King at parting wrung my hand,
(His eyes brim-full of tears) then sighing cry'd,
Pr'ythee be careful of my son!——his grief
Swell'd up so high, he could not utter more.

   Juba. Alas, thy story melts away my soul.
That best of fathers! how shall I discharge
The gratitude and duty which I owe him!

   Syphax. By laying up his counsels in your heart. 120

   Juba. His counsels bade me yield to thy directions:
Then, *Syphax*, chide me in severest terms,
Vent all thy passion, and I'll stand its shock,
Calm and unruffled as a summer-sea,
When not a breath of wind flies o'er its surface.

   Syphax. Alas, my Prince, I'd guide you to your
       safety.

   Juba. I do believe thou would'st: but tell me how?

   Syphax. Fly from the fate that follows *Cæsar*'s foes.

   Juba. My father scorn'd to do it.

   Syphax. And therefore dy'd.   130

   Juba. Better to die ten thousand thousand deaths,
Than wound my honour.

   Syphax. Rather say your love.

   Juba. *Syphax*, I've promis'd to preserve my temper.

Why wilt thou urge me to confess a flame,
I long have stifled, and would fain conceal?

   Syphax. Believe me, Prince, tho' hard to conquer love,
'Tis easie to divert and break its force:
Absence might cure it, or a second mistress
Light up another flame, and put out this.   140
The glowing dames of *Zama*'s royal court
Have faces flusht with more exalted charms;
The Sun, that rolls his chariot o'er their heads,
Works up more fire and colour in their cheeks:
Were you with these, my Prince, you'd soon forget
The pale unripen'd beauties of the *North*.

   Juba. 'Tis not a sett of features, or complexion,
The tincture of a skin, that I admire.
Beauty soon grows familiar to the lover,
Fades in his eye, and palls upon the sense.   150
The virtuous *Marcia* tow'rs above her sex:
True, she is fair, (Oh how divinely fair!)
But still the lovely maid improves her charms
With inward greatness, unaffected wisdom,
And sanctity of manners.   *Cato*'s soul
Shines out in every thing she acts or speaks,
While winning mildness and attractive smiles
Dwell in her looks, and with becoming grace
Soften the rigour of her father's virtues.

   Syphax. How does your tongue grow wanton in her praise!   160
But on my knees I beg you would consider——

   Juba. Hah! *Syphax*, is 't not she!——she moves this way:
And with her *Lucia*, *Lucius*'s fair daughter.
My heart beats thick—I pr'ythee *Syphax* leave me.

   Syphax. Ten thousand curses fasten on 'em both!
Now will this woman with a single glance
Undo, what I've been labouring all this while.

                             [*Exit.*

SCENE V.

Juba, Marcia, Lucia.

Juba. Hail charming Maid! how does thy beauty smooth
The face of war, and make even Horror smile!
At sight of thee my heart shakes off its sorrows;
I feel a dawn of joy break in upon me,
And for a while forget th' approach of *Cæsar*.
　　Marcia. I should be griev'd, young Prince, to think my presence
Unbent your thoughts, and slacken'd 'em to arms,
While, warm with slaughter, our victorious foe
Threatens aloud, and calls you to the field.
　　Juba. O *Marcia*, let me hope thy kind concerns　10
And gentle wishes follow me to battel!
The thought will give new vigour to my arm,
Add strength and weight to my descending sword,
And drive it in a tempest on the foe.
　　Marcia. My prayers and wishes always shall attend
The friends of *Rome*, the glorious cause of virtue,
And men approv'd of by the Gods and *Cato*.
　　Juba. That *Juba* may deserve thy pious cares,
I'll gaze for ever on thy godlike father,
Transplanting, one by one, into my life　　　20
His bright perfections, 'till I shine like him.
　　Marcia. My father never at a time like this
Would lay out his great soul in words, and waste
Such precious moments.
　　Juba. Thy reproofs are just,
Thou virtuous maid; I'll hasten to my troops,
And fire their languid souls with *Cato*'s virtue.
If e'er I lead them to the field, when all
The war shall stand ranged in its just array,
And dreadful pomp: then will I think on thee!　30
O lovely Maid, then will I think on thee!

And, in the shock of charging hosts, remember
What glorious deeds should grace the man, who hopes
For *Marcia*'s love.   [*Exit.*

SCENE VI.

LUCIA, MARCIA.

Lucia. *Marcia*, you're too severe:
How could you chide the young good-natured Prince,
And drive him from you with so stern an air,
A Prince that loves and doats on you to death?
   Marcia. 'Tis therefore, *Lucia*, that I chide him from
      me.
His air, his voice, his looks, and honest soul
Speak all so movingly in his behalf,
I dare not trust my self to hear him talk.
   Lucia. Why will you fight against so sweet a passion,
And steel your heart to such a world of charms.   10
   Marcia. How, *Lucia*! would'st thou have me sink away
In pleasing dreams, and lose my self in love,
When every moment *Cato*'s life 's at stake?
Cæsar comes arm'd with terror and revenge,
And aims his thunder at my father's head:
Should not the sad occasion swallow up
My other cares, and draw them all into it?
   Lucia. Why have not I this constancy of mind,
Who have so many griefs to try its force?
Sure, Nature form'd me of her softest mould,   20
Enfeebled all my soul with tender passions,
And sunk me even below my own weak sex:
Pity and love, by turns, oppress my heart.
   Marcia. *Lucia*, disburthen all thy cares on me,
And let me share thy most retired distress;
Tell me who raises up this conflict in thee?
   Lucia. I need not blush to name them, when I tell
      thee
They're *Marcia*'s brothers, and the sons of *Cato*.

Marcia. They both behold thee with their sister's
   eyes:
And often have reveal'd their passion to me.   30
But tell me, whose address thou favour'st most:
I long to know, and yet I dread to hear it.

Lucia. Which is it *Marcia* wishes for?

Marcia. For neither——
And yet for both——the youths have equal share
In *Marcia's* wishes, and divide their sister:
But tell me, which of them is *Lucia's* choice?

Lucia. Marcia, they both are high in my esteem,
But in my love——why wilt thou make me name him?
Thou know'st it is a blind and foolish passion,   40
Pleas'd and disgusted with it knows not what——

Marcia. O *Lucia*, I'm perplex'd, O tell me which
I must hereafter call my happy brother?

Lucia. Suppose 'twere *Portius*, could you blame my
   choice?
——O *Portius*, thou hast stol'n away my soul!
With what a graceful tenderness he loves!
And breathes the softest, the sincerest vows!
Complacency, and truth, and manly sweetness
Dwell ever on his tongue, and smooth his thoughts.
Marcus is over-warm, his fond complaints   50
Have so much earnestness and passion in them,
I hear him with a secret kind of horrour,
And tremble at his vehemence of temper.

Marcia. Alas poor youth! how can'st thou throw
   him from thee?
Lucia, thou know'st not half the love he bears thee;
Whene'er he speaks of thee, his heart's in flames,
He sends out all his soul in every word,
And thinks, and talks, and looks like one transported.
Unhappy youth! how will thy coldness raise
Tempests and storms in his afflicted bosom!   60
I dread the consequence.

Lucia. You seem to plead
Against your brother *Portius*.

Marcia. Heaven forbid!
Had *Portius* been the unsuccessful lover,
The same compassion shou'd have fall'n on him.
    Lucia. Was ever virgin love distress'd like mine!
Portius himself oft falls in tears before me,
As if he mourn'd his rival's ill success,
Then bids me hide the motions of my heart,   70
Nor show which way it turns. So much he fears
The sad effects that it would have on *Marcus.*
    Marcia. He knows too well how easily he 's fired,
And would not plunge his brother in despair,
But waits for happier times, and kinder moments.
    Lucia. Alas, too late I find my self involved
In endless griefs, and labyrinths of woe,
Born to afflict my *Marcia*'s family,
And sow dissention in the hearts of brothers.
Tormenting thought! it cuts into my soul.   80
    Marcia. Let us not, *Lucia*, aggravate our sorrows,
But to the Gods permit th' event of things.
Our lives, discolour'd with our present woes,
May still grow white, and smile with happier hours.

So the pure limpid stream when foul with stains,
Of rushing torrents, and descending rains,
Works it self clear, and as it runs, refines;
'Till by degrees, the floating mirrour shines,
Reflects each flow'r that on the border grows,
And a new Heaven in its fair bosom shows.   90
                         [Exeunt.

ACT II. SCENE I.

The SENATE.

Sempronius. Rome still survives in this assembled
    Senate!
Let us remember we are *Cato*'s friends,
And act like men who claim that glorious title.
    Lucius. *Cato* will soon be here, and open to us

Th' occasion of our meeting.　Heark! he comes!
　　　　　　　　　[*A sound of trumpets.*
May all the guardian gods of *Rome* direct him!

Enter CATO.

　Cato. Fathers, we once again are met in council.
Cæsar's approach has summon'd us together,
And *Rome* attends her fate from our resolves:
How shall we treat this bold aspiring man?　　　　10
Success still follows him, and backs his crimes:
Pharsalia gave him *Rome*; *Egypt* has since
Received his yoke, and the whole *Nile* is *Cæsar*'s.
　Why should I mention *Juba*'s overthrow,
And *Scipio*'s death? *Numidia*'s burning sands
Still smoke with blood. 'Tis time we should decree
What course to take.　Our foe advances on us,
And envies us even *Libya*'s sultry desarts.
Fathers, pronounce your thoughts, are they still fixt
To hold it out, and fight it to the last?　　　　20
Or are your hearts subdu'd at length, and wrought
By time and ill success to a submission?
Sempronius speak.
　Sempronius. My voice is still for war.
Gods, can a *Roman* Senate long debate
Which of the two to chuse, slavery or death!
No, let us rise at once, gird on our swords,
And, at the head of our remaining troops,
Attack the foe, break through the thick array
Of his throng'd legions, and charge home upon him.
Perhaps some arm, more lucky than the rest,　　31
May reach his heart, and free the world from
　bondage.
Rise, Fathers, rise! 'tis *Rome* demands your help;
Rise, and revenge her slaughter'd citizens,
Or share their fate! the corps of half her Senate
Manure the fields of *Thessaly*, while we
Sit here, deliberating in cold debates,
If we should sacrifice our lives to honour,

Or wear them out in servitude and chains.
Rouse up for shame! our brothers of *Pharsalia*   40
Point at their wounds, and cry aloud—To battel!
Great *Pompey*'s shade complains that we are slow,
And *Scipio*'s ghost walks unrevenged amongst us!

   Cato. Let not a torrent of impetuous zeal
Transport thee thus beyond the bounds of reason:
True fortitude is seen in great exploits
That justice warrants, and that wisdom guides,
All else is tow'ring frenzy and distraction.
Are not the lives of those, who draw the sword
In *Rome*'s defence, entrusted to our care?   50
Should we thus lead them to a field of slaughter,
Might not th' impartial world with reason say
We lavish'd at our deaths the blood of thousands,
To grace our fall, and make our ruine glorious?
Lucius, we next would know what's your opinion.

   Lucius. My thoughts, I must confess, are turn'd on
      peace.
Already have our quarrels fill'd the world
With widows and with orphans: *Scythia* mourns
Our guilty wars, and earth's remotest regions
Lie half unpeopled by the feuds of *Rome*:   60
'Tis time to sheath the sword, and spare mankind.
It is not *Cæsar*, but the Gods, my fathers,
The Gods declare against us, and repell
Our vain attempts. To urge the foe to battel,
(Prompted by blind revenge and wild despair)
Were to refuse th' awards of Providence,
And not to rest in Heaven's determination.
Already have we shown our love to *Rome*,
Now let us show submission to the Gods.
We took up arms, not to revenge our selves,   70
But free the common-wealth; when this end fails,
Arms have no further use: our country's cause,
That drew our swords, now wrests 'em from our
      hands,
And bids us not delight in *Roman* blood,

Unprofitably shed; what men could do
Is done already: Heaven and earth will witness,
If *Rome* must fall, that we are innocent.

   Sempronius. This smooth discourse and mild be-
      haviour oft
Conceal a traytor—something whispers me
All is not right—*Cato*, beware of *Lucius*.   80
                              [Aside to Cato.

   Cato. Let us appear nor rash nor diffident:
Immoderate valour swells into a fault,
And fear, admitted into publick counsels,
Betrays like treason. Let us shun 'em both.
Fathers, I cannot see that our affairs
Are grown thus desperate. We have bulwarks round
      us;
Within our walls are troops enured to toil
In *Africk*'s heats, and season'd to the sun;
Numidia's spacious kingdom lies behind us,
Ready to rise at its young Prince's call.   90
While there is hope, do not distrust the Gods;
But wait at least 'till *Cæsar*'s near approach
Force us to yield. 'Twill never be too late
To sue for chains, and own a conqueror.
Why should *Rome* fall a moment ere her time?
No, let us draw her term of freedom out
In its full length, and spin it to the last,
So shall we gain still one day's liberty;
And let me perish, but, in *Cato*'s judgment,
A day, an hour of virtuous liberty,   100
Is worth a whole eternity in bondage.

        Enter MARCUS.

  Marcus. Fathers, this moment, as I watch'd the
      gates
Lodg'd on my post, a herald is arrived
From *Cæsar*'s camp, and with him comes old *Decius*,
The *Roman* knight; he carries in his looks
Impatience, and demands to speak with *Cato*.

Cato. By your permission, fathers, bid him enter.

　　　　　　　　　　　　　　　　[Exit Marcus.

Decius was once my friend, but other prospects
Have loosed those ties, and bound him fast to *Cæsar.*
His message may determine our resolves.　　　110

SCENE II.

Decius, Cato, &c.

Decius. Cæsar sends health to *Cato.—*

　　Cato. Could he send it
To *Cato's* slaughter'd friends, it would be welcome.
Are not your orders to address the Senate?

　　Decius. My business is with *Cato: Cæsar* sees
The streights, to which you're driven; and, as he
　　knows
Cato's high worth, is anxious for your life.

　　Cato. My life is grafted on the fate of *Rome:*
Would he save *Cato?* bid him spare his country.
Tell your Dictator this: and tell him, *Cato*　　10
Disdains a life, which he has power to offer.

　　Decius. Rome and her Senators submit to *Cæsar;*
Her Generals and her Consuls are no more,
Who check'd his conquests, and denied his triumphs.
Why will not *Cato* be this *Cæsar's* friend?

　　Cato. Those very reasons, thou hast urged, forbid it.

　　Decius. Cato, I've orders to expostulate,
And reason with you, as from friend to friend:
Think on the storm that gathers o'er your head,
And threatens every hour to burst upon it;　　20
Still may you stand high in your country's honours,
Do but comply, and make your peace with *Cæsar.*
Rome will rejoice, and cast its eyes on *Cato,*
As on the second of mankind.

　　Cato. No more!
I must not think of life on such conditions.

　　Decius. Cæsar is well acquainted with your virtues,

And therefore sets this value on your life:
Let him but know the price of *Cato*'s friendship,
And name your terms.   30

    Cato. Bid him disband his legions,
Restore the common-wealth to liberty,
Submit his actions to the publick censure,
And stand the judgment of a *Roman* Senate.
Bid him do this, and *Cato* is his friend.

    Decius. Cato, the world talks loudly of your wis-
dom—

    Cato. Nay more, tho' *Cato*'s voice was ne'er
employ'd
To clear the guilty, and to vernish crimes,
My self will mount the *Rostrum* in his favour,
And strive to gain his pardon from the people.   40

    Decius. A stile, like this, becomes a Conqueror.

    Cato. Decius, a stile, like this, becomes a *Roman*.

    Decius. What is a *Roman*, that is *Cæsar*'s foe?

    Cato. Greater than *Cæsar*: he 's a friend to virtue.

    Decius. Consider, *Cato*, you're in *Utica*,
And at the head of your own little Senate;
You don't now thunder in the capitol,
With all the mouths of *Rome* to second you.

    Cato. Let him consider that, who drives us hither:
'Tis *Cæsar*'s sword has made *Rome*'s Senate little,   50
And thinn'd its ranks. Alas, thy dazled eye
Beholds this man in a false glaring light,
Which conquest and success have thrown upon him;
Didst thou but view him right, thou'dst see him black
With murder, treason, sacrilege, and crimes
That strike my soul with horror but to name 'em.
I know thou look'st on me, as on a wretch
Beset with ills, and cover'd with misfortunes;
But, by the Gods I swear, millions of worlds
Should never buy me to be like that *Cæsar*.   60

    Decius. Does *Cato* send this answer back to *Cæsar*,
For all his generous cares, and proffer'd friendship?

    Cato. His cares for me are insolent and vain:

Presumptuous man! the Gods take care of *Cato*.
Would *Cæsar* show the greatness of his soul?
Bid him employ his care for these my friends,
And make good use of his ill-gotten power,
By shelt'ring men much better than himself.

    Decius. Your high unconquer'd heart makes you forget
You are a Man. You rush on your destruction.   70
But I have done. When I relate hereafter
The tale of this unhappy embassie,
All *Rome* will be in tears.   [*Exit* Decius.

SCENE III.

Sempronius, Lucius, Cato, &c.

    Sempronius. *Cato*, we thank thee.
The mighty genius of immortal *Rome*
Speaks in thy voice, thy soul breathes liberty:
Cæsar will shrink to hear the words thou utter'st,
And shudder in the midst of all his conquests.

    Lucius. The Senate ownes its gratitude to *Cato*,
Who with so great a soul consults its safety,
And guards our lives, while he neglects his own.

    Sempronius. *Sempronius* gives no thanks on this account.
Lucius seems fond of life; but what is Life?   10
'Tis not to stalk about, and draw fresh air
From time to time, or gaze upon the Sun;
'Tis to be Free. When liberty is gone,
Life grows insipid, and has lost its relish.
O could my dying hand but lodge a sword
In *Cæsar*'s bosom, and revenge my country,
By Heavens I could enjoy the pangs of death,
And smile in agony.

    Lucius. Others perhaps
May serve their country with as warm a zeal,   20
Though 'tis not kindled into so much rage.

Sempronius. This sober conduct is a mighty virtue
In luke-warm Patriots.

Cato. Come! no more, *Sempronius*,
All here are friends to *Rome*, and to each other.
Let us not weaken still the weaker side,
By our divisions.

Sempronius. Cato, my resentments
Are sacrific'd to *Rome*——I stand reproved.

Cato. Fathers, 'tis time you come to a resolve.   30

Lucius. Cato, we all go into your opinion.
Cæsar's behaviour has convinced the Senate
We ought to hold it out 'till terms arrive.

Sempronius. We ought to hold it out 'till death; but,
   Cato,
My private voice is drown'd amid the Senate's.

Cato. Then let us rise, my friends, and strive to fill
This little interval, this pause of life,
(While yet our liberty and fates are doubtful)
With resolution, friendship, *Roman* bravery,
And all the virtues we can crowd into it;   40
That Heaven may say, it ought to be prolong'd.
Fathers, farewel——The young *Numidian* Prince
Comes forward, and expects to know our counsels.

SCENE IV.

CATO, JUBA.

Cato. Juba, the *Roman* Senate has resolv'd,
'Till time give better prospects, still to keep
The sword unsheath'd, and turn its edge on *Cæsar*.

Juba. The resolution fits a *Roman* Senate.
But, *Cato*, lend me for a while thy patience,
And condescend to hear a young man speak.

My father, when some days before his death
He order'd me to march for *Utica*
(Alas, I thought not then his death so near!)
Wept o'er me, prest me in his aged arms,   10

And, as his griefs gave way, my son, said he,
Whatever fortune shall befall thy father,
Be *Cato*'s friend, he'll train thee up to great
And virtuous deeds: do but observe him well,
Thou'lt shun misfortunes, or thou'lt learn to bear em.

Cato. *Juba*, thy father was a worthy Prince,
And merited, alas! a better fate;
But Heaven thought otherwise.

Juba. My father's fate,
In spight of all the fortitude, that shines   20
Before my face, in *Cato*'s great example,
Subdues my soul, and fills my eyes with tears.

Cato. It is an honest sorrow, and becomes thee.

Juba. My father drew respect from foreign climes:
The Kings of *Africk* sought him for their friend;
Kings far remote, that rule, as fame reports,
Behind the hidden sources of the *Nile*,
In distant worlds, on t'other side the Sun:
Oft have their black ambassadors appeared,
Loaden with gifts, and fill'd the courts of *Zama*.   30

Cato. I am no stranger to thy father's greatness!

Juba. I would not boast the greatness of my father,
But point out new alliances to *Cato*.
Had we not better leave this *Utica*,
To arm *Numidia* in our cause, and court
Th' assistance of my father's powerful friends?
Did they know *Cato*, our remotest Kings
Would pour embattled multitudes about him;
Their swarthy hosts would darken all our plains,
Doubling the native horrour of the war,   40
And making death more grim.

Cato. And canst thou think
Cato will fly before the sword of *Cæsar*?
Reduced like *Hannibal*, to seek relief
From court to court, and wander up and down,
A vagabond in *Africk*!

Juba. *Cato*, perhaps
I'm too officious, but my forward cares

Would fain preserve a life of so much value.
My heart is wounded, when I see such virtue   50
Afflicted by the weight of such misfortunes.

   Cato. Thy nobleness of soul obliges me.
But know, young Prince, that valour soars above
What the world calls misfortune and affliction.
These are not ills; else would they never fall
On Heaven's first favourites, and the best of men:
The Gods, in bounty, work up storms about us,
That give mankind occasion to exert
Their hidden strength, and throw out into practice
Virtues, which shun the day, and lie conceal'd   60
In the smooth seasons and the calms of life.

   Juba. I'm charm'd whene'er thou talk'st! I pant
      for virtue!
And all my soul endeavours at perfection.

   Cato. Dost thou love watchings, abstinence, and
      toil,
Laborious virtues all? learn them from *Cato*:
Success and fortune must thou learn from *Cæsar*.

   Juba. The best good fortune that can fall on *Juba*,
The whole success, at which my heart aspires,
Depends on *Cato*.

   Cato. What does *Juba* say?   70
Thy words confound me.

   Juba. I would fain retract them,
Give 'em me back again. They aim'd at nothing.

   Cato. Tell me thy wish, young Prince; make not
      my ear
A stranger to thy thoughts.

   Juba. Oh, they're extravagant;
Still let me hide them.

   Cato. What can *Juba* ask
That *Cato* will refuse!

   Juba. I fear to name it.   80
Marcia——inherits all her father's virtues.

   Cato. What would'st thou say?

   Juba. *Cato*, thou hast a daughter.

Cato. Adieu, young Prince: I would not hear a
　　word
Should lessen thee in my esteem: remember
The hand of fate is over us, and Heaven
Exacts severity from all our thoughts:
It is not now a time to talk of aught
But chains, or conquest; liberty, or death.

SCENE V.

SYPHAX, JUBA.

Syphax. How's this, my Prince! what, cover'd
　　with confusion?
You look as if yon stern Philosopher
Had just now chid you.
　Juba. Syphax, I'm undone!
　Syphax. I know it well.
　Juba. Cato thinks meanly of me.
　Syphax. And so will all mankind.
　Juba. I've opened to him
The weakness of my soul, my love for *Marcia.*
　Syphax. Cato's a proper person to entrust　　10
A love-tale with.
　Juba. Oh, I could pierce my heart,
My foolish heart! was ever wretch like *Juba?*
　Syphax. Alas, my Prince, how are you changed of
　　late!
I've known young *Juba* rise, before the Sun,
To beat the thicket where the Tiger slept,
Or seek the Lion in his dreadful haunts:
How did the colour mount into your cheeks,
When first you roused him to the chase! I've seen you,
Even in the *Libyan* Dog-days, hunt him down,　　20
Then charge him close, provoke him to the rage
Of fangs and claws, and stooping from your Horse
Rivet the panting savage to the ground.
　Juba. Pr'ythee, no more!

Syphax. How would the old King smile
To see you weigh the paws, when tipp'd with gold,
And throw the shaggy spoils about your shoulders!

Juba. *Syphax*, this old man's talk (tho' honey flow'd
In every word) would now lose all its sweetness.
Cato's displeas'd, and *Marcia* lost for ever!   30

Syphax. Young Prince, I yet could give you good
          advice.
Marcia might still be yours.

Juba. What say'st thou, *Syphax*?
By heavens, thou turn'st me all into attention.

Syphax. *Marcia* might still be yours.

Juba. As how, dear *Syphax*?

Syphax. *Juba* commands *Numidia*'s hardy troops,
Mounted on steeds, unused to the restraint
Of curbes or bittes, and fleeter than the winds:
Give but the word, we'll snatch this damsel up,   40
And bear her off.

Juba. Can such dishonest thoughts
Rise up in man! would'st thou seduce my youth
To do an act that would destroy my honour?

Syphax. Gods, I could tear my beard to hear you
          talk!
Honour's a fine imaginary notion,
That draws in raw and unexperienced men
To real mischiefs, while they hunt a shadow.

Juba. Would'st thou degrade thy Prince into a
          Ruffian?   49

Syphax. The boasted Ancestors of these great men,
Whose virtues you admire, were all such Ruffians.
This dread of nations, this almighty *Rome*,
That comprehends in her wide empire's bounds
All under Heaven, was founded on a Rape.
Your *Scipio*'s, *Cæsar*'s, *Pompey*'s, and your *Cato*'s,
(These Gods on earth) are all the spurious brood
Of violated maids, of ravish'd *Sabines*.

Juba. *Syphax*, I fear that hoary head of thine
Abounds too much in our *Numidian* wiles.

Syphax. Indeed, my Prince, you want to know the
 world;   60
You have not read mankind; your youth admires
The throws and swellings of a *Roman* soul,
Cato's bold flights, th' extravagance of virtue.
 Juba. If knowledge of the world makes man
  perfidious,
May *Juba* ever live in ignorance!
 Syphax. Go, go, you're young.
 Juba.   Gods, must I tamely bear
This arrogance unanswer'd! thou'rt a traitor,
A false old traitor.
 Syphax. I have gone too far.   [*Aside.*
 Juba. Cato shall know the baseness of thy soul. 71
 Syphax. I must appease this storm, or perish in it.
              [*Aside.*
Young Prince, behold these locks that are grown
 white
Beneath a helmet in your father's battels.
 Juba. Those locks shall ne'er protect thy insolence.
 Syphax. Must one rash word, th' infirmity of age,
Throw down the merit of my better years?
This the reward of a whole life of service!
——Curse on the boy! how steadily he hears me!
              [*Aside.*
 Juba. Is it because the throne of my fore-fathers
Still stands unfill'd, and that *Numidia*'s crown 81
Hangs doubtful yet, whose head it shall enclose,
Thou thus presumest to treat thy Prince with scorn?
 Syphax. Why will you rive my heart with such
  expressions?
Does not old *Syphax* follow you to war?
What are his aims? why does he load with darts
His trembling hand, and crush beneath a cask
His wrinkled brows? what is it he aspires to;
Is it not this? to shed the slow remains,
His last poor ebb of blood, in your defence? 90
 Juba. Syphax, no more! I would not hear you talk.

Syphax. Not hear me talk! what, when my faith to Juba,
My royal master's son, is call'd in question?
My Prince may strike me dead, and I'll be dumb:
But whilst I live I must not hold my tongue,
And languish out old age in his displeasure.

Juba. Thou know'st the way too well into my heart,
I do believe thee loyal to thy Prince.

Syphax. What greater instance can I give? I've offer'd
To do an action, which my soul abhors,   100
And gain you whom you love at any price.

Juba. Was this thy motive? I have been too hasty.

Syphax. And 'tis for this my Prince has called me traitor.

Juba. Sure thou mistakest; I did not call thee so.

Syphax. You did indeed, my Prince, you called me traitor:
Nay, further, threaten'd you'd complain to *Cato.*
Of what, my Prince, would you complain to *Cato*?
That *Syphax* loves you, and would sacrifice
His life, nay more, his honour in your service.

Juba. *Syphax*, I know thou lov'st me, but indeed
Thy zeal for *Juba* carried thee too far.   111
Honour's a sacred tie, the law of Kings,
The noble mind's distinguishing perfection,
That aids and strengthens virtue, where it meets her,
And imitates her actions, where she is not:
It ought not to be sported with.

Syphax. By Heavens
I'm ravish'd when you talk thus, tho' you chide me!
Alas, I've hitherto been used to think
A blind officious zeal to serve my King   120
The ruling principle, that ought to burn
And quench all others in a subject's heart.
Happy the people, who preserve their honour,
By the same duties, that oblige their Prince!

Juba. Syphax, thou now begin'st to speak thy self.
Numidia's grown a scorn among the nations
For breach of publick vows. Our *Punick* faith
Is infamous, and branded to a proverb.
Syphax, we'll join our cares, to purge away
Our country's crimes, and clear her reputation.   130

   Syphax. Believe me, Prince, you make old *Syphax* weep
To hear you talk——but 'tis with tears of joy.
If e'er your father's crown adorn your brows,
Numidia will be blest by *Cato*'s lectures.

   Juba. Syphax, thy hand! we'll mutually forget
The warmth of youth, and frowardness of age:
Thy Prince esteems thy worth, and loves thy person.
If e'er the scepter comes into my hand,
Syphax shall stand the second in my kingdom.

   Syphax. Why will you overwhelm my age with
    kindness?   140
My joy grows burdensome, I shan't support it.

   Juba. Syphax, farewel, I'll hence, and try to find
Some blest occasion that may set me right
In *Cato*'s thoughts. I'd rather have that man
Approve my deeds, than worlds for my admirers. [*Exit.*

   Syphax solus. Young men soon give, and soon
    forget affronts;
Old age is slow in both—A false old traitor!
Those words, rash boy, may chance to cost thee dear.
My heart had still some foolish fondness for thee:
But hence! 'tis gone: I give it to the winds:—— 150
Cæsar, I'm wholly thine——

SCENE VI.

SYPHAX, SEMPRONIUS.

   Syphax. All hail, *Sempronius*!
Well, *Cato*'s senate is resolv'd to wait
The fury of a siege, before it yields.

   Sempronius. Syphax, we both were on the verge of fate:
Lucius declared for Peace, and terms were offer'd

To *Cato* by a messenger from *Cæsar*.
Should they submit, e'er our designs are ripe,
We both must perish in the common wreck,
Lost in a general undistinguish'd ruine.

 Syphax. But how stands *Cato*?   10
 Sempronius. Thou hast seen mount *Atlas*:
While storms and tempests thunder on its brows,
And oceans break their billows at its feet,
It stands unmoved, and glories in its height.
Such is that haughty man; his towering soul,
'Midst all the shocks and injuries of fortune,
Rises superior, and looks down on *Cæsar*.

 Syphax. But what's this Messenger?
 Sempronius. I've practis'd with him,
And found a means to let the victor know   20
That *Syphax* and *Sempronius* are his friends.
But let me now examine in my turn:
Is *Juba* fixt?

 Syphax. Yes,——but it is to *Cato*.
I've try'd the force of every reason on him,
Sooth'd and caress'd, been angry, sooth'd again,
Laid safety, life, and interest in his sight,
But all are vain, he scorns them all for *Cato*.

 Sempronius. Come, 'tis no matter, we shall do
   without him.
He'll make a pretty figure in a triumph,   30
And serve to trip before the victor's chariot.
Syphax, I now may hope thou hast forsook
Thy *Juba*'s cause, and wishest *Marcia* mine.

 Syphax. May she be thine as fast as thou would'st
   have her!
 Sempronius. Syphax, I love that woman; though I
   curse
Her and my self, yet spight of me, I love her.

 Syphax. Make *Cato* sure, and give up *Utica*,
Cæsar will ne'er refuse thee such a trifle.
But are thy troops prepared for a revolt?
Does the sedition catch from man to man,   40

And run among their ranks?

   Sempronius. All, all is ready,
The factious leaders are our friends, that spread
Murmurs and discontents among the soldiers.
They count their toilsome marches, long fatigues,
Unusual fastings, and will bear no more
This medly of Philosophy and War.
Within an hour they'll storm the Senate-house.

   Syphax. Mean while I'll draw up my *Numidian*
     troops
Within the square, to exercise their arms,   50
And, as I see occasion, favour thee.
I laugh to think how your unshaken *Cato*
Will look aghast, while unforeseen destruction
Pours in upon him thus from every side.
So, where our wide *Numidian* wastes extend,
Sudden, th' impetuous hurricanes descend,
Wheel through the air, in circling eddies play,
Tear up the sands, and sweep whole plains away.
The helpless traveller, with wild surprize,   ⎫
Sees the dry desart all around him rise,   ⎬
And smother'd in the dusty whirlwind dies. ⎭

ACT III. SCENE I.

MARCUS *and* PORTIUS.

   Marcus. Thanks to my stars, I have not ranged
     about
The wilds of life, e'er I could find a friend;
Nature first pointed out my *Portius* to me,
And early taught me, by her secret force,
To love thy person, e'er I knew thy merit;
'Till, what was instinct, grew up into friendship.

   Portius. Marcus, the friendships of the world are oft
Confederacies in vice, or leagues of pleasure;
Ours has severest virtue for its basis,
And such a friendship ends not but with life.   10

Marcus. *Portius*, thou know'st my soul in all its
    weakness,
Then pr'ythee spare me on its tender side,
Indulge me but in love, my other passions
Shall rise and fall by virtue's nicest rules.
  Portius. When love's well-timed, 'tis not a fault to
    love.
The strong, the brave, the virtuous, and the wise,
Sink in the soft captivity together.
I would not urge thee to dismiss thy passion,
(I know 'twere vain) but to suppress its force,
'Till better times may make it look more graceful. 20
  Marcus. Alas; thou talk'st like one who never felt
Th' impatient throbbs and longings of a soul,
That pants, and reaches after distant good.
A lover does not live by vulgar time:
Believe me, *Portius*, in my *Lucia*'s absence
Life hangs upon me, and becomes a burden;
And yet, when I behold the charming maid,
I'm ten times more undone; while hope and fear,
And grief, and rage, and love, rise up at once,
And with variety of pain distract me.   30
  Portius. What can thy *Portius* do to give thee help?
  Marcus. *Portius*, thou oft enjoy'st the fair one's
    presence:
Then undertake my cause, and plead it to her
With all the strength and heats of eloquence
Fraternal love and friendship can inspire.
Tell her thy brother languishes to death,
And fades away, and withers in his bloom;
That he forgets his sleep, and loaths his food,
That youth, and health, and war are joyless to him:
Describe his anxious days, and restless nights,   40
And all the torments that thou seest me suffer.
  Portius. *Marcus*, I beg thee give me not an office,
That suits with me so ill. Thou know'st my temper.
  Marcus. Wilt thou behold me sinking in my woes?
And wilt thou not reach out a friendly arm,

To raise me from amidst this plunge of sorrows?

   Portius. *Marcus*, thou canst not ask what I'd refuse.
But here believe me I've a thousand reasons——

   Marcus. I know thou'lt say my passion's out of
   season,
That *Cato*'s great example and misfortunes   50
Should both conspire to drive it from my thoughts.
But what's all this to one who loves like me!
Oh *Portius*, *Portius*, from my soul I wish
Thou didst but know thy self what 'tis to love!
Then wouldst thou pity and assist thy brother.

   Portius. What should I do! if I disclose my passion
Our friendship's at an end: if I conceal it,
The world will call me false to a friend and brother.
                        [*Aside.*

   Marcus. But see where *Lucia*, at her wonted hour,
Amid the cool of yon high marble arch,   60
Enjoys the noon-day breeze! observe her, *Portius*!
That face, that shape, those eyes, that Heaven of
   beauty
Observe her well, and blame me if thou can'st.

   Portius. She sees us, and advances——

   Marcus. I'll withdraw,
And leave you for a while. Remember, *Portius*,
Thy brother's life depends upon thy tongue.

SCENE II.

LUCIA, PORTIUS.

   Lucia. Did not I see your brother *Marcus* here?
Why did he fly the place, and shun my presence?

   Portius. Oh, *Lucia*, language is too faint to show
His rage of love; it preys upon his life;
He pines, he sickens, he despairs, he dies
His passions and his virtues lie confused,
And mixt together in so wild a tumult,
That the whole man is quite disfigur'd in him.

Heavens! would one think 'twere possible for love
To make such ravage in a noble soul!   10
Oh, *Lucia*, I'm distrest! my heart bleeds for him;
Even now, while thus I stand blest in thy presence,
A secret damp of grief comes o'er my thoughts,
And I'm unhappy, tho' thou smilest upon me.

    Lucia. How wilt thou guard thy honour, in the
      shock
Of love and friendship! think betimes, my *Portius*,
Think how the nuptial tie, that might ensure
Our mutual bliss, would raise to such a height
Thy brother's griefs, as might perhaps destroy him.

    Portius. Alas, poor youth! what dost thou think,
      my *Lucia*?   20
His generous, open, undesigning heart
Has beg'd his rival to sollicit for him.
Then do not strike him dead with a denial,
But hold him up in life, and cheer his soul
With the faint glimmering of a doubtful hope:
Perhaps, when we have pass'd these gloomy hours,
And weather'd out the storm that beats upon us—

    Lucia. No, *Portius*, no! I see thy sister's tears,
Thy father's anguish, and thy brother's death,
In the pursuit of our ill-fated loves.   30
And, *Portius*, here I swear, to Heaven I swear,
To Heaven, and all the powers that judge mankind,
Never to mix my plighted hands with thine,
While such a cloud of mischiefs hangs about us,
But to forget our loves, and drive thee out
From all my thoughts, as far——as I am able.

    Portius. What hast thou said! I'm thunder-struck!
    —recall
Those hasty words, or I am lost for ever.

    Lucia. Has not the Vow already pass'd my lips?
The Gods have heard it, and 'tis seal'd in Heaven.
May all the vengeance that was ever pour'd   41
On perjur'd heads, o'erwhelm me, if I break it!

    Portius. Fixt in astonishment, I gaze upon thee;

Like one just blasted by a stroke from Heaven,
Who pants for breath, and stiffens, yet alive,
In dreadful looks: a monument of wrath!

 Lucia. At length I've acted my severest part,
I feel the woman breaking in upon me,
And melt about my heart! my tears will flow.
But oh I'll think no more! the hand of fate   50
Has torn thee from me, and I must forget thee.

 Portius. Hard-hearted, cruel maid!

 Lucia. Oh stop those sounds,
Those killing sounds! why dost thou frown upon me?
My blood runs cold, my heart forgets to heave,
And life it self goes out at thy displeasure.
The Gods forbid us to indulge our loves,
But oh! I cannot bear thy hate, and live!

 Portius. Talk not of love, thou never knew'st its
  force,
I've been deluded, led into a dream   60
Of fancied bliss. Oh *Lucia*, cruel maid!
Thy dreadful Vow, loaden with death, still sounds
In my stunn'd ears. What shall I say or do?
Quick, let us part! perdition 's in thy presence,
And horror dwells about thee!—hah, she faints!
Wretch that I am! what has my rashness done!
Lucia, thou injur'd innocence! thou best
And loveliest of thy sex! awake, my *Lucia*,
Or *Portius* rushes on his sword to join thee.
—Her imprecations reach not to the tomb, 70
They shut not out society in death——
But hah! she moves! life wanders up and down
Through all her face, and lights up every charm.

 Lucia. O *Portius*, was this well!—to frown on her
That lives upon thy smiles! to call in doubt
The faith of one expiring at thy feet,
That loves thee more than ever woman lov'd!
——What do I say? my half-recover'd sense
Forgets the Vow in which my soul is bound.
Destruction stands betwixt us! we must part. 80

Portius. Name not the word, my frighted **thoughts** run back,
And startle into madness at the sound.

Lucia. What would'st thou have me do? consider well
The train of ills our love would draw behind it.
Think, *Portius,* think, thou seest thy dying brother
Stabb'd at his heart, and all besmear'd with blood,
Storming at heaven and thee! thy awful Sire
Sternly demands the cause, th' accursed cause,
That robs him of his son! poor *Marcia* trembles,
Then tears her hair, and frantick in her griefs	90
Calls out on *Lucia*! what could *Lucia* answer?
Or how stand up in such a scene of sorrow!

Portius. To my confusion, and eternal grief,
I must approve the sentence that destroys me.
The mist, that hung about my mind, clears up;
And now, athwart the terrors that thy Vow
Has planted round thee, thou appear'st more fair,
More amiable, and risest in thy charms.
Loveliest of women! Heaven is in thy soul,
Beauty and virtue shine for ever round thee,	100
Bright'ning each other! thou art all divine!

Lucia. Portius, no more! thy words shoot through my heart,
Melt my resolves, and turn me all to love.
Why are those tears of fondness in thy eyes?
Why heaves thy heart? why swells thy soul with sorrow?
It softens me too much——farewel, my *Portius,*
Farewel, though death is in the word, For-ever!

Portius. Stay, *Lucia,* stay! what dost thou say? For-ever?

Lucia. Have I not sworn? if, *Portius,* thy success
Must throw thy brother on his fate, farewell,	110
Oh, how shall I repeat the word! For-ever!

Portius. Thus o'er the dying lamp th' unsteady flame

Hangs quivering on a point, leaps off by fits,
And falls again, as loath to quit its hold.
——Thou must not go, my soul still hovers o'er thee,
And can't get loose.

   Lucia. If the firm *Portius* shake
To hear of parting, think what *Lucia* suffers!

   Portius. 'Tis true; unruffled and serene I've met
The common accidents of life, but here   120
Such an unlook'd-for storm of ills falls on me,
It beats down all my strength. I cannot bear it.
We must not part.

   Lucia. What dost thou say? not part?
Hast thou forgot the Vow that I have made?
Are there not heavens, and gods, and thunder, o'er us!
——But see! thy brother *Marcus* bends this way!
I sicken at the sight. Once more, farewell,
Farewell, and know thou wrong'st me, if thou think'st
Ever was love, or ever grief, like mine.   130

SCENE III.

Marcus, Portius.

   Marcus. Portius, what hopes? how stands she? am
      I doom'd
To life or death?

   Portius. What would'st thou have me say?

   Marcus. What means this pensive posture? thou
      appear'st
Like one amazed and terrified.

   Portius. I've reason.

   Marcus. Thy down-cast looks, and thy disorder'd
      thoughts
Tell me my fate. I ask not the success
My cause has found.

   Portius. I'm griev'd I undertook it.   10

   Marcus. What? does the barbarous maid insult my
      heart,

My aking heart! and triumph in my pains?
That I could cast her from my thoughts for-ever?
    Portius. Away! you're too suspicious in your griefs;
Lucia, though sworn never to think of love,
Compassionates your pains, and pities you.
    Marcus. Compassionates my pains, and pities me!
What is compassion when 'tis void of love!
Fool that I was to chuse so cold a friend
To urge my cause! Compassionates my pains!   20
Pr'ythee what art, what rhetorick did'st thou use
To gain this mighty boon? She pities me!
To one that asks the warm return of love,
Compassion's cruelty, 'tis scorn, 'tis death——
    Portius. *Marcus*, no more! have I deserv'd this
        treatment?
    Marcus. What have I said! O *Portius*, O forgive me!
A soul exasperated in ills falls out
With every thing, its friend, its self——but hah!
What means that shout, big with the sounds of war?
What new alarm?   30
    Portius. A second, louder yet,
Swells in the winds, and comes more full upon us.
    Marcus. Oh, for some glorious cause to fall in battel!
Lucia, thou hast undone me! thy disdain
Has broke my heart: 'tis death must give me ease.
    Portius. Quick, let us hence; who knows if *Cato*'s life
Stand sure? O *Marcus*, I am warm'd, my heart
Leaps at the trumpet's voice, and burns for glory.

SCENE IV.

SEMPRONIUS *with the leaders of the mutiny.*

    Sempronius. At length the winds are rais'd, the
        storm blows high,
Be it your care, my friends, to keep it up
In its full fury, and direct it right,
'Till it has spent it self on *Cato*'s head.

Mean while I'll herd among his friends, and seem
One of the number, that what e'er arrive,
My friends and fellow-soldiers may be safe.

  1 *Leader.* We all are safe, *Sempronius* is our friend,
Sempronius is as brave a man as *Cato.*
But heark! he enters. Bear up boldly to him;   10
Be sure you beat him down, and bind him fast.
This day will end our toils, and give us rest!
Fear nothing, for *Sempronius* is our friend.

SCENE V.

CATO, SEMPRONIUS, LUCIUS, PORTIUS, MARCUS, &c.

  Cato. Where are these bold intrepid sons of war,
That greatly turn their backs upon the foe,
And to their General send a brave defiance?

  Sempronius. Curse on their dastard souls, they stand
      astonish'd !   [*Aside.*

  Cato. Perfidious men! and will you thus dishonour
Your past exploits, and sully all your wars?
Do you confess 'twas not a zeal for *Rome,*
Nor love of liberty, nor thirst of honour,
Drew you thus far; but hopes to share the spoil
Of conquer'd towns, and plunder'd provinces?   10
Fired with such motives you do well to join
With *Cato*'s foes, and follow *Cæsar*'s banners.
Why did I 'scape th' invenom'd Aspic's rage,
And all the fiery monsters of the desart,
To see this day? why could not *Cato* fall
Without your guilt? behold, ungrateful men,
Behold my bosom naked to your swords,
And let the man that 's injured strike the blow.
Which of you all suspects that he is wrong'd,
Or thinks he suffers greater ills than *Cato?*   20
Am I distinguish'd from you but by toils,

Superior toils, and heavier weight of cares!
Painful pre-eminence!

   Sempronius. By heavens they droop!
Confusion to the villains! all is lost.   [*Aside.*

   Cato. Have you forgotten *Libya*'s burning waste,
Its barren rocks, parch'd earth, and hills of sand,
Its tainted air, and all its broods of poison?
Who was the first to explore th' untrodden path,
When life was hazarded in every step?   30
Or, fainting in the long laborious march,
When on the banks of an unlook'd-for stream
You sunk the river with repeated draughts,
Who was the last in all your host that thirsted?

   Sempronius. If some penurious source by chance
    appear'd,
Scanty of waters, when you scoop'd it dry,
And offer'd the full helmet up to *Cato*,
Did he not dash th' untasted moisture from him?
Did not he lead you through the mid-day Sun,
And clouds of dust? did not his temples glow   40
In the same sultry winds, and scorching heats?

   Cato. Hence worthless men! hence! and complain
    to *Cæsar*
You could not undergo the toils of war,
Nor bear the hardships that your leader bore.

   Lucius. See, *Cato*, see, th' unhappy men! they
    weep!
Fear, and remorse, and sorrow for their crime,
Appear in every look, and plead for mercy.

   Cato. Learn to be honest men, give up your leaders,
And pardon shall descend on all the rest.

   Sempronius. *Cato*, commit these wretches to my care.
First let 'em each be broken on the rack,   51
Then, with what life remains, impaled and left
To writhe at leasure round the bloody stake.
There let 'em hang, and taint the southern wind.
The partners of their crime will learn obedience,
When they look up and see their fellow-traitors

Stuck on a fork, and blackening in the Sun.

Lucius. Sempronius, why, why wilt thou urge the fate
Of wretched men?

Sempronius. How! would'st thou clear rebellion!
Lucius (good man) pities the poor offenders, 61
That would imbrue their hands in *Cato's* blood.

Cato. Forbear, *Sempronius*!——see they suffer death,
But in their deaths remember they are Men.
Strain not the laws to make their tortures grievous.
Lucius, the base degenerate age requires
Severity, and justice in its rigour;
This awes an impious, bold, offending world,
Commands obedience, and gives force to laws.
When by just vengeance guilty mortals perish, 70
The Gods behold their punishment with pleasure,
And lay th' uplifted thunder-bolt aside.

Sempronius. Cato, I execute thy will with pleasure.

Cato. Mean-while we'll sacrifice to Liberty.
Remember, O my friends, the laws, the rights,
The generous plan of power deliver'd down,
From age to age, by your renown'd Fore-fathers,
(So dearly bought, the price of so much blood)
O let it never perish in your hands!
But piously transmit it to your children. 80
Do thou, great Liberty, inspire our souls,
And make our lives in thy possession happy,
Or our deaths glorious in thy just defence.

SCENE VI.

SEMPRONIUS *and the leaders of the mutiny.*

1 *Leader.* Sempronius, you have acted like your self,
One would have thought you had been half in earnest.

Sempronius. Villain, stand off! base groveling
worthless wretches,
Mongrils in faction, poor faint-hearted traitors!

2 *Leader.* Nay, now you carry it too far, *Sempronius*:

Throw off the mask, there are none here but friends.

  Sempronius. Know, villains, when such paltry slaves presume
To mix in treason, if the plot succeeds,
They're thrown neglected by: but if it fails,
They're sure to die like dogs, as you shall do.   10
Here, take these factious monsters, drag 'em forth
To sudden death.

Enter Guards.

  1 *Leader.* Nay, since it comes to this——
  Sempronius. Dispatch 'em quick, but first pluck out their tongues,
Least with their dying breath they sow sedition.

SCENE VII.

Syphax *and* Sempronius.

  Syphax. Our first design, my friend, has prov'd abortive;
Still there remains an after-game to play:
My troops are mounted; their *Numidian* steeds
Snuff up the wind, and long to scour the desart:
Let but *Sempronius* head us in our flight,
We'll force the gate where *Marcus* keeps his guard,
And hew down all that would oppose our passage.
A day will bring us into *Cæsar*'s camp.

  Sempronius. Confusion! I have fail'd of half my purpose:
Marcia, the charming *Marcia*'s left behind!   10

  Syphax. How? will *Sempronius* turn a woman's slave!

  Sempronius. Think not thy friend can ever feel the soft
Unmanly warmth, and tenderness of love.
Syphax, I long to clasp that haughty maid,
And bend her stubborn virtue to my passion:
When I have gone thus far, I'd cast her off.

Syphax. Well said! that's spoken like thy self,
 Sempronius.
What hinders then, but that thou find her out,
And hurry her away by manly force?

 Sempronius. But how to gain admission? for access
Is given to none but *Juba*, and her brothers. 21

 Syphax. Thou shalt have *Juba*'s dress, and *Juba*'s
 guards:
The doors will open, when *Numidia*'s Prince
Seems to appear before the slaves that watch them.

 Sempronius. Heavens what a thought is there!
 Marcia's my own!
How will my bosom swell with anxious joy,
When I behold her struggling in my arms,
With glowing beauty, and disorder'd charms,
While fear and anger, with alternate grace,
Pant in her breast, and vary in her face! 30
So *Pluto*, seiz'd of *Proserpine*, convey'd
To hell's tremendous gloom th' affrighted maid,
There grimly smil'd, pleas'd with the beauteous prize,
Nor envy'd *Jove* his sun-shine and his skies.

ACT IV. SCENE I.

LUCIA *and* MARCIA.

Lucia. Now tell me, *Marcia*, tell me from thy soul,
If thou believ'st 'tis possible for woman
To suffer greater ills than *Lucia* suffers?

 Marcia. O *Lucia*, *Lucia*, might my big-swoln heart
Vent all its griefs, and give a loose to sorrow:
Marcia could answer thee in sighs, keep pace
With all thy woes, and count out tear for tear.

 Lucia. I know thou'rt doom'd alike, to be belov'd
By *Juba*, and thy father's friend *Sempronius*;
But which of these has power to charm like *Portius*!

 Marcia. Still must I beg thee not to name *Sem-*
 pronius? 11

Lucia, I like not that loud boisterous man;
Juba to all the bravery of a Heroe
Adds softest love, and more than female sweetness;
Juba might make the proudest of our sex,
Any of woman-kind, but *Marcia*, happy.

   Lucia. And why not *Marcia*? come, you strive in vain
To hide your thoughts from one, who knows too well
The inward glowings of a heart in love.

   Marcia. While *Cato* lives, his daughter has no right
To love or hate, but as his choice directs.   21

   Lucia. But should this father give you to *Sempronius*?

   Marcia. I dare not think he will: but if he should—
Why wilt thou add to all the griefs I suffer
Imaginary ills, and fancy'd tortures?
I hear the sound of feet! they march this way!
Let us retire, and try if we can drown
Each softer thought in sense of present danger.
When love once pleads admission to our hearts
(In spight of all the virtue we can boast)   30
The woman that deliberates is lost.

SCENE II.

SEMPRONIUS, *dress'd like* JUBA, *with* Numidian *guards.*

   Sempronius. The Deer is lodg'd.   I've track'd her
     to her covert.
Be sure you mind the Word, and when I give it,
Rush in at once, and seize upon your prey.
Let not her cries or tears have force to move you.
—How will the young *Numidian* rave, to see
His mistress lost? if aught could glad my soul,
Beyond th' enjoyment of so bright a prize,
'Twould be to torture that young gay Barbarian.
—But heark, what noise! death to my hopes! 'tis he,
'Tis *Juba*'s self! there is but one way left——   10

He must be murder'd, and a passage cut
Through those his guards.—Hah, dastards, do you
    tremble!
Or act like men, or by yon' azure Heaven—

Enter Juba.

  Juba. What do I see? who 's this that dares usurp
The guards and habit of *Numidia*'s Prince?
  Sempronius. One that was born to scourge thy
    arrogance,
Presumptuous youth!
  Juba. What can this mean? *Sempronius!*
  Sempronius. My sword shall answer thee. Have at
    thy heart.   19
  Juba. Nay, then beware thy own, proud, barbarous
    man!   [*Semp. falls. His guards surrender.*
  Sempronius. Curse on my stars! am I then doom'd
    to fall
By a boy's hand? disfigur'd in a vile
Numidian dress, and for a worthless woman?
Gods, I'm distracted! this my close of life!
O for a peal of thunder that would make
Earth, sea, and air, and Heaven, and *Cato* tremble!
                              [*Dies.*
  Juba. With what a spring his furious soul broke
    loose,
And left the limbs still quivering on the ground!
Hence let us carry off those slaves to *Cato*,
That we may there at length unravel all   30
This dark design, this mystery of fate.

SCENE III.

Lucia *and* Marcia.

  Lucia. Sure 'twas the clash of swords; my troubled
    heart
Is so cast down, and sunk amidst its sorrows,
It throbs with fear, and akes at every sound.
O *Marcia*, should thy brothers for my sake!——

I die away with horror at the thought.

Marcia. See, *Lucia*, see! here's blood! here's blood
and murder!

Hah! a *Numidian*! Heavens preserve the Prince:
The face lies muffled up within the garment.
But hah! death to my sight! a diadem,
And purple robes! O Gods! 'tis he, 'tis he! 10
Juba, the loveliest youth that ever warm'd
A Virgin's heart, *Juba* lies dead before us!

Lucia. Now, *Marcia*, now call up to thy assistance
Thy wonted strength, and constancy of mind;
Thou can'st not put it to a greater tryal.

Marcia. Lucia, look there, and wonder at my
patience.

Have I not cause to rave, and beat my breast,
To rend my heart with grief, and run distracted!

Lucia. What can I think or say to give thee comfort?

Marcia. Talk not of comfort, 'tis for lighter ills; 20
Behold a sight, that strikes all comfort dead.

Enter JUBA *listening.*

I will indulge my sorrows, and give way
To all the pangs and fury of despair,
That man, that best of men, deserv'd it from me.

Juba. What do I hear? and was the false *Sempronius*
That best of men? O had I fallen like him,
And could have thus been mourn'd, I had been
happy!

Lucia. Here will I stand, companion in thy woes,
And help thee with my tears; when I behold
A loss like thine, I half forget my own. 30

Marcia. 'Tis not in fate to ease my tortur'd breast.
This empty world, to me a joyless desart,
Has nothing left to make poor *Marcia* happy.

Juba. I'm on the rack! was he so near her heart?

Marcia. Oh he was all made up of love and charms,
Whatever maid could wish, or man admire:

Delight of every eye! when he appear'd,
A secret pleasure gladned all that saw him;
But when he talk'd, the proudest *Roman* blush'd
To hear his virtues, and old age grew wise.   40

    Juba. I shall run mad——
    Marcia. O *Juba! Juba! Juba!*
    Juba. What means that voice? did she not call on
       Juba?
    Marcia. Why do I think on what he was! he's
       dead!
He's dead, and never knew how much I lov'd him.
Lucia, who knows but his poor bleeding heart,
Amidst its agonies, remember'd *Marcia*,
And the last words he utter'd call'd me Cruel!
Alas, he knew not, hapless youth, he knew not
Marcia's whole soul was full of love and *Juba?*   50

    Juba. Where am I! do I live! or am I indeed
What *Marcia* thinks! all is *Elisium* round me!

    Marcia. Ye dear remains of the most lov'd of
       men!
Nor modesty nor virtue here forbid
A last embrace, while thus——

    Juba. See, *Marcia*, see, [*Throwing himself before her.*
The happy *Juba* lives! he lives to catch
That dear embrace, and to return it too
With mutual warmth and eagerness of love.

    Marcia. With pleasure and amaze, I stand trans-
       ported!   60
Sure 'tis a dream! dead and alive at once!
If thou art *Juba*, who lies there?

    Juba. A wretch,
Disguised like *Juba* on a curs'd design.
The tale is long, nor have I heard it out.
Thy father knows it all. I could not bear
To leave thee in the neighbourhood of death,
But flew, in all the haste of love, to find thee,
I found thee weeping, and confess this once,
Am rapt with joy to see my *Marcia's* tears.   70

Marcia. I've been surprized in an unguarded hour,
But must not now go back: the love, that lay
Half smother'd in my breast, has broke through all
Its weak restraints, and burns in its full lustre,
I cannot, if I would, conceal it from thee.

Juba. I'm lost in ecstasie! and dost thou love,
Thou charming maid?

Marcia. And dost thou live to ask it?

Juba. This, this is life indeed! life worth preserving,
Such life as *Juba* never felt 'till now!   80

Marcia. Believe me, Prince, before I thought thee dead,
I did not know my self how much I lov'd thee.

Juba. O fortunate mistake!

Marcia. O happy *Marcia*!

Juba. My joy! my best beloved! my only wish!
How shall I speak the transport of my soul!

Marcia. *Lucia*, thy arm! Oh let me rest upon it!—
The vital blood, that had forsook my heart,
Returns again in such tumultuous tides,
It quite o'ercomes me. Lead to my apartment.——
O Prince! I blush to think what I have said,   91
But fate has wrested the confession from me;
Go on, and prosper in the paths of honour,
Thy virtue will excuse my passion for thee,
And make the gods propitious to our love.

Juba. I am so blest, I fear 'tis all a dream.
Fortune, thou now hast made amends for all
Thy past unkindness. I absolve my stars.
What though *Numidia* add her conquer'd towns
And provinces to swell the victor's triumph!   100
Juba will never at his fate repine;
Let *Cæsar* have the world, if *Marcia*'s mine.

SCENE IV.

A March at a Distance.

CATO *and* LUCIUS.

Lucius. I stand astonisht! what, the bold *Sempronius*!
That still broke foremost through the crowd of Patriots,
As with a hurricane of zeal transported,
And virtuous ev'n to madness——
    Cato. Trust me, *Lucius*,
Our civil discords have produced such crimes,
Such monstrous crimes, I am surprized at nothing.
——O *Lucius*, I am sick of this bad world!
The day-light and the Sun grow painful to me.

Enter PORTIUS.

But see where *Portius* comes! what means this haste?
Why are thy looks thus changed?   11
    Portius. My heart is griev'd.
I bring such news as will afflict my father.
    Cato. Has *Cæsar* shed more *Roman* blood?
    Portius. Not so.
The traytor *Syphax*, as within the square
He exercised his troops, the signal given,
Flew off at once with his *Numidian* horse
To the south gate, where *Marcus* holds the watch.
I saw, and call'd to stop him, but in vain,   20
He tost his arm aloft, and proudly told me,
He would not stay and perish like *Sempronius*.
    Cato. Perfidious men! but haste my son, and see
Thy brother *Marcus* acts a *Roman*'s part.
——*Lucius*, the torrent bears too hard upon me:
Justice gives way to force: the conquer'd world
Is *Cæsar*'s: *Cato* has no business in it.
    Lucius. While pride, oppression, and injustice reign,
The world will still demand her *Cato*'s presence.
In pity to mankind, submit to *Cæsar*,   30
And reconcile thy mighty soul to life.

Cato. Would *Lucius* have me live to swell the
  number
Of *Cæsar*'s slaves, or by a base submission
Give up the cause of *Rome*, and own a tyrant?
  Lucius. The victor never will impose on *Cato*
Ungen'rous terms. His enemies confess
The virtues of humanity are *Cæsar*'s.
  Cato. Curse on his virtues! they've undone his
  country.
Such popular humanity is treason——
But see young *Juba*! the good youth appears   40
Full of the guilt of his perfidious subjects.
  Lucius. Alas, poor Prince! his fate deserves com-
  passion.

Enter JUBA.

Juba. I blush, and am confounded to appear
Before thy presence, *Cato.*
  Cato. What's thy crime?
  Juba. I'm a *Numidian.*
  Cato. And a brave one too.
Thou hast a *Roman* soul.
  Juba. Hast thou not heard
Of my false countrymen?   50
  Cato. Alas, young Prince,
Falsehood and fraud shoot up in every soil,
The product of all climes—*Rome* has its *Cæsars.*
  Juba. 'Tis gen'rous thus to comfort the distrest.
  Cato. 'Tis just to give applause where 'tis deserv'd;
Thy virtue, Prince, has stood the test of fortune,
Like purest gold, that, tortur'd in the furnace,
Comes out more bright, and brings forth all its weight.
  Juba. What shall I answer thee? my ravish'd heart
O'erflows with secret joy: I'd rather gain   60
Thy praise, O *Cato*, than *Numidia*'s empire.

Re-enter PORTIUS.

Portius. Misfortune on misfortune! grief on grief!
My brother *Marcus*——

Cato. Hah! what has he done?
Has he forsook his post? has he given way?
Did he look tamely on, and let 'em pass?

Portius. Scarce had I left my father, but I met him
Borne on the shields of his surviving soldiers,
Breathless and pale, and cover'd o'er with wounds.
Long, at the head of his few faithful friends,   70
He stood the shock of a whole host of foes.
'Till obstinately brave, and bent on death,
Opprest with multitudes, he greatly fell.

Cato. I'm satisfy'd.

Portius. Nor did he fall before
His sword had pierc'd through the false heart of *Syphax*.
Yonder he lies. I saw the hoary traytor
Grin in the pangs of death, and bite the ground.

Cato. Thanks to the Gods! my boy has done his
     duty.
——*Portius*, when I am dead, be sure thou place   80
His urne near mine.

Portius. Long may they keep asunder!

Lucius. O *Cato*, arm thy soul with all its patience;
See where the corps of thy dead son approaches!
The citizens and senators, alarm'd,
Have gather'd round it, and attend it weeping.

CATO *meeting the corps.*

Welcome my son! here lay him down, my friends,
Full in my sight, that I may view at leisure
The bloody coarse, and count those glorious wounds.
——How beautiful is death, when earn'd by virtue!
Who would not be that youth? what pity is it   91
That we can die but once to serve our country!
——Why sits this sadness on your brows, my friends?
I should have blush'd if *Cato*'s house had stood
Secure, and flourish'd in a civil war.
——*Portius*, behold thy brother, and remember
Thy life is not thy own, when *Rome* demands it.

Juba. Was ever man like this!   [*Aside.*

Cato. Alas my friends!
Why mourn you thus? let not a private loss   100
Afflict your hearts. 'Tis *Rome* requires our tears.
The mistress of the world, the seat of empire,
The nurse of heroes, the delight of gods,
That humbled the proud tyrants of the earth,
And set the nations free, *Rome* is no more.
O liberty! O virtue! O my country!

Juba. Behold that upright man! *Rome* fills his eyes
With tears, that flow'd not o'er his own dead son.
                                                          [*Aside.*

Cato. Whate'er the *Roman* virtue has subdu'd,
The Sun's whole course, the day and year, are *Cæsar's*.
For him the self-devoted *Decii* dy'd,   111
The *Fabii* fell, and the great *Scipio* 's conquer'd:
Even *Pompey* fought for *Cæsar*. Oh my friends!
How is the toil of fate, the work of ages,
The *Roman* empire fallen! O curst ambition!
Fallen into *Cæsar's* hands! our great Fore-fathers
Had left him nought to conquer but his country.

Juba. While *Cato* lives, *Cæsar* will blush to see
Mankind enslaved, and be ashamed of empire.

Cato. *Cæsar* ashamed! has not he seen *Pharsalia*!   120

Lucius. *Cato*, 'tis time thou save thy self and us.

Cato. Lose not a thought on me, I'm out of danger.
Heaven will not leave me in the victor's hand.
Cæsar shall never say I conquer'd *Cato*.
But oh! my friends, your safety fills my heart
With anxious thoughts: a thousand secret terrors
Rise in my soul: how shall I save my friends!
'Tis now, O *Cæsar*, I begin to fear thee.

Lucius. *Cæsar* has mercy, if we ask it of him.

Cato. Then ask it, I conjure you! let him know
Whate'er was done against him, *Cato* did it.   131
Add, if you please, that I request it of him,
The virtue of my friends may pass unpunish'd.

Juba, my heart is troubled for thy sake.
Should I advise thee to regain *Numidia*,

Or seek the conqueror?——

Juba. If I forsake thee
Whilst I have life, may heaven abandon *Juba*!

Cato. Thy virtues, Prince, if I foresee aright,
Will one day make thee great; At *Rome*, hereafter,
'Twill be no crime to have been *Cato*'s friend.   141
Portius, draw near! My son, thou oft hast seen
Thy Sire engaged in a corrupted state,
Wrestling with vice and faction: now thou see'st me
Spent, overpower'd, despairing of success;
Let me advise thee to retreat betimes
To thy paternal seat, the *Sabine* field,
Where the great *Censor* toil'd with his own hands,
And all our frugal Ancestors were blest
In humble virtues, and a rural life.   150
There live retired, pray for the peace of *Rome*:
Content thy self to be obscurely good.
When vice prevails, and impious men bear sway,
The post of honour is a private station.

Portius. I hope, my father does not recommend
A life to *Portius*, that he scorns himself.

Cato. Farewel, my friends! if there be any of you
Who dare not trust the victor's clemency,
Know, there are ships prepared by my command,
(Their sails already opening to the winds)   160
That shall convey you to the wisht-for port.
Is there aught else, my friends, I can do for you?
The conqueror draws near. Once more farewel!
If e'er we meet hereafter, we shall meet
In happier climes, and on a safer shore,
Where *Cæsar* never shall approach us more.
                              [*Pointing to his dead son.*
There the brave youth, with love of virtue fired,
Who greatly in his country's cause expired,
Shall know he conquer'd. The firm Patriot there
(Who made the welfare of mankind his care)   170
Tho' still, by faction, vice, and fortune, crost,
Shall find the gen'rous labour was not lost.

ACT V. SCENE I.

CATO solus, *sitting in a thoughtful posture*: *In his hand*
Plato*'s book on the Immortality of the Soul. A drawn*
sword on the table by him.

It must be so——*Plato*, thou reason'st well!——
Else whence this pleasing hope, this fond desire,
This longing after immortality?
Or whence this secret dread, and inward horror,
Of falling into nought? why shrinks the soul
Back on her self, and startles at destruction?
'Tis the divinity that stirs within us;
'Tis heaven it self, that points out an Hereafter,
And intimates eternity to man.
Eternity! thou pleasing, dreadful, thought!　　10
Through what variety of untry'd being,
Through what new scenes and changes must we pass!
The wide, th' unbounded prospect, lyes before me;
But shadows, clouds, and darkness, rest upon it.
Here will I hold. If there 's a pow'r above us,
(And that there is all nature cries aloud
Through all her works) he must delight in virtue;
And that which he delights in, must be happy.
But when! or where!——This world was made for
　　Cæsar.
I'm weary of conjectures——This must end 'em.　20
　　[*Laying his hand on his sword.*
　Thus am I doubly arm'd: my death and life,
My bane and antidote are both before me:
This in a moment brings me to an end;
But this informs me I shall never die.
The soul, secured in her existence, smiles
At the drawn dagger, and defies its point.
The stars shall fade away, the sun himself
Grow dim with age, and nature sink in years,
But thou shalt flourish in immortal youth,
Unhurt amidst the war of elements,　　30

The wrecks of matter, and the crush of worlds.
　　What means this heaviness that hangs upon me?
This lethargy that creeps through all my senses?
Nature oppress'd, and harrass'd out with care,
Sinks down to rest. This once I'll favour her,
That my awaken'd soul may take her flight,
Renew'd in all her strength, and fresh with life,
An offering fit for heaven. Let guilt or fear
Disturb man's rest: *Cato* knows neither of 'em,
Indifferent in his choice to sleep or die.　　　　40

SCENE II.

Cato, Portius.

　　Cato. But hah! how's this, my son? why this
　　　　intrusion?
Were not my orders that I would be private?
Why am I disobey'd?
　　Portius. Alas, my father!
What means this sword? this instrument of death?
Let me convey it hence!
　　Cato. Rash youth, forbear!
　　Portius. O let the prayers, th' entreaties of your
　　　　friends,
Their tears, their common danger, wrest it from you.
　　Cato. Would'st thou betray me? would'st thou give
　　　　me up　　　　　　　　　　　　　　　　　10
A slave, a captive, into *Cæsar*'s hands?
Retire, and learn obedience to a father,
Or know, young man!——
　　Portius. Look not thus sternly on me;
You know I'd rather die than disobey you.
　　Cato. 'Tis well! again I'm master of my self.
Now, *Cæsar*, let thy troops beset our gates,
And barr each avenue, thy gathering fleets
O'erspread the sea, and stop up every port;
Cato shall open to himself a passage,　　　　20

And mock thy hopes——

Portius. O Sir, forgive your son,
Whose grief hangs heavy on him! O my father!
How am I sure it is not the last time
I e'er shall call you so! be not displeased,
O be not angry with me whilst I weep,
And, in the anguish of my heart, beseech you
To quit the dreadful purpose of your soul!

Cato. Thou hast been ever good and dutiful.

> [*Embracing him.*

Weep not, my son. All will be well again.   30
The righteous gods, whom I have sought to please,
Will succour *Cato*, and preserve his children.

Portius. Your words give comfort to my drooping
    heart.

Cato. *Portius*, thou may'st rely upon my conduct.
Thy father will not act what misbecomes him.
But go, my son, and see if aught be wanting
Among thy father's friends; see them embarked;
And tell me if the winds and seas befriend them.
My soul is quite weigh'd down with care, and asks
The soft refreshment of a moment's sleep.   40

Portius. My thoughts are more at ease, my heart
    revives.

S C E N E   I I I.

Portius *and* Marcia.

Portius. O *Marcia*, O my sister, still there 's hope!
Our father will not cast away a life
So needful to us all, and to his country.
He is retired to rest, and seems to cherish
Thoughts full of peace. He has dispatcht me hence
With orders, that bespeak a mind composed,
And studious for the safety of his friends.
Marcia, take care that none disturb his slumbers.

Marcia. O ye immortal powers, that guard the
    just,

Watch round his couch, and soften his repose,   10
Banish his sorrows, and becalm his soul
With easie dreams; remember all his virtues!
And show mankind that goodness is your care.

SCENE IV.

LUCIA *and* MARCIA.

Lucia. Where is your father, *Marcia*, where is *Cato*?
Marcia. Lucia, speak low, he is retired to rest.
Lucia, I feel a gently-dawning hope
Rise in my soul. We shall be happy still.
Lucia. Alas! I tremble when I think on *Cato*,
In every view, in every thought I tremble!
Cato is stern, and awful as a God,
He knows not how to wink at humane frailty,
Or pardon weakness, that he never felt.
Marcia. Though stern and awful to the foes of
    Rome,   10
He is all goodness, *Lucia*, always mild,
Compassionate, and gentle to his friends.
Fill'd with domestick tenderness, the best,
The kindest father! I have ever found him
Easie, and good, and bounteous to my wishes.
Lucia. 'Tis his consent alone can make us blest.
Marcia, we both are equally involv'd
In the same intricate, perplext, distress.
The cruel hand of fate, that has destroy'd
Thy brother *Marcus*, whom we both lament——   20
Marcia. And ever shall lament, unhappy youth!
Lucia. Has set my soul at large, and now I stand
Loose of my Vow. But who knows *Cato*'s thoughts?
Who knows how yet he may dispose of *Portius*,
Or how he has determin'd of thy self?
Marcia. Let him but live! commit the rest to
    heaven.

Enter LUCIUS.

Lucius. Sweet are the slumbers of the virtuous man!
O *Marcia*, I have seen thy godlike father:
Some power invisible supports his soul,
And bears it up in all its wonted greatness.   30
A kind refreshing sleep is fallen upon him:
I saw him stretcht at ease, his fancy lost
In pleasing dreams; as I drew near his couch,
He smiled, and cry'd, *Cæsar* thou canst not hurt me.
   Marcia. His mind still labours with some dreadful
     thought.
   Lucius. Lucia, why all this grief, these floods of
     sorrow?
Dry up thy tears, my child, we all are safe
While *Cato* lives——his presence will protect us.

Enter JUBA.

   Juba. Lucius, the horsemen are return'd from
     viewing
The number, strength, and posture of our foes,   40
Who now encamp within a short hour's march.
On the high point of yon bright western tower
We kenn them from afar, the setting Sun
Plays on their shining arms and burnish'd helmets,
And covers all the field with gleams of fire.
   Lucius. Marcia, 'tis time we should awake thy father,
Cæsar is still disposed to give us terms,
And waits at distance 'till he hears from *Cato*.

Enter PORTIUS.

Portius, thy looks speak somewhat of importance.
What tidings dost thou bring? methinks I see   50
Unusual gladness sparkling in thy eyes.
   Portius. As I was hasting to the port, where now
My father's friends, impatient for a passage,
Accuse the ling'ring winds, a sail arrived
From *Pompey*'s son, who through the realms of *Spain*
Calls out for vengeance on his father's death,

And rouses the whole nation up to arms.
Were *Cato* at their head, once more might *Rome*
Assert her rights, and claim her liberty.
But heark! what means that groan! O give me way,
And let me fly into my father's presence.   61

    Lucius. *Cato*, amidst his slumbers, thinks on *Rome*,
And in the wild disorder of his soul
Mourns o'er his country.——hah! a second groan!——
Heaven guard us all——

    Marcia. Alas, 'tis not the voice
Of one who sleeps! 'tis agonizing pain,
'Tis death is in that sound—

Re-enter PORTIUS.

    Portius. O sight of woe!
O *Marcia*, what we fear'd is come to pass!   70
Cato is fallen upon his sword——

    Lucius. O *Portius*,
Hide all the horrours of thy mournful tale,
And let us guess the rest.

    Portius. I've raised him up,
And placed him in his chair, where pale, and faint,
He gasps for breath, and, as his life flows from him,
Demands to see his friends. His servants weeping,
Obsequious to his orders, bear him hither.

         [*The back Scene opens, and discovers* Cato.
    Marcia. O heaven assist me in this dreadful hour
To pay the last sad duties to my father.   81

    Juba. These are thy triumphs, thy exploits, O
      Cæsar!

    Lucius. Now is *Rome* fallen indeed!——
         [Cato *brought forward in his chair.*
    Cato. Here set me down——
Portius come near me——are my friends embark'd?
Can any thing be thought of for their service?
Whilst I yet live, let me not live in vain.
——O *Lucius*, art thou here?——thou art too
    good!——

Let this our friendship live between our children;
Make *Portius* happy in thy daughter *Lucia*.   90
Alas   poor   man,   he   weeps!——*Marcia*,   my
     daughter——
——O bend me forward!——*Juba* loves thee, *Marcia*.
A Senator of *Rome*, while *Rome* survived,
Would not have match'd his Daughter with a King,
But *Cæsar*'s arms have thrown down all distinction;
Whoe'er is Brave and Virtuous, is a *Roman*.——
——I'm sick to death——O when shall I get loose
From this vain world, th' abode of guilt and sorrow!
——And yet methinks a beam of light breaks in
On my departing soul. Alas, I fear   100
I've been too hasty. O ye powers, that search
The heart of man, and weigh his inmost thoughts,
If I have done amiss, impute it not!——
The best may erre, but you are good, and——oh!
                                              [*Dies.*

    Lucius. There fled the greatest soul that ever
        warm'd
A *Roman* breast; O *Cato*! O my friend!
Thy will shall be religiously observ'd.
But let us bear this awful corps to *Cæsar*,
And lay it in his sight, that it may stand
A fence betwixt us and the victor's wrath;   110
Cato, tho' dead, shall still protect his friends.

    From hence, let fierce contending nations know
What dire effects from civil discord flow.
'Tis this that shakes our country with alarms,
And gives up *Rome* a prey to *Roman* arms,
Produces fraud, and cruelty, and strife,
And robs the Guilty world of *Cato*'s life.

EPILOGUE.

By Dr. *GARTH.*

Spoken by Mrs. *PORTER.*

What odd fantastick things we women do! ⎫
Who wou'd not listen when young lovers woo? ⎬
But die a maid, yet have the choice of two! ⎭
Ladies are often cruel to their cost;
To give you pain, themselves they punish most.
Vows of virginity should well be weigh'd;
Too oft they're cancell'd, tho' in convents made.
Would you revenge such rash resolves——you may: ⎫
Be spiteful——and believe the thing we say, ⎬
We hate you when you're easily said nay. ⎭
How needless, if you knew us, were your fears?   11
Let Love have eyes, and Beauty will have ears.
Our hearts are form'd as you your selves would chuse,
Too proud to ask, too humble to refuse:
We give to merit, and to wealth we sell;
He sighs with most success that settles well.
The woes of wedlock with the joys we mix;
'Tis best repenting in a coach and six.

Blame not our conduct, since we but pursue
Those lively lessons we have learn'd from you: 20
Your breasts no more the fire of beauty warms,
But wicked wealth usurps the power of charms;
What pains to get the gawdy thing you hate,
To swell in show, and be a wretch in state!
At plays you ogle, at the ring you bow;
Even churches are no sanctuaries now:
There, golden idols all your vows receive,
She is no goddess that has nought to give.

Garth] Samuel Garth (1661–1719), a well-known Kit-Cat, a humane doctor, and as Whig as Pope, who wrote the prologue, was Tory. He was the author of the once popular *The Dispensary.*

Oh, may once more the happy age appear,
When words were artless, and the thoughts sincere; 30
When gold and grandeur were unenvy'd things,
And courts less coveted than groves and springs.
Love then shall only mourn when truth complains,
And constancy feel transport in its chains.
Sighs with success their own soft anguish tell,
And eyes shall utter what the lips conceal:
Virtue again to its bright station climb,
And beauty fear no enemy but time,
The fair shall listen to desert alone,
And every Lucia *find a* Cato's *son.* 40

To Her ROYAL HIGHNESS the

PRINCESS of *WALES*,

With the Tragedy of *CATO, Nov.* 1714.

The Muse that oft, with sacred raptures fir'd,
Has gen'rous thoughts of Liberty inspir'd,
And, boldly rising for *Britannia*'s laws,
Engaged great *Cato* in her country's cause,
On You submissive waits, with hopes assur'd,
By whom the mighty blessing stands secur'd,
And all the glories, that our age adorn,
Are promis'd to a people yet unborn.
　No longer shall the widow'd land bemoan
A broken lineage, and a doubtful throne;　　　　10
But boast her royal progeny's increase,
And count the pledges of her future peace.
O born to strengthen and to grace our isle!
While you, fair PRINCESS, in your Off-spring smile
Supplying charms to the succeeding age,
Each heavenly Daughter's triumphs we presage;
Already see th' illustrious youths complain,
And pity Monarchs doom'd to sigh in vain.
　Thou too, the darling of our fond desires,
Whom *Albion*, opening wide her arms, requires,　　20
With manly valour and attractive air
Shalt quell the fierce, and captivate the fair.
O *England*'s younger hope! in whom conspire
The mother's sweetness, and the father's fire!
For thee perhaps, even now, of kingly race
Some dawning beauty blooms in every grace,

　Heading—The Princess of Wales] that is, of the new
Hanoverian dynasty, later Queen Caroline, who deserved
all the eulogies given her.

Some *Carolina,* to heaven's dictates true,
Who, while the scepter'd rivals vainly sue,
Thy inborn worth with conscious eyes shall see,
And slight th' Imperial diadem for thee.   30

 Pleas'd with the prospect of successive reigns,
The tuneful tribe no more in daring strains
Shall vindicate, with pious fears opprest,
Endanger'd rights, and liberty distrest:
To milder sounds each Muse shall tune the lyre,
And gratitude, and faith to Kings inspire,
And filial love; bid impious discord cease,
And sooth the madding factions into peace;
Or rise ambitious in more lofty lays,
And teach the nation their new Monarch's praise,
Describe his awful look, and godlike mind,   41
And *Caesar's* power with *Cato's* virtue join'd.

 Mean-while, bright PRINCESS, who, with graceful
  ease
And native majesty, are form'd to please,
Behold those Arts with a propitious eye,
That suppliant to their great protectress fly!
Then shall they triumph, and the *British* stage
Improve her manners, and refine her rage,
More noble characters expose to view,
And draw her finisht heroines from you.   50

 Nor you the kind indulgence will refuse,
Skill'd in the labours of the deathless Muse:
The deathless Muse with undiminisht rays
Through distant times the lovely dame conveys:
To *Gloriana Waller's* harp was strung;
The Queen still shines, because the Poet sung.

55 *Waller*] the famous poet (1606–87), at this time
regarded as the father of English verse, having, it was said,
introduced the smoothness then so much admired. In his
poem *Of the Queen,* he had written,
  Thither my Muse, like bold Prometheus, flies,
  To light her torch at Gloriana's eyes.
' thither ' meaning to the Court.

Even all those graces, in your frame combin'd,
The common fate of mortal charms may find;
(Content our short-lived praises to engage,
The joy and wonder of a single age,)   60
Unless some Poet in a lasting song
To late posterity their fame prolong,
Instruct our sons the radiant form to prize,
And see your beauty with their fathers' eyes.

SET IN
GREAT BRITAIN
AT THE
UNIVERSITY PRESS
OXFORD
AND
REPRINTED BY
ROBERT CUNNINGHAM
AND SONS LTD.
ALVA